THE
PINCH

About the author

David Willetts is President of the Resolution Foundation, a Visiting Professor at King's College, London and an Honorary Fellow of Nuffield College, Oxford. He was an official in HM Treasury and Margaret Thatcher's Number 10 Policy Unit. He served in the Coalition Cabinet as Minister for Universities and Science from 2010–2014. He was the Member of Parliament for Havant from 1992–2015 and is now a member of the House of Lords. He is a Fellow of the Academy of Social Sciences and an Honorary Fellow of the Royal Society and the Academy of Medical Sciences. He has written widely on economic and social policy. His book *A University Education* was published in 2017.

THE PINCH

HOW THE BABY BOOMERS TOOK THEIR CHILDREN'S FUTURE – AND WHY THEY SHOULD GIVE IT BACK

DAVID WILLETTS

Atlantic Books
London

First published in hardback in Great Britain in 2010 by Atlantic Books, an imprint of Atlantic Books Ltd.

This revised and updated edition published in 2019

10 9 8 7 6 5 4 3 2 1

A CIP catalogue record for this book is available from the British Library.

Paperback ISBN: 978 1 78649 122 0
E-book ISBN: 978 0 85789 142 6
Printed and bound in Great Britain by Clays Ltd, Elcograf S.p.A.

Atlantic Books
An imprint of Atlantic Books Ltd
Ormond House
26–27 Boswell Street
London
WC1N 3JZ

www.atlantic-books.co.uk

To Imogen and Matthew

CONTENTS

LIST OF TABLES AND CHARTS

Tables

Charts

ACKNOWLEDGEMENTS

This book started life years ago when I was the MP for Havant. I had a stream of young people coming to my surgery who were trying to do the right thing for their families but were unable to find an affordable place to live: that set me thinking about why this was happening and what our obligations were to the next generation.

I am very grateful to successive researchers who were of great assistance with the first edition, particularly Melanie Batley, Henry Cook, Ryan Shorthouse, and Laura Fox. Annie Winsbury and Helga Wright provided invaluable support. Gervas Huxley has been an encouraging friend throughout. Nick Hillman has been a great source of wisdom and advice. I have a particular debt to Chris Cook for his wide-ranging research when I was first writing the book. Georgina Capel, my agent, believed in the project from the beginning. Caroline Knight of Atlantic Books was a shrewd editor of the first edition; James Nightingale and James Pulford have urged me on to this second edition. Responsibility for any errors is of course mine alone.

When I stood down from the House of Commons in 2015, Sir Clive Cowdery asked me to join the Resolution Foundation as Chairman, particularly to develop a new strand of work on fairness between the generations. The Resolution Foundation has been a wonderful intellectual home since then. I chaired our

Intergenerational Commission, which reported in 2018, and the analysis we did has helped me update the book. The commissioners were: Vidhya Alakeson, Chief Executive of Power to Change; Kate Barker, Chairman of Trustees, British Coal Staff Superannuation Scheme; Torsten Bell, Director of the Resolution Foundation; Carolyn Fairbairn, Director General of the CBI; Geoffrey Filkin, Chairman of the Centre for Ageing Better; John Hills, Professor of Social Policy at the London School of Economics; Paul Johnson, Director of the Institute for Fiscal Studies; Sarah O'Connor, Investigations Correspondent and columnist at the *Financial Times*; Frances O'Grady, General Secretary of the TUC; Ben Page, Chief Executive of Ipsos MORI; and Nigel Wilson, Group Chief Executive of Legal & General. They were all an invaluable source of expertise and wisdom.

Matt Whittaker, Deputy Director of the Resolution Foundation, chaired the technical panel consisting of Kate Bell, Head of the Economic and Social Affairs Department at the TUC; Chris Curry, Director of the Pensions Policy Institute; Anna Dixon, Chief Executive of the Centre for Ageing Better; Bobby Duffy, Managing Director of the Ipsos MORI Social Research Institute; Frank Eich, Senior Adviser at the Bank of England; Laura Gardiner, Principal Researcher at the Resolution Foundation; Paul Gregg, Professor of Economic and Social Policy at Bath University; Andrew Hood, Senior Research Economist at the Institute for Fiscal Studies; David Kingman, Senior Researcher at the Intergenerational Foundation; Abigail McKnight, Associate Professorial Research Fellow, London School of Economics; Rain Newton-Smith, Director of Economics at the CBI; James Plunkett, Director of Policy & Advocacy at Citizens Advice; Jonathan Portes, Professor of Economics and Public Policy, King's College London; James Sefton, Professor of Economics at Imperial College London; Anna Vignoles, Professor of Education at Cambridge University; Kate Webb, Head of Policy at Shelter; and Duncan Weldon, Head of Research at Resolution Group.

Just about every researcher at the Resolution Foundation

contributed to the working papers which led to the Commission's report: George Bangham, Stephen Clarke, Adam Corlett, Conor D'Arcy, David Finch, Laura Gardiner, Kathleen Henehan, Lindsay Judge, Fahmida Rahman, Daniel Tomlinson, and Matthew Whittaker. They are a fantastic team. Co-authors were Paul Gregg, Brian Bell, Hannah Shrimpton, Gideon Skinner, Suzanne Hall, Donald Hirsch, Laura Valadez-Martinez, Toby Phillips, Patrick Thomson, and Anna Vignoles.

Much of the new evidence in this second edition comes from our excellent team at Resolution led by Torsten Bell, and I am grateful to them all. I owe a particular debt to Laura Gardiner, who was principal researcher for the Commission and has worked with great energy and intelligence on the project. Now we have created an Intergenerational Centre at the Resolution Foundation to continue to provide evidence on what is happening to the different generations; its annual generational audits are funded by the Nuffield Foundation. If you wish to keep up to date with our work then do visit the website: https://www.resolutionfoundation.org/major-programme/intergenerational-centre/

I have a further debt to the wider academic and research community in Britain and sometimes abroad as well. Rein Jansons of the LSE, Edmund Cannon of Bristol University, Alistair Muriel of the IFS, Bob Pannell of the Council of Mortgage Lenders, and the late Alan Holmans of Cambridge University provided research on specific issues for the first edition. But the debt goes wider than that. During my time as a Visiting Fellow at Nuffield College, Oxford, for example, John Goldthorpe generously gave time to educate me on social mobility, John Muellbauer on housing, and Paul Klemperer on game theory. Nuffield College subsequently elected me an Honorary Fellow and once again those friends, the Warden Sir Andrew Dilnot, and the community there have stimulated my thinking and helped keep me informed of the latest research. I have greatly benefitted from participating in the wide-ranging conferences held at the Ditchley Foundation.

Dr Paul Redmond at Liverpool University shared my fascination with the divergent attitudes of successive generations.

This edition has particularly benefitted from research by Ipsos MORI: the first edition got them thinking about generational attitudes and since then they have developed an illuminating research agenda which I have drawn on. Bobby Duffy who led this work is now a colleague at King's College, London, where I am a Visiting Professor. Social policy experts at the LSE, especially Nick Barr and John Hills, have helped me to think about the welfare state and the life cycle. John Ermisch, formerly of the Institute for Social and Economic Research and now at Oxford University, and Geoff Dench of the Young Foundation helped me to understand family change, distinguishing between cohort and life-cycle effects. Paul Gregg, now at Bath University, and Simon Burgess of the CMPO at Bristol University shared their researches on education and social mobility, as did Jo Blanden. Anna Vignoles, now the Professor of Education at the University of Cambridge, has long been an important source of research and advice on education and social mobility which I continue to draw on. Professor Ken Binmore of Bristol and UCL has thought deeply about game theory and its applications to public policy, and his work above all stimulated me to set out some ideas in an earlier lecture at the LSE. Daniel Finkelstein of *The Times* and Matthew Taylor of the Royal Society of Arts share my interest in trying to apply insights from this discipline and evolutionary biology to politics, an approach whose time has come. Matt Ridley has also helped guide me through the literature on this. Jonathan Gershuny has generously assisted with advice on his treasure trove of time-use data. Tim Gill has helped with evidence on how loss of time for free play has changed the character of childhood. Mark Bogard of the Family Building Society and Jonathan Haslam have shared with me their material on transfers within families. I have benefitted from many discussions on saving and investment with Martin Weale, formerly of the National Institute of Economic and Social Research, and Andrew Smithers of Smithers and Co. Together with Martin Wolf of the *Financial Times* they persuaded me early on of the importance of national saving rates in explaining what was going wrong with our economy. Dieter Helm of Oxford University links that to the importance of investment, especially in infrastructure. At events at the Royal Society and elsewhere Martin Rees and John Beddington introduced me to scientists' understanding of the challenges facing us over the next 40 years. James Sefton of Imperial College has helped with my understanding of generational accounts and kindly introduced me to Professor Ronald Lee of UC Berkeley and Laurence Kotlikoff of Boston University, two leading American experts.

Research institutes such as the Institute for Fiscal Studies and the Sutton Trust have been valuable research resources. Policy Exchange hosted the first event, back in 2005, when I attempted to set out some thinking on the shifts in wealth between the generations. More recently a new think tank, the Intergenerational Foundation, has become a lively contributor to the debate. Mervyn King when he was Governor of the Bank of England responded encouragingly to my interest in the links between demography and economics, and officials at the Bank have shared some of their data. Philip Booth of the IEA and Nick Bosanquet of Reform both tackled this issue as well. The National Centre of Social Research, and James Lloyd, then of the International Longevity Centre, provided their analyses of the distribution of income and assets, which the National Centre generously updated for the first edition of this book. Kate Barker took me through her work on housing. Adair Turner's reports on pensions provided excellent analytical material. David Coleman of Oxford University has shared his wide understanding of demography. Sitting on the Global Aging Commission run by the Center for Strategic and International Studies in Washington DC gave me an opportunity to think about demographic change as an international phenomenon.

Many other experts, especially from the worlds of education and pensions, have patiently shared their knowledge with me. Punter Southall gave me the opportunity to continue to think about pensions after my front-bench responsibilities on pensions ended. Jane Falkingham and her colleagues at the ESRC Centre for Population Change at the University of Southampton have welcomed me to discussions of these issues and provided valuable material to help update the discussions of demographic change for this edition.

There have also been the opportunities to hear directly the voices of young people. Sometimes it has been very direct indeed – students protesting about university fees for example. Sometimes it has been more structured in TV studios or consultations. Presidents of the National Union of Students have been smart and well-informed advocates for young people. And sometimes it has just been a young person buying the book to give to their parents or some other older adult, hoping that they will realize young people can't themselves be blamed for the problems they face.

More than a decade in Opposition after 1997 could have been sterile and frustrating. It was because of the generosity of so many people in universities and research institutes that I found them intellectually fruitful and I wish to acknowledge my debt and gratitude. After leaving government and then the House of Commons in 2015 I have similarly appreciated the stimulus of a surge in events and discussions on intergenerational issues which are too numerous to list. But every discussion always brings out a fresh angle on this fascinating and important issue, which ranges from the brutal economics of what makes us rich or poor through to the deepest questions of what holds a society together.

I should also acknowledge my debt to many friends in the much-maligned world of politics. They have recognized the problem and urged me on – hoping that books like this might broaden the range of what is politically possible.

My wife Sarah has shaped the thinking in this book more than she may know. She has always judged every family question by what is best for our two children. This book is dedicated to them.

PREFACE TO THE NEW EDITION

When this book came out, 10 years ago, it was the first to look at the post-War British political economy from the perspective of different generations and to argue that the Baby Boomers were doing very well – but at the expense of their children. We were familiar with the idea that social class or ethnicity or gender influenced our path through life, but I argued that there was also an increasingly important generational gap in the economic and social fundamentals of income, opportunity, and wealth. It challenged our assumption that things just got better for each successive generation.

I was able to draw on some data on the contrasting fortunes of different generations but it was limited and so the argument was more speculative. Now there is far more evidence, much of it obtained by the excellent researchers at the Resolution Foundation, and it enriches this second edition. In particular Chapters 4, 8, 11, and 12 have been completely revised and rewritten to include much more evidence from the past decade. The evidence is even more compelling: there clearly is a problem. The question is what we do about it, and that is tackled in the new Epilogue.

I first set out the argument in a speech in 2005,[1] and in the 15 years since then it has been tested in every possible way. But there are still sceptics. I think particularly of the courteous letters I receive from older people in neat copperplate handwriting on Basildon Bond paper explaining that they have had a much tougher life than young people nowadays. And in many ways that is true for an 80-year-old. But it is not so true for a 60-year-old Baby Boomer. Brexit has also added an extra intensity to these arguments because, on average, older people voted to Leave and younger people voted Remain. I have decided not to engage with Brexit in this book as it would overload it. But it has opened up a new generational divide in attitudes and voting behaviour which makes it even more important to understand and do something about the gap between the generations. There have been other arguments too – all part of the very lively debate which the book has stimulated. Here is a distillation of the main challenges, and my responses to them.

There is no problem for the younger generation – and if there is it is only temporary

First there are the sceptics who claim there is no real evidence of a problem and the younger generations are all fine. But the latest evidence is overwhelming – and it is not just one or two economic indicators. Both major components of income – pay and the transfers from the welfare state – are heading in the wrong direction for the younger generation. Household income after housing costs for a 30-year-old Millennial born in 1990 is no higher than it was for a 30-year-old member of Generation X born in 1980. It also shows up in the key elements of wealth – housing and pensions – as the Boomers are still enjoying surges in wealth whereas the younger generation are finding it much harder to get started on the housing ladder or build up a decent pension.

The problems tended to emerge in the 1990s and early noughties and then got worse after the financial crash of 2008, though they did not all develop simultaneously. By and large the younger generation lost ground on asset ownership before they then lost ground on income. Nor are the problems all on the same scale. And there are of course nuances and qualifications. Home ownership fell first and fell heavily, but just possibly may have bottomed out. The loss of defined benefit pensions is a heavy blow to younger generations, but at least now there is auto-enrolment into defined contribution pension pots. Pay has been doing badly and a 30-year-old today earns no more than 10 or 15 years ago, but their pay is still more than a Boomer 40 years ago. State pensions are increasing in value while working-age benefits are being cut, but the pensions age is rising to offset some of the extra costs of the state pension. However, none of these qualifications disprove the core proposition that Millennials, born between 1981 and 2000, are having a tough time compared with the post-War Boomers.

The biggest special factor has been the 2008 crash. The decade since has been tough, especially for young people launching themselves into the jobs market. One argument is that this is the real story, and without the crash we would not have a problem. But most of the trends hitting young people began before then. They were already losing ground in the jobs market. Company pensions were already closing to them. The trends are deep-seated, and many span both the favourable decade before the crash of 2008 and the tougher one after it. The real story of the crash is that when sacrifices had to be made it was young people above all who made them – we were already in a political and social environment which ranked their claims behind the rest of us. The older people whose pensions and annuities depended on assets held by banks were protected at the expense of younger taxpayers. We are now emerging from that but the scars will last for a long time – some of the loss of income and productive potential may never be regained.

Nobody likes too much pessimism. It can be debilitating. It is better that young people believe they can shape their own future rather than being passive victims of fate. That is one reason why we welcome the rational optimists such as Steven Pinker in *The Better Angels of Our Nature: Why Violence Has Declined*, Matt Ridley (*The Rational Optimist: How Prosperity Evolves*), and Hans Rosling's *Factfulness: Ten Reasons We're Wrong About the World – and Why*

Things Are Better Than You Think. Their books do what they say on the tin, and show how more people across the world have escaped from poverty into better lives in the past 40 years than in any previous period of human history. They are right to remind us that humanity is still advancing. The wheels of modern capitalism and scientific progress have not stopped turning. A young person today enjoys a wider range of technologies than ever, from extraordinary IT to modern medicine. And for anyone who thinks things were better in the old days there is that most compelling one-word riposte – *dentistry*. But such progress is not a unique benefit enjoyed by this generation today. Successive generations were already enjoying really significant technological advances on their predecessors. For the Boomers it was access to TVs, washing machines, and motor cars. Indeed one school of thought argues that the spread of technology then was at least as rapid as it is now.[2] It is the backdrop against which every generation has lived their lives in the West since the Industrial Revolution.

The question is how the benefits and the costs are distributed, and here it looks as if today's young people are losing out. Boomers are using smartphones and the Internet at least as much as our kids, whose job is often to provide unpaid technical support so their parents can fully reap the benefits. And there look to be long-term costs associated with technological advances which we are loading on to younger generations. Climate change is ever more real and intense. Pervasive access to social media does look to be a driver of the worrying growth of mental illness among younger people.[3] The Boomers have been enjoying the benefits of a wide range of technologies while the costs are dumped on generations coming after.

I hope and believe that human ingenuity and advances in science and technology will see us through, but it is not going to be easy. In fact it is going to be a lot harder because of all the other heavy burdens the younger generation are having to face as well.

Yes, there might be a problem, but it is just a matter of bad luck – and if it is anyone's fault it is not the Boomers but the younger generation themselves or Margaret Thatcher or migrants or...

You might be persuaded so far and accept that young people do face significant problems, but believe it is all just a matter of luck. I was lucky to be born in 1956 and not to have to go to war, unlike my grandfather and father who were shot at in the First and Second World Wars. Maybe the younger generation are just unlucky to be faced with economic risks. Global economic trends are not under any one generation's control. But neither can the Boomers come over all powerless and innocent because they play such a significant role in our national life, and ultimately we do all have some power to shape the lives of future generations. We can decide how we respond to external shocks and global economic trends. We can decide how much we invest in infrastructure and skills for the future. We can decide whether we are going to make it easy or hard to build houses where young people want to live. We can decide whether the Boomers' pension schemes are going to be so expensive that they close for future generations. We can decide how much government debt we are going to leave them and how to spend the money we borrow. Moreover, we would not regard it as remotely acceptable to say it is just bad luck if you are having a tough time because of your gender or your ethnicity or your social background. Bad luck won't do as a justification of a raw deal for younger people either.

There are versions of this intergenerational problem in other countries too. But there is still something unique about the British problem. There are other countries where the younger generation are doing badly but nowhere else has the reversal of generation-on-generation progress been so precipitate as in the UK. It is not just a matter of some uncomfortable changes in the world economy affecting everyone.

There is one other form of the sceptics' argument about luck. Perhaps it is not that the younger generation are unlucky. Perhaps they are having a typical deal in a tough world. Is it instead that the Boomers have had unusually good luck? Are the Boomers the aberration? This line of thinking has some of the melancholy about the human condition that is captured in the story of the Russian peasant who describes the harvest as 'about average' and when asked what that means, replies 'not as good as last year but better than next year'. One can accept that there are some very special factors at play which took the Boomers to the top of the charts, after which decline was unavoidable. The most vivid example is the spread of home ownership, which reached exceptionally high peaks sooner than for any other generation.

But if it is all a matter of exceptional luck then the Boomers have been very lucky indeed. Here are examples of the luck they have enjoyed: inflation was high when they had big debts and low when they became richer; house-building was high when they needed houses but much lower when they had their own homes; credit was easy when they needed to get started on the housing ladder but much stricter afterwards; pension promises were weak when they were joining pension schemes but then were turned into gold-plated guarantees for them, after which companies stopped making such promises for future generations; benefits for old people were low when the Boomers were young but are worth much more relative to benefits for young people now the Boomers are old; consumption was high among young people when they were young and now is lower among young people and higher for older people; the Boomers' parents stuck together for them but then the Boomers were much more likely to split up once they themselves were parents. There is a suspiciously clear pattern to this luck. If the roulette ball keeps landing in the same place, we must begin to suspect it is not just luck.

We are not entirely the playthings of fate and fortune. And that opens up another defence of the Boomers – if anyone is to blame, it is the young. In this argument the misfortunes facing the younger generation are their own fault, and blaming the Boomers for problems they have brought on themselves by their own behaviour is just typical of a self-pitying hypersensitive snowflake generation who should stop whingeing and get a grip. But what is the behaviour of the younger generation which has had such dire consequences for them? They study harder and for longer than Boomers did. As their incomes are squeezed they don't borrow more but instead cut back on their consumption. They are more sceptical of the welfare state and much more likely to accept it is their responsibility to go out and get a job.[4] If you want to find a group which broke with prudence and raided the piggy bank for themselves, it is not the younger generation but the Baby Boomers.

There is another argument against the charge that we Boomers broke the intergenerational contract. OK, maybe something has gone wrong for the younger generation which is not their fault but that does not mean it is our fault. There are other culprits. Indeed some critics on both Left and Right regard this stuff about the generations as a dangerous diversionary tactic. For some on the Left the real culprit is Thatcherism and neo-liberalism. There are some on the Right for whom mass migration is to blame. Both views have a certain similarity: that the bonds tying us together as a national community have been weakened, but not by the Boomers; instead it is by an external shock, be it ideological or demographic.

But it is wrong to blame Thatcherism when many of the indicators on which young people are now doing badly – ownership of houses and pensions – were actually Thatcherite priorities, where progress was made in the 1980s but has since been reversed. Moreover the power to shape the welfare state was used very differently in Margaret Thatcher's day – compare the real cuts in the state pension then with the triple lock now.

As for those on the Right who claim mass migration is the reason why pay has not increased – our assessment at the Resolution Foundation is that at most migration has had a very small negative impact on the pay of native workers.[5] I am regularly told by opponents of more housing that the only reason we have housing pressures is because of migrants and that if they could be confident new houses were really for their own kids they would support house-building. But there would be housing pressures even without migration, because we have not been building enough houses for people born here in the places where they want to live.

There is one other version of the argument: that to focus on the generations is a distraction when the real problems are elsewhere. Fairness within generations is claimed to be much more of a problem than intergenerational unfairness. It is this sort of objection to which we now must turn.

There is nothing here – there are no generations and there is no such thing as an intergenerational contract – and even if there are generations and exchanges between them that does not matter compared with injustice within generations

The challenge from these sceptics is that this generational analysis cannot bear the weight which is being put on it. Gender or social class or ethnicity come freighted with enormous historical and cultural significance, but attaching weight to the accident of when you were born is by contrast just rather trivial. They argue that something so banal is no real basis for political economy, and that as soon as we go back to looking at Britain from other perspectives we see that the real issues are within the generations rather than between them.

But the life cycle matters, and changes in the number of people at different stages of the life cycle is a very substantial change in how a society and an economy function. Serious political thinkers such as Thomas Malthus, Auguste Comte, Karl Mannheim, and Richard Easterlin have seen the changing sizes of different generations as one of the key drivers of human history. They did however tend to assume that it was big generations that faced the problems, whereas the unusual twist in my argument is that it is the big generation which has the advantage. This is because in the modern economy the consumer (and hence cultural) power of a big generation is so great. And in a modern democracy, where the state distributes resources through the welfare state, the voting power of a big cohort is very significant.

We are not self-sufficient through our lives: in particular young and old depend on others who are at different stages of their lives. Exchanges between the generations are crucial. Indeed it is at the heart of the social contract which holds a society together. That is why we understand that we have obligations to other generations: 50 per cent agree that the success of our society is measured by how well we provide for older generations, and 59 per cent agree that every generation should have a higher standard of living than the one that came before it.[6] These beliefs show there is a contract between the generations, and different generations can do better or worse from these exchanges.

Some of the critics might concede that these are important arguments in principle but then claim that in practice the gaps between the generations are less significant than those within them. So they say we must not be distracted by these intergenerational appeals which are like the chaff put out by fighter planes to distract enemy radar – they just take our eye off the target. It is the gaps within the generations which we should focus on. There are indeed real differences within generations, and some of them are very big indeed. Those classic measures of disadvantage by class, gender, and ethnicity do matter. But we were so sensitized to these forms of unfairness that we failed to spot what was happening to the younger generation as a whole – even young people who appear to have every conventional advantage in life might still find themselves stuck in grotty rented accommodation with little prospect of getting started on the housing ladder. So alongside the masses of analysis and the thousands of books on those issues, it is right to add something from a generational perspective.

Moreover, some of the key differences within generations – such as in wealth – are getting worse generation by generation. That is indeed one of the problems facing the younger generation. One reason may be that if it is harder for younger people to build up income and assets of their own, what is inherited from parents matters more. Here we are beginning to see the close links between inter- and intra-generational issues. We might hope that each generation lives in a society with more social mobility not less. But individual families might be so worried about the prospects for the young that they tackle it the only way they can – by putting extra effort into their own children. This is part of the growth in the significance of the family and creates a society where property ownership and wider advantages are increasingly hereditary. So even if it is intra-generational unfairness you really care about, you ought to be tracking intergenerational unfairness because it can exacerbate the problems you most worry about.

You are promoting generational warfare – we are divided quite enough already without your making things worse, thank you very much

I believe that appeals to intergenerational fairness are powerful and desirable. Indeed I devote a whole chapter to trying to prove that these claims are at the base of those great projects for human co-operation: the family and the nation state. But one of the most widespread criticisms and the one which I really take to heart is that I am promoting intergenerational warfare. It is, they say, inflammatory to blame one generation for the problems of another: it turns the generations against each other. But the whole point of this book is to appeal to one generation which has done exceptionally well – the Boomers – to do more to help those generations coming after them. I do believe that the behaviour of the Boomers has made things tougher for the younger generation – consider those campaigns against house-building and the regulations which turned our defined pension schemes into a one-off special offer. But I don't believe that the Boomers did this with the deliberate intention of damaging the younger generation. It is a disaster caused by a failure to consider properly the interests of the younger generation rather than driven by active hostility to them. Indeed, this book is an appeal to the better instincts of the older generation who genuinely care about the prospects of the younger generation. The more we understand what we are doing, the greater the chance we will do something about it.

———

The Baby Boomers do have an extraordinary capacity to come up with alternative explanations when the evidence for their responsibility is overwhelming. Like Macavity, T. S. Eliot's mystery cat, whenever there is a problem the Boomers are not there:

> He always has an alibi, and one or two to spare:
> At whatever time the deed took place – MACAVITY
> WASN'T THERE!

But as we shall see, the evidence shows the Boomers were there. They can't escape their responsibility. It is time to do something about it.

David Willetts
July 2019

THE BIRTH RATE OVER THE PAST HUNDRED YEARS

The chart below shows the number of babies born each year in the UK over the past century. This basic information is one of the most important predictors of the changing shape of our society and our economy. It shows when there are going to be surges in the number of children needing more places in school. It shows when there are big increases in the number of young adults – disrupting the old order and looking for work. It shows when a big cohort is going to be in middle age – paying most tax and using public services the least. And it shows when we can expect to see surges of older people getting older and using the NHS more. And, of course, it shows how big the twin peaks of the post-War baby boom were. The chart is a particular focus of Chapter 3, but is referred to throughout the book.

Figure 1: UK births 1896–2016 defining the generations[7]

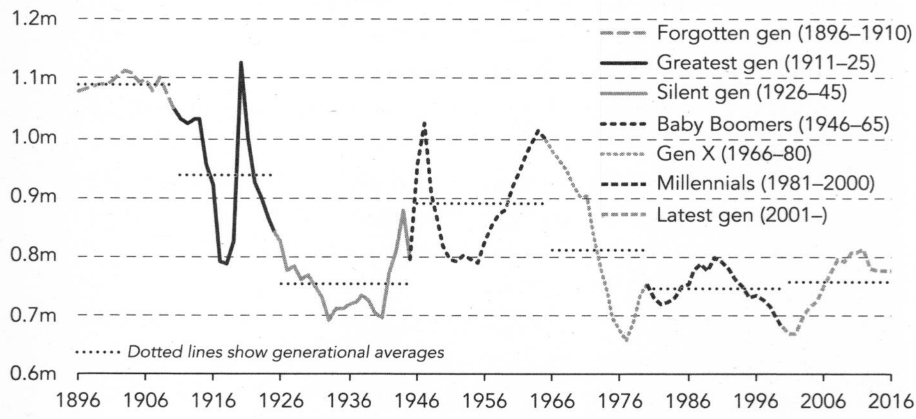
1.2m
1.1m
1.0m
0.9m
0.8m
0.7m
0.6m
Forgotten gen (1896–1910)
Greatest gen (1911–25)
Silent gen (1926–45)
Baby Boomers (1946–65)
Gen X (1966–80)
Millennials (1981–2000)
Latest gen (2001–)
Dotted lines show generational averages
1896
1906
1916
1926
1936
1946
1956
1966
1976
1986
1996
2006
2016

INTRODUCTION TO THE FIRST EDITION

We all know the story. The parents return home from a night away to find a teenage party has got out of hand and the house has been trashed. Every few months a particularly dramatic episode gets into the media – with distraught parents tidying up a mess left by a swarm of young people summoned on Facebook. It plays to a deep-seated fear that younger people will not appreciate and protect what has been achieved by the older generation. This is the eternal anxiety of each generation about what comes after. But what if, when it comes to many of the big things that matter for our futures, it is the other way round? What if it is actually the older generation, the Baby Boomers, who have been throwing the party and leaving behind a mess for the next generation to sort out?

The Boomers – roughly those born between the end of the Second World War and 1965 – have done and continue to do some great things, but now the bills are coming in and it is the younger generation who will pay them. We have a good idea of what at least some of these future costs are: the cost of climate change; the cost of investing in the infrastructure our economy will need if we are to prosper; the cost of paying pensions when the big Boomer cohort retires; all on top of servicing the debt the government has built up. The charge is that the Boomers have been guilty of a monumental failure to protect the interests of future generations.

The Baby Boomers have concentrated wealth in the hands of their own generation. It is far harder for the younger generation to get started on the housing ladder or save for the future in a decent company pension. This leaves them more dependent on their parents for longer. That in turn means new barriers to the spread of opportunity and ownership. Growing to adulthood and starting a family take longer and are more difficult. And young people found themselves by far the biggest victims of the recession – unable to find a job or a mortgage. We are rightly sensitive to the injustices and inequities of life chances within a generation but we ignore the injustices between generations, perhaps because they are harder to measure.

I had better declare where I fit in here. I was born in 1956, in the middle of the baby boom, and in Birmingham, in the middle of England. It was the year of the Suez Crisis and the Soviet invasion of Hungary. My mother remembers being worried about the dreadful, dangerous world into which she had brought me. So far, however, my age group has turned out to be, by and large, a lucky generation. Over the past 10 years I have spent a lot of my time involved in education and pensions. I have come to see how they are linked – they are about the obligations of the generation in the middle to the generation coming after and the one which went before. That set me to applying my interest in economic policy to the links between the generations, and how some get a better deal than others.

What if instead of being born in 1956 I had been born 50 years earlier, in 1906? Then a mother, depending of course on her social class, might have felt things were looking pretty good for her newborn child. Britain was rich and powerful, with social reform on the way as well. She could not have expected that her son's father would die in the trenches of the First World War, that this young man would then not be able to find work in the Great Depression, be conscripted in the Second World War and endure austerity after it. He would finally have retired in 1971 only to find his modest savings destroyed by the worst 10 years of inflation in our nation's history. It was an unlucky generation.

So what of a child born now? These two examples warn us that of course we cannot know. But many Boomers are guiltily aware of the heavy burdens being piled on their children and grandchildren. Try asking a group of people who are middle-aged or older whether they have enjoyed greater opportunities and prosperity than their parents. Almost everyone will say they have. But then ask them whether life will similarly be better for their children or grandchildren. They are not so sure. It is what, deep down, most parents are most anxious about – the life chances of their children.

How has this happened? It would be easy to slide into generational name-calling. But that gets us nowhere. It is not that some generations are good and others bad; it is that some are big and others are small. That is why Chapters 2, 3, and 4 track the demographics of boom and bust and what this means for the distribution of wealth and power. Being a great big generation makes you a powerful disruptive force: you pour through society like a flooding river breaking its banks.

We can make sense of the economic and social changes around us if we see them as the continuing story of the extraordinary impact of this massive post-War generation. Some economists thought it would be a disadvantage to be in a big generation; with more crowding and competition at every stage, it would be like travelling through life in economy class rather than business class. But, so far at least, being big has turned out to be a fantastic advantage, enabling that generation to dominate marketplaces and shape politics.

Successive generations at different stages of our lives have different needs and different things to offer. That is why it makes sense for different generations to co-operate – so we educate the younger generation now and then hope to benefit from what they produce in the future. What you get back need not be a direct exchange but instead an expectation that the next generation will do the same for you, so for example you care for your parents now and hope your children care for you when you are older. These types of exchanges between the generations, explored in Chapters 5 and 6, are how families and whole societies function. I try to get down to the fundamentals of human co-operation, drawing on recent insights coming from game theory and evolutionary biology. They help us to understand how these ties between the generations, the implicit contracts between them, can actually work.

I believe that a lot of our social and economic problems can be seen as the failure to understand and value these contracts between the generations. Much of what we see as social breakdown is in fact the breakdown of relations between the generations; much mistrust is mistrust between generations; much of what has gone wrong with our economy is a failure to get the balance right between generations. This is what low savings and big deficits are all about, and it is what environmental degradation is about too. Sometimes we do not even appear to understand what we are doing to future generations nor how much we owe to previous ones.

The great French thinker Alexis de Tocqueville put the charge as powerfully as anyone:

> Among democratic nations new families are constantly springing up, others are constantly falling away, and all that remain change their condition; the woof of time is every instant broken, and the track of generations effaced. Those who went before are soon forgotten; of those who will come after, no one has any idea; the interest of man is confined to those in close propinquity to himself... Thus not only does democracy make every man forget his ancestors, but it hides his descendants and separates his contemporaries from him; it throws him back forever upon

himself alone, and threatens in the end to confine him
entirely within the solitude of his own heart.[1]

There is one obvious explanation why we are failing to protect
the interests of future generations. We can reasonably hope that
successive generations will be more affluent, unless the entire
mechanism of economic growth since the Industrial Revolution
is turned off. In Chapter 7 we look at the argument that economic
growth means we do not have to worry about future generations
as they should be richer than us. But I do not believe this does
remove our obligation. We each of us benefit from what we inherit
from previous generations and we must do our best to leave
something worthwhile for the next.

Think of life as a relay race. We are handed a baton to run our
lap and then pass it on to someone else. We may be able to run
faster than the earlier runners, perhaps because we have better
kit or better training, and we might expect that later runners
coming after us will do better than us. But we still have to try to
do the best lap we can. We cannot escape our obligations to future
generations just because we think they might be richer, any more
than previous generations could decide not to educate us or build
roads and sewers or leave great public buildings because we would
be rich enough to do all this for ourselves. Indeed the only reason
to assume that successive generations will be better off is if we
invest in the future – if there is one thing which would turn that
process off it would be a belief that the future did not matter.

Moreover we do actually depend on future generations. Just as
we were provided for in our childhood by the older generation,
so in our old age we are provided for by the younger generation.
What we will live on in our old age is not produced now; it will be
produced then. The bread we will eat is not baked now and stored
in the garden shed; it will be baked by the younger generation and
we will hope to get some of it, either by taxing them or by owning
a stake in what they produce. The challenge is how we can stake a

claim now to that future output in a way which ensures that claim is honoured. If the younger generation feel they have had a raw deal, they will not protect the Boomers in their old age.

It is the contract between the generations which binds these two interests together. This is where government fits in too: maintaining the balance between the generations, as we will see in Chapter 8. Native American peoples have a rule that they should consider the impact of every decision for the next seven generations. Good government values the future; bad government takes from it.

There is nothing more natural in human affairs than the eternal repeating cycle of childhood, adulthood, and old age – or what used to be called the seven ages of man. This cycle gives a deep pattern to our lives which we can all recognize whatever our political and ethical views. The basis for co-operation between the generations is that we can exchange to mutual benefit because we are at different points in the cycle and have different needs and capabilities. In the final four chapters I focus on particular stages of our lives to see what they reveal about the relations between the generations.

We immediately confront an important paradox here. If anything, relations between parents and their children are better than they used to be – what was called the generation gap is disappearing. There is striking evidence of the enormous effort most parents are now putting in to raising their children: they are closer to their children than parents were a generation ago. Many children are now dependent on their parents for longer than ever – and it is unwise to row with your banker. The dependence of the generations on each other in the family is more mutual as well, perhaps because of the speed of technological change – neatly captured in the cartoon of a mother holding a gadget like a TV remote and calling out desperately to her baby: 'How do I get it to work?' But however close we are to our families, we cannot just do our best for the next generation one by one. We also have to offer a fair share of power and wealth to the younger generation as a whole. This is where the gap between the generations is getting wider, and it is a different sort of generation gap from the one we are used to. We may be better parents than we are citizens.

This is the challenge for the Baby Boomers. At the moment this generation dominates just about every important institution in the country: it has most of the wealth and power. How will this generation discharge its obligations to the younger generation? Will the Boomers be selfish with their luck, or will they pass that luck on to the next generation? So far the evidence is not good. The Baby Boomers, having so far enjoyed a spectacularly good deal, are dumping too many problems on the younger generation. It has the great advantage of being a giant generation, but how will it use that power? At the moment it looks like a selfish giant.

The Boomers are a rich and powerful generation. They are now past the halfway stage but it is not certain their luck will last. Solon, the great Athenian statesman, visited Croesus, the richest and most powerful man of his day. Croesus was surprised that Solon was not more impressed by his good fortune. 'Call no man happy until he is dead' was Solon's dry response. Subsequently, Croesus lost his wealth, his kingdom, and his family, and died a captive.[2] So this is a challenge to the Boomers to value not just future generations but also their own future. It is a matter not just of other people's futures but of what – for today's long-lived generations – has been called the Long Now.[3]

Britain is at an unusual point of generational equipoise. Now is a good moment to judge the balance between the generations. If you line up the British population today by order of age, the middle person in Britain would be aged 40. Their life expectancy is 80. So the middle person is likely to be almost exactly halfway through their life. What happens in the next 40 years matters to them even if they do not feel any obligation to other generations.

One of our deepest human instincts, somewhere between a desire and an obligation, is to transmit something worthwhile to the next generation. It is not just wealth but a body of knowledge, a set of values, an understanding of how to lead a good life. We know that each generation is going to move on, and we hope that it will do better than us, but we know its chances of doing better than us are greatest if it is standing on our shoulders. Much of this experience, wisdom, and values is transmitted within the family. This is where the contract between the generations is played out most personally for each one of us.

So we will start in Chapter 1 with families, and how they shape the deepest features of our society.

1

WHO WE ARE

Picture a family gathered around steaming plates of pasta on a massive trestle table under a tree in a Tuscan garden, with uncles, aunts, brothers, daughters-in-law, elderly sisters all engaged in an excited, voluble hubbub. That is a real family, the kind of family in the film *My Big Fat Greek Wedding*. It is easy to assume – I certainly used to – that at some point in the past the English lived like this too. Even if the food was not so good we surely lived in big, extended peasant families, and in those times all the land belonged to a feudal lord as well. Then there came a great transformation – perhaps the rise of Protestantism, or the Civil War, or the Industrial Revolution – which drove the spread of private property and the modern nuclear family. But the truth is that England was never a society of peasants living in extended families, and we never had true serfdom. As far back as 1250, and probably even earlier, it looks as if England had a very different social structure, different even from the rest of the British Isles. Forget everything you think you know about extended families, arranged marriages, serfdom, and seigneurs. As far as we know none of that happened in England – ever. When it comes to families, England was the first nuclear power.

Instead, think of England as being like this for at least 750 years... We live in small families. We buy and sell houses. We go out to work for a wage. Our parents expect us to leave home for paid work when we are in our teens. If you are a boy you go off to be an apprentice, and if a girl perhaps to be a servant in another house. You try to save up some money from your wages so that you can afford to get married. You are not dependent on inheriting property from your parents so they have a limited hold over you and you can choose your spouse. Indeed, when it comes to choosing your partner what matters is love, actually. It takes a long time to build up some savings from your work and find the right person with whom to settle down, so marriage comes quite late, possibly in your late twenties. If a man gets a girl pregnant before then he might well have to marry her but they tend to avoid full sex, settling instead for elaborate forms of heavy petting.

Because we marry quite late and the two parents then bear a large part of the burden of raising the children, we do not have many of them.[1] If a society has extended families or clans then this spreads the costs of raising children across more adults, who then have more children younger. That means there is a danger of cycles of population boom and bust as surges in the birth rate are followed by famine and collapse. But that is not the English model. Our population grows slowly but steadily after the catastrophe of the Black Death in the fourteenth century, which may have reduced it to 2.5 million. Britain's first great economic statistician, Gregory King, estimated that the population of England in 1688 totalled 5.5 million. His key table includes estimates of average family size.[2] The upper-class 'heads of families' do indeed have many family dependents. But where the wider population is concentrated – categories such as the 750,000 'freeholders of the lesser sort' or the 1,275,000 'labouring people and outservants' – estimated family sizes are 5, 4, or 3.5. This first demographic analysis of England offers further evidence that we have long had small nuclear families.

There are a few rich families with an enormous amount of land for whom arranged marriages matter for dynastic settlements and inheritance, but it is a mistake to assume they are typical of everyone else. Most people are, of course, peasants, in the sense that they work on the land from generation to generation. But they are not under the exclusive control of a feudal landlord, let alone his property. They can make themselves available for hire at the great seasonal fairs. They are probably paid in cash not in kind. Money matters. There is borrowing and lending and mortgages and, to keep all this going, quite a sophisticated law of contracts. In turn, these contracts are enforced by an independent judiciary.

———————

Here is an account of England in the flat language of modern sociology. It is a familiar picture of who we are and how we live: 'The majority of ordinary people in England... are rampant individuals, highly mobile both geographically and socially, economically "rational", market-oriented and acquisitive, egocentred in kinship and social life.'

Some figures for typical English towns and villages confirm that, and capture vividly how markets seem to matter more than roots. In Leighton Buzzard, out of 909 transfers of land, 66 per cent are outside the family; only 15 per cent go to the family in the owner's lifetime and another 10 per cent at death. Another study, of a village near Huntingdon, finds on 43 occasions the property is passed on within the family and, of these, 24 are direct blood inheritance. But there are 21 cases of the property being conveyed to someone outside the family and 98 cases of an open market sale. A third study shows 87 per cent of land transactions taking place between people not related to each other through kinship. And a host of studies show lots of buying and selling of property. This is just what we would expect – a nation of cash, contracts, and commerce. The key question is supposed to be whether or not these modern patterns of behaviour are desirable. Has this turbulent individualism eroded our ties of family and community? But there is just one hitch. The statistics for Leighton Buzzard are for the period 1464 to 1508; for the village near Huntingdon the period studied is 1397 to 1457; and the 87 per cent non-family transactions occurred in a manor in about 1400. The quotation is from a description of England back to the thirteenth century by Alan Macfarlane, the historian who above all has revived this understanding of England, and whose influence pervades this chapter.[3]

The power of local barons over peasants was limited by an effective national government too. Insofar as medieval England was 'feudal', its feudalism took an unusually centralized form. The Normans successfully increased the power of central government and subordinated local magnates. Peasants could not be called up for military service directly by a local landlord. In the words of Frederic William Maitland, the great Victorian historian, the king could directly tax his subjects, 'their lands and their goods, without the intervention of their lords'.[4]

There was local administration of the common law, that exceptional English creation of the early medieval period. But the common law was crucially not local law. You were bound by precedent, a body of case law that was consistent across the country. That is what 'common' means. Royal authority was used to limit the power of barons to administer the law in their own interests. Indeed, the crown kept direct control of justice in the regions by sending travelling assize courts around the country. This made it much harder to do special favours for kith and kin and so helped to ensure protection for the small nuclear family without extended networks of relatives. The standardization was not, however, achieved simply by royal fiat: it was achieved by lawyers meeting at their London Inns to compare notes and establish through these self-governing institutions a shared understanding of the law, built up through precedent – the role of precedent and its limit on discretion being a difference between the English legal system and the more Roman-influenced legal traditions which flourished on the Continent.

An effective national government and a national framework of law made geographical and, hence, social mobility much easier. Internal migration was easier than in the rest of Europe: not least because you were not tied to an extensive network of favours and reciprocal obligations. Indeed, geographical mobility has been another exceptional feature of the English model – and one which America shares with us.

This adds up to an extraordinarily balanced political and social system in which an effective national government protected the rights of individuals and families and stopped the creation of local clans and concentrations of baronial power. It was not, by and large, possible for local feuds to develop into private wars. Local barons were not able to extract tax at will. And administration of justice remained broadly fair, without special favours to networks of relatives.

This was the eighteenth-century English polity when Adam Smith wrote *The Wealth of Nations*, but its roots go back at least 500 years. It might be called merely a nightwatchman state. But this is to underestimate the crucial role of effective national government. It was not a libertarian utopia. Maintaining an effective framework of national law and stopping local magnates being too powerful were both crucial national responsibilities, discharged by virtually no other government at the time. This is the paradox of strong but limited government. This strong government protected small families.

These small families were very unusual. Unlike many other cultures, we lack specific words for particular types of uncles, grandparents, and cousins. (How many people could work out what relation a second cousin, twice removed, would be to them?) There is no framework of law setting out obligations between them. Even our earliest law code, King Alfred's, placed very weak obligations on families. In the words of one historian of Anglo-Saxon society, 'the duties kinsmen had with respect to [a given family member] were few'.[5] These small families could be extraordinarily strong,

5

held together by powerful attachments between a couple and with marriage increasingly recognized in canon and civil law as a pre-eminent institution. But their unusually small size also made them vulnerable to external shocks. An extended family can offer more by way of support and mutual insurance.

This model of law and society is quite different from models in many other parts of the world. In parts of Asia, for example, it is assumed that if one member of a large extended family gets a good job, his responsibility is to distribute the benefits to his relatives and ideally get them a similar job in the same organization. Helping relatives with contracts and jobs is not seen as corruption but as a moral obligation. Big, clan-style families are better than nuclear ones at spreading advantage and pooling risks, but for them to be effective people have to stay close to each other, so there is less mobility.[6]

Sometimes we may regret that England does not enjoy the advantages of these clan-style families, and look back to an age when supposedly we did. The earliest recorded example of this sort of nostalgia is a sermon given by Bishop Wulfstan in 1014, in which he expressed regret that vendettas were not what they used to be, as family members just would not join in – 'too often a kinsman does not protect a kinsman any more than a stranger'.[7]

These mobile individuals and small families had to look outwards and create alternative networks for support and insurance. So they were very effective at creating local and civic institutions. With small families, people needed more of these civil networks in order to sustain a given level of social insurance. Medieval guilds are one early example. And early means early – these societies were being created more than a thousand years ago. The rules of the Thegns' Guild in Cambridge in the late tenth century describe the obligations between 'guild-brothers'; for example, 'If any guild-brother dies outside the district, or is taken ill, his guild-brothers are to fetch him and bring him, dead or alive, to where he wishes, on pain of the same fine which has been stated in the event of his dying at home and a guild-brother failing to attend the body.'[8] Instead of families discharging what Bishop Wulfstan thought were their responsibilities, outside groups such as guilds were providing mutual insurance of a sort we can recognize today.

The 'guild-brothers' were not blood brothers. These guilds were not family-based or closed shops. They were usually open to new members: 'if our lord or any of our reeves can suggest to us any addition to our peace guild; [rather] let us accept it joyfully, as becomes us all and is necessary for us'.[9] For the next thousand years the English carried on creating these groups and societies. Thomas Babington Macaulay, the great nineteenth-century politician and historian, looked at them with a hint of amusement: 'This is the age of societies. There is scarcely one Englishman in ten who has not belonged to some association for distributing books, or for prosecuting them; for sending invalids to the hospital or beggars to the treadmill; for giving plate to the rich or blankets to the poor.'[10]

Small families need civil society more. But it is not just voluntary societies which provide mutual support. You need markets and commercial services too. Instead of the mutual exchanges of the extended family, small families must buy services. For example, insurance schemes, annuities, and savings help protect you when there is no wider family with any such obligation. This is one reason why England has a long history in financial services.

Small families meant there was a role for government too. By Tudor times the national government had already stepped in with the Poor Law, after the dissolution of those powerful civic welfare institutions, the monasteries.[11] The Elizabethan Poor Law required the provision of welfare, which was delivered and financed locally. Despite its harshness and injustices, it was a far more ambitious nationally legislated welfare provision than existed anywhere else in Europe. It set out the entire local parish's obligations to people who could not care for themselves, as they were old or infirm or not in work. Unlike in most other countries then or now, it was provided independently of employers or relatives. This left people unencumbered and mobile. When, centuries later, his government was trying to reform welfare, Lord Liverpool, the prime minister after the Napoleonic Wars, summarized this unique combination very neatly: 'The legislature of no other country has shown so vigilant and constant a solicitude for the welfare of the poorer classes; no other has so generally abstained from the interference with the details and operation of trade.'[12]

This is a very unusual social and political structure indeed. England has had unusually small families, unusually strong national government, unusually weak local magnates, and unusually free peasants. It is not just different from Papua New Guinea or Pakistan; it is also quite different from France and Italy and most of Continental Europe. This difference was recognized by foreigners. After visiting England in 1730, that shrewd French observer of human cultures, Montesquieu, observed: 'I too have been a traveller, and have seen the country in the world which is most worthy of our curiosity – I mean England.'[13]

It is not that England is better or that foreigners are wrong. But England is certainly distinct. How come? One possible explanation, suggested by Alan Macfarlane, is that almost a millennium and a half ago the Anglo-Saxons brought with them the social, legal, and family arrangements of the German tribes. Perhaps because they were frequently on the move, they did not have the sense of land held perpetually by some family or group. Instead it was always being exchanged between individuals. The original Germanic model then disappeared on the Continent as Roman law extended its way back across Northern Europe in the Middle Ages. However, it survived in England, to which it had emigrated. This idea was neatly caught by Benjamin Franklin when he wrote that 'Britain was formerly the America of the Germans'.[14] Montesquieu had a similar thought when he wrote that 'In perusing the admirable treatise of Tacitus on the manners of the Germans we find it is from that nation the English have borrowed their idea of political government. This beautiful system was invented first in the woods."[15] The reference to the woods may be a crucial clue – one suggestion is that the need to cut down trees to create small clearings is why families were small rather than large and clan-based. It is indeed in Central Germany where archaeologists have found the first genetically identifiable nuclear family – a mother, father, son, and daughter buried facing each other in graves dating back 4,600 years. The mother was not genetically related to the father and had spent her childhood in a different region, suggesting that the relationship was not based on membership of the same clan.[16]

The range of family structures around the world has been mapped on to political structures by the great contemporary French thinker Emmanuel Todd.[17] The correlation is uncanny and its historical roots deep. The other European countries with the Anglo-Saxon model of the nuclear family are the Netherlands and Denmark. Todd casually notes that these happen to be the areas of Europe once ruled by King Canute, which itself indicates the timescale over which we must think about these family structures. Todd shows the fundamental importance – not just for social structures but also for shaping political systems – of the difference between endogamous societies, where marriages are often arranged and with relatives (looking inwards to reinforce the clan), and exogamous societies, where marriages are to outsiders and partners may be freely chosen. The second key distinction is between societies where inheritance is egalitarian, with all children having an equal claim, and societies where it is inegalitarian, with no obligation to treat all children alike. Many other European countries have exogamous marriage but they do not usually have inegalitarian inheritance as well. (The exact legal form and force of marriage may change over time, as common law marriage thrived before the Church of England got greater control over marriage in the eighteenth century.)

Thus the Anglo-Saxon model is unusual in being both exogamous and inegalitarian. Instead of all the property belonging to the family as a whole and being automatically divided between many children when the parents died; in England the older son usually inherited. This pushed out waves of property-less younger sons to make their way in the world. At the same time, it made it easier to accumulate wealth in the hands of an individual because it was not endlessly being divided among many heirs. Hence you get that distinctive English combination of a society that is both mobile and unequal.

So far we have been painting a picture of England as a marketplace – perhaps the world's first and most sophisticated market economy. Inevitably that means we have focused on patterns of behaviour that are rational, calculating, and acquisitive. But that is not the full picture. The market relationships described so far are complemented by, and indeed create an intense need for, emotional relationships outside the market economy as well. A small, simple family structure not driven by the need to pass on an inheritance or to sustain ties with brothers and cousins in a clan can be more personal, intense, and emotional – a clue to England's Romantic tradition. Foreign observers have long remarked how the English love their gardens and their countryside. This may be because we were more urban and then more industrial than the rest of Europe. As we were the first country to move from dependence on agriculture, that perhaps explains some of the emotions we now invest in our pets – and the proud claim of the English to be the inventors of pet food. Charles Dickens captures all this brilliantly with his picture in *Great Expectations* of Wemmick retreating over his drawbridge to his little domestic arcadia, away from the hurly-burly of market transactions. England displays that strange mixture of calculation and sentiment which marks so many modern societies.

There is an obvious romantic appeal in tracing our origins to German tribes from the woods and plains of Northern Europe.

But is this just nostalgia for a pre-industrial world? Because this account of national identity goes all the way back to the Middle Ages, it is open to the charge that, even if it were once true, now it is out of date. Didn't the Industrial Revolution and class politics change all that? It is easy to assume that Britain had the Industrial Revolution and then became the world's first modern commercial society. The truth is exactly the other way round. We were already the world's first market society and were therefore ripe for the Industrial Revolution. We have rightly been described as enjoying 'capitalism without factories' for many centuries before the Industrial Revolution. That the Industrial Revolution began in England is a crucial piece of evidence in support of the argument that we have a distinctive economic and social structure.

One way of assessing the impact of the Industrial Revolution in Britain is through the historical equivalent of the *Sunday Times* Rich List. The historian W. D. Rubinstein has studied the estates left by the richest families before, during, and after the Industrial Revolution.[18] In the early eighteenth century the wealth of the British middle and upper classes came from commerce, finance, the law – and the global trading networks they serviced. Then came the Industrial Revolution, and Lancashire and Yorkshire rose from providing 10 per cent of business and professional incomes in 1810 to a peak of 22 per cent in 1860. They made their wealth differently from the way anyone had made money in the past – by manufacturing – and they created a proud civic culture in the cities of the Midlands and the North. But after that the North of England began to decline as a proportion of the richest families. By the early twentieth century, patterns of income and wealth in Britain had reverted to what they were before the Industrial Revolution. Once again it was trade, finance, commerce, and the great professions.

A similar pattern can be seen in demography. We have seen how, traditionally, England had an unusually low birth rate and hence a degree of protection from the worst of all possible boom-and-bust cycles – that of human lives. After the Black Death, the population of England appears to have been on a slow upward trajectory for the next 400 years or so, rising perhaps to 8.3 million by the end of the eighteenth century. But the nineteenth century was an exception to this steadiness, as our population soared to 30 million by the century's end. As we industrialized there was a mass movement of population into towns, and at the same time some of the traditional constraints of the English family system broke down. People had more babies and had them earlier. And, of course, in the conditions of living then, many of them were sadly to die. Indeed, because our pre-industrial birth rate was so low, it actually rose during the early stages of industrialization: this is another unusual feature of English demography.[19] By the end of the nineteenth century, mortality in our towns was falling and then the birth rate fell as well. After the Industrial Revolution we therefore went through the two classic phases of the demographic transition which most societies go through as they modernize. It can be summarized very simply – first, we stop dying like flies, and then we stop breeding like rabbits. By the early twentieth century we had resumed a pattern of later marriage and lower birth rate, of the sort we can recognize from Alan Macfarlane's account of early medieval England.

––––––––––

Just as aerial photography can reveal the outlines of some long-lost medieval village, so, if we know how to look, we can discern deep features of English society that endure to this day. Here is an example. A series of reports have attributed the long-standing weaknesses in the productivity of the British economy to our lack of a *Mittelstand*, the strong medium-sized family businesses of the sort they have in Germany and France.[20] We appear to be very good at starting small businesses, and some of our big companies are very strong indeed. It is the high-performance, solid, long-term, high-investment medium-sized companies in the middle that we seem to lack. It is not that we have fewer family-owned firms – about 30 per cent of mid-sized British firms are owned by a family, very similar to those in France and Germany. But we run them differently. Perhaps England's family structure helps to explain this.

A key difference is that land is not owned by kin groups but by named individuals with unrestricted power over what happens to their property. This is one reason why, from medieval times, if you had property you were expected to leave a will. Friedrich Engels recognized that this made England's family law very different: 'In those countries where a legitimate portion of parental wealth is assured to children and where they cannot be disinherited – in Germany, in countries with French law and elsewhere – the children are obliged to obtain their parents' consent to their marriage. In countries with English law... the parents have full liberty to bequeath their wealth to anyone and may disinherit their children at will...'[21]

French law reflects a very different view of the family. In France, neither land nor a firm is the freehold property of the individual, belonging rather to the family's bloodline with an automatic right of inheritance within the family for all the children. This is how the principle of equal inheritance is delivered in practice. In England, the firm – like other property – belongs absolutely to the individual to do with it as they wish. It may be passed on to one child who will have control of the company. In France an asset such as a family firm is not the absolute property of one individual. A father has no right to cut his children out of his will; they (and to almost the same extent, the spouse) are *héritiers réservataires*, 'protected heirs'. If any part of the property or land is willed to someone other than the children of the deceased, forced heirship rights kick in and can override any bequest regarding the property.[22]

In England, therefore, family firms are more likely to be run as the personal property of an individual, who often manages the business themselves. In France and Germany family firms are more likely to be held in common by a whole family and seen as the long-term property of a dynasty across several generations. This means the family is more willing to bring in professional managers to run the business on its behalf: 31 per cent of family-owned firms in France are run by an external manager, as against only 23 per cent in the UK. (It is 60 per cent in Germany.) Of family-owned firms still owned by the founder, 44 per cent in France are externally managed; whereas it is only 14 per cent in the UK (again, it is 60 per cent in Germany).[23] A report in the *Economist* makes the same point: 'A survey of the manufacturing industry by the Office for National Statistics showed that family-owned and -run companies are about 19% less productive than others. Family-owned companies that have non-family management do better, but still lag the rest.'[24]

This has a big effect on economic performance[25] – if an inherited family firm brings in an outside manager, it raises returns by 6 percentage points, a significant improvement in return on capital.[26] One factor is that external managers in family-owned firms are more likely to be graduates than managers in family-run firms are.[27]

If you go further afield the differences are far greater, and show up even more starkly the links between the social, the political, and the economic. Why is it so hard to establish liberal democracies and effective governments in large parts of the Middle East? It is not ultimately a matter of religion but of the cultural traditions associated with some versions of Islam. Their family structure may help explain why Western-style democratic government is so rare in parts of the Muslim world. In Pakistan, 50 per cent of marriages are to first cousins. In Saudi Arabia this figure is 36 per cent.[28] The political structure of a society of extended families is completely different from that of a society with small families. It means that voting is by clans: it is hard to have neutral contracts enforced by an independent judiciary when family obligations are so wide-ranging and so strong.

It is no accident that there is a Muslim Brotherhood – brotherhood really does mean something in parts of the Muslim world. It weakens national governments and makes it hard for the neutral contractual arrangements of a modern market economy to be created. In England, by contrast, as Dr Johnson observed: 'Sir, in a country as commercial as ours, when every man can do for himself, there is not much occasion for that attachment. No man is thought the worse of here whose brother was hanged.'[29] The French Revolutionaries ignored the uncomfortable truth that liberty and equality before the law are hard to reconcile with fraternity. That is why it is such a challenge to integrate communities based on fraternity into a host society where the dominant principles are liberty and equality.

England's closest neighbours understood more clearly than the English themselves the components of this distinctive Englishness. A whole stream of French observers were fascinated by this extraordinary English political and social experiment – from Voltaire and Montesquieu in the eighteenth century to Alexis de Tocqueville and Hippolyte Taine in the nineteenth. But it was above all the Scottish thinkers of the eighteenth century who reflected on this English model. David Hume, Adam Smith, and Adam Ferguson put markets, contracts, and civil society at the centre of their thought, and in doing so created the political economy of the modern world. As well as political and moral philosophy, Hume wrote a history of England. Smith drew heavily on English evidence throughout *The Wealth of Nations* and his *Theory of Moral Sentiments*. Scottish intellectuals reflecting on England's economy and society created what Gertrude Himmelfarb has boldly called the British Enlightenment.[30]

Britishness is emphatically not the same thing as Englishness. The English model is just one within the British Isles. Scotland has a distinctive history, with a separate legal system and educational arrangements and a different culture. Great Britain provides the political institutions which linked these two nations in an outward-looking endeavour of trade and conquest: it is the British army, the British Empire, and the British pound. That connection made both nations different and better than they would have been on their own; and in the early excitement after the Act of Union of 1707, Scots such as David Hume were willing to describe themselves as living in North Britain. Britishness is a weaker cultural identity than Englishness or Scottishness. That is why H. G. Wells could say that 'The great advantage of being British is that we do not have a national dress.'

That Britishness is essentially an institutional concept makes it very well suited for today, when empire and conquest have long gone. It helps ensure our national identity is not ethnic, giving it a marvellous openness. Instead it is a political identity, resting above all in a set of political institutions. Most non-white ethnic groups describe themselves as British rather than English, whereas it is very different for white people. Sixty per cent of non-whites identify as British and 20 per cent as English, whereas for whites it is 38 per cent who identify as British and 60 per cent as English.[31]

So British patriotism is not a nationalism of blood and soil. It is a celebration of the institutions that shaped our country and which should be open to everyone. In fact, successive waves of migration brought distinctive ideas and institutions that between them developed into what we now call Britishness.

Winston Churchill wrote his *History of the English-Speaking Peoples* in this tradition, including North America and beyond in his celebration of these political institutions. Andrew Roberts has carried that tradition forward, adding an extra volume to Churchill's history.[32] Niall Ferguson has also argued for the distinctive identity of what is now called the Anglosphere. These formidable historians show very clearly that in everything from economic structures to cultural attitudes, there is a close link between Great Britain, the US, Canada, and Australia. But they do not fully resolve the question of what makes the Anglosphere distinctive.

It is easy to think of the English language as what unites this group – after all, the Anglosphere was formerly known as the English-speaking peoples. But this does not tell anything like the whole story. The unusual importance of civil society is crucial. Now, we immediately face a paradox. Alexis de Tocqueville was one of the first people to see that the youthful America derived much of its dynamism from its extraordinarily rich and self-reliant civil society, as a contrast with pre-Revolutionary France: 'When the Revolution started, it would have been impossible to find, in most parts of France, even ten men used to acting in concert and defending their interests without appealing to the central power for aid.'[33] But his most influential book fails to recognize that this is what the US and England share, or why. His analysis suffers from one massive disadvantage – he went to America before he visited England. When he wrote his great book *Democracy in America* in the 1830s he was completely unaware of the English origins of the American model. In fact, he thought that England was trapped in an aristocratic and feudal past and that the vigour of civil society in America was unique. This is a crucial mistake. It obstructs the understanding of what links Britain and America, and leaves Brits, metaphorically at least, forever playing aristocrats and butlers in American films.

When he finally visited England, Tocqueville was trying to work out when the revolution which America and France had already experienced would also strike England and lead to the overthrow of powerful concentrations of aristocratic wealth. He expected some revolution in favour of agricultural smallholdings belonging to people like the soldier-citizens who were the backbone of Jefferson's America. Free-market English economists had to explain that we had big farms because they were more efficient.

Tocqueville only came to appreciate that what he had seen in America could also be found in England after two visits – the moment of epiphany coming when he visited the city where I was born and brought up, Birmingham, in the full vigour of the

Industrial Revolution. He noted in his diary that its inhabitants were 'generally very intelligent people but intelligent in the American Way'.[34] Tocqueville thought at first that America was the future for everywhere – and indeed that France, having already had its revolution, was further on the way than England. But slowly he came to realize that this model was not right. The vigour of civil society in England or the US is not some universal historic trend. It depends on some very unusual and shared features of our two countries.

Civil society in England and America is similar because we share the same (rather unusual) family structure. Tocqueville eventually made the connection between this social mobility and exceptional family structure, observing that 'England was the only country in which the system of caste had not been changed but effectively destroyed. The nobles and the middle classes in England followed together the same courses of business, entered the same professions, and what is much more significant, inter-married.'[35]

But there are frustrating misunderstandings which obscure this crucial point. The leading history of the American family, *Public Vows* by Nancy Cott, talks of the nuclear family as the 'republican family' – showing how it was seen as an example of republican virtue in contrast with the decadence of the European model, which was thought to be oppressive both domestically and politically.[36] Meanwhile, one of the best books on the nuclear family, Ferdinand Mount's *The Subversive Family*, treats the nuclear family essentially as a human universal. But the real dividing line is to be drawn differently. American family structure is similar to the English model, and different from much of Continental Europe. This explains the strength of US and British civil society and the pervasiveness of the market economy in the Anglosphere. The special relationship depends on a special relationship.

Tocqueville appears to have believed that it was political structure which shaped family life. On a visit to Algiers he was shocked by the blank walls of houses turning their backs to the street and attributed it to 'a tyrannous and shadowy government which forces its subjects to hide from the world and tightly encloses all passions in the interior world of the family'.[37] But it could be the other way round, because the extended, non-nuclear family behind its walls is self-sufficient and turns its back on civil society. Generally, nuclear families mean a stronger civil society because individuals need support outside the family and turn to a rich network of clubs and friendly societies. A recent study of European families showed that these patterns continue to matter today.[38] People in inegalitarian nuclear family societies, like England, Denmark, and the Netherlands, are the likeliest to join clubs and associations.

We also look out to the market to buy services with contracts instead of the mutual exchanges of the extended family. This requires respect for contracts, for property, and for marketplaces. This, too, changes the nature of society. It makes it open and market-facing and literally more mobile. We were delivering good opportunities for younger people to do better than their parents. But, as we shall see in Chapter 4, this promise has not been delivered in the 20 years or so since the Millennium. No other major Western country has done so well and then so badly.[39]

The Anglosphere economies are outward-looking and flexible, so they are good early adopters of new technologies. But they may not be so good at steady incremental improvements in performance with a given technology. And sometimes, as we have seen with new financial instruments, their sheer restless innovativeness can do catastrophic damage. Nevertheless, their flexibility can sustain them in the long run.

———————

It is easy to caricature all this as a picture of sturdy yeoman farmers and individualistic offshore islanders. Julian Barnes's novel *England, England* imagines the custodians of Englishness retreating to the Isle of Wight, which becomes a theme park dedicated to a cosy

England-land. Some contemporary historians would see the account in this chapter as just one way in which a national 'narrative' is 'constructed', traditions are 'invented', communities are 'imagined', and nations are 'forged'.[40] A modern liberal society is indeed going to see different versions of its own history endlessly contested. And modern Western societies are converging. Nevertheless, I believe this account of Englishness is empirically rooted and conceptually rigorous. It is right under our noses. It is, quite simply, the main school of English historical writing, from its emergence as a serious discipline. David Hume and Sir William Blackstone were key founding figures in the eighteenth century. It includes the leading Victorian historians Sir Henry Maine and Frederic William Maitland. Maitland was the mentor of one of the leading founders of the Political Studies Association, Sir Ernest Barker, who wrote of the distinctive strength of our civil society, and whose influence carried on to the Second World War.

Theirs is not just the dominant strand of English historical understanding; it shapes our political thought too. It is why England saw the first flourishing of classical liberalism. The first great liberal political philosopher, John Locke, celebrated the freedom of the individual, and understood property not as something that belonged to a family or a group but as something created by an individual's own efforts. Locke did not construct such an extraordinary new political theory in a vacuum – it was an abridgement of the political and social arrangements he saw around him. The theory followed the practice.

This English political tradition emphasizes the strength and importance of civil society, our country's historic freedoms, and a legitimate role for government in providing equitable justice accessible to all, together with a faith in evolutionary social progress. It sustained a political programme – spreading the rights of citizenship widely and generously – which still matters today. That meant widening the franchise and also spreading what William Beveridge called (in his great wartime report) social security, providing mutual insurance against the giant evils of Want, Ignorance, Disease, Squalor, and Idleness. Democracy and the modern welfare state rested on a powerful sense of the birthright of British citizens which did not depend on who your parents were. But that whole tradition was worn smooth and came to seem too complacent. Our weak economic performance after the Second World War showed it just wasn't strenuous enough. And now we fear that, despite the achievements of the welfare state, our society is becoming less cohesive and less mobile.

We hope that our children will have better lives than us. Instead of thinking just of the horizontal obligations we have to fellow citizens now, we need to think also about the vertical obligations we have to our children and grandchildren and future generations. We think of haves and have-nots. But what if the haves are us now, and the have-nots are our children and grandchildren in the future? We need to do much better at weighing the claims of the Nows versus the Laters. This is the promise of a modern, open, mobile society. But there is increasing concern that we are failing to deliver on that promise.

Figure 2: Opinions about whether young people will have a better life than their parents, 2017[41]

This concern is widespread across many countries. But there is a range – from China, with most optimism for the prospects of their children, to France with the greatest pessimism. Britain is towards the pessimistic end of the scale. And as we gradually assemble the evidence (especially in Chapter 4) we will see that this concern is rooted in reality.

The danger is that if we are failing to pass on full opportunities in life to all our citizens, then we may respond by concentrating only on what we can do for our own children. That is an understandable and indeed admirable instinct. But it is not, as we have seen, an instinct that gets automatic protection in the British system. A shrewd nineteenth-century French observer, Hippolyte Taine, was shocked by this feature of the English system: 'they owe nothing but education to their children; the daughters marry without a dowry, the sons shift for themselves'.[42]

Our great tradition has one very important lesson for us: we do not just want to pass on opportunities for our own children. We inherit not just a particular set of possessions that belonged to our parents. We also inherit a claim to participate in an extraordinary political, social, and economic system that gives us a chance in life. That is a part of the inheritance that we are obliged to pass on to the next generation; that is the obligation which I fear we are failing to discharge, not just as parents but as citizens. And to understand our failure to discharge this obligation, we need to see how the tumultuous social and economic changes since the War have shifted the balance between the generations.

2

BREAKING UP

Imagine a society where people live together in quite large nuclear families with traditional roles. The father goes out to work. His wife may work part-time but mostly she is busy running the house and caring for the two kids and her elderly widowed mother who lives with them. She is as much a worker as he is but her work has no direct financial reward. Although it is much smaller than an extended family, nevertheless it is still a kind of mini-welfare state. The man's earnings are transferred to four dependants. It is a transfer from man to woman. It is also a transfer across the generations, from the middle-aged man to children and a pensioner. Even if he is earning quite a lot, he may not feel very affluent as he has so many commitments. Indeed, the official measures of income and poverty allow for this by counting his income as much less than that of someone with the same earnings who lives on his own ('equivalizing'). The tax system recognizes this too, with special allowances to reduce your income tax if you are married or if you have children, resting on the doctrine that the man we are describing has less 'taxable capacity' than a single person with the same earnings. In this society there is a benefit system too, and its main purpose is to compensate men for loss of earnings – through unemployment, disability, or retirement. He will also get higher benefits such as more unemployment benefit or state pension if he is married, so that he can still, in both senses of the word, keep his wife. This further enforces the dependence of women and young people on the male breadwinner, because even state benefits come via the man. There might also be labour market regulations aimed at protecting the jobs this paterfamilias does, even if as a result it is harder for women or young people to get employment.

This was the British model in the earlier part of the twentieth century. People may disagree about whether it made our community stronger or sustained a monstrous and oppressive paternalism. Perhaps it is pushing the point to include the elderly relative in the house, but these arrangements were quite common for a time after the War because there was such a housing shortage. It is broadly what Japan and Italy are still like today. These are countries with high unemployment benefits, low benefits for single parents, high pensions, and high proportions of pensioners living with their children. (They are also, incidentally, countries with exceptionally low birth rates, suggesting that when women are expected to discharge traditional caring roles for an extended family in an inflexible labour market, they refuse to raise children as well. This is why access to birth control poses a particular demographic challenge for these societies with extended families: it gives women the opportunity to escape one of their many obligations.)[1]

Then a massive social change fragments millions of families like these – the ultra-individualism unleashed by the post-War Baby Boomers. The nuclear family always depended on a personal emotional commitment between two adults – in this sense, it was always individualistic. But in the past it had been sustained by economic dependence, social pressure, and stern personal morality. From the 1960s onwards all these supports fell away. Instead, each of us focused on our own personal needs because, in the words of the L'Oréal advert, 'I'm worth it.' Or, if instead of L'Oréal you prefer Hegel, whose *Philosophy of Right* is one of the few major works of philosophy to focus on the family, marriage declines into 'reciprocal caprice'. Britain and America were particularly susceptible to this fragmentation because, as we have seen, marriage in the Anglosphere relies particularly on its emotional value to each partner.

Let's go back to our opening example. The marriage breaks up in the 1970s or 1980s when the divorce rate surges. The man moves out. His wife becomes a lone parent. The mother-in-law has to go into a flat with some domiciliary care. The lone mother starts to claim benefits. The elderly widow was already getting a basic pension but now she needs a top-up means-tested benefit as well. As they all have their own housing costs to meet with very little income, new benefits have to cover these costs as well. To pay for all these benefits the man finds that his income tax bill goes up. Those special allowances for marriage now seem strangely out of date so they are gradually taken away and the income tax bill goes up even for the couples who have stuck together.

Let's take stock of what this new world is like. Instead of one household there are several. That means we need more housing, though households are smaller. (England's population rose by 19 per cent in the 35 years from 1971 to 2016 but the number of households rose by 45 per cent, though household size was shrinking faster earlier on than more recently.)[2]

Table 1: Household size: UK

1961	3.01
1971	2.84
1981	2.65
1991	2.45
2001	2.37
2011	2.37

As it is more expensive to run multiple households than one, people will feel poorer even if there is the same amount of money to go round as before. At the same time these demographic pressures – combined with restrictions on supply and easy credit

– put up house prices much faster than inflation. So people find themselves asset-rich but cash-poor. They stop saving and instead they borrow against the equity in their properties. So, in our example, there was previously just one working household. But after all these changes there are two workless households as well, one of which is headed by a person of working age.

Official unemployment doesn't change but workless households are up. People start worrying that children are being brought up without seeing a parent going out to work and that this can damage their own employment prospects in turn.[3] There is pressure to tackle the problem of worklessness by getting tougher on adults such as those single parents who aren't working.

Benefits spending has gone up and so has the tax burden. A welfare system that was originally designed to compensate men for loss of earnings is slowly and messily redesigned to compensate women for the loss of men.

The labour market is deregulated so as to get more women and young people into work. The employment rate rises, though there may still be more workless households than before. This reinforces the trend for individuals to be less dependent on each other as more people earn an income for themselves. At the same time there is less deference to tradition and authority, and the very idea of the paterfamilias disappears into history.

This model helps us to understand the economic and social changes which were at their most intense in the 1980s and 1990s and still have an influence on Britain today. (The proportion of workless households peaked in the early 1990s at over 20 per cent, and Universal Credit was designed on the basis it was a big problem.)[4] In fact much of our domestic politics is an argument about these changes and their consequences. Why, for example, did Britain become a more unequal society in the 1980s especially, with such pressure on the tax and benefits system to redistribute from rich to poor? Our example provides a clue. The man is counted as richer after the break-up, even though his actual income has not changed. His ex-wife and the children are counted as poorer. The man's equivalized income appears to have risen, as he has fewer family responsibilities. Two new low-income households have been created as well. There were of course other forces at work in the 1980s – rising pay inequality, distribution of the tax burden, and changes in the structure of the economy. But here it is the demographic backdrop which we are focusing on.

In a modern market economy there may well be big gaps in individual earnings (and in Britain and America they are wider than most). We tend to focus on this diversity of individual earnings. But you see things very differently if you measure incomes not by individuals but by whole households. A society where well-paid individuals are sharing their income with other members of the family who are not working can end up quite equal. One difference between more-equal and less-equal societies is that, by and large, more-equal societies have bigger households. Indeed the big rise in UK inequality in the 1980s coincided with an increased rate of family break-up, which has since stopped growing so fast (while on most measures, inequality has stopped rising).

People talk sometimes as if inequality and poverty are a result of changes in tax rates and the value of benefits. These have certainly played a role – such as the recent cash freeze, cutting the real value of benefits for working families. But at least as important in the 1980s and 1990s were changes in the family. One way of measuring this is to take the tax and benefit rates and the employment patterns of Britain in 1997 and then impose on them the family structure of Britain in 1979. Then we get less poverty and inequality than the actual outcome. Indeed researchers calculated the different factors behind the increase in the proportion of families below 60 per cent of median income from 15 per cent in 1979 to 30 per cent in 1997. Changes in government benefits, other things being equal, actually reduced the poverty rate on this measure by 3 percentage points. But it was more than offset by a demographic change which pushed up the poverty rate by 9 percentage points, by far the biggest single factor behind the increase in their model. This demographic change was higher rates of family break-up and more lone parenthood.[5]

There is quite a lot of argument about why these changes occurred. Did the tax and benefits system drive them? Did it at least make them possible? Or was it just passive, responding to much deeper changes in people's willingness to commit to each other and stick together? Are they just an inevitable consequence of living in a society where personal fulfilment matters above all? And are they a good thing? Politicians find it hard to fit these changes into the conventional political arguments. In a sense, people have become more free as taboos and ties are eroded, so it becomes easier to leave a relationship that is not fulfilling. But by becoming more independent of each other we have also become more dependent on the state, which has to take on the financial responsibilities no longer discharged by the traditional male breadwinners. This means there is a growing celebration of personal independence and freedom, but it is combined with higher public spending and tax. So it feels as if the government is failing to match our individualist values when it is actually picking up the consequences of them.

The irony is that it is hunger for personal fulfilment and happiness which drives these changes, but after all this people are no happier than they were before. In fact, the research suggests that the very arrangements from which some are fleeing seem to offer more happiness for most people.[6] There are also growing gaps between different countries – Denmark has got a lot happier, and now 72 per cent of Danes are very satisfied with the life they lead and 27 per cent fairly satisfied. The UK is not bad, with 42 per cent very satisfied and 51 per cent fairly. Italy is however rather unhappy, with only 6 per cent very satisfied and 61 per cent fairly. This suggests that Italy's attempt to keep the old model is not going well; Denmark's combination of a high level of equality, high marriage rate, and high levels of happiness looks a lot better.[7]

There are ambitious attempts to try to measure the wider effects of the fragmentation of the family on quality of life and well-being. American researchers have even tried to calculate their environmental impact as smaller households are more energy-intensive per person. They estimate that 'Divorced households in the US could have saved more than 38 million rooms, 73 billion kilowatt-hours of electricity, and 627 billion gallons of water in 2005 alone if their resource-use efficiency had been comparable to married households.'[8]

The old model did work quite well, at least for some – and especially for men. Marriage is certainly good for keeping men healthy; when the man in our example moves out to live on his own he starts drinking more, smoking more, and going to bed late, so his health suffers. His life expectancy falls now he is on his own. Some evidence even suggests that married men are more productive at work.[9] (About half the higher wages of married men can be attributed to a selection effect – as women choose men they think will perform better in the jobs market – but the rest appears to arise because the greater commitment in marriage means it is more worthwhile for a spouse to invest time and effort in improving their partner's performance at work. When individual American states moved to easier no-fault divorce, the marriage premium in wages fell as the commitment device had been weakened.)

But the traditional model also involved massive sacrifices of opportunities of jobs and careers by women. It wasn't such a good deal for the woman who sacrificed her career to raise the kids and then found herself on her own without either her husband's earnings or her own. The whole model depended on very high levels of trust and commitment and it was women and children above all who lost out when the commitment was not kept.

So the lesson which the next generation of women took from all this was not to get a man but first to get a qualification and a career. That is the real pre-nup. Only then can you risk getting married. The feminists would add that it is not just that women cannot trust men to stick to their side of the old marriage contract. Women want to enjoy the same freedom to get a job and make their careers which men have long taken for granted. And before we get too misty-eyed about the traditional family model, we should recognize that it was women who did most of the work keeping it going while men earned most of the money. So the new family contract involves a rather different share of responsibilities and burdens between men and women than before – as we shall see in Chapter 9.

The political economist who created the first and most coherent account of the effects of greater individualism was Joseph Schumpeter. In *Capitalism, Socialism and Democracy*, published in 1942, he offered a powerful critique of capitalism. Marx had said that capitalism would collapse because people got poorer and poorer and would eventually revolt against the sheer misery of their conditions. But Schumpeter argued that capitalism would be destroyed not by its failure but by its success. It would spread material well-being and a consumer culture in which people abandoned projects for the future in favour of living for today. Instead of living by solid bourgeois virtues of prudence and foresight, a counter-culture would mock and then overwhelm them.

Schumpeter predicted the decay of the two most powerful forms of commitment to the future. He argued that saving and investment would decline to catastrophically low levels. Secondly, he believed that the birth rate would decline because children, our ultimate project for the future, get in the way of consuming today. Both his predictions have become true across the West, though in very different combinations from country to country. On the

Continent they still save but have fewer babies. In the Anglosphere our savings rate fell much lower, but the birth rate is rather higher.

On this model, divorce and single parenthood are but transitional stages to a world of full-blown childless singletons: we are on our way to an atomized society of weaker families, transient relationships, and fewer children.[10] We can certainly see this social change in the great world cities of New York, London, and Paris. In London, single households are unlike those on, say, the south coast because many of them comprise a single person, quite possibly a man, under 60. (London has smaller households and more inequality than the rest of Britain. The ratio of income for the 90th to the 10th income percentile is 4.66 across the country, but it is 6.26 for London.)[11] Within London there is one area where almost half of all households comprise one person living on his or her own. It is the greatest concentration of under-60 singletons to be found in Great Britain.[12] It is Kensington and Chelsea. If you want to see the future as a cosmopolitan, mobile, rootless, unattached, affluent network of under-60s, living on their own in flats and socializing outside them, then go to Kensington. That is where, as they say, people are thinnest, richest, and singlest.

The impact of the turbulence of the 1980s and 1990s is now showing up across the UK in the growth of older singletons. In 1985, 10 per cent of men aged 60–64 were living alone; by 2009 that had risen to 22 per cent.[13] Nationally there is greater inequality between singleton incomes, which is what one would expect considering this chapter's account of social change. The gap between the income of the top and the bottom 20 per cent of singleton incomes is 3.02 as against 2.58 for couples with children and 2.48 for couples.[14]

The thinker who did most to provide a theory for all this is the sociologist Professor Anthony Giddens. He astutely identified a gap in classical liberalism. On the one hand it praises choice and freedom, but on the other it rarely asks what the people doing all this choosing are like and how they are created. It just assumes a benign history and culture that shape these robust individuals – and, as we saw earlier, liberalism first flourished in England because of just such a culture. But Professor Giddens argued it was absurd for the economic liberals to think we can restrict choice to holidays and cars: we can choose who we are as well. He argued that our identities are no longer fixed and unchanging but instead are deliberately adopted. And that changes the nature of our relations to others. The pure relationship is one which is chosen and can be 'unchosen'. 'A pure relationship is one in which external criteria have become dissolved: the relationship exists solely for whatever rewards that relationship as such can deliver' instead of ties of 'kinship, social duty, or traditional obligation'.[15] It is not clear where obligations to children or parents fit into this model.

Giddens's argument is very important for understanding the intellectual currents around us. It is a kind of explanation for ultra-individualism It reduces all traditions to equally valid costumes in the fancy-dress party of life. It sees all unreflective and unquestioned identities as equally anachronistic and equally threatening to the pure untrammelled choice which it values above all. Life becomes like channel-surfing, with the TV remote in our hands. (Indeed one of the many differences between the generations is that older people tend to watch a single programme, while younger people channel-surf, holding several different narratives in their head at the same time – at least until the arrival of TV on demand.)[16] Choice and freedom are everything. We might argue about whether we like it or dislike it but the liberal progressives and the moral pessimists agree on the trend.[17] In that case it looks as if there really is little chance of society meaning much apart from perhaps, if we are lucky, a feeble agreement on how we are going to disagree with each other.

Alexis de Tocqueville was one of the first people to spot this trend: he traced it back to the breakdown of the contract between the generations, as we saw in the Introduction. The rise of identity politics shows that if liberalism has such a tepid account of what makes us who we are then much more red-blooded accounts will supplant it. One of the many reasons why the intergenerational contract matters so much is that it offers a deeply rooted account of who we are – children and parents located in families.

These changes in family patterns were most marked in the 1980s and to some extent the 1990s. Since then, many of them have stabilized – such as rates of lone parenthood and marriage break-up. Others have significantly improved: employment has risen to a record proportion of the adult population, and the proportion of households that are workless has fallen from 20 per cent to 15 per cent. But we also face new problems, notably the poor progress of young people in getting a well-paid job and a foot on the housing ladder.

We think that the problems of the young must be caused by 'bad' behaviour when actually the Boomers drove these changes in behaviour. And they had a big welfare state to protect them from the worst consequences of their risky behaviour. But now young people bear more risk and behave with greater prudence. They are not relaxed hedonists but suffer from higher levels of mental illness. The economic and social challenges they face cannot be attributed to their behaving like the Boomers – if anything it is the opposite. Today's young people have conventional aspirations and are really rather conservative – with less sex, less drink, more study, and more work. The failure to fulfil their aspirations is not because of their behaviour.

In the next two chapters we will look at how changes in the balance between the generations have reshaped Britain and other Western societies since the War. We will look first at the social changes driven by the sheer size of the Baby Boomer generation, and then at the shifts of income and wealth between the generations. It might help us see what the Baby Boomers really did and why.

3

THE BABY BOOM

From Bust to Boom

The pressures on families were just too much. People were getting married later (aged 26 or more) and having fewer children (down to 690,000 births[1]). One of the popular bestsellers of the day warned of *The Twilight of Parenthood*.[2] How could parents afford all these new consumer goods and raise children as well? It was called the dilemma of the pram or the car. Government advisers warned that by the year 2000 the population could fall to 34 million.[3] Pessimism about the future was pervasive. Welcome to Britain in the 1930s.

The greatest minds of the period worried about the long-term effects of this shift towards fewer children and later marriage than in Victorian times. T. S. Eliot feared in 1939 that 'a wave of terror of the consequences of depopulation might lead to legislation having the effect of compulsory breeding'.[4] Aldous Huxley envisaged in *Brave New World* a society where sex was for fun and nothing to do with producing children. In such a future the raising and care of children would be taken over by the state, leaving individuals unattached and free to consume.

John Maynard Keynes's *General Theory of Employment, Interest and Money* was written at the same time as he was wrestling with what he called 'the economic consequences of a declining population' – the title of a lecture he delivered in 1937. He boldly reversed the obvious but incorrect conventional wisdom that a growing population is more likely to lead to unemployment because of too many workers – the so-called lump of labour fallacy. Keynes argued the opposite: a population that was shrinking would be at greater risk of unemployment. A youthful and growing population borrowed more and consumed more, thus stimulating demand and using resources to the full. By contrast, he argued, a shrinking and ageing population diminished demand, leaving resources unemployed. Keynes's lecture on population began with a statement of what then looked obvious:

> We know much more securely than we know almost any other social or economic factor relating to the future that, in the place of the steady and indeed steeply rising level of population which we have experienced for a great number of decades, we should be faced in a very short time with a stationary or a declining level.[5]

Those confident words were of course proved wrong by the post-War baby boom, reminding us of the need for some humility in the face of apparently inevitable demographic change. But it was a decade before Keynes's forecast, based on the low interwar birth rate, was to be challenged.

In France and Britain fear of depopulation led to new proposals for supporting families – the origins of family allowances (which later became Child Benefit). But it was the fascist governments of Germany and Italy which worried most about low birth rates and were most successful in reversing the trend; this linked pro-natalism with fascism and left the issue politically untouchable for half a century. Only since the turn of the century have the Organisation for Economic Co-operation and Development (OECD) and the European Union been willing to look at the consequences of demographic decline and policies that might raise birth rates.

The Attlee government of 1945–51 and its Conservative successor commissioned earnest reports into the problems of an ageing population and a low birth rate. Indeed one of the Treasury's main fears about the costs of the post-War welfare state was that there would not be enough workers to pay for it. A Royal Commission on Population reported in 1949. A National Advisory Committee on the Employment of Older Men and Women produced a series of reports urging employers not to miss out on the talents of older people. The Phillips Committee warned in 1954 that by 1979 the dependency ratio of pensioners to workers would become unsustainable.[6] Their main proposal was to increase the state pension age for women from 60 to 63 and for men from 65 to 68. On the latest plan, a pension age of 68 for both men and women is supposed to be reached in 2046. It will be almost a hundred years after it was first proposed in a government report – a record even by the standards of Whitehall.[7]

Life was tough in the 1930s. But the actuaries have calculated that 1931 was the best year to have been born in order to have enjoyed the greatest improvement in life expectancy Britain has ever experienced. The austerity of those years and the surge in life expectancy may even be linked – our diet was low in calories, sugar, and fat in the 1930s and 1940s, and scientists now believe that this can prolong life.[8] Another reason that generation did well is the decline in smoking since the 1970s. Of the 750,000 people born in the UK in 1931, more than half – 425,000 – got to the age of 75. But not many people were born in the 1930s and during the War. That means, contrary to popular myth, that the increase in pensioners in Britain was, if anything, unusually modest during the nineties and noughties. It sped up as the post-War Boomers grew old. The number of pensioners went through the 9 million mark in 1990, and eventually surpassed 10 million in 2009. It reached 11 million in 2013, 12 million in 2017, and will exceed 13 million in 2025. That is a clear acceleration in the upward trend, even after being softened by increases in the pension age.

In the 1940s, contrary to all the official forecasts, the baby boom got underway. The opening chart on page xxx shows the size of the change. The first surge had already started during the War, with births rising from below 700,000 in the early 1940s to reach an exceptional peak of more than 1 million in 1947. Four key factors led to this dramatic rise in fertility rates. First, after the low fertility of the 1930s, women faced the choice of either not having children at all or getting on with it even in the unpropitious circumstances of the War. Think of the decline and surges in birth rates as like someone playing an accordion. Births can be low and spread out as people put off having children, but then births get compressed together in a few years. Second, high wartime employment for women (as well as men) provided financial security that encouraged more children. Third, the Second World War saw a sudden and enormous increase in government-funded local authority nurseries on a scale not to be seen again for at least 50 years. Fourth, there was a direct financial incentive, as a soldier's pay was increased if he had children.[9] Britain had a pro-natalist policy without even realizing it.

After the first baby boom peak there was then a modest decline during the early 1950s – though it remained at a high plateau, never falling below 800,000 – before the boom reached a second peak of over a million births in 1964 before declining steadily over the next decade. These twin peaks are very different from the American post-War baby boom, which grew steadily to one sustained high plateau in 1957–61.

With all these babies, the shortage of family homes was a big problem. Churchill wanted to see 'the smoke rising from the chimney of an Englishman's cottage' and won the 1951 election partly because of the dramatic pledge to build 300,000 houses. Harold Macmillan made his reputation by delivering that. In turn, the availability of affordable housing helped to keep the baby boom going. Harold Macmillan went on to become the British prime minister and famously said in 1957: 'Most of our people have never had it so good.' Nowadays we may hear a sexual innuendo in that and, whatever Macmillan's intentions, we are right. The age of first sexual intercourse fell by two years in the fifties, from 21 to 19, a drop more than at any other time in Britain's history.[10] Macmillan's remark could be roughly translated as 'go forth and multiply'. The second phase of the baby boom was underway.

Philip Larkin famously wrote:

> Sexual intercourse began
> In nineteen sixty-three
> (which was rather late for me) –
> Between the end of the *Chatterley* ban
> And the Beatles' first LP.[11]

He got the year exactly right. In 1964, births across the UK peaked at 1.015 million – the only time they have exceeded a million since 1947.

Delaying gratification is crucial in a society where there is not much to go round. But in the words of one advertisement for a credit card, a modern consumer society takes the waiting out of wanting. There is no more primal example of gratification and our need to manage it than sexual desire. For much of our history and for most people, whatever heavy petting or bundling they might have enjoyed, full sexual activity was delayed. It does indeed look as if by the 1960s we were having more sex and having it earlier. The conventional explanation is the Pill, but the big change in sexual behaviour was in the 10 years from the mid-1950s to the mid-1960s, whereas the Pill only became widely available after the NHS Family Planning Act of 1967. A better explanation is that there were more young men in good jobs at an early age than at any other time in the twentieth century. Moreover, marriage as a cultural idea and an economic institution was as powerful as ever: it was still the model for bringing up and providing for a child. If a man got a woman pregnant he was expected to marry her. This meant there was an insurance policy behind the sexual relationship. So there was a host of reliable men with a steady income and a commitment to marrying a woman if they got her pregnant. It was, in a very different sense from today, safe sex. This was the environment which created the most extraordinary surge in the birth rate that modern Britain has seen.

And Britons were not just having more sex and getting pregnant. What they were also doing in the Swinging Sixties was getting married. In each year from 1964 to 1971 there were more than 300,000 first marriages in England and Wales – the highest level ever, apart from during the Second World War. And the average age of brides reached a record low of 22 in 1964. One crucial piece of evidence supports the explanation of early marriage as a kind of insurance claim after earlier sex: 22 per cent of brides were pregnant in 1965, a historic peak compared with 15 per cent in 1955 and 6 per cent in 2015.[12]

As well as a baby boom, the sixties saw a marriage boom. In particular, the two extraordinary years of 1964 and 1965 saw a record number of marriages, a record number of pregnant brides, and record numbers of babies born. It was a frenzy of mating, like a scene from a David Attenborough nature film – with perhaps a touch of *Romeo and Juliet* as well. After all, one in seven brides in the 1960s was a teenager.

This was a disaster for marriage, brilliantly disguised as a success. It put enormous pressure on such unions. The pressure arose not because people were abandoning marriage but because so many people were piling into it so young. Something that had worked for centuries as a contract that adults chose to commit to in their mid- or late twenties was now being entered into by people who were more youthful – and more pregnant – than ever before. Sadly, people who marry young or marry pregnant are most at risk of breaking up. These marriages were fragile. People searched for escape routes, either to avoid getting married in the first place or to get out from marriage more easily.

The first taboo to go was abortion, legalized in 1967. Many of these abortions were to unmarried women: abortion was a way of avoiding the need to marry. But divorce law was still restrictive, and again the pressure for liberalization proved irresistible. Divorce law reform was introduced in 1969 followed by an immediate big increase in divorces. Divorces rose from 25,000 in 1960 to 120,000 by 1972. Five times as many 1960s marriages collapsed within 10 years as 1950s marriages. Abortion and divorce, key features of the 'permissive society', were a response to the boom in fragile marriages.

The origins of the permissive society lie, paradoxically, in the marriage boom of the 1960s. Instead of deferring marriage, people surged into it earlier. But marriage simply could not bear the pressures that were put on it by so many people. Then came the bust. This cycle, in turn, was magnified by economic boom and bust as well.

The Economics of the Family

Once upon a time, 50 years ago, there were what traditionalists still look back on as real jobs and real families. Men were breadwinners. Women, once they married, became housewives. There were steady jobs in manufacturing which paid enough for a man to keep a family. By and large the old Left looks back nostalgically to the traditional industrial jobs and the old Right looks back nostalgically to the traditional role of women. In reality they were dependent on each other, and both were the product of an unusual set of economic circumstances.

This model was itself only perhaps 50 years old. Women had been in paid work for much of the nineteenth century. But as real wages rose it became possible for a man to keep a family on one income, and women stopped working when they married. Only one quarter of women were not in paid work in 1851; in 1911, 90 per cent of wives were not in paid employment.[13] Responsibility for childcare shifted from older siblings (which was then the traditional model) to mothers. The 're-moralization' of late-Victorian society and the surge of voluntary activity may well be linked to these economic forces taking women out of the labour market and making them more available for childcare and voluntary work. Large organizations such as the Civil Service even had rules specifically requiring that women cease work when they got married – a rule which was only abandoned in 1946. Marriage was reinforced by economic dependency. If one partner (usually a man) has a paid job and the other does not, that makes the marriage less likely to break up, even today.[14] As late as 1964, only 40 per cent of British women were in employment.

The economic crisis of the decade following the oil price shock of 1973 destroyed the economic environment on which the twentieth-century model rested. As unemployment rose in Britain in the 1970s and 1980s, the big losers were men in traditional industries. The collapse of reliable male industrial employment weakened marriages and families. It is difficult being an unemployed paterfamilias. It is uncomfortable to confront the evidence that the family is affected by its economic environment, as a family rests above all on the intense personal feelings that hold a relationship together. But evidence is now becoming available which shows how these changes in the jobs market affected families. A man losing his job increased the risk of the marriage breaking up by 70 per cent.[15] One expert estimates that 'the fall in male employment explains between 38 per cent and 59 per cent of the 1.16 m increase in lone parent families over the period 1971– 2001'.[16] Men were less able to discharge their traditional breadwinner role so more women gave up on them.

Some other countries tried to protect traditional male jobs. They still have higher rates of employment among men in traditional jobs; it is women and young people who are unemployed. But in Britain it was older men who lost out from economic change in the 1980s, and the young Baby Boomers who did relatively better. Why was Britain different? A key factor was that we had generous company pension schemes with substantial assets behind them. Employers who made older workers redundant could treat this as early retirement and make the cost a charge on the pension scheme, without the company having to pay anything directly itself. Pension schemes therefore helped finance the social costs of the recessions of the 1970s and 1980s and paid for the restructuring of the British economy, but only by targeting unemployment on older workers.[17] It was the traditional breadwinner who lost out.

The unusual strength of Britain's funded pensions thus contributed to the unusual weakness of our families. There was even a specific programme, the Job Release Scheme of 1977–8, in which older workers were permitted to retire early on condition that their jobs were filled by unemployed school-leavers. It was a vivid example of the use of company pension schemes to fund unemployment for the old and jobs for the young. It has been called 'the most explicit policy of generational substitution yet seen on the statute book'.[18]

Young workers may not be so skilled but they are more flexible, precisely because they have not built up particular know-how tying them to specific industries. They are what you need if you are going through a big change in the structure of your economy – employees who will easily adapt to new technologies. And the peak in the birth rate in the mid-1960s meant there was a surge of young, flexible workers in the mid-1980s. This flow of new workers helped make possible the dramatic structural changes in the British economy as we shifted from traditional manufacturing to services. At the same time there was only a very modest increase in the number of pensioners ahead of them, and a fall in the number of children behind them. (The number of pensioners only went up by 400,000 between 1985 and 1995, while the number of under-18s fell by 600,000.) So the total number of dependants was falling, making control of public expenditure easier. This combination of a surge in flexible young workers and unusually low public spending pressures was crucial to Thatcherism.

More women went into the jobs market too. One reason was the financial pressure of needing a second income to maintain living standards. It was also an insurance policy as more and more marriages broke down. But above all there was simply the urge for personal fulfilment through education and work. Women have indeed been liberated. Any account of generational changes in Britain in the War has to welcome the significant advances enjoyed by successive generations of women.

The story is taking shape. A couple get married young in the 1960s because they think it is the only thing to do if you or your partner are pregnant, and they are both confident that the husband, the breadwinner, will keep them. But he loses his job. Or maybe he just turns out not to be the husband his wife hoped for when she married him at 18. Then his wife gets a part-time job. But she still has to do the housework as well. He does not bring any money in and does not help her around the house either. More and more women are deciding the feminists are right, and that a woman needs a husband as much as a fish needs a bicycle, so she divorces him.[19] (Three-quarters of all divorces are initiated by women, and the rise in divorces since the 1969 reforms matches the increase in female employment.)[20]

The tough economic conditions of the 1970s and 1980s did not just have an impact on marriages; they affected the birth rate too. In 1977, the year after Britain had to be bailed out by the IMF, our birth rate reached a historic low. Those who are more interested in the weather than in economics might also observe that the birth rate peaked after the cold winters of 1946–7 and 1962–3, and reached a low point after the long hot summer of 1976.[21]

Immigration

If an economy has not got many young people, the temptation is to import them. The Labour government took a deliberate decision that East Europeans would be an ideal group to encourage to settle here to plug gaps in the labour market. Within a few years, several hundred thousand Poles and other East Europeans had come over in one of the biggest deliberately engineered movements of immigrants this country has ever seen.

This was, of course, the scheme set up at the end of the Second World War by the British government to recruit potential workers from the Continent to work in Britain and overcome labour shortages. In the 1940s, 350,000 people entered Britain under the European Volunteer Workers Scheme. There was some controversy immediately after the War about all these Poles arriving. The Attlee government set up a Committee for the Education of Public Opinion on Foreign Workers, and the Ministry of Labour helped produce a leaflet entitled 'What the Poles Have Done for You'.[22]

Demographics drove the policy. The War had claimed approximately 400,000 British lives, military and civilian – mostly young adults. It is, however, striking evidence of the power of demographic trends that, even if every British person who died in the War had been aged between 20 and 30, this would have had less of an effect in reducing the size of that age group than the fall in the birth rate in the interwar years. It was this earlier baby bust which meant there was a serious shortage of young people entering the labour market in the 1950s. (It was also one reason why their wages were rising strongly, which in turn created the conditions for the baby boom – and so the cycle turns.) The Royal Commission on Population, which reported in 1949, was quite explicit about the demographic challenge. It calculated that Britain needed to recruit some 140,000 young immigrants, and went on, in the language of the day, to say that they should be 'of good human stock and... not prevented by their religion or race from inter-marrying with the host population and becoming merged in it'.[23] These immigrants were assumed to be coming to settle permanently.

The European Volunteer Workers Scheme was not enough to plug the gap in the jobs market. The first group of immigrants from the West Indies arrived on the *Empire Windrush* in 1948.

Unlike the Workers Scheme, this migration had not been deliberately planned by the government, and there was some Cabinet hostility to 'coloured immigration'. However, the migrants were Commonwealth citizens with a legal right to travel to the mother country.[24]

It is easy to assume that there is a steady and constant supply of new workers coming into the labour market, but looking at the figures generated by earlier birth rates, the truth is very different. The number of 20- to 30-year-olds fell by 1.3 million in the decade from 1950 to 1960; almost as massive as the fall of 1.5 million between 1995 and 2005.[25] This in turn influenced attitudes to immigration. As the first young people from the wartime baby boom began to enter the jobs market, we find more hostility than in the 1950s. The first serious restriction on Commonwealth immigration came in 1962. The National Front was established in 1967 and Enoch Powell's 'Rivers of Blood' speech was delivered in 1968. That year's Immigration Act was also the most dramatic single tightening of immigration controls in the post-War period. Twenty years after the first peak in the birth rate, 1968 would have seen intense competition for jobs, as a very large cohort of young people entered the labour market. From the mid-1960s through to the late 1990s, Britain enjoyed the boost from the post-War Baby Boomers entering the jobs market. In particular 1980 to 1990 saw an unprecedented surge of 1.4 million extra young workers when immigration was tightly controlled. But the low point of the birth rate in the mid-1970s meant that early in the twenty-first century the experience of immigration immediately after the Second World War repeated itself and the Blair government opened up the labour market to the new members of the EU in Eastern Europe. The average age of new immigrants in 2005 was 29, neatly matching the low point in the birth rate 29 years earlier.[26]

The rate of migration stayed high over the following decade because of Britain's flexible labour market, the high pound maximizing the value of remittances back home, and high housing costs giving an advantage to migrants willing to be housed more densely. This coincided with the slowdown in pay and so fed the popular narrative that migration drove down wages. But it is one of those apparently common-sense propositions which may not actually be true. Analysis by the Resolution Foundation suggests a very low impact from immigration on wages.[27] We will investigate all this further in Chapter 11.

Meanwhile the cycle of births rising and falling carried on, though with nothing as massive as the post-War boom. Even during the plateau in the middle of that boom, the number of births did not fall below 800,000. But since then it has rarely reached that level. After falling to an extraordinary low of 660,000 in 1977 the number of births then began to rise slowly, reaching a peak of 800,000 in 1990. Since then we have had a further cycle. The number of births fell to a new low of 670,000 in 2002, almost as low as the low point in 1977 and lower than the low point in 1933. After that, barely remarked upon at first, a new baby boom got underway. It really was a significant birth surge – with the number of babies born in the UK rising above the 800,000 level for three years in succession and hitting a historic high of 810,000 in 2012. Since then it has declined, and was at 750,000 in 2017.

It makes sense to focus on crude birth numbers because that tells us the actual size of a birth cohort, which is what matters for actual market power, democratic power, and pressures on public services. But there is a similar story for the total fertility rate.[28] This rate (the number of children per woman) rose from a low of 1.63 in 2001 to 1.95 in 2008, the highest rate since 1973, when it was 2.0.[29] (If you want to get a sense of the scale of the original baby boom, however, it hit a peak of 2.95 in 1964.) It looks as if the increase is spread across women of most ages, but especially older women. The birth rate for women aged 35–39 has now, for the first time in our history, overtaken the teenage birth rate.

There are two different effects here – one involving women born abroad and another for women born in Britain, but both contributing to the birth surge. The total fertility rate among women born abroad is about 2.5. That rate has remained stable. But the number of women born abroad of child-bearing age has increased from 10 per cent to 15 per cent of all women of childbearing age since 2001. Given their higher birth rate they are now responsible for about 20 per cent of all births in the UK. The number of British-born women of childbearing age has actually been falling slightly – because of that low birth rate in the 1970s and early 1980s. But their fertility rate per person has risen from 1.7 to 1.8, which has more than offset the slight decline in their numbers, and has been 'since 2004... the largest single factor increasing the overall number of births'. It is the women born abroad who push our overall fertility rate up even higher, to 1.9.[30]

The increase in the birth rate took most of the experts by surprise.[31] High house prices were thought to be a powerful contraceptive, keeping the birth rate down and pushing it to the historic low of 2002, so the surge in births might be called 'unplanned' – at least from the perspective of public services and government. But the baby boom peaking in 2008 is less surprising if we go back to the four reasons we gave for that first post-War boom; they all applied in the new Millennium as well. Women who delayed having children finally got round to it. Female employment reached a record high of over 70 per cent in early 2008, before they were hit by the rise in unemployment. With flexible working, access to childcare, and proper maternity leave, female employment does actually raise the birth rate. There was also more provision for the under-5s. Perhaps most significant is the modern equivalent of the wartime scheme whereby soldiers with children got higher pay. Tax credits meant there was a more significant financial reward for having children if you were in work. One estimate was that we might have been having an extra 45,000 babies a year as a result.[32] The recent decline in the number of births may be attributed to reductions in the real value of family benefits and adjustments to lower living standards after the crash.[33]

Now our debate about population is the opposite of the one in the 1930s. The new debate in Britain is not about demographic decline but about the pressures of living on a crowded island. Our population reached 60 million in, by my reckoning, May 2005[34] and it has kept on growing since because of – in the words of the Office for National Statistics – 'births outnumbering deaths (by 148,000 in 2017) and immigration exceeding emigration (by 282,000 in 2017)'. It really is a very substantial and sustained increase in the population to record levels. The British population rose to 50 million in 1948, after which it took almost 60 years to get to 60 million. But we are now growing fast, having reached 66 million already and we are forecast to reach 70 million in 2029. This will excite you if you think big is beautiful. But what matters more for living standards and GDP per head is the composition of this population. Here the news is not so good.

The Ageing of the Baby Boomers

We had an extraordinary demographic bonus from the 1980s through to roughly the financial crash of 2008. There was a bulge of workers in the middle with no real increase in the number of pensioners, and quite a low birth rate. Now that bulge in the middle is sagging and instead the bulges are at the ends of the cycle, among children and pensioners. The Baby Boomers have been a big generation in the middle of the age range – economically productive and with few dependants either younger or older than them.

Between 1985 and 1995 the working-age population increased by 3 million as the Baby Boomers replaced the older small cohort ahead of them. Earnings peak between the ages of 30 and 45, presumably because historically people reach a productivity plateau at that age. So the 1964 birth rate peak had its most positive impact on Britain's economic growth between 1994 and 2009. This matches pretty neatly our successive quarters of economic

growth starting in 1992, the longest run since the Second World
War. We had a combination of a modest increase in the number
of pensioners because of the low birth rate in the 1930s, a positive
impact on the labour market because of the surging population
at their peak earnings, and a modest demand for services for
children because of another smaller cohort behind. It added
up to a very favourable demographic background. The number
of pensioners rose by 0.9 million in the 20 years from 1985 to
2005. But because of the ageing of the post-War Baby Boomers
it then rose by 1.6 million in the 10 years to 2015 (it would have
been 2.1 million but for the increase in the women's pension age
from 2010). The women born in the first baby boom peak of 1947
became pensioners in 2007, and the men in 2012.[35]

The demographic environment is now changing – and it will be
one of the biggest shocks to our economy since the War. Having
had easy sailing with favourable tailwinds, for the next 20 or 30
years we will be battling against demographic headwinds. More of
our growing population will be old people and children; a smaller
proportion will be of working age.

We are getting closer to the key question. Which generations
are doing well out of these demographic fluctuations, and which
are doing badly? Who is going to be well protected in these
tougher times, and who is going to find themselves exposed? That
is the subject of our next chapter. But there is just one more thing
to clear up first – who exactly are these Baby Boomers, and why
should the generation you were born into matter at all?

The Generations

Nowadays we think of adults as if we are year groups at school, with
each successive generation making our way through the system.
This is not how people used to understand their world. The first
great thinker to set out this way of thinking was Karl Mannheim
in his essay 'The Problem of Generations', published in 1928.[36]

His argument was that vertical ties across the generations were weakening. We were all becoming more mobile, and he predicted that increasingly our crucial social and cultural links would be horizontal ties to our contemporaries and our friends, not vertical links to our elders and betters – and not even to our parents. It was a challenge to the then-conventional wisdom that it was the conflict of classes that would shape the future. And Mannheim was broadly right; a key feature of our society is the limited contact between the generations, with the one important exception of the family. Work, for example, is increasingly segregated by age, with more and more of us working exclusively with people of the same age (as we shall see in Chapter 6).

In modern societies, our identities are supposed to be shaped by the generation we belong to. Of course, we do not all follow this generational determinism. One traditionalist wanted to claim in a speech that he was a child of the 1960s until an adviser warned him that really he had gone through the 1950s twice and then moved straight to the 1970s. Nevertheless the model is thought to apply to most of us. We think that we can track each distinctive birth cohort through the system. Each generation creates its own world. We assume that the members of a generation will carry with them through their lives distinctive patterns of behaviour learned in their formative years. Social and political change is supposed to be recorded like tree rings, eternally imprinted with the effects of a drought or a volcanic explosion. Indeed part of the appeal of this model is that it looks as if we can understand the present and predict the future by seeing where each generation has got to. Sometimes it gets perilously close to astrology, as we work out which generational sign you were born under. No one has yet written a history of Britain explicitly in terms of successive generations, but Neil Howe and William Strauss have written a fascinating history of the US by tracking its 13 generations:[37] it is only a matter of time before their approach reaches us.

We are reaching a shared view of how we define the different British generations. Mannheim argued there are two different ways of doing this. One is by hard demographic facts. That would mean focusing on, for example, the turning points in the birth rate. Alternatively you can go for softer cultural measures – intangible shifts in social attitudes, as successive generations have different experiences of the world. The most convincing accounts link hard and soft accounts, and one way to do this is through the pattern of cohort size. The cycle of big and small cohorts is not unlike boom and bust in economics, and the experience of being in a big cohort may be very different from being in a small one. (Here, and on occasions when the distinction matters, I use 'cohort' to refer to successive defined age groups covering the same number of years, such as five-year birth cohorts. I use 'generations' to refer to age groups of varying size defined by a mix of demographic facts and cultural background.)

One way of defining generations demographically is to treat them rather like economic cycles. There is a clear pattern with cycles of births around the post-War average annual birth rate of 750,000 for the UK as a whole. This figure then defines the low point of some cycles and the high point of others. On this approach the baby boom begins with the mini-dip in 1945 (795,000). Then it runs up to a peak in 1947 (1,025,000) and down to a dip in 1955 (790,000), with 235,000 fewer births than at the peak. The second phase of the baby boom then runs from 1956 (825,000) up to a peak in 1964 (1,015,000). The birth rate then falls steadily. It crosses below its post-War average in 1972 to a low in 1977 (660,000) which is 350,000 fewer births than its peak only 13 years earlier. This is Generation X. Unlike the Boomers, shaped around high points in the birth rate, this generation is shaped around a post-War low point in the birth rate. We then have a muted echo of the baby boom with a modest peak in 1990 (800,000) and then moving down to a low in 2002 (670,000). This cycle – roughly from 1981 to 2000 and centred on the modest peak of 1990 – defines the Millennials, sometimes called Generation Y, who came to adulthood after the Millennium.

It is tempting to avoid hard chronological definitions because there is no neat and tidy distinction between these generations. There must inevitably be fuzziness around the edges. Some generations cover more years than others, which makes intuitive sense but also makes comparison harder. But we need to set down real dates and real figures so that arguments and assertions can be tested. So, in the interests of accountability and testability, here is a summary of this rather mechanistic model. (The first figures after each generation are the average numbers of babies born each year for that generation, and the second figure is the total number from each generation surviving to 2015.)

Table 2: Defining the generations[38]

Generation		Average births per year	Total population of generation in 2015
1911–1925	The Greatest Generation	940,000	555,000
1926–1945	The Silent Generation	755,000	7,440,000
1946–1965	Baby Boomers	890,000	15,630,000
1966–1980	Generation X	811,000	13,010,000
1981–2000	The Millennials	745,000	16,940,000
2001–	The Latest Generation	760,000	11,530,000

People believe that unless you bought the Beatles' first single, were at the Summer of Love and Woodstock, bought your bell-bottoms in Carnaby Street and marched against Vietnam and capitalism as a *soixante-huitard* then you can't be a Baby Boomer. That restricts the Baby Boomers to the young people who were enjoying the sixties so much that they can't remember them. That surge of people, born in a few years in the second half of the 1940s, produced an exciting teenage movement in the mid-sixties with extraordinary optimism and youthfulness. For many of them it was brought to an abrupt end with marriage and children, as we saw. But we are not just trying to pin down these narrow and intense cultural moments; we are trying to identify bigger economic and demographic changes. That means focusing on the birth surge which carried on from the 1940s to a second peak in the early 1960s. Looked at as a demographic and economic phenomenon, the baby boom covers the 20 years after the War to 1965.

The upswing of a boom feels very different from the downswing. The cutting edge feels very different from the trailing edge. These far-less-optimistic late Boomers had punk and the Poll Tax riots. Their emblems were not flower power and psychedelic colours but nose studs and Mohicans – their icon was not Tariq Ali but Johnny Rotten. Indeed many of the big social changes of the permissive era which we attribute to the 1960s, from divorce and lone parenthood to real violent radicalism, actually happened in the following decade – the 1970s were a product of the baby boom too.[39] It may be that Britain's Baby Boomers do not have as strong a collective identity as in America because we have two peaks linked by a more modest surge. This is a contrast to the single high plateau of the American baby boom in the period from 1957 to 1961.

It is hard to pin down the baby boom culturally because there is such variation within an age group. Here is one account, from Emma Soames, who writes *Saga* magazine's 'Boomer at Large' column:

> You are a Baby Boomer if you can do the twist... if you wore crushed velvet trousers in the daytime, if you heard Pink Floyd perform *Dark Side of the Moon* at the Roundhouse and saw the Beatles anywhere: you probably spent a certain amount of time under the influence of exotic cheroots talking about *2001: A Space Odyssey*... if you think you are still groovy and that, whatever the mirror may say, you are a cool young dude.

But there is a very different account of a Boomer growing up in the 1960s: 'prefabs, Formica, Scalextric, crowded classrooms and walking to school, then being expected to join a trade union and vouching for your behaviour to get to the head of the queue for a mortgage from a building society'. It is because of these divergences that the argument here rests not on cultural generalizations but measurable underlying economic and social trends.

The post-Boomers are the product of the low birth rates and the tough times of the 1970s. This is a shorter generation, centring on the historic low in the birth rate in 1976. They are sometimes called the lost generation, though Douglas Coupland popularized a better name in his novel *Generation X*.[40] It is a small generation covering a demographic trough from the mid-sixties to a low point in 1976, through to the arrival of Margaret Thatcher as prime minister in 1979, after which we enter a modest demographic recovery. Generation X were born in a recession and hit by successive recessions as they moved into adulthood. The financial pressures they faced are one reason why this is the first generation where women expected to work and have careers like men. As the children of tough times they are seen as tough-minded, even cynical, in contrast to the optimistic Baby Boomers.

The next group, the Millennials, born between 1981 and 2000, are in many ways an echo of the baby boom, growing up during more sustained economic growth and sharing some of the optimism of the Baby Boomers. They are also a demographic echo, as the surge of Boomers to early adulthood produced a second but weaker boom with a modest birth-rate peak in 1990, after which the birth rate declined again to a new low around the Millennium. They are digital natives not digital immigrants – they don't print off a document to read it. They may see all knowledge as a matter of opinion and contentious. (Indeed, one suggestion is that some of them may not believe that man landed on the moon; the web is full of accounts of how it was all faked by the authorities and they cannot believe that a previous generation could have achieved anything technological beyond what they have experienced.)[41]

The exposure to social media as a teenager looks like an increasingly significant distinguishing factor between the generations. It may well be the driver of the significant increase in mental health problems for young people now. That suggests an alternative definition, with a new generation starting in about 1995. It captures those who were early adolescents when in 2006 Facebook opened up to anyone over 13, and when the iPhone was introduced in 2007 and then the iPad in 2010.[42] This restriction of the Millennials to those born up to 1995 also appeals to the tidy-minded by reinforcing a pattern of 15-year generations. But so far this remains a minority view.

The Latest Generation take us up from the low in the birth rate at the start of the Millennium. They are the products of the surprise multicultural baby boom which is pushing the British population up from 60 million to 70 million and changing our country massively in the process. Their impact has already been felt in new pressures on maternity units, childcare centres, and for places at primary school.

We have offered an alternative demographic history of post-War Britain. The conventional approach is to explain a big shift in values in the 1960s and 1970s by claims about affluence or permissiveness. But these do not really explain much. The patterns of demography and their impact on economics and the family can help to explain the shift in a much more real way. Why did attitudes to abortion and divorce change so much in the 1960s and 1970s? After all, there had been assaults on bourgeois values before. The sixties counter-culture was not unique, but what was extraordinary was that it had an effect on wider society in a way that previous bohemian revolts against the bourgeois did not. The issue is not that there was a bohemian counter-culture but that it was so successful. Demographics help explain this. The Baby Boomers were beginning to make themselves felt. But that was only the beginning, as we shall see in the next chapter.

4

SPENDING THE KIDS' INHERITANCE

Hunter-gatherers

Imagine a primitive family of hunter-gatherers in which everything they kill is eaten. Children and elderly people need to be fed out of the surplus food caught or picked by the adult hunters. When they hunt successfully there is more than enough meat for the hunters themselves so it is shared out. This is the simplest form of redistribution across the generations. At any one point in time it might look like it is one generation – the one that works and does the hunting – paying out to the others. But over their lives everyone would be a contributor and a beneficiary, so the food they catch and the food they consume would roughly net out to a balance. Each generation would eventually consume an amount equal to what it produced.

Living together in a tribe enables consumption to be spread across our lives in this way. This informal contract between the generations is fundamental to the family and to society. If we could always just live on what we ourselves killed we would have little need for society.

The tribe in our scenario is stable until there are some mild winters and more babies survive infancy. It has a baby boom on its hands. What happens? The conventional answer has been that it is bad luck to be a big generation because there are more mouths to feed. There are more children fighting for scraps of food from their harassed parents. And then, as the baby boom generation become hunters themselves, there are more hunters chasing the same prey. So life is more competitive and times are tougher. Indeed a big generation is so busy fighting for scarce resources that they have fewer children themselves. As a result, big generations are followed by smaller ones. This is what Thomas Malthus famously argued in his *Essay on the Principle of Population* of 1798. Subsequent thinkers such as Auguste Comte treated this as the fundamental cycle in human affairs. It is why Richard Easterlin, the first great contemporary demographer to consider the impact of the Baby Boomers, predicted that they would have an unusually hard time.[1] We can recognize some of the patterns these thinkers identified, but they are not the whole story.

For a start, we may hope that when there are more hunters they can hunt more mammoths. This is the contemporary response to Malthusian pessimism – that there is no shortage of mammoths, only a shortage of hunters. Human skill and ingenuity is such that we should think of ourselves not just as consumers but as producers and creators.

Moreover, the surge in the number of hunters means that there are more of them relative to the elderly members of the tribe who are not hunters. This is the demographic sweet spot when life seems particularly good. Even though they may hunt just as hunters always did, there is a greater feeling of prosperity as each of them has to distribute less to other members of the tribe. They can spend this gain on higher living standards for working hunters, and may even spread the benefits out more widely to others. They can devote more time to cave painting. They can cut back on the frequency of hunting and gather exotic berries and grasses which do not provide much nutrition for hunting but make them feel good at their tribal festivals. It is an age of plenty and of experiment. The young hunters are quite contemptuous of the confined and conventional lives led by their parents. They try to raise their children differently.

There is an even more optimistic version in which our hunter-gatherers can hunt more effectively when there are more of them. They can take on bigger mammoths. The increase in the size of the mammoths the hunters can kill turns out to be more than proportionate to the increase in the number of hunters. Malthus may have worried about the increase in the number of mouths to feed but there is also an increase in the amount of food they can successfully hunt. So big generations enjoy surges of prosperity because of genuine improvements in performance. Our primitive Boomers are naturally very susceptible to these arguments about what great hunters they are and how the tribe has increased its hunting performance in their generation. It is only a few tribal elders who worry about the future, but it seems perverse to argue there is a problem when everyone can see there is more meat to go round.

Then this big generation of hunters start to grow old and want to hand their spears over to the younger generation. Even if they each had just as many children as before, there is no avoiding the fact that there are more old ex-hunters to be maintained. So the next generation of hunters finds that more of what they catch needs to be taken for other members of the tribe. Life seems tougher. Some of the retired hunters argue that the younger ones just aren't as good at hunting as they were in the old days.

There is a final twist. The clan is run by a democratic tribal council. That big generation therefore finds it has the most votes. It uses this power to protect itself, especially as the younger members of the tribe are too busy decorating themselves with woad to turn up for boring tribal meetings. While they were in their prime, the baby-boom hunters were not very keen on the redistribution of mammoth meat to non-productive members of the clan and were more keen on the rights of hunters to keep as much as possible of what they caught. But as they get older they become more interested in the respect due to senior retired hunters and start voting for more tribute from new young hunters.

Younger hunters face a double squeeze, with more retired hunters to support and more expected from each one of them. They have to spend more time hunting. They want to raise their kids in the same generous way their parents raised them, but it seems harder to achieve and as a result they don't have so many of them.

Our thought experiment shows a society which worked until a big generation came along that took more of what it produced during its prime and then tried to take more from later generations when it was in need. It was partly just because of its size. Maybe it was also because of how it used the power that came with its size. But, whatever the reason, the principle of fairness across the generations was broken. And that threatened to break the society.

If you could choose, would you rather be part of a big generation like the Boomers or a small one? The standard answer from the economists has actually been that it is better to be in a small cohort. A big group means more competition for jobs, which drives down wages. And public services can be very crowded if you are a big generation – I think of the 48 children in my primary school class in the sixties. It may be that, like the rest of life, sometimes you want to be in a crowd and sometimes you want to be on your own. It might be that in a small generation you have less competition from your contemporaries so your wages may be higher. But in a big generation you have much greater power to shape the political and cultural environment around you.

One of the advantages of being a big, prosperous generation is the power you can exercise as consumers. Your music and your cultural tastes carry on being celebrated through your lives – the Baby Boomers can still go to Rolling Stones concerts, get Beatles CDs, and drive versions of the Volkswagen Beetle and the Mini. That far smaller group who were teenagers in the 1950s, not the 1960s, are still waiting for a trendy repro version of the Triumph Mayflower. We sent soldiers to Korea and stayed out of Vietnam. But Vietnam happened during the formative years of the Boomers and so casts a far longer shadow than Korea, which was only a decade earlier and actually saw British soldiers fighting and dying.

It is hard to measure these cultural effects from changes in the size of generations but here is an attempt. Compare the top 100 albums as selected in a poll of the general public (*Daily Mirror*) and the top 100 albums as selected by music enthusiasts (*Q* magazine).[2] There are only 38 albums in common. Moreover, there is not even any similarity in the rankings of the 38 albums between the two lists. The enthusiasts and the general public deeply disagree. How can such a gap open up?

Let us try an explanation. Most new albums are listened to and bought by young people. Our musical tastes are fixed by those first tracks we bought as teenagers. (I still prefer the real Monkees to the Arctic ones.) So if there were more teenagers around when a pop group was in its prime, it will do better in popular ratings regardless of its quality.

Therefore let us weight the rankings of the albums as voted for by the public so they take into account how many teenagers there were when the album was released. Hence, albums in the *Mirror* chart released in years when there were more young consumers are given a handicap, and albums released in years when there were fewer youngsters are given a boost. Once you do that, musicians and the general public start to agree – they agree about which albums are better than others roughly three-fifths of the time.[3] This is a first stab at explaining how our culture is weighted towards the Baby Boomers.[4]

There is a further effect favouring the Baby Boomers. Albums from the Boomers' adolescence do extremely well, even on a demographically adjusted basis. The years when the Boomers were youthful consumers are remarkably strong performers, accounting for two-thirds of the critics' top 100. This, too, is a cohort effect, but of a different kind. In the years with lots of teenage music-buyers it was easier to sell enough records to break even. You needed a smaller proportion of the total market. So it is easier for more experimental or innovative bands to make a living in a niche market. This means big cohorts enjoy far deeper musical markets with much greater diversity than their colleagues in other cohorts do. As a consequence, a big cohort may actually deliver a genuine improvement in performance that is more than proportionate to its size. So the Baby Boomers did have something special going for them and this may have magnified their cultural impact. Another survey, on the 40th anniversary of Woodstock in 2009, shows how in America the Boomers' musical tastes have spread to other generations. The great bands of the sixties have an extraordinarily wide appeal – the Beatles in particular are in the top four of the most popular musical performers for every age group, with the Rolling Stones not far behind.[5]

Snapshots of Today's Cohorts

The cultural power of the Baby Boomers reflects their economic power as a big group of consumers. We can investigate that economic power by tracking the shifting fortunes of successive generations. We will start by drawing on data from three different five-year cohorts, each 25 years apart: members of the Silent Generation born 1931–5; a cohort born 1956–60 in the middle of the baby boom; and early Millennials born 1981–5.

The Silent Generation, largely born in the 1930s and during the War, may well feel they had a tough start in life. They certainly had unusually low calorie consumption during the Depression and the War. But more of them are still around than anyone forecast. Indeed that frugal diet may be one reason why they have enjoyed the most dramatic surge in life expectancy ever recorded in Britain. They then benefitted from the long, steady post-War growth in pay, which together with the improving access to housing meant they had lots of kids – the Baby Boomers. Someone born in that cohort in the early 1930s saw their real household income more than double over their working lives. It rose steadily from £8,900 in the early 1960s to £10,800 in the early 1970s and £15,100 in the early 1980s, and peaked at £18,000 in 1990 (all figures in 2017 prices).[6]

Three-quarters of this pre-War cohort ended up owning their own home but it took them a long time, with steady saving out of gradually rising wages, and then came a big boost from council house sales in the 1980s. The 1931–5 cohort reached 52 per cent home ownership aged 40 in the early 1970s, but then advanced further to 71 per cent home ownership 20 years later, aged 60.[7] An average couple ended up with housing wealth of about £300,000 (74 per cent of people born 1936–40 were homeowners in 2015, with mean housing wealth per person of £145,000).[8] The other big asset they built up was a pension. Company pension schemes were not particularly generous at first but also gradually spread so this cohort ended up with pension wealth of £45,000 for a couple. And they benefitted from generous welfare-state spending promises, so even after they retired their income continued to rise. (The real value of pensioner benefits per pensioner has gone up by more than 10 per cent in the decade since the crash of 2008.)

The post-War Boomers had much higher incomes than the generation before them, and they rose faster. So the cohort born in 1956–60 earned £533 per week when they were aged 45 (in 2001–5, in 2017 prices), compared with £324 earned 25 years earlier by the cohort born in 1931–5, when they were aged 45.[9] The Boomers' advance in home ownership is even more striking. The cohort born in 1956–60 reached a high plateau of about 70 per cent home ownership when they were aged 40 in the late 1990s, a much higher rate than enjoyed by the previous generation at the same age. That is similar to the level eventually achieved by the cohort 25 years older than them, but the Boomers got to 70 per cent home ownership almost 20 years sooner.[10] We can see why the older pre-War generation think life was tough for them and that their income and wealth came as a reward for years of steady slog. By contrast the Boomers got high wages and home ownership earlier, which looked to the older generation as if it all fell into their lap with less sustained effort. This is the economic backdrop to the cultural gap between the Boomers and their parents.

The earnings of the early Millennials did advance on the Baby Boomer generation, but on nothing like the scale of the Boomer advance. So, aged 30, the cohort born 1981–5 were earning £496 a week as against £428 by Boomers born 1956–60 at the same age.[11] This is a much smaller improvement on the Boomers than the gain the Boomers enjoyed on the cohort 25 years older than them. And this early cohort of the Millennials really is behind when it comes to home ownership. By their early thirties 58 per cent of 1956–60 Boomers were homeowners; a big advance on 39 per cent for the pre-War cohort. But both of them are substantially ahead of the cohort born 1981–5 who were down to 33 per cent home ownership by age 30.

These comparisons of three five-year cohorts stretching out over 50 years give a sense of how incomes and wealth have changed for different age groups in Britain since the War. We can also focus more tightly on the contrasting fortunes of people entering two very different ages in the last 20 years. We have more detailed data for different age cohorts in 1995, 2005, and 2015, and can use this to measure how the experience of someone reaching the 25–29 age group has changed over two decades. We can also compare it with someone entering a very different group, aged 75–79, over the same period. These 20 years straddle a decade of strong growth up to the crash of 2008 and then a second decade of post-crash underperformance. The wider economic backdrop is the same for everyone, but young and old have been affected in very different ways.

The tables below tell a very striking story. They show that as successive waves of older people reach their late seventies, their living standards and home ownership rates go up compared with their immediate predecessors. But as successive waves of young people reach their late twenties, their living standards and home ownership rates are going down. We think we should live in a society where it is young people who are optimistic about the spread of progress, but on these trends it is the old people who experience progress for successive age groups while younger people experience decline.

Table 3: Median real household annual net income after housing costs by birth cohort: GB[12]

	Aged 25–29	Aged 75-79
1995	£17,200	£10,800
2005	£21,700	£17,100
2015	£17,800	£19,400

This shows the massive change in the relative incomes of young and old over these crucial two decades. Old used to mean poor. We still assume that old people are less well off, and public policy is certainly still designed on that basis. But now old does not mean poor. For the first time, the typical living standards of an old person have overtaken those of a working-age person. The trends in home ownership shown in the table below are even more dramatic.

Table 4: Family home ownership rates of successive birth cohorts: UK[13]

	Aged 25-29	Aged 75-79
1995	37%	57%
2005	28%	70%
2015	17%	74%

As the Boomer generation who have achieved high levels of home ownership age, so old people are more likely than ever to be homeowners. But the chances of a young person being a homeowner have collapsed. The share of under-35s in the homeowner population has halved in the last 15 years.[14]

This account of the different fortunes of different age groups includes both their assets and their incomes. But the two shifts did not happen simultaneously. The spread of asset ownership went into reverse first. Home ownership by young people peaked in the late 1980s and then went into reverse from the early 1990s. House prices kept rising and young people could not keep up. The growth of earnings of young people changed more than a decade later: the pay of young people stagnated from about 2005 and has fallen since 2009 after the crash.

We will match this chronology in our analysis, looking more closely at what is happening to the assets of successive generations and then their earnings and incomes.

The Surge in Household Wealth

Together, all the assets held by British people are worth about £12.8tn (£12,800bn).[15] Our gross housing wealth is £5.7tn, slightly ahead of the other major asset owned by many households – the pension, which has also been shooting up in value. Once one deducts about £1.1tn of mortgages, our private pensions (excluding state benefits) are worth more than our housing. Before council house sales and the great housing booms of the past 40 years, housing was less than one-fifth of total wealth, and a lot less than the funds we had saved up for our pension. By 1997 our housing had risen to be worth about the same as our pensions. In fact in 1997, by an extraordinary statistical fluke, the net value of these two crucial assets was identical, at £1,301bn each.[16] Both of these crucial assets have since increased more than four times in the past 20 years. This surge in wealth has changed our society because it is much greater than the increase in national income, so assets matter more – and who owns them matters more as well.

Nothing captures more vividly the theme of this book than the mixed emotions of a Baby Boomer contemplating the rise in the value of their house in the successive house price booms of the past 40 years. When prices were rising we experienced a combination of amazement at our own good fortune together with anxiety about how our children were ever going to be able to afford to get on to the housing ladder themselves. Whenever there is a fall in house prices and our wealth declines, we console ourselves with the thought that at least now houses will be more affordable for young homebuyers. But even with house prices lower, access to credit is so difficult that first-time buyers may not benefit much – instead, the main beneficiaries are well-off Boomers who have easier access to credit and can afford to buy a second home. Already, 17 per cent of 50-year-olds live in families with more than one property.[17] Baby Boomers own half of all the wealth held in additional properties.

Housing wealth is now falling – the boost to its total value from the increase in the total number of houses is not enough to offset lower prices. Pensions are doing better as auto-enrolment is successfully boosting what we are saving, so current trends suggest pensions pulling further ahead of housing wealth.

We directly hold about £1.6tn of wealth as financial assets – in bank and building society deposits and stocks and shares.[18] These assets account for about a tenth of all our wealth. This type of wealth belongs almost entirely to people in their fifties and sixties. It is a classic pattern of wealth ascending, with roughly £100bn held by under-45s, £200bn by 45- to 54-year-olds, £400bn by 55- to 64-year-olds, and £700bn by the over-65s.[19] We do not really build this wealth up until the children have left home, and then we run it down in the early stages of retirement when we use the money to go diving on the Great Barrier Reef. We do not appear to want to pass it on to our kids. It is the most transient form of wealth, like the flowers after rain falls on the savannah.

Then there is about £1.2tn of physical wealth: the self-assessed value of house contents and of motor cars, etc. It is the smallest element of our wealth. It is also hardest to measure and attribute between generations, so it is excluded from the table below.

This table shows how £11.3tn of personal wealth is broken down between different age groups. The Boomers own £6.5tn of this wealth – almost 60 per cent of the total.

Table 5: Distribution of private wealth between generations in £tn, 2014–16, GB (excluding physical wealth)[20]

	Silent	Boomers	Gen X	Millennials	Total
Financial (net)	0.6	0.8	0.2	0.03	1.6
Housing (net)	1.1	2.3	1.0	0.2	4.6
Pensions	0.6	3.4	1.1	0.2	5.3
Total	2.3	6.5	2.2	0.4	

There are just over 60 million of us, so the overall total averages out at about £210,000 of personal wealth for every man, woman, and child in the country. Most toddlers do not own anything but most 50-year-olds do. So we should expect big disparities in wealth by age, just because most people acquire some property as they go through life. But are there greater gaps between the generations than there used to be? Is there a lucky generation of Baby Boomers who have ended up unusually wealthy compared with the generation before or after them? And if so, why?

These questions matter now more than ever because the most important single change in Britain's entire political economy over the past 30 years has been the rise in the value of assets relative to income. Our economic output is now about £2tn per year, so our wealth is over six times our GDP. But through the post-War period until the 1980s our personal wealth was steady, at just under three times our GDP.[21]

So the past 40 years have seen a doubling of the value of our wealth relative to income. (And taxes on capital have not risen to reflect this – an issue we return to later.) This has had profound effects. It weakens the value of work, as earning your way to wealth is harder. It reduces equality because wealth is less evenly distributed than income. It reduces the significance of conventional public policy, which has historically focused much more on compensating people for low incomes than for low assets. It is bad for social

Figure 3: Wealth has risen in relation to GDP[22]

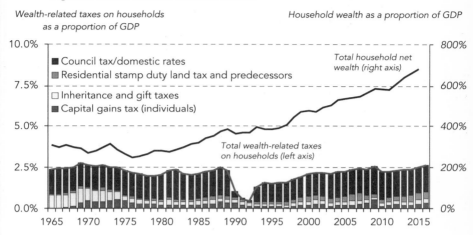

Wealth-related taxes on households as a proportion of GDP

Household wealth as a proportion of GDP

mobility, as assets are often inherited whereas incomes aren't – inheritance matters more and earnings matter less. (The real value of estates passing on death has doubled over the past 20 years, from £38bn to £87bn.)[23] It also changes the balance between the generations. Imagine a society where the income of the typical person aged 60 is twice that of someone aged 30. But the wealth of someone aged 60 is four times someone aged 30. The value of wealth in that society doubles relative to income. Even with no change in the distribution of either incomes or wealth, it massively shifts the balance between the generations just by making wealth more significant. This scenario shows why the ratio of wealth to national income matters. Even if there is no change in anything else, it can reshape a society and change its values. Add in real changes in the distribution of both wealth and earnings and you get very significant changes indeed.

There is one engagingly simple account of what has happened to drive this surge in the value of wealth – quantitative easing (QE). After the crash, monetary policy was eased and this pushed up the value of assets. It is a clear and economically sound account. And it has had a big impact on the relative position of different generations. Since 2007 all of the £2.7bn increase in wealth has accrued to the over-45s, with two-thirds accrued by the over-65s. There has actually been a 10 per cent fall in the wealth of those aged 16–34. QE does not account on its own for these passive increases in the value of assets, however, because the bulk of the increase in asset values happened before the crash.

The chart below shows real house prices going back to the late 1960s. It shows that house prices in the UK have gone up by 418 per cent (after inflation) since the late 1960s and London house prices by 764 per cent – 82 per cent of the UK rise happened before QE and 63 per cent of the London rise. Indeed, average UK house prices in real terms are below where they were before the crash. To understand what happened we need to investigate particular pressures pushing up the value of houses and pensions.

Figure 4: Real house prices, UK and London[24]

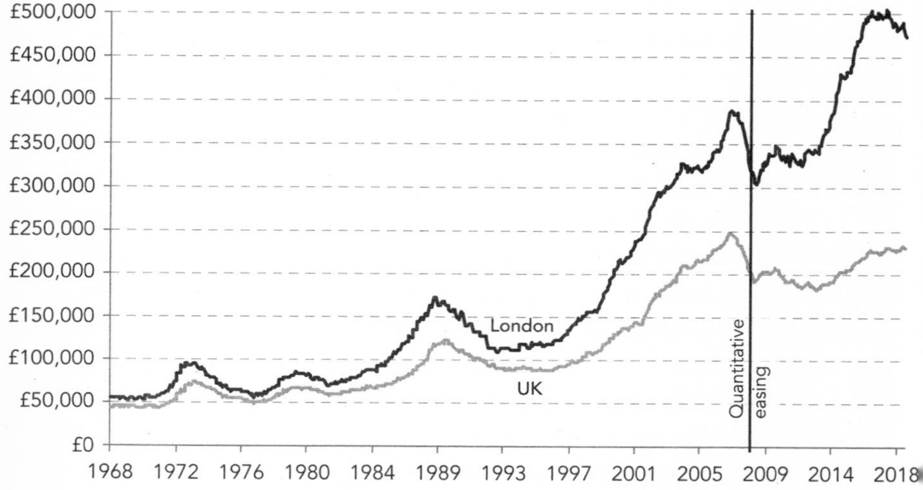

QE is however a vivid example of a wider truth – these increases in wealth are passive gains. It is not a result of an increase in saving, though there was some paying down of debt after the crash. Over the longer period from 1993 to 2014, 82 per cent of the increase in housing wealth – £2.3tn – was the result of house prices rising by more than inflation, and that enormous increase did not arise because homeowners added a conservatory. It is not that the older generation are richer because we were more prudent – we have just had more house price inflation. (These passive rises in house prices may however partly reflect increased productivity in dense clusters like London, but in that case housing supply should adjust – and it has not.) The average windfall from higher house prices is worth £80,000 to people born in the 1950s as against just £35,000 for those born in the 1970s. It is unlikely such a surge in wealth will be repeated in the foreseeable future. And if it were, it would still be the Baby Boomers who would gain as they own much more of the housing than younger generations.[25]

There is a similar story behind the increase in pension wealth. A company pension promise to pay a certain income after a certain age is worth more if your life expectancy increases – you would in effect need a bigger pension pot to yield such a promised income. These valuation changes account for 74 per cent of growth in private pension wealth – about £800bn – just in the period from 2006–8 to 2012–14. That is worth about £45,000 for adults born in the 1950s cohort but only £10,000 for those born in the 1970s. And again it is unlikely that younger generations will ever be able to enjoy such gains as they don't have that sort of company pension. Instead they have fixed personal pension pots, which means the individual has to cover the cost of increased life expectancy by for example taking less income per year – there is no automatic pension promise to cover it.[26]

These sorts of trends are the reason the wealth of the recently retired (aged 65–74) has overtaken the entire population of under-45s (a group twice their size) over the period 2008–12.[27] It is such changes in the relative position of different age groups which really matter. It is OK that old people are usually richer than young people. But if old people are getting richer and young people aren't, something else much more worrying is going on. The two tables below are snapshots of wealth in 2006–8 and then 2014–16.[28] They show extraordinarily big changes in the relative positions of different age groups over a short space of time.

Table 6: Distribution of total wealth by age, 2006–8 (£bn): GB

	Net property wealth	Net financial wealth	Private pension wealth	Total wealth
Under 35	160	40	70	270
35–44	540	130	310	980
45–54	790	220	680	1,690
55–64	890	290	990	2,170
65+	1,150	360	840	2,340
Total	3,530	1,040	2,890	7,450

Table 7: Distribution of total wealth by age, 2014–16 (£bn): GB

	Net property wealth	Net financial wealth	Private pension wealth	Total wealth
Under 35	130	20	130	290
35-44	480	110	420	1,010
45-54	880	230	1,200	2,310
55-64	1,120	400	1,790	3,310
65+	1,910	710	1,770	4,390
Total	4,520	1,470	5,310	11,310

The assets which really matter are housing and pensions and we will look at these in turn.

Housing

Historically, home ownership has spread wealth more widely and reduced inequality because housing wealth is distributed more evenly than most other forms of wealth. But the fall in home ownership for younger generations has reversed this trend. Indeed the past 15 years or so have been very unusual, with inequality in housing wealth rising but offset by the successful spreading of pension wealth through auto-enrolment. Less affluent younger people have been the main losers from falling home ownership. Just between 2006–8 and 2012–14, home ownership fell by 12 per cent among the poorest half of the population while only falling 3 per cent among the affluent half.[29]

The chart below shows how different patterns of home ownership are for different generations. Today's young people are half as likely to own a home aged 30 as Boomers at the same age. Every group has felt it. It is certainly a problem which extends beyond London to many bigger cities.[30] It has been most acute for those without wealthy parents, but even affluent families have been affected (though it shows up more as an increase in support from the bank of mum and dad than big falls in their home ownership). It is one reason why the cause of intergenerational fairness is one which strikes a chord with people in such diverse circumstances.

Figure 5: Home ownership rates for each generation[31]

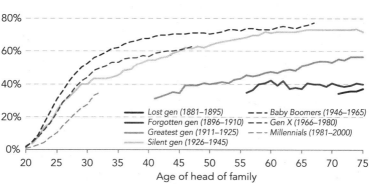

Home ownership overall peaked in 2004 – before then, the decline in home ownership among young people was offset by the rise among older people. Of all Western countries, Britain is unique in having achieved high levels of home ownership and then suffering a rapid reverse. (Only Australia gets even close, and there the declines have been slower though longer.) Baby Boomers aged 45–49 had home ownership rates that were a very significant 29 per cent higher than the generation before them. But after that big boost there comes a substantial reverse, with home ownership rates 27 per cent lower for Millennials aged 25–29 than for Baby Boomers at the same age.

The table below gives estimates of the distribution of housing wealth across the generations. It only covers owner-occupied housing. The exclusion of second homes and buy-to-let property is the reason why it shows net housing wealth rather less than total housing wealth: that extra wealth is of course very likely to belong to the Boomers.

Table 8: Distribution of housing wealth by age, 2014–16 (£bn): GB[32]

	Under-35s	35–44	45–54	55–64	65+	Total
Gross	320	860	1220	1270	1970	5,640
Mortgage	180	380	340	150	60	1,120
Net housing wealth	130	480	880	1120	1910	4,530

The table shows two-thirds of all wealth in owner-occupied housing belongs to the over-55s, and only about 15 per cent to everyone aged under 44.

Housing is fundamental to shifts in power and wealth between generations. The house price boom of the past 40 years drove the biggest shift in wealth between the generations since the War. The chart earlier in the chapter shows how house prices have shot up, particularly in the late 1980s and then in the noughties. Which generation will have benefitted most from these booms? It would be a group that achieved high rates of home ownership early on – say by the age of 40 so they could then gain from the subsequent boom. The two main surges in house prices match the twin peaks of the baby boom 40 years earlier. The timing of the booms has been perfectly targeted to deliver massive wealth gains to the Boomers.

In the cautious words of the Bank of England: 'Changes in house prices redistribute wealth. When house prices rise, those who plan to trade down gain while those who intend to trade up lose... In practice, households planning to trade up tend to be younger households and those planning to trade down are often older homeowners.'[33]

The Baby Boomers who were buying their houses and trading up did not just see the value of their house rise; they have also got a mortgage that could well have shrunk to a fraction of its former size because of inflation. Inflation redistributes income as powerfully as any tax; it favours the young at the expense of the old. Younger and middle-aged people are borrowers – above all with mortgages – and it is quite helpful for them if inflation wipes out their debts. But it wipes out savings too. Older people are savers and a low-inflation world is better for them as it protects their savings while they try to live on a fixed income. Inflation was 4 per cent in the 1950s and 3.5 per cent in the 1960s. Then, when the Boomers had big mortgages, it shot up to 13 per cent in the 1970s and 7.5 per cent in the 1980s. Now they are entering retirement and quite possibly their income may be fixed in money terms so they want price stability, and inflation has been at historic lows for over a decade. Ultra-low interest rates do however reduce the income received by savers on the deposits they have in the bank, while of course low inflation protects their real value – this dampening of the incomes of savers was cited by the coalition government as one justification for the triple lock protecting the value of the state pension. Meanwhile, for the younger generation trying to borrow to finance a house today, the borrowings they take on are likely to be almost as burdensome in 20 years' time as they are now if inflation remains low. It was all well and good moving to a low-inflation world, but it is very convenient for the Baby Boomers that it was achieved after their debts had effectively been written off by inflation.

The changes in income and wealth between different generations we are looking at in this chapter lead to very significant changes in how those generations lead their lives. As younger generations get priced out of home ownership for example, so their lives are more uncertain as private renters. As housing becomes more expensive, the time spent commuting rises. We will look further at these issues in Chapter 11.

Pensions

There have been stark shifts in pension wealth between the generations. The total value of our savings in company pension schemes and personal pensions is about £5.3tn.[34] Many of the big pension schemes are now maturing, with more and more pensioners and fewer and fewer active contributors. They are closing to new young members. Less than 10 per cent of private-sector employees born in the early 1980s were active members of a defined benefit scheme in their early thirties; this compares with more than 15 per cent of those born in the 1970s and nearly 40 per cent of those born in the 1960s.[35] It is older workers who have this increasingly rare and precious form of pension provision: about 30 per cent of men in their fifties are members of such generous schemes but almost no men in their twenties. We can see who gains and who loses when a company announces it is closing its pension scheme to new members, plugging the deficit with an injection of funds and setting up a new, much less valuable, defined contribution pension for new employees. This adds up to a substantial redistribution of resources across the generations. The traditional final salary scheme remains almost only for pensioners and perhaps established older employees. Even if it is closed for future accruals, the pension rights that pensioners and older employees have already built up are protected. Revenues from the company as a whole, earned by employees of all ages, are diverted into the pension scheme and are not available to the younger staff. New employees who are much younger have a much less generous pension to look forward to – or rather *not* to look forward to. It is the young new recruits who are the poor bloody infantry being sacrificed as the generals fight the pensions crisis. And the gap between the pensions of older employees and younger employees gets even wider.[36]

The table below shows the percentage of each age group with pension wealth, and its median value for that age group.

Table 9: Distribution of pension assets across different age groups, 2014–16[37]

Age	Percentage with wealth in current pension	Average amount of wealth held in current pension
16–24	29%	£3,500
25–34	62%	£12,000
35–44	70%	£35,000
45–54	71%	£66,900
55–64	64%	£104,000
65-plus	23%	£97,900
All	62%	£31,100

Older people will usually have more pension wealth than younger people. That itself is not shocking. But the balance between the generations in pensions is changing, and that does matter. Between 2006–8 and 2014–16 the pension wealth of those aged 55–64 increased from 3.2 times that of those aged 35–44 to 4.2 times.[38]

Two big events of the last 30 years – lower inflation and greater longevity – have between them delivered a massive shift in the relative pensions wealth of different generations that we have barely begun to understand let alone address. Changes in life expectancy have increased the value of pension rights. Even the most lurid theory of intergenerational selfishness could not attribute this improvement in life expectancy to a deliberate plot by the Baby Boomers. Nevertheless it does have a big impact on the relative wealth of the generations. It means that people who have already got pension rights are going to enjoy them for much longer, increasing their total lifetime value way beyond what was intended when the pension promise was made. It is the interaction of improved life expectancy with low inflation which is particularly potent, especially in impact on pension wealth – if you live longer but inflation is high your pension may lose much of its value. But if you live longer in an age of low inflation your income may keep its value and the total lifetime value of your pension goes up – a big passive gain in wealth.

When economists try to think through the implications of an increase in the money supply they imagine what would happen if a helicopter dropped £10 notes on the population and attempted to track the effects both on prices and, temporarily, on economic output. But imagine instead that the helicopter is dropping pills which increase everyone's life expectancy by 10 years. One way it would affect us is very similar to the way inflation works, by changing the real value of a contract fixed by a nominal price or by a chronological age. High inflation redistributed resources because some people (such as elderly savers) had their incomes fixed but the incomes of other people (such as wage-earners) could adjust every year to keep their value. Increased life expectancy redistributes resources when contracts are fixed on specific ages. That in turn redistributes money across the life cycle, as anything you are entitled to from, say, the age of 60 or 65 is worth a lot more. The value of contracts which are based on a chronological age goes up. If we index future pension age to life expectancy we can offset the effect for younger generations, but meanwhile it is older people who gain from an unanticipated increase in the lifetime value of their pension promise.

This is a massive concentration of property ownership. It would not matter so much if this were just a repeat of the usual cycle, with the younger generation always owning less; but what has happened is the younger generation have much worse prospects of building up their property. That is the real injustice. There is a common pattern behind what is happening both to pensions and to housing. In both cases we find the Baby Boomers awarding themselves a one-off special offer. The value of their pensions has shot up as the promise of an income above a certain age applies for much longer than ever expected. But employers are not going to fall into that trap again and future generations will have a fixed pension pot to be eked out for longer if life expectancy improves. The Baby Boomers also enjoyed surges in home ownership and house prices partly driven by historically low levels of house-building and the one-off sale of the council house stock. Again it is hard to see these conditions returning.

Increased Assets Have Reduced Saving

It felt marvellous as the Baby Boomers' houses shot up in value, some years earning more than they did. The Boomers increasingly came to think of their houses as not just a place to live but their own personal gold mine which could pay for holidays or cars, or be their pension. One estimate was that when the housing boom was at its peak, just before the 2008 financial crash, the annual yield on property was 22 per cent – so housing became a profitable investment for the Boomers at the expense of the young.[39] It was essentially an increase in the price of land (as they say: 'Buy land; they're not making it any more'). It was not wealth we had produced. It was not that our work was more productive. However, we thought we were richer and acted accordingly. As financial services became more sophisticated we all became alchemists, converting paper increases in the value of our homes into extra money to spend.

Sometimes the conversion of the asset into spending was direct and simple – we borrowed against the house and spent the money.

Equally it could be indirect. People felt richer and did not feel they needed to save. It is rather like the holidays from pensions contributions taken by some British companies when the stock market was booming in the 1990s. And saving is net, so even when we carried on putting £5,000 a year into a pension, if at the same time we were re-mortgaging our house for £5,000 our net saving was zero – it was like paying pension contributions on our credit card.

We did not feel we needed to save so much as we were richer, and when we retired we could eat our house, using it to pay for our retirement. The Treasury were shockingly complacent about this. Indeed, they explained in the following notorious passage why this asset price bubble meant we did not need to save like we used to:

> The Government is committed to a policy framework that enables people to choose how and when to save across the full range of asset-building activities. Traditional measures of aggregate saving, such as the saving ratio, often fail both to reflect this variety and to highlight the positive impact asset growth has had on households' balance sheets in recent years. Broader measures, for example including capital growth, indicate that saving behaviour has been more robust in recent years than is often appreciated.[40]

Translated, that means that instead of measuring saving just as a proportion of your income, house price rises really should count as saving too. This was a catastrophic misreading of what was happening to the economy. The Treasury failed to understand the economic cycle – perhaps because the then Chancellor claimed to have abolished it. As a result they treated a boom as a structural change in the growth rate and an asset price bubble as part of saving. It was a kind of financial levitation in which we appeared to save without actually putting any income aside. It happened above all because of the rise in house prices. It would have been far better to have stuck to the wise words of Adam Smith:

> Though a house... may yield a revenue to its proprietor, and thereby serve in the function of a capital to him, it cannot yield any to the public, nor serve in the function of a capital to it, and the revenue of the whole body of the people can never be in the smallest degree increased by it.[41]

Before the crash, the proportion of income that UK households saved fell to a record low – as the table below shows. After the crash there were attempts to pay off debt and the savings ratio rose. But then the UK returned to normality, which for us means a low savings ratio.

Table 10: Net household savings rates, selected countries[42]

	France	Germany	US	UK
2000	8.7	9.0	5.0	5.7
2005	8.5	10.1	3.3	2.8
2010	10.5	10.0	6.8	6.5
2015	8.4	9.7	7.8	4.6

These figures from the OECD show extraordinarily low levels of saving by British households – not just lower than the virtuous French and Germans but also lower than the Americans, with whom we are often compared. They also tell us that, before the 2008 crash, British households borrowed so much against their increased property value that they basically stopped saving. This, incidentally, is one reason British mortgage lenders like Northern Rock were so vulnerable in the credit crunch – they did not have a savings base but were still lending; they relied on wholesale lending from abroad rather than retail depositors.

The house price boom led to a fall in the saving ratio, and that in turn imposed a heavy burden on our children. Here's why. The swings in house prices can have a big impact on the distribution of wealth between generations – but the effect depends on what we do. Let us start with the case in which we respond to higher house prices with true wisdom and do absolutely nothing. We realize that we have not created any more wealth and have nothing extra to spend or to save. We just leave our house unencumbered for our children to inherit. There are of course tricky questions about equality and social mobility, as different houses have different values, but at least we as a generation have not imposed any further burden on our children.

We did not behave with such wise self-control. Instead we borrowed against the house, or did not save as much as we would otherwise have done – expecting to finance our retirement by borrowing against it in the future. That is why the low saving ratio was so important; it was telling us how we responded to the house price boom. And where does this money that we thought we had come from? From our children. By increasing our spending because our houses have gone up in value, we are taking from the younger generation. They have to spend more for their house and there is less of an inheritance to pay for it. So they have to pay more for their house out of their lifetime earnings. The flow of resource is from children to parents, not the other way round.

Imagine a country where every couple has two children, and where every house was previously un-mortgaged and worth £300,000 and houses were passed on, debt-free, from generation to generation. But each now increases in value to £500,000. We do not see that extra £200,000 as just an increase in the price of land but instead we see it more as a performance bonus, a testament to the extraordinary skills and virtues of our generation. We spend it now or plan to spend it during our retirement. Somehow or other we intend to release that wealth for our use. That means that when we die our children will find that, instead of an inheritance of £500,000 to get a house like ours, there is a mortgage on it and between them they get only £300,000. That means that they have to lower their living standards so they can service a mortgage to enable them to borrow the money to buy a house like their parents', or accept lower living standards in the form of smaller and cheaper accommodation. It is like opening a treasure chest, to discover a pile of IOUs which you are obliged to pay.

A single generation has had a one-off wealth gain as the price of land shoots up relative to everything else. That one generation is converting this one-off wealth effect into higher consumption. If we thought house prices were going to stay high, our children would need the money to pay for their houses. If we thought they would fall, then it was never there to spend.

Martin Weale has calculated the scale of what we are talking about here. House prices rose between 1987 and 2016 at 2.0 per cent per annum faster than earnings. That adds up to an extra £2,200bn of housing wealth on top of what would have matched the growth in our incomes. That is more than 100 per cent of GDP transferred to current homeowners from future homeowners (107 per cent to be precise). This is a heavy burden for the next generation – in fact, it is as if the government had increased the national debt by that amount and left the younger generation to pay it off with higher taxes.[43] The international comparison in the table below shows that land values have grown over twice as fast as GDP in the UK over these two decades. Only France and Australia were faster.

Table 11: Land value growth over and above GDP growth, 1995–2015[44]

France	1.94	Netherlands	0.83
Australia	1.47	United States	0.31
United Kingdom	1.35	Germany	0.09
Sweden	0.94	Japan	-1.50
Canada	0.94		

The crash might have changed all this, but it did not. The fall in house prices in 2008–9 did not reverse the house price increase of the past two decades – it only reversed about two years of house price inflation and they then started moving up again before falling after the Brexit referendum (as Figure 4 on page 70 showed). This still leaves a big gain for the possessor generation. Even if we went back to the level of 2001, first-time buyers then paid £48,000 more for the average house in real terms than the Baby Boomers who bought the house in 1975.[45] And it has not helped the younger generation get started in the housing market – as we shall see in Chapter 11.

This low saving rate is associated with a shift in the distribution of assets from public sector to private sector. There is a lively controversy about this: I have historically been on the side of those who support the shift of assets out of the public sector. The evidence suggests that competitive open markets and the profit performance area is the best way to maximize returns from these assets. The state claims resources for public services by its power to tax, not by direct ownership of assets. And similarly it can use tools, from regulation to public procurement, to achieve wider economic objectives – it does not need to own stuff. But the state as owner does hold assets in common for all of us and for generations as yet unborn. If transferred to the private sector, there is a danger that they instead become the possession of one generation which happened to be holding power at the time the transfer occurred. Then the shift to private ownership can exacerbate a shift in power and wealth between the generations.

Pay and Incomes

Richard Easterlin's path-breaking *Birth and Fortune* remains one of the few serious attempts to think through the economic impact of successive cohorts of different sizes. The book, which came out in 1980, argues that you would be better off in a small cohort than a big one. He does not really focus on the value of housing and pension wealth – the book was written just before the great asset price boom which so enriched the Baby Boomers. Instead he looks at wages and proposes, very plausibly, that if you are in a big cohort you will have so many more people competing for jobs with you that wages will be bid down. By contrast, a small cohort of workers is in a much stronger bargaining position and so can bid up wages. That was not a stupid forecast. Indeed, the weight of economic theory is with him. But things have not quite turned out like that.

The chart below shows what has happened to the median real weekly earnings of successive generations of British employees.

Figure 6: Median real weekly employee pay by age and generation: UK, 1975–2017[46]

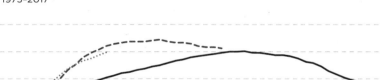

It shows that the Boomers enjoyed big increases in earnings on the generations before them right from the start. After them this advance in pay slowed down – Gen X and the Millennials have not yet shown any gain at all. (We return to a more detailed analysis of the pay of successive five-year cohorts on page 247.) Other figures reinforce the point. In 2015, at age 27, those born in 1988 were earning the same as 27-year-olds a quarter of a century before. The typical Millennial working throughout their twenties has earned £8,000 less than a typical person in Generation X.[47] And these problems are not just the result of the particular vulnerability of younger workers to the crash. Between 2005 and 2009 the pay of those aged 22–29 grew by just 2 per cent, whereas it grew by 6 per cent for those in their thirties and forties.[48] This trend is partly due to a decline in the growth of productivity per hour worked, which in turn may be linked to a decline in the rate at which educational qualifications were increasing. The 2008 crash then exacerbated the problem: it hit young people particularly hard, as recessions always do. The unemployment rate for under-25s subsequently rose to 14 per cent – double the rate for those aged 25–64. The number of young people not in education, employment, or training (NEET) rose to over 1 million by late 2009 – over 15 per cent of all 16- to 24-year-olds.[49] But the good news is that employment of young people then recovered much faster than many had feared. The NEET numbers are down to about three-quarters of a million.[50] The danger is, however, that young people are particularly vulnerable to long-term damage to their future earnings from periods of unemployment early in their working lives, so the last recession could have blighted the earnings prospects of an entire generation of young people – the scarring effect.[51] We will investigate further the reasons for the poor performance of pay in Chapter 11.

Behind the averages, women have done rather better than men. Women in particular have benefitted from increased educational opportunities and the removal of barriers to work and promotion. Household income has been boosted by the improved performance of a female second earner – it was one of the main drivers of rising living standards before the crisis, particularly in the bottom half of the income distribution.[52] This process began with the Boomers. One study, for example, compares US data for people aged 25–34 and 35–44 in 1962 and in 1989.[53] The 1962 data measures the incomes and wealth of the Boomers' parents, and the 1989 data measures the incomes and wealth of

Boomers themselves. To boost their living standards the Boomers postponed marriage, had fewer children, and above all more women went to work. Their wages performed less well in the US than the UK but, even so, total household income rose because of the shift of women into better-paid work. This trend has carried on, and in the UK is more significant for later cohorts. But as the earnings and labour participation rates of women aged under 30 have now caught up with men it is hard to see how this benign social transformation can do much more to boost household incomes of younger generations as they enter the jobs market.

The smaller generations coming along behind the Baby Boomers have not enjoyed the wage premium they might expect on the Easterlin argument. Globalization is crucial here. It happened at just the right moment for the Boomers. As they grew older they needed an infusion of young workers into the jobs market, or else wages would rise behind them and shift resources to the next generation. Bang on cue, hundreds of millions of workers from China and India joined the world trading system, driving down wages of the younger cohort of British workers competing with them. This argument has been put by Charles Goodhart and Manoj Pradhan, who argue that the glut of labour from globalization 'reduced the need for labour saving, productivity enhancing capital investment in the West', with the result of 'less inflationary pressure from wages'. It meant that there was downward pressure on wages, inflation, and interest rates, and inequality rose. Thomas Piketty's claim that returns on capital exceeded returns to labour (thus increasing inequality) is not a universal truth, but an account which depends on the specific circumstances of a surge in the global workforce.[54]

Goodhart is arguing that classic economic theory is right, and being a big generation should drive down wages relative to being a small one. But what is the relevant geographical measure of the size of a generation when it comes to work – national or international? The Boomers were competing in an international labour market just comprising Western Europe and North America, which is far smaller than the competition facing younger British workers today. The opening up of the global economy, notably to China and India, meant that the relatively small Western cohorts coming after them were actually part of a much bigger global labour market.

The timings make sense. China's opening up began under Deng Xiaoping in 1978 – but it took at least a decade before it had any impact beyond agriculture, and another decade before it reached much beyond their territory. So, meanwhile, back in the UK Generation X did pretty well. China only joined the World Trade Organization in 2001 which is when their exports really started shooting up, and that matches quite neatly the evidence of a slowdown in pay of younger cohorts entering the jobs market. It precedes the crash of 2008, which comes a bit late to explain what is going on.

The Boomers gain two ways. When it comes to political power and all the decisions taken by national governments, they are a big cohort. But when it comes to the global labour market they were part of a small cohort; they were a scarce resource that could get away with charging a higher price for their labour. The smaller British cohorts coming after them are actually competing with many more other workers across the globe: their wages are lower as the global labour supply is growing.

This argument is supported by the widening pay gap between young workers and older ones. One detailed estimate, this time with British data, is that between an earlier cohort born in 1958 and a later cohort born in 1970 there was a 10–12 percentage point decline in the full-time gross weekly earnings of young men aged 21–29 compared to all working men.[55] Other evidence from the Resolution Foundation confirms this clear trend. In 1975 the average 25- to 29-year-old male employee earned 15 per cent more than the average 60- to 64-year-old. He was still significantly ahead in the late 1980s, but in 2008 the older employee caught up and by 2017 on average earned 10 per cent more than the younger man. In 1975 the average 50- to 59-year-old earned about the same as the 25- to 29-year-old – by 2008 it was 20 per cent more and by 2017 it was 26 per cent more.[56]

We have already seen that this pay slowdown started before the crash, and now we can see it broadly matches the timing of globalization.

Consumption and Living Standards

Beyond jobs and pay there are the fundamentals of living standards. This is where the shift in both incomes and assets between generations comes together and really hits the younger generation hard. The rise in the value of assets relative to incomes directly affects individuals when it comes to trying to buy a house out of current income. And the high cost of a house feeds through into high rents, so incomes after housing costs suffer. The younger generation, many of whom are renters, feel this particularly badly. Older generations who may own their house with the mortgage paid off are insulated from these effects – for them the rise in house prices boosts their assets without hitting their living standards.

A year after *The Pinch* was first published in 2010, typical pensioner incomes after housing costs overtook the income of non-pensioners for the first time: it was a historic shift in the incomes of different generations. The chart below shows that, during the first decade of the twenty-first century, pensioner incomes after housing costs grew on average by 28 per cent, while over the same period working-age incomes grew by only 6 per cent. Although life can be tough for pensioners on low incomes, working-age families are doing worse. Pensioners used to be a disproportionately high proportion of low-income households (40 per cent in 1961), whereas now they are a much lower proportion of low-income households (12 per cent in 2015) than their share of the overall population. A poor pensioner at the bottom twenty per cent point on their income scale has an income which is now higher than a working age family at a similar point.[57]

Figure 7: Real net incomes after housing costs: pensioners and working age households, UK[58]

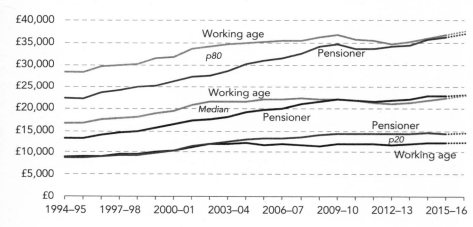

This divergence in disposable incomes shows up in the basics of consumer spending. The chart below shows the shifts in spending between different age groups. In 1963, people aged 25–34 spent 3 per cent less than those aged 55–64, but by 1989 they were spending 11 per cent more. In 2000–1, people aged 25–34 were spending 13 per cent more than those aged 55–64, but in 2014 they were spending 1 per cent less. One of the key factors was the rise in housing costs. As housing spend has gone up particularly for the younger generation, it means the rest of spend goes down even more – non-housing spend was the same across generations in 2000–1 but by 2014 it was 15 per cent less for 25- to 34-year-olds than for 55- to 64-year-olds.

Figure 8: Average household housing and non-housing consumption expenditure over time by age[59]

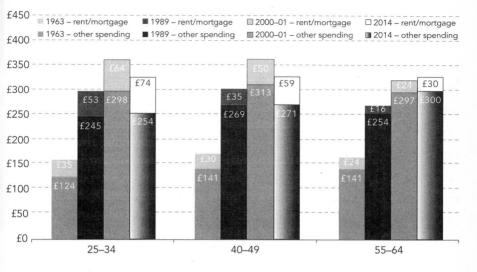

When the Boomers were young, their younger age group enjoyed the greatest surge in consumer spending. But now they are old it is again their age group which is doing best. So in the 1960s the non-housing spend of people aged 25–34 grew by 12 per cent more than the average for all adults aged 25–64. By 2014 it was those aged 55–64 whose spending improved most – on average 11 per cent faster than for those in the 25–64 bracket. It is a vivid example of the Baby Boomer phenomenon: the Boomers always contrive to be on the right side of any generational divide – young when the young are doing well and old when the old are.

It is argued that Millennials eat avocado toast in cafés and go on holiday rather than saving, so their living standards are higher than income measures suggest. But it is not true that young people have high incomes and have cut back on their saving. Their saving rate is low but no lower than it has been for a long time. It is their incomes which have changed. Boomers are tempted by elaborate accounts of changes in behaviour by young people reacting against materialism or ownership. But that is a device to avoid the uncomfortable and simple truth that young people are spending less because they have less money.

Research commissioned by the Resolution Foundation enables us to answer the classic questions about the consumption of different age groups.[60] It does not support the caricature of high-spending Millennials. And the variation in types of spend between different age groups is not as big as one might expect. Eating out? Those aged 25–34 do spend more on eating out than 55- to 64-year-olds but this is entirely offset by less spent eating in. And there has been a bigger growth in consumption on eating out by older working-age adults than for the young.

Is there a younger iPhone generation spending all their money on the latest digital devices? It does not show up in consumer spending, where spending on mobile phones is very similar at about £11 per week across different age groups. Leisure is 11 per cent of spending for those aged 25–34, 14 per cent for ages 40–49, and 17 per cent for ages 55–64. And the real growth is not partying on Ibiza but on cruises for the over-50s.

Experiences such as eating out and going on holiday have become more important than acquiring household goods – but this applies across generations. It is actually 55- to 64-year-olds who are enjoying the biggest growth in eating out at restaurants and cafés and in foreign holidays. The older generation seem to be doing the best in accessing the experiential economy.

Big Generation or Small Generation?

Let us go back to that opening question – if you had a choice, would you rather be born into a large generation or a small generation? The classic argument is that if you are born into a large generation you will find that things will be tougher. At every stage of the life cycle you will need to compete harder – for a traineeship, for your place at university, for your first job. At every moment in your economic life you personally may be poorer than people in smaller generations. As a result you may have fewer children, thus driving the cycle in which big generations are followed by small ones.

We have seen, however, that you actually gain enormous advantages from being in a big generation, with incomes and wealth growing faster than in the lifetimes of other, smaller generations. And if you shift your behaviour compared with the generations immediately before you – so for example you cut down on saving or your partner goes out to work – you can achieve a one-off improvement in household income, boosting it even more. But the benefits for the Baby Boomers seem to have gone much further than this. Be it the effects of globalization on wages, the shift to lower inflation, the impact of improved life expectancy, or the house price boom, the Baby Boomers seem to have had all the luck. Or is there more to it than that? Perhaps the Boomers have helped make their luck because being a big generation gives you a lot of power. Your large generation will dominate marketplaces. You will be kings and queens among consumers. Elections will be pitched to you. In fact, your values and tastes will shape the world around you – you will be able to spend your life in a generational bubble, always outvoting and outspending the generations before and after you. That is what it means to be a Baby Boomer; unless of course you see yourself as part of a wider network of obligations that tie you to other generations. It is to these obligations which we now turn.

5

THE SOCIAL
CONTRACT

The ultra-individualism with which we began Chapter 2 was not some chance event; we saw in Chapter 3 that it could be traced back to a series of demographic and economic changes driven above all by the Baby Boomers. We then saw in Chapter 4 how this big cohort was also shifting power and wealth to themselves and away from the young generation coming on behind. These changes are one reason for the widespread belief that the inevitable trajectory of any modern society must inevitably be towards ever-greater fragmentation. The trends towards more atomization look unstoppable.

But, and it is the biggest 'but' in this book, this will not do. There is nothing inevitable about this development. Every man for himself (and every generation for itself) is not a well-founded account of what it is to be fully human and to lead a good life. It does not even accurately describe what our own society is really like. Many thinkers have been trying to find a contemporary way of expressing the deep human instinct for co-operation. It has been called social responsibility, social justice, communitarianism. I called it civic conservatism. Religious leaders like Rabbi Lord Jonathan Sacks and the former Archbishop of Canterbury Rowan Williams, and thinkers of the Left such as David Selbourne have made distinguished contributions to this debate, as have philosophers such as Alasdair MacIntyre and Michael Sandel.

The Nobel Prize in Economics was awarded in 2009 to Elinor Ostrom, whose book *Governing the Commons: The Evolution of Institutions for Collective Action* is a path-breaking example of this genre of thought.[1]

Co-operation is a good thing and it is easy just to call for more of it. But that does not get us very far. We have to understand where co-operation comes from and how it works. I myself believe that co-operation between the generations is the most important form of co-operation. It is the key to the social contract and has the enormous advantage that it does not depend on a particular set of religious or cultural beliefs. Wanting the best for one's children and grandchildren is a deep-seated, natural human instinct. It is a powerful unifying principle in a society, however diverse it is becoming. We will be better able to judge the importance of relations between the generations when we have a deeper understanding of how a society is held together. And we are fortunate that there has been an extraordinary surge in research on how co-operation works. Even better, it starts with us as free individuals, not with airy appeals to a common interest.

We can start by going back to our hunter-gatherers. Two great political thinkers, David Hume and Jean-Jacques Rousseau, were close friends until a terrible falling out (it was, by the way, Rousseau's fault).[2] Both tried to root their political thought in an account of how primitive societies could have evolved.

Rousseau formulated one of the classic versions of the problem of co-operation – the stag hunt.[3] The story is briefly told in his *Discourse on Inequality*: 'If it was a matter of hunting a deer, everyone well realized that he must remain faithful to his post; but if a hare happened to pass within reach of one of them, we cannot doubt that he would have gone off in pursuit of it without scruple...'[4]

If we hunt on our own we have a good chance of catching a hare; if we hunt together we might get a stag, a much better return for our effort. But if everyone else gets distracted by pursuing individual hares, hunting on your own for a stag is the worst option of all. So what stops us chasing after hares individually and instead co-operate to hunt a stag?

David Hume wrestled with a similar problem and described it rather pessimistically:

> Your corn is ripe today; mine will be so tomorrow. 'Tis profitable for us both, that I should labour with you today, and that you should aid me tomorrow. I have no kindness for you, and know you have as little for me. I will not, therefore, take any pains upon your account; and should I labour with you upon my own account, in expectation of a return, I know I should be disappointed, and that I should in vain depend upon your gratitude. Here then I leave you to labour alone: you treat me in the same manner. The seasons change; and both of us lose our harvests for want of mutual confidence and security.[5]

Hume's response was a deliberately naturalistic account of society and morality – very different from the appeals to an external divine or ethical obligation which appear to solve such tricky problems by some *deus ex machina*. And now leading thinkers are following in his footsteps and trying to understand co-operation and morality as natural human behaviour, drawing on evolutionary biology, neuroscience, and game theory.[6]

Game theory has suffered from some terrible PR. Two geniuses of game theory have featured in famous films. The inventor of game theory, John von Neumann, was the model for the eponymous character in *Dr Strangelove*, acted by Peter Sellers as a mad Nazi who can barely restrain his arm's indiscriminate urge to give a Hitler salute. John Nash does slightly better with Russell Crowe's performance in *A Beautiful Mind* but the film's one attempt to define a Nash equilibrium gets it completely wrong. Perhaps it is not surprising that people are baffled by this strange discipline which seems to be dominated by tortured geniuses. And as for evolutionary biology, it has had nasty hints of 'the devil take the hindmost'.

But we need to break free from these caricatures because these are some of the most exciting areas of intellectual advance today: they help us understand how humans interact, institutions emerge, and co-operation flourishes. We can tell it as a story of human progress, which is incidentally how David Hume himself approached it.[7] He called it a move from natural to artificial virtues – and now the standard theory does, in a more sophisticated way, show how primitive impulses can lead to complex and pro-social patterns of behaviour.

We are starting with minimal assumptions to see how far we can get in explaining our pro-social behaviour without just appealing to our good nature. A good place to start therefore is with what Richard Dawkins famously called the selfish gene. The doctrine was formulated with classical precision by J. B. S. Haldane in what may have been a joke – 'I will jump into the river to save two brothers or eight cousins.' Now it has been tested with an ingenious if rather odd experiment: participants knew that the longer they remained in an uncomfortable ski-training-type position, the more money would be given to a beneficiary. In each case they knew the beneficiary but they did not know that the key variable being tested was their genetic link to the beneficiary. And they did hold the position for longer the closer they were genetically to the beneficiary. The length of time did not depend on whether they liked the relative. There were broadly similar results in England and with Zulus in South Africa, though with some differences in sensitivity to distant relatives, which may be to do with our account of different family structures in the opening chapter. So culture matters too; it is not just genetic determinism.[8]

We could just leave it there. But that would risk repeating the mistake of those nineteenth-century Social Darwinists who thought there was just a brutal struggle for survival everywhere and at all levels, and therefore Darwin's explanation of the evolution of the finch could justify the colonial powers massacring natives in the Congo because they believed they were winning out in the competition between nations. There is far more to human nature than just 'Genes-R-Us'. One way out is to appeal to some external moral or religious obligation to overcome these selfish genes. But what if there is no *deus ex machina* or so-called sky-hook we can appeal to? Or what if there are so many such beliefs in a diverse modern society that appeals to them are not the basis for a wider social contract?[9]

The classic example of game theory, the famous 'Prisoners' Dilemma', can give a rather bleak interpretation of the human condition. Imagine that two bank robbers are charged with their crime and held in separate cells. If they both implicate the other, each gets nine years. If one bank robber betrays the other and the other bank robber refuses to do so, the snitch gets off scot-free and his partner gets ten years. If they hold out and refuse to confess they face a minor tax-evasion charge and each gets one year. Suppose that our partners in crime had an understanding that if caught they will remain silent and will refuse to confess. Will they honour their agreement? Suppose that your partner has implicated you. If you stay quiet, you will end up in prison for ten years. In that case, the best thing to do is to implicate them so you only get nine years. Now, suppose your partner has stayed quiet. In that case, if you stay quiet you will get one year in prison. But if you implicate them, you can escape the charge altogether. It does not matter what your partner has done; the structure of the game is such that you will always be better off betraying the other person. That is the best strategy to choose, whatever the other player has chosen to do. According to game theorists there is only one possible outcome: both players betray their partners. In doing so, they both receive a prison term of nine years. This makes it what the evolutionary biologists call an evolutionarily stable strategy. The game theorists call it the unique Nash equilibrium. It is a set of solutions in a game where no one player can improve their position by changing their strategy. It is a *unique* Nash equilibrium because, in this case, there is only one such equilibrium.

The choice between betraying and remaining silent has become a metaphor for our ability to co-operate, share burdens, and generally be a good citizen. The implication that we will not be good citizens and that the two partners will not co-operate with each other is what all the fuss is about. The outcome of the Prisoners' Dilemma might seem 'nasty', but this is a consequence of the payoffs built into the structure of the game. Change the payoffs and you change the game and its outcome. The dilemma does not tell us anything very profound about human nature except that in some circumstances co-operation is difficult to sustain. You can also use the tools of game theory for the opposite effect – to show how co-operation can be sustained. To see how this is possible we need to go to a place where such behaviour seems inconceivable.

We can imagine few places more hellish than the trenches of the First World War. But they have helped us understand how human co-operation can emerge. Even in those terrible circumstances, co-operative strategies emerged between soldiers on the two front lines to make life more bearable. There were of course extraordinary acts of bravery. But there is evidence of co-operation too. Snipers would shoot to miss because otherwise neither side would ever be able to get out of their trench. They would not fire at certain areas marked out by flags. Bombardments would not happen at certain prearranged times. You did not shell supply trains coming to the front line. One account from a British soldier captures it very well:

> I was having tea with A Company when we heard a lot of
> shouting and went out to investigate. We found our men
> and the Germans standing on their respective parapets.
> Suddenly a salvo arrived but did no damage. Naturally
> both sides got down and our men started swearing at the
> Germans, when all at once a brave German got up and
> shouted out: 'We are very sorry about that; we hope no
> one was hurt. It is not our fault, it is that damned Prussian
> artillery.'[10]

Tony Ashworth calls these arrangements the 'live and let live'
system. They show how co-operation can emerge even without
explicit agreements, because frequent interaction permits us to
adopt strategies that reward co-operation and punish a failure
to co-operate. This is an example of reciprocal altruism. Each
individual act of one of the soldiers refraining from firing may
on its own seem altruistic, but it was part of a system in which
reciprocity was assured. It was sustained because it was in
everyone's rational self-interest. It shows how co-operation can
emerge without anyone appealing to a sense of community – in
fact all the appeals were the other way. Even in these uniquely
unfavourable circumstances, repeated interaction meant that
co-operation did emerge.

This is the crucial clue which transforms the classic Prisoners'
Dilemma. Things look different if we change the game in one
crucial respect: imagine that rather than this being a one-off
decision, you face the same dilemma with the same partner in
crime over and over again. In this new situation it is possible
that cooperation between players can emerge and be rewarded. If
the prisoners were brought back to a similar situation again and
again, they would have the opportunity to 'punish' one another
for betraying them by doing so themselves in subsequent games.
This means it becomes possible to enforce agreements. Robert
Axelrod arranged a tournament between computer programs

playing Prisoners' Dilemma–style games again and again.[11] He showed that the most effective strategy was a program called TIT FOR TAT. It would co-operate with the computer it was playing against, but if it was betrayed, it would punish the betrayer on a subsequent turn. If the other computer program reverted to co-operating, it would revert back too. In effect, it would mirror the other player one turn later. The Prisoners' Dilemma can be resolved if instead of playing the game once, we find ourselves repeatedly playing the same game.

This is how institutions work – they are places where people interact with each other sufficiently frequently for co-operation to emerge as a rational strategy. Values are not worth much unless they are embodied and sustained in real live institutions which shape how people behave. The generals in their chateaus behind the lines in the First World War deliberately moved the troops around from trench to trench so as to destroy co-operation between them and the enemy.

Exchange and reciprocity are very powerful – so powerful they can be exploited by people like the philosopher Schopenhauer, who is supposed to have left a tip on the table at the beginning of a meal and removed it at the end.[12] It lies behind many of the fascinating examples of persuasion which Robert Cialdini, the expert on influence, has analysed. A lot of persuasion works by creating a sense of reciprocity – it is what the followers of Hare Krishna are doing when they give us a flower for free but promptly expect something from us in return. David Hume put it very neatly: 'I learn to do a service to another, without bearing him any real kindness; because I foresee that he will return my service, in expectation of another of the same kind, and in order to maintain the same correspondence of good offices with me or with others.'[13]

The co-operative behaviour institutions sustain is not necessarily for a good purpose. Classic psychological experiments have shown their power to make us behave badly, as well as their power for good.[14] As the philosopher Michael Oakeshott observed, 'We do not first decide that certain behaviour is right or desirable and then express our approval or disapproval of it in an institution; our knowledge of how to behave well is, at this point, the institution.'[15] Areas dominated by gangs and where people refuse to speak to the police are a nasty equilibrium, largely based on the fear of future contact with local criminals. One role of government is to break up these unpleasant arrangements.

So far we have seen how reciprocity generates co-operation. But direct reciprocity isn't enough. That is the awkward issue behind the homely advice: 'If you don't go to his funeral, he won't go to yours.' We need to escape being dependent on repeat encounters. Direct exchange is the equivalent of a barter economy; we need a currency.[16] That currency is reputation – how we are regarded by others. Reputation allows us to enjoy indirect reciprocity. And if we go further and punish another person by refusing to help them because they refused to help another person, we can build a virtuous circle.

This requires that their reputation be known to us, hence we need memory and gossip too. Adam Smith rightly identified how we are regarded by others as a key source of human well-being: 'What are the advantages which we propose to gain by that great purpose of human life which we call bettering our condition? To be observed, to be attended to, to be taken notice of with sympathy, complacency, and approbation, are the advantages which we can propose to derive from it.'[17]

This is a clue to the power of social media, as people come to depend on their 'likes'. This basic element in human experience is intensified and magnified to such an extent that it threatens well-being and can even lead to depression and suicide. It is why one of the defining features of the younger generations is their smartphones, and hence ubiquitous continuous access to social media such as Facebook.[18]

Small institutions are particularly effective for generating these networks of indirect reciprocity. US college students are the lab rats of the social sciences, so it is no surprise that one of the best pieces of evidence on this comes from American student dorms. Researchers dropped addressed letters and measured what percentage of letters are picked up and returned. The score was 100 per cent returned in a small dorm, 87 per cent in one which is medium-sized, and 63 per cent in a large one.[19] My own research showed much worse problems of discipline and behaviour in English schools if they were larger.[20]

We put a lot of effort into identifying defectors and impose lots of minor punishments for doing that. We spot cheaters in social contexts better than if the same situations were presented as pure logical problems.[21] This is what humans are particularly good at. Infant children at two and a half years old have similar cognitive skills to chimps and orangutans of that age but already have better social skills.[22] Reputation, good and bad, works because of willingness to approve or punish people whose behaviour has not directly affected us. And failure to punish must itself be punished. This may sound unpleasant but it is the subtle expressions of approval and disapproval that convey a sense of what we think of people's behaviour, and even the most non-judgemental of us would be hard put to avoid these. It is how social values are protected. If you doubt this then why not pause to enjoy Jane Austen's *Pride and Prejudice*.[23] The malefactors are a philanderer, Mr Wickham, and the youngest of the Bennet sisters, Lydia. They set up house together, 'living in sin'. The family is of course shocked and faces the dilemma of ostracizing them or being ostracized themselves: '... this false step in one daughter, will be injurious to the fortunes of all the others, for who... will connect themselves with such a family... Let me advise you... to throw off your unworthy child... and leave her to reap the fruits of her own heinous offence,' writes Mr Collins to Mr Bennet.

Then, later: 'This unfortunate affair will, I fear, prevent my sister's having the pleasure of seeing you at Pemberley today,' says Mr Darcy to Elizabeth Bennet.

The reader's sympathy is directed towards Lydia's sisters and the obvious injustice involved in the need to punish them: *who... will connect themselves with such a family?* Unless of course they in turn punish their sister: *Let me advise you... to throw off your unworthy child.*[24]

Frequently there is a strong reciprocator in these novels – somebody who derives pleasure from enforcing society's rules. In *Pride and Prejudice* it is Mr Collins, the clergyman. However, he is the least sympathetic character in the novel. His unseemly enthusiasm for punishment is treated with derision and contempt. Elizabeth is if anything rather pleased that she will no longer enjoy his company. Mr Darcy, on the other hand, complies with the rules only with the greatest reluctance. He obeys out of a sense of duty – a duty that derives from the importance he attaches to his standing in society (which he has every right to defend). The reader is left in no doubt who has the more important role in enforcing society's rules, Mr Collins or Mr Darcy.

Jane Austen was profoundly ambivalent in her attitude towards the subject of her novels: the moral codes by which society is governed. This ambivalence results not because she is a twenty-first-century liberal who thinks that sex outside marriage is OK, but rather because her greatness lies in her subtle treatment of the roles we all play and the dilemmas we face. The world of the nineteenth-century novel may seem to be far removed from society today and sounds severe, but Austen's genius is to capture something timeless about human nature. Even though society's particular moral codes have varied over time, we enforce our contemporary morality – be it about racism or drinking and driving – with similar disapproval.

––––––

We are trying to construct an account of how we co-operate with others drawing on limited assumptions about human nature. So far we have got from selfishness through reciprocal exchanges to indirect reciprocity and the importance of how we are regarded by others. The next stage is to consider how competition rewards different patterns of behaviour. We will go back to our hunter-gatherers, and this time we have uncomfortable news. Nearly two-thirds of hunter-gatherer groups for which records exist waged war at least every two years.[25] Archaeological data suggests 15 per cent of people in primitive societies died violently.[26] Darwin described what he thought would be the effect of such competition:

> When two tribes of primeval man, living in the same country, came into competition, if the one tribe included (other circumstances being equal) a greater number of courageous, sympathetic, and faithful members, who were always ready to warn each other of danger, to aid and defend each other, this tribe would without doubt succeed best and conquer the other.[27]

This idea of group selection is controversial. Some experts do not believe this step in the argument is correct or necessary.[28] But we can see how a competitive environment can create the conditions for co-operation, regardless of whether or not you think it goes beyond rational individual self-interest. A very good example is the behaviour of vampire bats. As we know from all the best horror movies, vampire bats need regular supplies of fresh blood. We now know that the vampire bats which come back from a night's hunting with lots of blood regurgitate some to share it with other vampire bats who were less successful. The vampire bat colonies which survive through tough times are the ones which are capable of this pooling of risk. So competition for limited resources rewards co-operation. Maybe vampire bats are caring, sharing creatures after all, or as Professor Binmore puts it: 'Although vampire genes are selfish, reciprocal sharing turns out to be sustainable as an equilibrium in the vampire game of life.'[29]

This works best if everyone in the colony keeps an eye out for vampire bat free-riders who take blood but do not give – so, who knows, they may have bat squeaks of gossip too.[30]

This is where group selection gets tricky. Some scientists dispute this account, claiming that vampire bat blood-sharing is just restricted to immediate relatives. But actually the evidence is that those bats with wider networks, including non-relatives, do better in times of adversity than with smaller deeper groups of reciprocators.[31]

There is also a subversive challenge from the feminists who point out quite correctly that it is female bats who do most of the sharing of blood. In fact, women seem historically to have borne more of the burden of maintaining such contracts, perhaps because they live longer and so are likely to be recipients of more informal care later. Ingenious research by anthropologist Robin Dunbar using mobile phone records does suggest older women devote more time on the phone to daughters than to husbands, perhaps because they invest in their grandchildren via close contact with their daughters. Phone calls from men to their adult children run at half the rate of mothers and are more gender-neutral, whereas mothers' calls are particularly focused on daughters when they are of an age likely to have children. So there is a strong matrilineal element to the contract between the generations.[32]

Overall this account of reciprocity generating co-operation does seem to match the empirical evidence on our moral values. If you ask people to endorse one of several classic moral codes for living, reciprocal altruism scores highest. The one which gets the greatest endorsement, from over three-quarters of adults, is 'Do to others as you would have others do to you' (77 per cent). Next is 'Be true to yourself in all things' (72 per cent). Only 41 per cent endorse 'Always do what you want as long as you don't hurt anybody'.[33]

There is a paradox behind this model – we are trying to explain good features of human behaviour like empathy or co-operation with a very limited set of assumptions about human behaviour, which may put some people off the whole exercise. They may feel we are 'taking the altruism out of altruism'. There is not some social glue to be poured over us to make us more co-operative: it is how institutions and incentives work.

A good example comes from Mediterranean trade in the Middle Ages. To an outsider it must have looked very trusting indeed – merchants sent goods around the Mediterranean not necessarily paid in advance, sometimes to people they did not know and had never met and all without an enforceable law of contract. How did they do it? Were they just more trusting?

We now know how it worked from an extraordinary cache of eleventh-century documents found in an ancient synagogue in old Cairo. It all depended on a network of traders. An agent who defrauded one trader would lose business with all of them, as the traders had a reciprocal network in which they would all exclude an agent who defrauded any one of them. It was in the interests of the traders to preserve the coalition against rogue agents – all contracts were short-term and so they could be penalized by other members of the coalition if they did not enforce action against a delinquent agent.[34]

This is a case study in how ingenuity in designing an institution creates 'trust'. We do not need to rely on personal moral improvement, desirable though that is, nor worry that we are somehow worse people than we are. We need to give institutions the space to emerge and to function and to create their own networks of reciprocity. Governments can be like those First World War generals, disrupting the inner life of an institution and stopping co-operation. And the demographic disruption wrought by the Baby Boomers has eroded the contract between the generations which is at the heart of a healthy society. It is something we instinctively value and is strong within the family, but as we saw in the last chapter we may not be so good at delivering it when it comes to wider society.

Politics is not therefore about pouring social cement over atomized citizens to try to stick them together so they co-operate with each other. Instead we can think of co-operative behaviour as being like drystone walling held together by its inner structure – Hume's image was the stones held together in a well-designed stone arch. In the words of Ken Binmore in his powerful book *Natural Justice,* 'social capital isn't a *thing* – it's just a word we use when talking about the properties of an equilibrium that has evolved along with our game of life'.[35]

***

Reciprocity involves empathy – being able to put yourself in someone else's shoes even when their feet are a different size. Sympathy is feeling for someone else; empathy is making the leap to understanding someone else even if your emotions are not directly involved. When Adam Smith put sympathy at the heart of his *Theory of Moral Sentiments* he meant what we would now call empathy: this is the key that unlocks the argument in that great book – otherwise it is just about being nice to each other.

Other mammals with sufficient social structure and mental powers to practise reciprocity also have some capacity for empathy. Rhesus monkeys do. Here is an account of an experiment which involves monkeys in two separate cages side by side:

> One would have a chain and a trough. If they pulled the chain, food would be delivered to the monkey. However, at the same time, the other monkey would receive an electric shock. Having realised the connection, monkeys in these cages refused to ask for more food for five days and for 12 days. They starved themselves to avoid shocking a peer.[36]

Scientists have even tracked down the chemical which governs this behaviour. Paul Zak has shown that infusing the human brain with moderate doses of oxytocin can induce people to trust strangers with their money.[37] It is sometimes called the 'lust and trust' chemical. Or if you prefer the same thought in a rather more spiritual way, Thomas Jefferson put it beautifully: 'The Creator would indeed have been a bungling artist, had he intended man for a social animal, without planting in him social dispositions.'[38] And if you want to put it in the language of modern neuroscience, there is a concentration of processing power in those parts of the brain we need for empathy. It takes a lot of high-power neurological activity to act empathetically. We have to be able to distinguish between what we want and others want.

Nicholas Humphrey, the evolutionary psychologist, argues this is where self-consciousness comes from – we have to be able to think ourselves into other people's heads in order to function socially, and that generates a sense of what is different about what is going on in our own heads.[39] Our empathetic interaction with others creates our sense of who we are.

Instinct and emotion fit in here too. We are not desiccated calculating machines. Apart from all the other problems, that just wouldn't work. We would endlessly be doing intricate calculations about what other people might do; life would be like playing an elaborate game of chess. We would be incapable of actually doing anything until our computations were complete. So we need shortcuts, instinctive rules of thumb. Apparently irrational anger also has a place – it is a good way of showing we will protect our reciprocal understandings and not be patsies who can be exploited.[40] Professor Binmore argues that emotion helps to police – more rapidly than rational calculation can – primeval social contracts. It protects co-operation.[41] And the emotion which polices and sustains these particular arrangements and understandings is linked to our most physical responses: disgust and nausea. The evolutionary biologists suggest that we took the most basic aversions, which had developed to protect us from eating stuff that would kill us, and used what were literally gut feelings to protect and enforce our social contracts – as argued by Jonathan Haidt in *The Righteous Mind*.[42]

Our emotions are particularly engaged in defence of fairness: anger makes us irrationally committed to deals we think are fair. The Ultimatum Game captures this very neatly. In its simplest form there are two players. One, the proposer, is given a sum of money and distributes some of it to the second player. If the responder rejects the offer then there is no deal and the money is lost to both of them. The experiment has been played in many forms and there is a clear pattern – a responder offered less than about 30 per cent of the money rejects the deal and both players lose everything.

It is hard for conventional economics to explain this behaviour because economists assume something is better than nothing. But the game is telling us that fairness matters so much to us that we will make sacrifices for it. One explanation is that we are behaving as if the negotiation is to be repeated even if it is not – so we kind of overshoot, thinking we can generate reciprocal altruism even when we can't. Neuroscientists have also identified the part of the brain that controls our behaviour in the Ultimatum Game, and can temporarily disable it with waves of the right frequency aimed specifically at it so that when we play the game we accept lower offers.[43]

The Ultimatum Game does not just apply to humans. Capuchin monkeys can learn the value of a token, which they exchange for barter at different values – so a low-value token gets a cucumber and a high-value one gets a grape. Capuchins who observed their peers receiving a high-value item for a given token or price would ignore the reward or refuse to make the exchange if offered a lower-value one.[44]

We are beginning to see how our hunter-gatherers got to hunt stags not rabbits. They would have needed a deal about sharing out the stag which they believed was fair. A convention for sharing consumption was essential for co-operative production. And it would be policed by knowing that someone you betrayed would be so angry about it that he would be willing to stop everyone else having the stag.

———————

We have got a long way in understanding co-operation, empathy, and fairness. It is an exciting and productive research programme which is gradually being absorbed into our wider culture. Yuval Noah Harari's *Sapiens* has popularized this type of approach by arguing that our capacity for imaginative belief in gods, institutions, money, etc. enables our species to co-operate on a scale no other species can match.[45] I believe this naturalistic account of morality is increasingly going to contribute to public discourse about the many ethical issues in public policy. It does not resolve all our dilemmas but it helps us understand them. And it enables us to talk about them in a way which reaches across the different religious or ethical views now represented in open Western countries.

The most profound dilemma arises from what has been called the move from 'tribal brotherhood to universal otherhood'.[46] It is the tension between the intimate experience of a community and the abstract rules of a modern market economy. We have seen how we develop our understandings and reciprocity within a particular community and within an institution. What about people who are outside our group? How do we co-operate with them? Is fairness just for us or does it include them too? What happens when the local and the universal collide? Institutions provide the framework in which we co-operate – and that often involves defining others as outsiders, hence what has been described as the 'antagonism between social tribes who must maintain their internal solidarity – through bonds of loyalty, religion, language and so on'.[47] And how do other generations count in all this – are they part of our community or outside it?

There are deep philosophical issues here. But rather than tackle them head on we can look at the evidence of how our moral attitudes are actually formed. One survey showed the top influences on people's moral values were parents (95 per cent) and family (91 per cent), way ahead of teachers (75 per cent) or religion (46 per cent).[48] The family is the first place where we experience these reciprocal exchanges, particularly between the generations. The good news is that early experience of strong reciprocity yields a belief in universal values. The evidence suggests that strong families (where children are particularly close to their parents) are unusually effective at generating a willingness to reach out beyond the particular group. One researcher studied the Germans who had the courage to shelter Jews in Nazi Germany and found that they had one key thing in common – they all came from strong families. The same is true of people who were willing to stand up against discrimination and against the Vietnam War in America in the 1960s.[49] Low levels of father contact lower altruism.[50] Interaction with siblings also appears to be a good way of learning how reciprocity works.

Individuals' behaviour is not of course determined by these factors, and a community can be rich in other types of ways of experiencing reciprocity and altruism. But the good news is that the experience of family life suggests that strong, tightly focused reciprocity can provide the basis for wider moral understandings too – the dilemma which looms so large in theory does not appear to be so bad in practice.

One reason why families matter so much is that many family exchanges are across different generations. This has been one of the great weaknesses of social contract thinking – it treats the contract as between a group of middle-aged men, like those illustrations of the American founding fathers or members of a Victorian club. The challenge is to extend it across generations.

Indeed we may think that what makes nationhood and family so important to us is that both are communities which link generations. (Universities, transmitting a critical understanding of a body of knowledge from one generation to the next, are also very strongly represented in lists of those very special institutions which have lasted more than 500 years. By contrast, it is striking evidence of the sheer dynamic turbulence of the marketplace that very few companies last more than a hundred years.)

If we want to understand contracts between generations, the family is a good place to start. Here are four implicit contracts between members of successive generations:

i   if we care for our children when they are young, they will care for us when we are old (a direct exchange);

ii   if we care for our parents now they are old, our children will copy us, and similarly care for us when we are old (replication of our behaviour to our benefit);

iii if we care for our children, they will copy us and care similarly for their children, our grandchildren (replication of our behaviour to the benefit of future generations);

iv   our parents helped care for our children so we have got to copy them and help our children when they have children (we have to replicate behaviour from which we have benefitted).

It is this cat's cradle of relationships between the generations – half exchange and half obligation – which makes the world go round. They do, however, come with very different emotional overtones, captured in the proverb: 'When the father helps the son, they both laugh. When the son helps the father, they both cry.'

Those four key commitments between the generations are still more likely to be discharged by women than men. Indeed, the blindness of conventional social contract thinking to what have been the distinct roles of men and women may be one reason why it has also been so weak on the contract between the generations.

The list comprised examples of reciprocity or exchange, but we think that this is not what morality should be like – it should just be absolute injunctions. Look at the Ten Commandments. They take this unconditional form – *thou shalts* and *thou shalt nots*. If they say anything about consequences, they are in the next world, not this one. But the commandment on relations between the generations is unique. It alone explains what should happen in this world as a result of complying with it: 'Honour thy father and thy mother: that thy days may be long upon the Earth which the Lord thy God giveth thee.'[51] It is saying you will do better and live longer yourself if you have cared for the older generation. There will be a benefit back to you from honouring your parents, presumably as you are more likely to be so honoured yourself. So even the Bible is implying some kind of reciprocity between the generations, and one which is not direct exchange.

There are indeed links between intergenerational caring and improved life expectancy. There is also strong evidence for children boosting the life expectancy of their parents. Research into broadly similar adults participating in IVF fertility treatment found that those who go on to become parents live longer than those who do not – the death rate for childless women was four times higher and for men two times higher. One reason we look after ourselves is so we can look after our children.[52] A separate study showed that, at 60 years of age, the difference in life expectancy between people with and without children was 2 years for men and 1.5 years for women. There was an even bigger gain for lone parents – perhaps because in the absence of a partner, care from children is even more important.[53]

The four relationships in our list are all examples of reciprocity, but only one is a direct exchange between two generations. Behaviour is copied or cascades across the generations.[54] These exchanges are not necessarily between the same people. They are less like a conventional exchange than like someone passing the baton in a relay race. The pattern of obligations can become so complex it looks more like the links in a TV soap or a particularly elaborate family line. But all of us start benefiting from an enormous investment of care and education, and if we are not betrayed then we should not betray the next generation. We know where babies come from, but even more important is where adults come from. And they are shaped by their experience of these intergenerational exchanges.

Moral philosophers are much better at neighbourhood ethics – obligations to fellow citizens now – than they are at obligations across the generations. And we can see why it is much harder for them. These exchanges are not a classic set of contracts entered into at one moment in time. We can think of them as a special case of the Prisoners' Dilemma, where co-operation is even harder to obtain as the iterations occur across time with people who may not yet exist. And even if you do not think in terms of contracts, the problems still remain. Nowadays much of our moral reasoning is based on the assertion of rights – captured by the cartoon showing the lawn with the notice: 'Please respect the rights of the grass'. But it is hard to think of the rights of people who do not yet exist.

Such questions understandably trouble the philosophers.[55] But perhaps our original model of the interests of the selfish gene can help for our purposes. Let us go back to Haldane's neat remark about our genetic interests: 'I will jump into the river to save two brothers or eight cousins.' What would the calculation of the interest of a selfish gene look like across four generations? Your child has half of your genes, your grandchild a quarter, and your great-grandchild an eighth. 4/8 + 2/8 + 1/8 adds up to 7/8 in total.

After one more generation it adds up to 15/16ths and carries on getting closer and closer to 1. So even if all you care about is your own gene's future, you soon find that the interests of the aggregate of descendants in the future weigh very heavily indeed – more heavily than any one contemporary, however close they are to you.[56]

There is strong empirical evidence for these sorts of intergenerational exchanges. Imagine that you are a harassed middle-aged woman with an elderly parent as well as children. If you think of these as conflicting claims then you would expect that the more time you have to spend on your parents or parents-in-law, the less you have for your children – and it may be that we cannot devote maximum attention to both generations. But some evidence suggests that the more you do for your parents, the more you do for your children as well – and this is after allowing for class, income, etc. One study found that 'British women who provided help to a child were twice as likely to help a parent as those who were not helping a child (and conversely those helping a parent were twice as likely to be helping a child).'[57] The best way to explain this is that the intergenerational contract suggests these are complementary activities. What you give to the next generation depends partly on what you received from the previous ones. And it looks as if young people are willing to accept they have obligations to elderly parents, whereas as parents age they grow increasingly concerned about imposing burdens on their children.[58]

Simulated games in which volunteers are put into situations where they have to decide how to act in dilemmas involving future generations confirm that our behaviour to future generations is influenced by how previous generations treated us. For example, they are running a commercial fishing company and have to decide how to respond to a request to voluntarily reduce their catch to protect fish stocks for the future but sacrificing income now. When these dilemmas are modelled, participants are more willing to make cuts if they are told that previous generations ensured fish stocks survived by making voluntary cuts, but are much less willing to do so if told that previous generations did not. The sacrifice of income called for now was the same in both cases, but those who were told that previous generations had made sacrifices were far more willing to make cuts themselves – by 84 per cent to 37 per cent. This is a potentially powerful way of 'nudging' our behaviour; our decisions about how to treat future generations are shaped by how we believe past ones treated us.[59]

Here we are moving way beyond transfers between generations within the family – these are across generations as a whole. Can we think of the whole social contract as being intergenerational?

———

The social contract has a long tradition in political thought: its greatest recent exponent is John Rawls in his book *A Theory of Justice*.[60] He asks us to imagine that we are choosing in advance a set of political and economic arrangements from behind a veil of ignorance. We do not know whether we will be rich or poor, man or woman, talented or not. In fact, for his thought experiment to work we do not really have anything distinctive about us at all – we cannot have a culture or a religious faith. If you assume away all those things then you end up with the classic modern state – tolerant of an extraordinary diversity of lifestyles and beliefs, but licensed to intervene to reduce diversity of income.

The classic objection to this type of social contract theory is that it invites us to think of ourselves as somehow existing outside society, history, and culture. We cannot even have a language, which does after all embody a set of values. We are just bearers of some genes: 'selfish' ones. Rawls might as well ask us all to imagine that we are sheep. But Rawls, to his credit, is one of the few political philosophers who has seriously wrestled with intergenerational fairness. Even more to his credit, he recognizes that the problem of justice between generations 'subjects any ethical theory to severe if not impossible tests'.[61]

The idea of obligations across the generations radically changes the implications of Rawls's account of justice. He argues that any particular difference of outcomes would need to be justified as helping the least well off in society – the so-called difference principle. But he says that this should be applied to 'the longer-term prospects of the least-favoured extended over future generations. Each generation must not only preserve the gains of culture and civilization, and maintain intact those just institutions that have been established, but it must also put aside in each period of time a suitable amount of real capital accumulation.'[62] That opens up a host of arguments for saving, enterprise, and cultural traditions that are often ignored. And it happens as a direct result of his brave attempt to include future generations in his model.

Rawls is saying we have to look to the future, and that might limit what we feel able to spend on ourselves today. He is going out of his way to avoid the criticism of so much liberalism that it does not understand our obligation to transmit a culture and capital from one generation to the next. This attitude was captured by J. M. Keynes, who dismissed concern about the long-term consequences of his economic theories by saying 'in the long run we are all dead'. As his model broke down in the 1960s and 1970s the riposte came back: 'Now Keynes is dead, and we are in the long run.'

Rawls does not want to be open to the same line of criticism. That means he has to explain why these long-term consequences for future generations should matter for the liberal individuals entering into his social contract behind the veil of ignorance. He solves his problem by an extraordinary move – he describes the contracting parties as 'heads of families'. 'The parties are thought of as representing continuous lines of claims, as being, so to speak, deputies for a kind of everlasting moral agent or institution.' He expressly says this is necessary so that they will think of the consequences of their actions for 'at least two generations'.[63] This enables him to include obligations across the generations. But it comes at the price of sacrificing the integrity of his theory. These people behind the veil of ignorance who are not allowed a language or a religion or a nationality are supposed to have children. And these children are not just products of chance sexual encounters and abandoned at birth. They are part of something called a family.

Rawls, even though he is willing to shed every other feature of our lives as a social animal, cannot abandon the family, otherwise our obligations to future generations would not have a firm foothold in his theory. Rawls has to put people into some kind of institutional framework after all, in order to create the moral obligations without which his theory of justice would collapse – and what drives him to it is the need to include obligations to future generations. This shows that any worthwhile social contract has to be between the generations.

Just as the Old Testament has to make an exception for the intergenerational contract in the otherwise-unconditional structure of the Ten Commandments, so the great liberal thinker, Rawls, has to make an exception in his theory too. This tells us how important these contracts between the generations are, even if they are hard to pin down in conventional form. These intergenerational transactions are deeply embedded in our nature. Intergenerational exchange is at the heart of the social contract. And they are as natural as it is possible to be – if we want to understand what ties us together in a way that bridges the gaps of culture and age then a commitment to the future of our children and grandchildren is the most powerful appeal we have. The social contract is, at root, a contract between the generations.

6

AGES AND STAGES

Three Different Effects: Period, Cohort and Life Cycle

The little old lady on her own in her flat is genuinely anxious about what she fears is the threat from a group of teenagers outside her window. The police are called. Sometimes it is very serious indeed but other times they find a disconsolate gang of youths hanging around who feel they are being harassed by older people when they are just bored. They can be dispersed for good by installing a Mosquito, the device which emits a high-pitched note that can be heard by teenagers but not older people, so as to drive them away from areas where they are not welcome. This ingenious British invention is in effect a declaration of intergenerational warfare. Imagine the outrage if the sound could only be heard by pensioners and was being used to exclude them.

Such misunderstandings reflect a breakdown of trust between the generations. This erodes a nation's sense of well-being and hope for the future. The good news is that there is widespread support for the social contract between the generations. Research by Ipsos MORI found that 50 per cent of people agree that the success of our society is measured by how we provide for older generations. But there is also a growing concern that we are letting down the younger generation. Only 22 per cent believe young people will have a better life than their parents, as against 48 per cent who believe it will be worse. These are extraordinarily pessimistic figures given that modern liberal democratic societies and technological advances are supposed to deliver material progress and personal well-being. Overall, 59 per cent thought every generation should have a higher standard of living than the one that came before it: 64 per cent of those aged 25–34 and 55 per cent of people aged 55–75 were in agreement with this. There is a larger difference between the cohorts on the obligations to generations that have come before: 45 per cent of 25- to 34-year-olds agree the success of our society is measured by how we provide for older generations, as against 64 per cent of 55- to 75-year-olds.[1]

We described in Chapter 3 the disruptive demographic changes since the War that lie behind this growing pessimism. In Chapter 4 we provided the economic evidence of what has gone wrong: we are indeed spending the kids' inheritance. We could just pack up and go home, conceding that deep social and economic trends are moving inexorably against us. But that won't do. It is not inevitable that the intergenerational contract must break down. We tried in Chapter 5 to show how even a modern secular society can still understand and value a social contract, at the heart of which is a contract between the generations. We can now go further and look at what our attitudes and values actually are, not just what we assume they are, so we can see to what extent there really is a generation gap and how it might be bridged.

We have to start, as always, with the Baby Boomers. The Boomers have led a big change in attitudes towards work and domestic life. Of people aged 65 or over in 2006, 55 per cent agreed with the proposition that 'being a housewife is just as fulfilling as working for pay'. The big change came with the Boomers: only 42 per cent of early Boomers, people aged 50–64 in 2006, agreed with the proposition, and the proportion agreeing remains just about identical at 40 per cent for subsequent cohorts. Of the oldest cohort, 43 per cent agreed that 'a job is all right but what most women really want is a home and children'. That falls to 26 per cent for early Boomers and again remains pretty much the same for subsequent generations.[2] Later research by Ipsos MORI shows the same pattern: similarly high percentages of Millennials, Gen Xers and Baby Boomers are opposed to propositions such as 'it is the husband's job to earn money while the wife stays at home' and 'sexual relations between two adults of the same sex are always wrong'. The big gap is between the Boomers and the generations before them, though even among the oldest generations there has been some modest shift in attitudes over time.[3] So the Boomers led a change in attitudes and these have remained broadly stable for subsequent generations. A conspicuous exception is attitudes to immigration, where there was a surge in concern but it was very much concentrated among the older generations including the Boomers with the big gap between them and Gen X and Millennials who are much less worried.[4]

A change in the culture affecting most age groups is a 'period effect'. That is why one way of thinking of these changes is a general trend to greater individualism, led by the Boomers but affecting most of us. Individualism can mean many different things. When it comes to the economic prospects of younger generations it can mean a shift away from mutual insurance to personal risk-bearing. This can create an exhilarating sense of personal liberation from, for example, a company pension scheme or a big welfare state. But greater exposure to risk in a personal pension scheme can yield a lower future income if a pension pot is annuitized at a bad moment. And if there is a limit to our appetite for risk then we may become more risk-averse in some other area. Acrobats make bolder moves when there is a safety net underneath them. We may just feel we are more on our own as we face the risks and challenges of our existence. As so often in life, good and bad are intimately linked. We are more tolerant (a good thing) but also more disengaged (a bad thing). And, anyway, this wider cultural trend to individualism is not the same as irresponsibility.

The TV series *Absolutely Fabulous* had a distinctive take on the contrast between the generations. Edina and Patsy are fun-loving, liberal-minded Baby Boomers, but Edina's daughter is earnest and straitlaced. She has little time for the irresponsibility of the older generation, who as children of the sixties seem to have had life far easier. And as we look at the way in which the younger generation assemble their CVs, make the most use of their gap years, and are so driven by moral concerns, it is clear that *Ab Fab* was on to something. Maybe the Boomers are different but, once again, have constructed a world in their own image and claimed for it the status of a universal truth.

There is some empirical evidence from attitude surveys of a special sixties generation that is far more liberal in its attitudes than its successors as well as its predecessors. The cohort whose formative years were in the 1960s might have a different view of the world because of the exceptional events of that decade. The flood of the Baby Boomers into early marriage and then out to divorce may have been deeply disruptive for them.

The evidence bears this out. The cohort whose formative years were in the 1960s have even more liberal attitudes than previous or succeeding cohorts. Thus, for example, 49 per cent of the cohort of those who were young in the 1960s disapprove of extramarital sex, as against 56 per cent of people who are 10 years younger and 63 per cent who are 10 years older.[5] Another survey showed that it was the youngest age groups who were most likely to agree that life in Britain would improve if people were more sexually faithful.[6] Today's youngsters have been called Generation Sensible – or even, rather cruelly, Generation Yawn. The evidence is that overall they are extraordinarily well-behaved. The number of people aged 10 to 17 convicted or given a police caution for a first offence in England and Wales was 110,000 in 2007 and down to 28,000 in 2017. Around 75,000 children and young people (aged 10–17) were arrested by the police in England and Wales in 2016–17, down by 79 per cent on 10 years earlier.[7] In 2005 around two-thirds of British 18- to 24-year-olds had drunk alcohol in the previous week. By 2017 that was down to around a half. And binge-drinking was down from one in three to one in four. The percentage of cigarette smokers in the same age group is down from 35 per cent to less than 25 per cent over the same period.[8] It suggests a growing aversion to risky behaviour. They are more aware of safety. In America, too, they drink less, have a lower rate of teenage pregnancy and are more likely to wear seat belts. Fewer of them agree with the statement 'I like to test myself every now and then by doing something a little risky'.[9] Maybe what is really shocking about the younger generation is how much more cautious they are than the much more cavalier Boomers.

Researchers asked participants when they last completely changed the way they styled their hair or the way they dressed. This is, if you like, a question about how fixed our identities are. You might expect a clear pattern with the youngest generation – those who are most likely to be changing all the time. But the evidence is subtly different. Pensioners do indeed live up to the stereotype. The average older person has not changed his or her hairstyle since the age of 41, the way they dress since the age of 36, or their diet since the age of 38. Those who came of age in the 1960s are the opposite. Of all the different cohorts studied they are the ones who are most likely to have completely changed their hairstyle or the way they dress.[10]

It was said of Winston Churchill's book on the First World War that he had written a book about himself and called it *The World Crisis*. The Baby Boomers have done something similar for our cultural and political understandings. As the key generation in the challenge to social institutions in the 1960s and the transformation of our economy in the 1980s, they have created a picture of the world which applies their experiences to everyone else as well. They are behind this assumption of a simple trend to ever-greater individualism. But you could see things very differently. Think instead of each generation as distinctive, imprinted with the experiences of their youth and carrying them through life. Generations are more like slices in one of those ice cores they drill in Antarctica – forever imprinted with the unique features of the period. That was Mannheim's way of thinking, which we applied in Chapter 3 as we described different cohorts.

There is some evidence of particularly influential stages of our lives when these attitudes are shaped. What happened when you were aged 17–25 is likely to be reported by you for the rest of your life as a very important event – which is one reason why it makes sense to look at society from the perspective of different birth cohorts who share distinct formative experiences. The major national or world events recalled by Americans as especially important 'refer back disproportionately to a time when the respondents were in their teens or early twenties'.[11] Another researcher has found that savers' decisions about what to invest in were shaped for a period of 20 or 30 years by the performance of different assets when they started saving in their youth.[12] Similarly, an early experience of unemployment is a scar whose effects can be found in higher risks of unemployment and lower wages 20 years later.[13] The Millennials were starting their adult careers around the time of the crash and this has scarred them. Young adults with only GCSE-level qualifications who left education in the depths of the crisis were up to 35 per cent less likely to be in work a couple of years later than their counterparts beginning careers in rosier economic times, and their chance of being in employment has remained depressed for a decade.

Highly educated young people had much better chances of staying in work, but they bear the scars in their pay and the types of jobs they do. After the crash, the chance of a graduate working in a low-paid occupation rose by 30 per cent compared to graduates who left education into a stronger labour market, and this figure remained elevated a full seven years later. And pay for those graduating in the midst of a recession took 50 per cent longer to recover this time round (with scarring evident for six or seven years) than it did after the 1990s recession.[14] (The current evidence of graduates appearing to do less well in the labour market than their predecessors is about this particular post-crash cohort.) So these years in your teens and early twenties are as formative as the early years on which so much attention is focused.

The idea of distinctive generations, each with its own character, is a very fruitful one. It liberates us from the idea that there is an inexorable trend in one direction. Each generation could be shaped by rather different events and respond to them. So, for example, in a world of economic slowdown, Islamist extremism, and environmental damage, there might be a hunger for more security, community, and a recognition of the ties that hold the West together. Instead of an inexorable trend towards greater individualism, perhaps we should instead think of a society of successive generations, each imprinted with its own values and carrying them through life.

This model, however, raises a new set of problems. Are there no experiences which link us to the generations before and after us? If the past is a different country and so is the future, then what obligations do we have to the different generations who live in those different countries? What do we share with the people coming before or after us? To answer that question, we need to think instead about the life cycle.

The classical model, the seven ages of man, was dominant before generational thinking came along. It assumes that what matters above all is not which generation you belong to but where you are in relation to the big experiences of life. It is also similar to the way in which economists explain individuals' patterns of income, borrowing, and saving over time.[15] This thesis says it is the real experiences of getting a job, becoming a parent, indeed becoming a grandparent, that shape attitudes. And the old, rather rigid concept of the life cycle is being overtaken by the idea of the life course. This allows for a much greater range of experiences, such as first sexual encounter, leaving home, the first death of a significant elder, the first death of a contemporary, and widowhood. These are fundamental human experiences which change us as we go through our lives.[16] Personal learning and growth, often around the big events of one's life, are what many novels are about. If economists and novelists agree on this way of viewing the world, it just might be true.

There is evidence of the life cycle shaping people's attitudes. Take, say, attitudes to sex, especially outside marriage. We have already seen there is quite an interesting cohort effect, with the 1960s generation apparently more tolerant of extramarital sex. But also, as people get older and get married and see what damage can be done by extramarital relationships, they become more disapproving. It is a good example of both a cohort effect and a life-cycle effect

Having children is the key event in changing people's attitudes. That is the point at which we stop just living for ourselves and suddenly start connecting with others across the generations. It is our first experience of life repeating itself through the next generation. We may get more self-knowledge as we reflect on our own childhood. And we get a personal measure of how the world has changed. The other event, whose significance is not properly appreciated, is having grandchildren.

Let us go back to the evidence at the beginning of this chapter, which suggested that the Boomers led a big change in social attitudes that has affected subsequent generations. Geoff Dench has ingeniously analysed the data between parents and childless people.[17] He finds that the oldest cohort of parents had rather less traditional attitudes than their childless contemporaries, who were very traditional, whereas younger cohorts of parents had less liberal attitudes than their childless contemporaries. The biggest swings in social attitudes occurred among successive cohorts of childless people; they were more susceptible to changes in the culture. But when people had children, their attitudes were shaped in similar ways by the fundamental experience of parenthood, no matter which cohort they were born into.

The significance of the family is shown when you ask people about crucial events that have happened during the previous year. Top of the list are family events, with 23 per cent of first mentions and 41 per cent of total mentions. Second is work, with 11 per cent of first mentions and 24 per cent of total mentions. Leisure and holidays are third, with 10 per cent of first mentions and 23 per cent of total mentions.

Table 12: Highly mentioned life events and happenings (%)[18]

Life events	First mentions	Total mentions
Family	23	41
Employment	11	24
Leisure	10	23
Health	9	19
Education	6	14
Consumption	4	10

Politicians should note that national and world events get 0.5 per cent of first mentions and 2 per cent of total mentions.

This evidence does not just tell us how important the family is for people; it also reveals a lot about the significance of life-course events. The family events most commonly mentioned are births, weddings, and deaths. In the words of a character in T. S. Eliot's verse play *Sweeney Agonistes*: 'Birth, and copulation, and death. That's all the facts when you come to brass tacks'.[19] Moreover, events apparently unrelated to family life may actually derive their significance from the life course, such as holidays.

Consumption comes a low 4 per cent on the table. We know from separate research for General Motors that purchases of cars are often linked to life-course events – 80 per cent of people who have recently married or divorced, become parents, or suffered a bereavement buy a car within one year of the event.[20]

There is one other important piece of evidence from this

research which shows how we change as we go through the life course. Younger people are much more likely to mention events affecting themselves (81 per cent of 16- to 24-year-old men and 76 per cent of 16- to 24-year-old women mention something that has happened to them personally). But above the age of about 40, references to oneself decline. And only 47 per cent of men and 39 per cent of women aged over 65 mention events affecting themselves. They are beginning to live through the younger generations coming after them. There is an important paradox here. It is older people who are the most future-oriented. They are thinking about the world their children and grandchildren will inherit. It is young people who have the luxury of living in the present, because when you are young you think that the present will carry on for ever. That is why it would be entirely wrong to think the issue of justice across the generations is some kind of appeal targeted on younger people. If anything it is the opposite – it is an appeal to the Baby Boomers. It is an appeal to the old world to redress the balance for the new.

We must not get carried away, however. As we get older we do not become completely altruistic. There is clear evidence of a life-cycle impact on attitudes to public spending. In general, more older people support public spending – perhaps because they depend more on public services. This is shown in, for example, a very clear increase in support for public spending on healthcare as people get older. When it comes to education spending, if anything it is the other way around. It is one of the few areas of public spending that is strongly supported by younger people and where support declines as people get older.[21]

There does look however to have been a shift in attitudes to the welfare state among the young, as shown in a 2019 report by Onward:

Though all age groups agree, young people are particularly likely to say that being able to keep your own money is more important than taxing more to increase equality. People under the age of 35 are more likely to say we should reform schools and hospitals to make them more efficient, rather than spend more. While all age groups generally favour more rather than less regulation of business, younger people are more favourable to deregulation.[22]

This may partly reflect the failure of the welfare state to do much for them.

There is also one other very significant life-cycle effect. One of the most fruitful areas of research at the moment is happiness and well-being. There are a host of influences on our happiness – from the state of our marriage to our income. But happiness is also heavily influenced by the stage we are at in our lives. If you draw a graph of how happy people are it is a very strong U-shaped curve. You are happy when you are young and you are happy when you are old but it is when you have all the burdens of middle age that your happiness level plummets. The least happy age is about 50, when self-reported happiness is 7–8 per cent lower than the happiest age, which is about 70. Those in middle age are the people who bear the burdens of the intergenerational contract, with obligations to children and to older people.

But as well as this, it does look as if there has been a gradual upward trend in well-being since about 2011, when it really started being measured in a consistent way over time in the UK. That means even the mid-life low point is now rising (leaving the mid-life low point of Boomers as the lowest low point – so not everything goes the Boomers' way). Around age 45 the cohort born in 1966–70 had levels of life satisfaction about 5 per cent higher than the cohort of Boomers born in 1961–5. But as successive age groups emerge from that mid-life low, those Boomers have had some of the biggest gains in happiness and well-being – Boomers in their late fifties shoot up into what must seem by contrast an almost exuberant sense of well-being. There is however one important exception to the pattern of underlying improvements in well-being across all age groups. People in their late teens and early twenties are unusually unhappy. There does look to be an unhappy iGen coming to adulthood.[23]

So the life cycle matters. It is not just which generation you were born into. The events that matter in your life, what you think of public spending programmes, even how happy you are all depend on the stage you are at in your life. Our social attitudes are like an intricate Bach fugue with three distinct strands. First, as our society changes, all of us are influenced by the same trends – the period effect. But each cohort has a different character because of its different experiences – the cohort effect. And then, the different stages of the life cycle shape our values. We can make more sense of our society if we understand these three effects. One estimate is that two-thirds of changes in social attitudes are due to change within the cohort as they go through the life cycle, and one-third are due to successive cohorts having different attitudes.[24] This is a much richer view than a simple model of an underlying trend towards social breakdown as each generation succeeds the next.

There is no law of social entropy that the beliefs which successive generations hold must diverge or that the ties which bind us must break. In fact, as we go through our lives we create and understand more of these ties – both with friends within our own generation, and across generations within the family.

Social Capital and Trust

Now we can use these tools to get to grips with what is happening to the connections between us. Robert Putnam, the leading expert on the subject, describes social capital as the 'networks, norms, and trust that enable participants to act together more effectively to pursue shared objectives'.[25] It is the trust and social co-operation we analysed in the previous chapter when we showed we could think of it not as a social cement but instead as the sum of our co-operative strategies.

A good starting point is the classic question: 'Would you say that most people can be trusted?' 'Yes,' said 44 per cent in the UK in one survey, compared with 38 per cent in the US. 'How often would people try to be fair or would they take advantage if they got the chance?'; 53 per cent in Britain and 57 per cent in the US said most people try to be fair most of the time.[26]

Those who say most people can be trusted also belong to voluntary groups. Of people who belong to no such organizations, 44 per cent say people can be trusted most of the time, compared with 48 per cent of people belonging to one and 75 per cent of people belonging to two or more organizations. There is a similar pattern when it comes to willingness to ask a neighbour to collect a prescription when out shopping. So, involvement in institutions builds trust, confirming the account we offered in the previous chapter.[27]

Younger people appear to be less trusting. Is this telling us that successive cohorts are less trusting or that we start off not very trusting and then become more trusting as we become older? Robert Putnam explains it as changes between successive cohorts. He says that: 'the decline in social trust in America is entirely generational, that is if you look at any birth cohort, average trust has not changed over time, but each successive birth cohort over the last thirty–forty years has become adult with a lower level of social trust'.[28] A study in the nineties found that of people who were born before 1914, 45 per cent agreed most people can be trusted; as against 31 per cent of those born after 1959.[29] It is as if this hole in society opened up with the baby boom.

Putnam detected a decline in trust in other people in successive cohorts of Americans and argued it is a result of changes in the contract between the generations. The GI Bill of 1944, which provided a massive expansion of places at colleges and universities paid for out of taxes, was a fantastic investment in the young men who came back from the Second World War – fighting for your country in your youth is a powerful way for your generation to stake a claim. The claim was honoured with a transformation of education opportunities for young Americans. This in turn gave them a sense of obligation which has left them the most civic generation in America's history. It is a potent piece of evidence of the power of the intergenerational contract. When I see a disconsolate 20-year-old I imagine him wading ashore on D-Day and the debt we would then owe his generation. Do we have any less of an obligation to the young man today?

The trouble is that, especially in the US, the battles fought by the next generation, the Boomers, were much more divisive than the battles fought in the Second World War. The Boomers' civil rights campaigns and cultural wars divided people by age and attitudes, whereas the soldiers of the Second World War had fought on behalf of whole nations and united different generations. So the Boomers' battles, however justified, were more destructive of social capital. Indeed, one of their deliberate aims was to open up institutions to greater diversity: they wanted less conformity and for institutions to be more porous. This made it easier to join them and also to leave, but at the price of generating less trust.[30]

We saw in Chapter 5 how important institutions are in generating reciprocity and hence altruism. But there is some rather uncomfortable evidence of what happens to reciprocal altruism when institutions become more diverse. One ingenious experiment involves two partners in a game: the first player is given an opening stake, and he can give any proportion of this to the second player; this amount is doubled by the experimenter, and the second player then decides how much to return. He sends back less if the first player is of a different race or nationality, and so, in the words of the experimenters, 'heterogeneity may reduce trust' – perhaps because there is less expectation of reciprocal altruism. In particular, white Americans return little to Asians – cynics might say this appears to have become American economic policy. The better news is that the amount returned rises more than one for one with the amount sent, which is good evidence of reciprocal altruism.[31]

Evidence from the US is that politics gets very messy when the claims of different generations are overlaid with ethnic differences too. William Frey of Brookings has measured this cultural/generation gap in different states. It is greatest in Arizona, where 43 per cent of the population under 18 is white as against 83 per cent of the population over 65. California is not far behind, with 30 per cent of the under-18 population white, and 63 per cent of the over-65s. This is America's very own challenge, a potent mix of culture, age, and demographics. Arizona is also the US state which spends the least per head on its school students.[32]

In these circumstances, Boomers may find it tempting to be libertarian tax-cutters when it comes to public services for the younger generation, and socialist spenders when it comes to Social Security and Medicare. In his book *Diversity Explosion*, Frey says:

> this youth-driven diversity surge is also creating a 'cultural generation gap' between the diverse youth population and the growing, older, still predominately white population. This gap is reflected in negative attitudes among many older whites toward immigration, new minority growth, and big government programs that cater to the real economic and educational needs of America's younger, more diverse population.

According to Frey: 'This gap is not a result of racist attitudes per se. It reflects the social distance between minority youth and an older population that does not feel a personal connection with young adults and children who are not "their" children and grandchildren.'[33]

America is now becoming minority-majority, with more than 50 per cent of under-fives from minorities. Britain does not have the same fraught racial politics, but sometimes when I present my arguments for doing more to help young people the response from Boomers is 'If I knew I had to do this for my children and people like them I would, but it isn't like that. The real reason we need more houses and to spend more on education is for the migrants.' The evidence is that actually migrants are net contributors to the funding of public services, though the increased population does add to housing and infrastructure pressures.

The good news is that the latest British evidence shows quite a high level of trust in institutions among Millennials. Younger people actually have slightly higher levels of trust in experts and practitioners such as civil servants, business leaders, and police. This even extends to economists: 55 per cent of Millennials trust economists, compared with 50 per cent of Gen X and 40 per cent of Boomers.[34]

But it is very different for trust in other people in general. Between 50 and 60 per cent of successive generations believe that generally you can trust the man/woman in the street to tell the truth. If anything, this has been on a gently rising trend. However the jarring exception is the Millennials, who have a much lower trust in other people. Just 56 per cent of this generation say other people can be trusted to tell the truth, compared with 68 per cent of Gen X and 77 per cent of Boomers.[35] Overall, the Millennials appear to have a more technocratic view of society – trusting experts to do their specialized work but less trusting of the generality of their fellow citizens. Maybe another reason is just the worse treatment that younger people get. Over half of 18- to 29-year-olds report having been treated with prejudice because of their age, the highest of any group. This compares with just a fifth of those aged 60–69.[36]

There could also be a life-cycle effect, with people becoming more trusting as they become older. Indeed, Peter Hall's survey of social capital in Britain suggests that 'levels of social capital generally seem to have remained reasonably high in Britain', this being disguised by the tendency of social capital to appear low among the young.[37] As we go through stages of the life cycle, so we build up social capital – at least until we become very old, when we may be more isolated. So young people may appear to be less trusting than older people, but as they settle down and become rooted in a community we might expect their levels of trust to grow. Marriage and home ownership increase civic engagement, for example, as measured by voting behaviour.[38] Parenthood is a key moment too. Having children can increase civic engagement as parents become more involved in the local community and create new networks through playgroup and sharing the school run. A key figure in all this is the grandmother. We have already seen from the compelling evidence of the people she phones that she is the custodian of a family's roots and traditions and a source of wisdom and advice, and we will investigate this further in Chapter 12.

This is a reason to hope successive generations will indeed put down roots and rebuild social capital. The only trouble is that our move through the life cycle is slower and messier than it used to be. Education is a good example. The evidence suggests that the longer you are in education the more friends and acquaintances you build up. More people are in education for longer so this should be good for social capital. But the amount of extra social capital you get out of each year of education is not as great as it was, so you need longer in education to accumulate the same network of friends. For example, Americans used to acquire 0.15 of a confidant for every year of education, but this figure then went down to 0.08.[39]

It is harder for the younger generation to move through the stages of the life cycle but their aspirations remain surprisingly conventional. Most young people say they want to settle down with someone they love in a marriage, with kids, a decent job, and a home of their own. The evidence from attitude surveys shows how resilient and widespread marriage is as an aspiration: 25-year-old women revealed thoroughly modern attitudes to sex. They had an average of eight partners: two-thirds had had a one-night stand. But 90 per cent said that they would like to get married and that they then expected their marriage to be faithful.[40]

There is no revolution against these bourgeois values. What is happening is that we are finding it harder to achieve them. What was previously a normal rite of passage to adulthood has instead become like scaling a distant peak that can only be conquered after years of effort and preparation. We find it harder to navigate the stages of the life cycle. Then we interpret what is really a delay in doing the big things of life as a wholesale abandonment of them. We think modern life is fast and urgent, but when it comes to the things that really matter, modern life is very slow. Getting started in the housing market, for example, is much harder than a generation ago – if it isn't high house prices it is the sheer difficulty of getting a mortgage. That means you are more dependent on your parents. Then there is the jobs market and the slow process of getting a job paying a living wage, as the earnings of young people have fallen relative to older workers.

We saw in Chapter 4 how hard it has become to get started on the housing ladder. This means people are renting for longer – especially renting privately. This affects their wider participation in society; for example, registration to vote is harder. This in turn reduces voter turnout among younger people. So what is often interpreted as political disengagement by them is largely the result of external conditions. Sixty-two per cent of Millennial households were renting at age 28 as against 35 per cent of Boomer households at the same age, and this affects voting behaviour. Changes in the voter registration rules also made it harder for younger people to vote. And if they do not vote when they first have the opportunity, a bad habit is formed and it is harder to get them to engage later. The Boomers' electoral advantage from being a big cohort is reinforced by these other factors. For every Baby Boomer there are another 530,000 voters of the same age, whereas for every Millennial it is another 400,000.[41]

These tough conditions for owning a home of your own in turn affect relationships. One reason is that it takes longer to work out what kind of life you might have with your partner. So you cohabit, as neither partner feels they know enough to commit. Cohabitation can be a route to marriage but the relationship can easily break up and you boomerang back to your parents. This in turn means extra dependence on your parents for longer. (The company advertising Lynx deodorant to young men on the proposition it made them sexy discovered that it is actually bought by mothers for their 20-something sons who are still at home.) All this pushes back the average age of marriage, which has risen steadily. For single men marrying women it is up from about 24 in 1970 to almost 34 in 2015, and for single women marrying men it is up from about 22 to about 32.[42] (One explanation sometimes put forward for delayed marriage is that weddings have become more expensive, but cause and effect may be the other way round: weddings have become more expensive as a commitment device to show how serious we are about our relationship.) Sixteen per cent of people in relationships say housing problems have led them to postpone marriage, and 22 per cent say housing issues have put them off having children.[43] In fact, the delay from housing problems is so great it has been claimed housing now causes a seven-year hitch in marriage.[44]

As a result we have become even more dependent on our families for longer. So parents with more money can afford to support their children and then pay for them to go out into the big wide world. It means a more divided society. We do our best for our own children even while our society gives a raw deal to young people as a whole – this is a reason for the decline in social mobility.

It is not that marriage has been rejected. If anything, we have higher hopes of marriage than ever before. We are taking longer to find the right partner, but we are still searching for that person with whom we want to spend the rest of our lives. Just ask Bridget Jones. Or how about Carrie, Samantha, Miranda, and Charlotte from *Sex and the City*? Here is Rosie Boycott's take on the series:

The real secret of the show's appeal was that it gave confidence and reassurance in spades to the... growing world of singletons... [that] being single is just a brief state to be got through as best you can so make the most of it. But beneath this well polished liberation... At the end of the day, the girl wants the boy and she wants him loyal, faithful and – preferably – bearing a ring.[45]

Changes in Median Ages and Relative Size of Different Cohorts

Younger cohorts who may feel the intergenerational contract has not been honoured may be less trusting – at least in the capacity of the welfare state to help them. As we move through the life cycle we build up trust, but this process itself has become slower and messier. There is something else going on, too, which helps explain these shifting patterns of trust and the disruption wrought by the Boomers: changes in the relative size of successive cohorts.

We saw in Chapter 4 how thinkers such as Auguste Comte and more recently Richard Easterlin saw the different sizes of successive cohorts as giving a fundamental pattern to human affairs. They thought this gave the cohorts their different characters, as they were imprinted with different economic experiences. We need not go as far as this, but the shift in balance of ages in a population shapes the character of a society and changes relations between generations. We can measure changes from small to big cohorts through the way they change median age (the age of the middle person in a population). Imagine there has been a surge in the birth rate, creating an unusually big cohort. When this extra-large cohort is young, your society as a whole feels younger even while the steady process of improving life expectancy is underway. That is one reason we look back to the 1960s as a time when the country was young – 1968 was when those born in the first post-War baby boom peak got to 21. Such youthfulness is intoxicating. It also brings turmoil and even war.

What do Afghanistan, Yemen, Congo, Palestine, South Sudan, Zimbabwe, and Somalia have in common – apart from being a list of the world's trouble spots? They are all teenage countries. They all have a median age of 19 or under. Afghanistan is one of the youngest countries in the world: its median age is 17. This makes it far harder for tribal elders to exercise authority over the youthful Taliban. The median ages of the young countries (estimated for 2015 by the United Nations) are Iraq (19), Yemen (19), Democratic Republic of Congo (19), Palestine (19), South Sudan (18), Zimbabwe (19), and Somalia (17).[46]

The CIA attach a lot of importance to this demographic analysis, and estimate that of the world's 25 youngest countries, 16 have experienced war and civil bloodshed These young countries in particular have massive surges of teenage males. Their young men need food and worthwhile jobs – a challenge in itself. And how will they secure a position in society? One theory is that they will fight for it – either within their countries or by being sent abroad to fight – which was Europe's solution to its similar demographic challenges in the nineteenth century.[47]

China's population growth meant it was at its most youthful at the time of the Cultural Revolution. For Iran it was the time of the fall of the Shah. The median age of Russia in 1917 was 15. France was going through this sort of demographic turbulence at the time of the 1789 Revolution. Riding such a demographic surge of young people is the greatest single challenge to any social and political system – most do not survive it. The frustrations of a surging number of young people unable to find productive work or political expression led to the Arab Spring. Now the world faces just such a surge, with 1.2 billion young people aged 15–24. They make up 16 per cent of the world's population and many of them are in developing countries.[48]

So unlike our own dear country now, you may think. And if you look at the median of advanced Western nations, the picture is indeed very different.

Table 13: Median ages of selected countries, 1950–2050[49]

	1950	1980	2015	2050
UK	34.6	34.4	40.2	43.9
US	30.0	30.1	37.6	42.0
China	23.9	22.1	37.0	48.0
World	24.0	23.0	29.6	36.1

The table shows that China's extraordinary demographic slowdown caused by its one-child policy will by 2050 make it one of the oldest countries the world has ever seen. In fact, by the time you read this China will have become an older country than the US. After India, the world's second-largest population will be Chinese pensioners.

The UK is also growing older, with our median age rising. But this isn't the whole story. We have been clustering in places with people the same age as ourselves, a tendency reinforced by social-housing allocation policies. We have about 14 million children under 16 out of a population of around 67 million. On average, therefore, across the country, there is approximately one child to four adults. But we are not evenly spread by age. On the tough estates there are such large numbers of children relative to adults that demographically they are closer to some of the poorest and youngest parts of the world. Some of our social housing projects have ended up with three children to every two adults – six times the national average. Research by a leading housing expert suggests that changes in the age mix on estates were crucial in explaining the growth of antisocial behaviour: 'There is considerable evidence that the ratio of children to adults on estates affects the amount of bad or antisocial behaviour experienced.'[50]

Although the two bodies of research – one on instability in the developing world and the other on antisocial behaviour on housing estates – have developed entirely separately from each other, they have reached the same demographic explanation.

The best account of the impact of all these young people is not to be found in the works of the demographers but in William Golding's novel *Lord of the Flies*. It is a vivid and all-too-credible account of children turning feral when, after a plane crash, they find themselves trapped on an island without an adult. It was a deliberate counterpoint to the Victorian idyll of R. M. Ballantyne's *The Coral Island*, in which youngsters on their own are shown as being intrepid and co-operative. But even *Lord of the Flies* reaches a kind of happy ending when it only takes the arrival of a few adults to stop the savage blood-letting and to restore order.

It is a tough job socializing successive generations of children, especially when there are lots of them. Even in sober, law-abiding Britain we saw the turmoil that resulted when the Baby Boomers were coming to adulthood. The two most violent riots in post-War London were the Grosvenor Square riots of 1968 and the Brixton and Broadwater Farm riots of 1985. They occurred around 20 years after each of the post-War baby boom peaks. The mini-peak of 1990 was then followed by the London riots of 2011.[51]

Age Segregation

Strengthening civil society means strengthening contact and the contract between the generations. But we are increasingly segregated by age. Age segregation is worst in rural areas but there have been big increases in the former industrial towns of the North of England, as older people stay and younger people leave. So, 'whereas only 9.4% of all districts (33) displayed moderate or high age segregation in 1991, by 2011 the proportion had reached 56.8% (198 districts)'.[52]

In 1991, just 3 per cent of 18- to 19-year-olds would have had to move in order to distribute themselves evenly across local authority boundaries. By 2001 this had gone up to 8 per cent. For 20- to 24-year-olds it went up from 8 per cent to 12 per cent.[53] This is partly driven by 'studentification'. But it is not just where we live. We work with our contemporaries too. One survey showed 9 per cent of employees in workplaces were aged between 16 and 21, but 15 per cent of workplaces had at least one-quarter of their workforce in this age group... and employees aged 50+ made up 20 per cent of the workforce but were at least a quarter of the workplace in 32 per cent of establishments.[54] Our friends tend to be contemporaries too. The family is one of the few places where this sort of intergenerational experience is still possible. We socialize as they do in *Friends* and live in families like the Simpsons. One reason why *The Simpsons* is so much deeper and more satisfying than *Friends* is that *The Simpsons* does show people of different ages interacting. *Friends*, by contrast, focused narrowly on one 20-something age group. Individual age cohorts may have a strong sense of collective identity, shaped by shared formative events, but it is not quite a full, real community. Something precious is lost.

There does appear to have been a decline in social networks, both of family and of friends. But networks of friends are shrinking faster, so the family is becoming relatively more important. Researchers have compared confidants with whom Americans discuss important matters in 1985 and 2004. Mean network size, including both family and friends, has fallen from 2.94 to 2.08. The number saying they have no confidant has trebled. And the number speaking regularly to at least one non-relative fell from 80 per cent to 57 per cent.[55] Numbers both of kin and non-kin have declined, but as non-kin has fallen more this increases the relative importance of kin.

One piece of British research asked respondents to whom they would turn with the sorts of problems that can happen to anyone.[56] The results were striking.

Table 14: People turned to for various problems (% of respondents)

	Job	Help while ill	Borrowing money	Marital problem	Depression
Spouse/partner	58	61	21	9	47
Parent	8	13	20	15	8
Child	13	11	6	17	7
Sibling	4	3	4	12	6
Friend	7	5	2	27	21

Then researchers went on explicitly to ask about comparisons between family and friends.

Table 15: Attitudes towards the family (% of respondents)

	Agree	Disagree	Neither
People should keep in touch with close family members even if they do not have much in common	70	18	12
People should always turn to their family before asking the state for help	48	19	33
I would rather spend time with my friends than my family	13	23	64
On the whole my friends are more important to me than members of my family	7	12	81

When asked about who they would turn to for advice or to borrow money, most people put fellow members of the family, often from a different age group, ahead of friends, who are often contemporaries. It is those links across the generations, through families, which matter. If anything, the family is becoming more important as trust in others declines. It is partly because if you spread out across the generations there is much more you can do to shift money and the burdens of care, whereas within your own generation everybody is facing the same struggles and the same problems at the same time. So the intergenerational cover provided by the family makes it better as an insurance scheme. Economists think of families as an imperfect annuities market. They have calculated that even small Anglo-Saxon families can do more than 70 per cent of the job of an annuity in enabling you to spread the risk of living longer than your savings.[57]

There is an important paradox here. In the rest of our lives we are divided more horizontally by our age group, working with and living in communities of people our age. But the shrinking of the family is taking it in the opposite direction, to a beanpole with fewer siblings and cousins. If, to take one extreme example, Italy's fertility rate of 1.2 continues for two generations, then, Nicholas Eberstadt has calculated, 'Almost three-fifths of the nation's children will have no siblings, cousins, aunts, or uncles; they will have only parents, grandparents, and perhaps great-grandparents.'[58] The future is tall, thin families as the only link between generations in a wide, flat, age-segregated world. This is why the family is becoming so important for delivering the intergenerational contract.

Strong families are very powerful ways of passing on advantage from generation to generation. It is a genuine and legitimate source of deep fulfilment for many people. Studies of changing values also show us the ability to provide for one's family is a key driver of self-worth. In four surveys from 1968 to 1981, 'family security' came in second or first as a life goal, leading 'companionship' or 'a comfortable life'. It is surely no coincidence that the people most likely to be unhappy are divorced or unemployed – both events sever that sense of keeping a family and discharging our obligations across the generations.[59] These are very powerful findings. They are just as powerful as the earlier evidence from the research project into who people turned to for various problems, which again shows it is these deep and real ties across the generations that matter to people. In the 1960s and 1970s there was a lot of worry about the generation gap, and the rows and tensions above all within the family as different generations could not seem to get on. That gap has largely gone, to be replaced by an economic gap between the generations.

The best single advantage you can have is parents who are committed to the project of investing in you and your future. That probably means they are married, an important form of commitment to this project. That advantage tends to go with many others. Poor families are far more vulnerable to breakdown than well-off families. Kay Hymowitz has analysed this phenomenon in America and shown that family structure is creating what she calls a 'new caste society'.[60] The well-educated and well-off stick together, whereas poorer families find it harder.

British evidence from the Millennium cohort study shows that 5 per cent of degree-educated mothers split from their partner before their child's third birthday, compared to 42 per cent of mothers without qualifications.[61] This is not simply an education effect – the biggest factor influencing whether couples stay together is marriage, followed by age; then come education, income, ethnic group, and being on benefits. A separate study showed that by a child's fifth birthday, 8 per cent of married parents have split up, 57 per cent of cohabitees, and 25 per cent of those who married after the birth.[62] Whatever the exact pattern of cause and effect, the conclusion is clear: families powerfully transmit advantage from one generation to the next. We are better at providing for our own children than looking after the interests of the next generation as a whole. We are indeed better parents than we are citizens. We shall pursue the implications in Chapters 9 and 10.

7

WHY BOTHER ABOUT THE FUTURE?

The Optimists versus the Malthusians

He was a liberal-minded aristocratic reformer who played a big role in the early stages of the French Revolution – but, like the reformers in Russia in 1917 or Iran in 1979, he himself was then consumed by the Revolution. He was condemned by Robespierre and went into hiding before being captured and dying in mysterious circumstances while in detention. Knowing he did not have long to live, he scribbled notes on the back of revolutionary posters in which he dreamed of humanity moving to perfection. And what was this utopia? It was a world where people become ever more prosperous, freedom and democracy are assured, foreign colonies gain self-government, free secular education spreads equality of opportunity, there is no discrimination by race, class, or gender, and a benign government insures you against the risks of poverty, ill-health, and old age.

Of all the eccentric utopias envisaged by political thinkers, Condorcet's *Sketch for a Historical Picture of the Progress of the Human Mind* has the distinction of being the one that got closest to the hopes – and in many ways the reality – of the modern world. At the same time William Godwin, an English radical, was writing his *Enquiry Concerning Political Justice and Its Influence on General Virtue and Happiness*. He envisaged a society where it would be understood that vice and evil are not individual failures but a consequence of social problems, and as we improve social conditions so vice would be eliminated and we could achieve ever more freedom and happiness.

A young Anglican parson with a formidable mathematical mind read these two revolutionary texts and concluded that their utopias rested on a simple fallacy. Thomas Malthus replied in his *Essay on the Principle of Population*[1] that the population would grow much faster than the resources, notably the food, which they needed. He thought their utopias were mathematically impossible: the population would grow geometrically (multiplying every generation) but the food supply would only grow arithmetically (adding a fixed amount per generation).[2] The result of such population growth would not be human perfection but misery and vice. By 'misery', Malthus means starvation. By 'vice' he means sex outside marriage and without children.

All three books were published in the 1790s but we are still arguing about them now. In many ways the optimists have won – even conservative economists now subscribe to a world view closer to those eccentric utopian revolutionaries. Worries about the future are denounced as Malthusianism. Malthus himself is accused of the fallacy of failing to realize that if the human population could multiply, so might the resources of the natural world – such as for example agricultural crops in the Green Revolution, and domesticated animals. And even when there are constraints on natural resources, advances in technology can overcome them – hence the observation that the Stone Age did not end because they ran out of stones. These are the rational optimists such as Johan Norberg, Hans Rosling, and Matt Ridley.[3] Thus Moore's law that the number of transistors which can be placed on an integrated circuit doubles approximately every two years captures the modern attitude, though interestingly Gordon Moore himself was speculating by 2015 that his law might be ceasing to apply.[4]

Modern optimists take the original Malthusian model of multiplying growth of population and turn it around by applying the same mathematical relationship to our technological capacities. It culminates, literally, in Ray Kurzweil's 'Singularity', when innovations in digital and genetic technologies converge and accelerate.

Such optimism about long-term growth has a profound effect on the contract between the generations. Imagine that each generation of our tribe of primitive hunter-gatherers became more skilled at making straighter spears that were better for hunting, and sharper scythes better for gathering berries and wheat. Then each generation would believe its successors were going to be better off. The deliberations of the tribal elders would be very different. They might be willing to take larger contributions from the younger generation coming along behind, expecting they would have more to live on when they were older.

In a country growing at 5 per cent per annum, GDP will double every 15 years. A 20-year-old would expect that at the age of 50 he or she would live in a society four times as wealthy, and by the age of 65 it would be eight times so. Any attempt to help future generations appears to be a shift from the poor (us now) to the rich (them then). Instead of worrying about our grandchildren we think we can take from them some of the extra wealth they are going to enjoy. Disraeli may have denounced an opponent because: 'He thinks posterity is a pack-horse, always ready to be loaded.' But we have to face the response that in the future the pack-horse will be far sturdier than anything we have now, so we should worry about the here and now – where there are quite enough problems, thank you very much.

The Discount Rate – What the Future Holds

Conventional market economics has a powerful mechanism for putting a value today on future income and costs. The social discount rate is the way economists describe how much a pound in a year's time would be worth to you now. Imagine a world with no inflation and no risk. If you were due to receive £105 in a year's time, how much would you settle for right now instead? If, under these conditions, you attach the same value to £105 in a year's time as £100 today then you have got a typical social discount rate of 5 per cent. It is an essential tool for an economist trying to work out what the payback is from any kind of investment. If you set a discount rate at 5 per cent then costs and benefits more than 20 or 30 years out do not have much value today. It tells us that the future more than a generation or so ahead counts for little. Environmental economics, with its powerful concept of sustainability, is changing all this. In his 2006 report on climate change, Nicholas Stern explicitly sets a very low social discount rate of 0.1 per cent.[5] Indeed, he argues that really we should value costs and benefits in the future at exactly the same value as they have today – there is no rational basis for pure time preference. It is only 0.1 rather than zero because, being the rigorous economist that he is, he wants to allow for the modest risk of the extinction of the human race. The 0.1 per cent is to allow for the slight chance of there being nobody around in the future to enjoy it. It is as if he looks at the distant future through a powerful telescope, so it suddenly looms much larger.

That means £1bn of cost in the future is as expensive as £1bn today. The critics of Stern argue that he should assume a more typical, higher discount rate so that future environmental costs do not look so expensive. He argues that conventional economic analysis might work for appraising particular investment projects but it does not work when we are assessing fundamental issues such as limited natural resources, and the value of special places – be they natural such as the Great Barrier Reef or ones we have created such as Venice. It is the same thought as Margaret Thatcher's: 'No generation has a freehold on this earth. All we have is a life tenancy – with a full repairing lease.'[6]

We may admire Nick Stern's moral judgement that we cannot value future generations any lower than ourselves. It does not sound very moral for us to say that we should prefer our pleasure now to the pleasure of our great-grandchildren. But we have to recognize our own inconvenient truth – distance in both space and time does affect the claims people have on us. Stern's unusually low discount rate is indeed like a telescope, offsetting our natural tendency to focus on the here and now. Dickens mocks such an attitude in the famous portrait of Mrs Jellyby, the 'telescopic philanthropist' who devotes all her energies to 'Borrioboola-gha' and ignores the wretched children around her.[7] And if we are to stick with the naturalistic morality we described in Chapter 5, this may be one area where we find our local loyalties do not stretch so far out into the future. There are good reasons why we do not behave as Stern wants us to – we would be paralyzed by endlessly having to attach the same value to everything and everybody, however far away in the future. So the criticism of Stern is that he is not describing how we currently value the future but proposing a very different standard, far removed from everyday life.

We have a dilemma. There is the conventional economic device of the discount rate, which basically says we do not need to attach much weight to anything more than a generation or so out. And we have an attempt to argue that we should calibrate it so we attach equal value to the future, which appears to be implausible. But this smart dismissal of Stern leaves us uneasy that future generations might curse us for our insouciance. Even John Locke, the ultimate classical liberal, had the principle that enough and as good should be left for future generations, and we do appear to be breaching that principle. Is there a way out of this dilemma?

One way is to go back to the realities of human psychology and look at how we actually behave. Then we liberate ourselves from the tyranny of the straight line. We see that when it comes to short-term decisions over the next few years, we do indeed have quite a high discount rate – so money now is worth quite a bit more than money in, say, four years' time. These are the typical short-term decisions for which conventional discount rates work quite well.

But then we appear to attach continuing value to costs and benefits
10 or 20 or more years out – we do not continue discounting
them at the same rate. So we can draw a discount rate not as a
straight line but as a hyperbola, with the value of the future falling
sharply at first and then flattening out. This enables us to combine
conventional discount rates for normal purposes and also to attach
some value to what our grandchildren face. (This in turn leads
to some imaginative proposals for nudging our behaviour – for
example, it might be hard to get people to save more out of their
current income, but they are more willing to commit to saving a
significant part of pay increases a few years out.)[8]

Stern still faces the challenge that we will be richer in the future.
Even if we value £1,000 in the future the same as £1,000 today,
he still accepts people will be better off in the future so they will
command more resources than us now and so be able to do more.
But he replies that 1 per cent of GDP in the future will only yield
the same amount of happiness to people in the future as 1 per
cent of GDP today, so they will not really be better off than we are.
It is combining this assumption with his ultra-low discount rate
that has really generated the controversy among economists. If we
believed that future generations would not really feel any better
off, and that it will take greater resources for them to achieve any
given level of happiness, we would do an enormous amount of
saving for future generations. But that isn't how we behave. Stern
has not just offered a neutral economic analysis; he has in effect
called for us to attach more value to the future than we do at the
moment.[9]

The Stern Review accepts we will still enjoy strong economic
growth, but it also wants to argue we should spend money on
protecting the environment now, not in the future when we
will be richer. The assumptions Stern uses to generate these
conclusions are what have proved so controversial.[10] Instead we
could just challenge the assumption that the next generation is
bound to be so much richer than us. That is what they do in an

episode of *South Park* – 'Goobacks'. Time travellers start arriving from the future because life is tough there and they are looking for work. Everything Americans say in the real world about Mexican immigrants is run as an argument about whether to let in these impoverished time travellers.[11]

Such fears immediately face the charge of neo-Malthusian pessimism. We certainly have to recognize that the innovative power of the almost 8 billion humans alive today is a resource which dwarfs all others. And the future may be a world transformed for the better, just as Condorcet expected. But if we just look out over the next 50 years we can already see the problems facing advanced Western nations like our own. These are not speculations, but trends which are happening now. We know that the bulge of post-War Baby Boomers in many advanced Western countries is growing old, and those Boomers are reaching a point when they want to command a lot of resources without working to generate them. We also know that since the crash there has been a massive increase in public debt, which will have to be paid for out of our taxes. Above all, we have come to accept the reality of climate change, which will impose a massive cost on future generations unless we can slow it down. And if we can't slow it down, then adapting to it is going to be very expensive indeed.

These are good reasons why the next generation may not be as much better off as we like to think. And time is pressing. The latest advice from the UN's Intergovernmental Panel on Climate Change is that we have to cut carbon emissions by 45 per cent by 2030 to limit the global temperature increase to 1.5 degrees.

But even climate change is only one of a series of interacting pressures on the environment.[12] There is indeed a pinch point coming. The rate of growth of the world's population is levelling off, but the UN's central forecast is still that it will rise to almost 10 billion by 2050.[13]

The growth of total demand for food may slow a bit as population growth slows. But if people enjoy rising incomes, as we hope, then that means much greater demand for meat and dairy products – as we have already seen in China. One forecast is a doubling of demand for meat by 2050. That means more deforestation and more methane emissions, exacerbating climate change.[14] We could deliver big increases in agricultural output, but that might in turn mean big increases in water needed for agriculture. Already 1.2 billion people are affected by water scarcity, and that could get much worse. Much of the water we are using in some key agricultural areas is being extracted from depleting aquifers. It is hard to predict total water demand, but the UN forecasts the number of people experiencing physical shortages of water could rise to 1.8 billion by 2025.[15]

Desalination is one obvious technology to tackle water shortages, and again one instinctively trusts human ingenuity to develop this and other solutions. But desalinating water, like making fertilizer, is energy-intensive – so it will put yet more pressure on energy demand. We can look to ingenious solutions to demands on land for agriculture such as GM crops, which could lead to another Green Revolution; but, especially in Europe, there are objections to introducing some of the very technologies which we need. It is the sheer interconnectedness of these pressures – population, food, water, energy – which makes the global challenge all the greater.

Climate change itself threatens some of the world's most productive agricultural areas, such as California. Africa is already affected by desertification, one factor behind surges in migration. Extreme weather is becoming more frequent as warmer air holds more moisture, which is then released in more violent storms. Globally, climate change dwarfs all the other challenges we face.

It is the most vivid example of the burdens older generations are placing on younger generations, as they have to adjust to using much less carbon compared with the cavalier insouciance of previous generations. The table below shows how much carbon successive generations will be able to use, and how a child born today will have to emit a fraction of the carbon generated by a Boomer. One estimate is that 'In a world where warming is limited to 1.5C, the average person born today can emit only an eighth of the lifetime emissions of someone born in 1950.'[16]

Table 16: Lifetime carbon budget in a 1.5C world, broken down by generation (tonnes of CO_2)[17]

	Pre-Boomer (pre-1946)	Boomers (1946–1964)	Gen X (1965–1980)	Millennials (1981–1996)	Gen Z (1997–2012)	Post-Gen Z (post-2012)
Global	275	325	276	202	118	56
US	1494	1464	1191	846	472	238
Europe	686	698	582	398	218	105
China	119	255	256	220	151	71
India	38	64	61	52	23	18

The most effective contemporary protests – the *Skolstrejk för klimatet* ('School strike for climate') led by the extraordinary Greta Thunberg – have shown that the single most powerful way to get us to act is to show vividly the burden of climate change on future generations.

We can reasonably hope that human ingenuity will see us through and world GDP will continue to grow. But it might not feel much like growth as we know it. Imagine that you were told your income was going to double by 2040 – pretty good, you might think. But then you are told that a lot of that extra income will be going on higher energy bills, higher food prices (with meat especially affected), and higher levies to pay for flood protection, and that the water meter in your house will rattle up costs like a taxi meter in Central London. Then you would not be quite so sure that this growth automatically meant greater prosperity. And you might wish that a lot more had been done sooner to prepare for all this. But we aren't doing that.

Saving for the future in Britain and America shrank to catastrophically low levels during the boom years, when we should have been setting money aside for a rainy day (as we saw in Chapter 4). This has affected levels of investment. You need a lot of basic infrastructure to enable a modern economy to function effectively.[18] It is key to the technological innovation we are relying on, because people have to be able to cluster together – and modern cities are very creative, very energy efficient, and very expensive. And we also need business investment to ensure we can work productively. But the UK invests relatively little by international standards. Taking averages across the two decades from 1997, the UK sits bottom of the OECD table for total investment as a share of GDP. Our average of 16.7 per cent is 2.9 percentage points lower than Italy's – the next lowest-placed country. It is way behind the 20-year averages of 20.8 per cent in the US, 21.7 per cent in France, and 30.8 per cent in South Korea.[19]

As an advanced, services-based economy, the UK might be expected to be investing less than economies with larger manufacturing bases. And we do invest in intangibles such as research and development, branding and design, which do not show up in these figures.[20] But, nevertheless, physical kit does still matter, and the chart below shows that investment in the UK has been on a downward trend for the last 45 years. If I were obsessed with the irresponsibility of the Boomers I would observe that this covers the period of their adulthood, when they would have been the main generation paying for the investment. But I am not. So I won't.

Figure 9: Gross fixed capital formation as a share of GDP[21]

We can now see how financial innovation has eroded the commitment devices needed to save and invest for the future. Imagine an island where there is a goose that lays a golden egg every month. By selling the gold every month and investing some of the proceeds, the family that own the goose gradually become more prosperous. Then some innovative bankers sail into harbour and everything changes. For them the flow of golden eggs is a guaranteed income stream. You do not have to wait for anything as vulgar as the goose actually laying the egg before you enjoy the income from it. You can write contracts promising to pay an income out of future golden eggs and sell those contracts today. The goose and her eggs can be priced, leased, mortgaged, and securitized. They say to the goose's owners that the family should be able to control their own flow of income to meet their own needs, which are quite independent of the goose's egg-laying habits. This is all very plausible.

But it has a consequence, which we are confronting now. David Laibson has shown, using sophisticated calculations which he calls, of course, the 'golden eggs model', how an economy can move from above the amount of savings needed to sustain its growth to below it, by the simple expedient of increasing credit availability. Increasing liquidity effectively diminishes the effectiveness of savings vehicles as commitment devices, and so reduces personal welfare. He shows that when access to credit rose dramatically in the US in the 1980s and 1990s, savings fell from an average of 7.3 per cent in 1946–83 to 5.3 per cent in 1985–94.[22]

Borrowing against your goose's future egg-laying worked fine for a time. You enjoyed higher living standards as you borrowed against future golden eggs. And you might even have persuaded yourself that you were spending the extra money on really worthwhile things that would make you more prosperous in the long run. But the losers if your gamble goes wrong are your children and grandchildren, because they inherit the family goose and find that its income is allocated to pay off various bond-holders who now appear to have a bigger stake in your goose than you do. The next generation find that they have to work harder for longer to pay their debts. This is why future generations were the biggest losers from the financial crisis.

What Do We Owe the Future?

An implacable sceptic might concede that perhaps future generations are not going to be so much better off after all, but still say, 'So what? Stuff happens.' Different generations born at different times get dealt a good hand or a bad hand by history. Life is hard enough for us without bearing the burden of providing for generations who may not even be born yet. Future generations have no claim on us, any more than we have a claim on generations that came before us. Even if we are getting a particularly good deal and our successors a raw deal, that is their problem not ours and does not put us under any moral obligation to do anything about it. In the famous words of one Irish MP: 'Why should we do anything for posterity; for what has posterity done for us?'[23]

The answer is of course that we are the posterity of previous generations, and they did a lot for us – from fighting for us and building schools, to advancing scientific understanding to make modern technology possible. That is why it was so important to establish in Chapter 5 that there is indirect as well as direct reciprocity.

The argument in earlier chapters that the social contract is a contract between the generations is one answer to this challenge. But we can go further in explaining how valuing the future is fundamental to us as humans and how our society works. It helps to look at it in three stages.

First, there are the claims of future generations as yet unborn. There are tricky philosophical issues about attributing rights to people who do not yet exist, though the implicit contracts which we listed in Chapter 5 could still apply. We are not, after all, talking about legal documents but the social contracts that keep families and nations going. You might, for example, think it was wrong to borrow against the buy-to-let flat which you hope to give to your potential grandchildren, some of whom are as yet unborn.

Then there is the second stage: our obligations to the next generation – young people who are already born. And there are people alive today who will live into the twenty-second century. Just protecting them as current members of society demands policies for the long term. The longevity revolution requires we look much further ahead. And this is not pure altruism, because today's ageing adults will rely on the next generation. The intergenerational exchanges we set out in Chapter 5 have certainly begun. We are assuming that in future they will produce wealth and pay taxes to fund services we will need. For example, the pensions we hope to live on are claims on future resources which they will have to create for us at the time. We are not squirrels setting aside nuts now. The bread we will eat in the future does not yet exist. Ultimately, we just have claims on the bread that the younger generation will be baking. Some of those claims rest on the state's power to tax future income, and others rest on our shares in businesses giving us a claim on their future earnings. Either way, we need to behave fairly towards them now so that they will share their bread with us in the future. The reciprocity is becoming clear.

Third, just think of us in the future. The median age in Britain today is 40. Rather neatly, a person of that age can expect to live for roughly another 40 years. So the middle person in Britain is at the midpoint of their lives. As a nation we are on the cusp, perfectly balanced between past and future. The big challenges we face – the costs of adjusting to environmental change; demographic burdens as the Boomers age; the taxes to service massive public debt – are all issues that will arise well within the next 40 years. A key date is 2050, when the middle person in Britain today might be getting to the end of their working life and the youngest Boomer will be 85. Perhaps we cannot expect people to look forward for the rest of their lives, but even a selfish majority should care about our circumstances to 2030. That is getting very close – it is less than one generation ahead. It is the early pinch point when many of the pressures we have identified come together. It is when the survivors of the million people born in the first peak year of our baby boom get to 83, and at this rate half of the babies born back in 1947 will still be alive and may well be needing more care.[24]

It is a global pinch point too, when the challenge of global population movements from areas of environmental distress looks potentially quite serious; and as we saw earlier it is a crucial tipping point if we are to stop global temperatures rising by more than 1.5 degrees. But it is too soon for transformational technologies like nuclear fusion to be harnessed for us. Even if valuing other people's future is too much to ask, the Boomers might be expected to care about the risks they are running with their own futures – unless of course we are all going the way of Phineas Gage.

Phineas Gage was by all accounts a sober, prudent, gratification-deferring working man, blasting a route for the American railroads in the 1840s. That was until he had a horrific industrial accident in which an iron spike went into his head, destroying some of his brain. He survived but thereafter he was totally impulsive; his capacity to plan for the future had been lost.[25] A lot of our problems arise from our difficulty in valuing the future and deferring gratification. This can be a problem for us personally too – the obesity crisis is a vivid example of the challenge we face trying to resist our appetites today in the cause of something better in the future.

What we are talking about here is prudence. Here is Adam Smith's account:

> The qualities most useful to ourselves are, first of all, superior reason and understanding, by which we are capable of discerning the remote consequences of all our actions, and of foreseeing the advantage or detriment which is likely to result from them: and secondly, self-command, by which we are enabled to abstain from present pleasure or to endure present pain, in order to obtain a greater pleasure or to avoid a greater pain in some future time. In the union of those two qualities consists the virtue of prudence, of all the virtues that which is most useful to the individual.[26]

We have more choices and more temptations than ever, so our capacity for such self-command matters: it is the ultimate soft skill. Gray's 'Elegy' is treated nowadays as an ode to social mobility. As the poet reflects on the lives that are marked in the churchyard, he does think of the missed opportunities – an appeal that particularly touches our modern sensibility. But he goes on to make a rather different point: about evil averted because of the absence of temptation. Modern life is full of new temptations. Our self-control is tested in a way that was not possible until Britain emerged from austerity after the War – when one of the first responses was, of course, a baby boom.

There is a permanent battle for self-control in a modern consumer culture. With all these temptations we need to signal that we possess it. One reason for our obsession with being thin is that we want to offer evidence of self-control in an age of temptations.[27] It would be very convenient if it were like a muscle which got stronger the more it was used. But some evidence suggests that it resembles more a scarce natural resource – like water in a flask, you can use it up. Researchers asked a group of people to regulate or suppress some thought while watching a film clip, and a control group were given no such instruction. Then they were all asked to squeeze a handgrip hard for as long as possible. The group asked to regulate their thoughts gave up much sooner on the hand grip.[28] So self-control may be in limited supply. Resisting temptation once does not appear to get easier.

One of the most famous tests of our capacity for self-control is the experiment conducted by Walter Mischel in the 1960s.[29] He offered children aged four the choice between one marshmallow now or two in 20 minutes' time. The ones who were able to wait for the second marshmallow subsequently massively outperformed the other group in America's Scholastic Aptitude Test. The value children place on the future has also been measured in a study engagingly entitled *Economic Experiments That You Can Perform at Home on Your Children*.[30] A child loses a tooth and leaves it under their pillow night after night. Each day that they delay handing it over to their parents, an extra dime accrues for them. So you start off with high percentage returns but they fall relative to the amount you have built up in your tooth deposit. The research shows children do indeed have very high discount rates – 3 per cent per day – which fall as they get older.

The good news is that individually we do behave prudently. As we saw in the previous chapter, young people are really rather earnest – drinking less and having less sex. Teenage pregnancy rates are down. We may not agree with the worst caricatures of the 'snowflake generation'[31] but it is striking how safety has become their watchword rather than risk; 'safe spaces' may be their emblematic expression. And the surge in parental investment in their children which we will investigate further in Chapters 9 and 10 shows that the family is if anything getting stronger, and that is certainly a project for the future.

The capacity to defer gratification is clearly very important. But instead of just telling people to pull their socks up we need to think about the circumstances in which this capacity flourishes. How do we resist temptations and exercise prudence? Dieters provide a useful clue. Dieters need a plan for the future which makes it all worthwhile. People who find it hard to diet lack a sense of how it is all part of a long-term plan, so the sacrifice seems meaningless to them. Evidence for this came after 9/11, when Americans were deeply uncertain about their future and many gave up their diets, observing, 'Life is too short to suffer again through... celery sticks.'[32]

This is the clue that enables us to get back to the tricky philosophical question that has been hovering over our discussion since Chapter 5. The most metaphysical of all the challenges to this concern about the future comes from the late philosopher Derek Parfit. He deployed some of the most trenchant challenges to the idea of obligations across the generations, arguing that we cannot have obligations to people who do not yet exist. But he went further with his scepticism – he would not even be satisfied with our more modest appeal to our own futures 10 or 30 years out. Parfit's radical challenge to our conventional notions of personal identity was to ask whether me in 10 years' time is really the same person as me now.[33]

His ideas have now been tested empirically by asking people of different ages how similar they are to what they used to be like, and how similar they expect their future selves to be. One thing old and young have in common is greater expectation of change in the next 10 years. It is the middle-aged who are most connected to their other selves. They are also the ones who are most linked in to the different stages of the life cycle and bear the greatest burden of other generations.[34] As we saw in Chapter 6, the young live in the present, and although older people do worry about the future they are sadly not going to be around for so long to shape it. The younger Baby Boomers and Generation X are at the stage of the life cycle when they should be most susceptible to these appeals to the future. (And separate research shows that we make the most rational calculations of future risk when we are aged around 53.)[35] The key issue in our ability to control ourselves may be connectedness – the links between us now and how we think we might be in the future.

The narrative we need to link us to ourselves in the past and the future is not that different from the one linking us to other people. Indeed, it might be like our evidence on empathy and consciousness – we first learn to value the future in relation to others and then apply it to ourselves. We can see this if we go back to that evidence on deferring gratification. One classic study by Mischel appeared to show East Asians in Trinidad were willing to forego a dollar today for a dollar and 50 cents tomorrow, but the black population preferred the dollar today. What lies behind this? It isn't ethnic. His research suggested one factor was father absence, which was found to be higher in that black community – if you had lacked an authority figure you trusted to do things for you in the future, you found it much harder to have your own plans for the future and make sacrifices for them. So, once again, the intergenerational exchange within the family proves to be crucial to shaping our character. Inability to defer gratification is not a psychological – let alone a moral – defect in a child; it is an understandable response to particular circumstances which make it difficult to trust in a project for the future. And we can learn to get better at it. Indeed, children's performances in versions of the marshmallow test that involve how long the child will wait have been improving at the rate of about a minute per decade over the 50 years since Mischel's first experiment.[36] One factor could be that IQ is rising, and as we get smarter we are more able to see the long-term consequences of our actions.

Ability to plan for the future is very closely linked to the reciprocal altruism we focused on in Chapter 5. Reciprocity depends on being able to value future benefits in return for sacrifices today. And the neuroscientists have indeed established that the same part of the brain which makes decisions on intertemporal choices is used for altruism and fairness. The limbic system lights up for immediate rewards, whereas the lateral prefrontal cortex is lit up by intertemporal choices. This is also the bit of the brain which protects our sense of fairness, and which the scientists temporarily disabled in the Ultimatum Game experiment. This tends to confirm our explanation of our behaviour in that game – we reject the unfair deal because we think we are part of a set of long-term exchanges.[37] The capacity to engage in long-term reciprocal exchange with others and our ability to have a long-term plan for ourselves are linked.

We need an environment rich in commitment devices, and that includes institutions with long and stable histories where we can be confident of rewards and indeed penalties out into the future. These will work to protect not just our own futures but those of future generations too. It is hard to imagine a society where individuals are good at deferring gratification for themselves but uninterested in others. Indeed, future generations can be the project which causes us to exercise self-control. The family is the most powerful of those commitment devices, and one of the themes of this book is that it is growing in importance. But the family should not be on its own. Civic institutions can do this too.

The Nobel Prize-winning economist James Tobin put it very well: 'The trustees of an endowed institution are the guardians of the future against the claims of the present. Their task is to preserve equity among generations.'[38] But a lot of young people would say that social institutions in the UK such as trade unions, residents' associations, and political parties tend to defend the vested interests of older people, rather than being the guardians of the future. The very institutions supposed to uphold the intergenerational contract may instead betray it.

Game theorists wrestle with the problem of the individual defector destabilizing an arrangement which only works if everyone complies. Institutions can help promote co-operation with the future by stopping individual defectors. Democracies can do this. They provide legitimacy for personal sacrifices and confidence that others will be obliged to make similar sacrifices. And one piece of evidence suggests that countries that are more democratic have more-sustainable energy policies.[39] But it might be that the growing importance of the family as the device for co-operating across the generations partly reflects the weakness of the other civic institutions that should also be able to do this.

The link can also be thought of as operating through the stages of the life cycle. Those exchanges we analysed in Chapter 5 are also between us now and us in the future – the contracts are between us at different stages of the life cycle. Perhaps Charles Dickens can help us bring all this together. In A Christmas Carol, Scrooge is forced to observe himself at other stages of his life (and after), and that leads him to change his behaviour now.

Alfred Nobel, the inventor of dynamite, had an experience not unlike that which Dickens created for Scrooge. His brother died but a French newspaper got them confused and reported it was Alfred who had died, so he found himself reading his own obituary, entitled 'The merchant of death is dead'. It was this which led him to change the direction of his life and give away most of his fortune to endow the Nobel Prizes.

We give meaning to our lives by trying to leave something for future generations coming after. Reflecting on our mortality encourages this. If you conduct interviews with people near a funeral parlour about how much they would give to charity, they will volunteer to give more than when in a more neutral environment.[40]

Thinking about future generations, instead of being like a particularly superhuman exercise in virtue, may actually be so strong that it encourages us to be altruistic. An interesting experiment to test this asked people to imagine they were running a logging company which this year makes bigger profits the more trees it cuts down. But there is a choice about how many to cut down. In fact there are three different trade-offs, each of which invites a sacrifice of some income and profit this year. One says that if the participants cut down fewer trees this year they would make more profits in the future, as the forest will continue to generate income for them – a trade-off between personal prosperity now and in the future. The second trade-off is that if they do not chop down so many trees, more of the forest could be made available to the community to enjoy now. This is a trade-off between self-interest now and altruism now and is the classic form of Right versus Left party politics. But neither of these appeals is as strong as the third type of appeal: that if they do not cut down so many trees, future generations can enjoy them. When people played these roles they were most susceptible to an appeal to restrain their logging to protect the interests of future generations. If people have to make sacrifices, they are most willing to do so if it is for future generations.

8

WHAT GOVERNMENTS DO

Hunter-gatherers

A nation is, along with the family, a way of transmitting a body of knowledge and culture from one generation to the next. We may do our best as individuals to pass on something worthwhile to our own children; it is a powerful and benign instinct. But we cannot rely on individual families to do it all, and indeed too much dependence on family inheritance weakens progress to a more open and mobile society. We cannot just respond to the challenge of justice across the generations individually, family by family. Governments matter too. They have the power to sustain or break the contract between the generations.

If our account of the pattern of people's lives is on the right lines, then it should help us make sense of how the modern welfare state does this. We don't need a complicated account of tax rules and benefit entitlements. Such detail can all too often obscure any sense of the structure that lies behind them. We won't start with finance or politics either. We can grasp the basics from tribes of hunter-gatherers.

We will start with the food they obtain and consume. They do not yet have money or government, so we can look behind these to the fundamentals of calorie consumption. Humans spend much longer dependent for their calorie intake on parents and other adults than chimpanzees do. The family is a commitment to share food; indeed, sharing meals remains at the heart of family life and its decline into serial grazing is a trend we worry about.

Studies of surviving groups of hunter-gatherers show that until the children reach the age of five they are heavy consumers of the energy generated by others – which any parent knows. They then have a long period when they are semi-independent, generating some calories but not adding up to a net contribution. Compared to other mammals, humans go much more for food which is hard to obtain but high in nutritional value. It takes a long time to learn the skills to get this. That is one reason why we have always been dependent on our parents for an exceptionally long time.

The calorific value of the food youngsters produce takes a long time to catch up with and overtake the value of their food consumption: when that happens, they reach adulthood. They then contribute through a long life of hunting and gathering in which they reach their peak net contribution quite late on – especially the more skilled hunters. Old age starts reducing their performance and they become once again net recipients of calories generated by others. One study of three surviving foraging groups, the Ache and the Hiwi of South America, and the Hadza, one of the last remaining hunter-gatherers in Africa, calculated when these transitions occurred. You might just recognize the key ages for these shifts in surviving hunter-gatherer tribes to being a net producer and then once more becoming dependent – 18 and 65.[1]

These late ages of transition may be surprising because child labour has been widespread in primitive societies and in the developing world. Some researchers might indeed place the age when a youth becomes a net contributor a bit earlier, perhaps 15. But one study of a contemporary developing country, the Ivory Coast, also showed a surprisingly high age when young people became net producers in the rural economy (over 20 years old). It was even higher in the town than the countryside (closer to 30 years old) because their urban consumption was higher when they were young. Even though young people were producing, it was less than what they were consuming. This tells us something very important. In most societies, families deliver big net transfers to young people that carry on well into their teens and quite possibly beyond. These transfers predate modern government. The general pattern has been for a substantial flow of resources in the family down to the young people. Older people carry on working but with less efficiency, so they eventually also become net recipients. But the scale of these receipts is modest compared with what young people receive.[2]

We like to think of the modern state as redistributing from rich to poor. But that doesn't really give us a full sense of what it is all about. The welfare state is also supplementing or even displacing the family as a device for transmitting resources across the generations. It takes money from us at times when we are earning a lot, and provides for us at times when we are not; that means transferring money from the middle-aged to the young and old.[3] The key ages for transfers of resources in the modern welfare state match broadly the calorie transfers of our hunter-gatherers, though the trend is for the age you start full-time paid work and the age you retire to shift later. You get educated up to about the age of 18 or more. Then you become a net taxpayer. When you are older you are once more a recipient of public resources, delivered as your pension and also as healthcare.

The Modern Welfare State

The figures for the British welfare state show the scale of these transfers between the generations. Most social security benefits and tax credits are paid to old people or for children. In fact, pensioners alone account for about 59 per cent of all such spending, whereas spending on unemployment benefits, which looms so large in the public imagination, is about 1 per cent of total social security benefits.[4] There is also a transfer to women, particularly as mothers or those, such as widows or lone parents, who are not living with a man. Men get more per person from, for example, the contributory state pension, but as there are many fewer male than female pensioners, the total pensions budget is still balanced towards women – 62 per cent of pension spending goes to women.[5] The only exception to these general rules is compensation for people of working age who are not able to work, notably unemployment and disability benefits, which does go disproportionately to middle-aged men.

Setting this pattern of spending on benefits alongside the income taxes we pay shows how money is redistributed by government. It is a neat comparison, because total income-tax revenues of approximately £181bn in 2017–18 were not too far from total spending on benefits and tax credits of approximately £206bn in the same year.[6] Income tax is above all a tax on middle-aged men: men aged 35–55 paid £71bn, two-fifths of the total from all tax-paying men and women.[7]

Some men may think this proves that they bear the heaviest burden. Others may think it is powerful evidence that women's earnings are still far too low compared with men's. But the message from the figures is clear. Overall, the tax and benefits system shifts resources from the middle-aged to the old and the young, and to some extent from men to women. Sometimes critics say that the tax and benefits system just robs Peter to pay Paul – it churns money around for no real purpose. But really it is doing something else – the system takes from Peter to pay Kylie and Edith.

It is not just tax and benefits which redistribute resources between different age groups. Much of healthcare and all pensions are the debt we owe our parents; education is what we owe our children. In the UK we devote about £75bn of public spending to educating the under-18s. Add to that the £45bn or so of Child Benefit and tax credits for families.[8] That total is broadly similar to the £120bn we spend on benefits for pensioners. So far, that is a broad balance between young and old. But that is before we include the total NHS budget of about £140bn, most of which goes on older people.[9] We devote about £1,500 a year of public spending on healthcare for a person in their thirties and forties compared with £7,000 on someone over 65.[10] Put all this together and public spending is heavily tilted towards the old over the young – and increasingly so as the NHS budget grows relative to total public spending. The table below summarizes all this.

Table 17: Average spend/revenue (£ thousand per head) by age of recipient and type of public spending, 2020[11]

	0–18	19–30	31–50	51–64	65+
Health	1.73	1.11	1.45	2.24	7.02
Education	4.76	1.58			
Social security	2.83	1.24	1.42	1.68	11.25
Total tax	0.55	10.36	20.31	17.14	5.93

Education, healthcare, and benefits together account for over 60 per cent of all public spending. The overall pattern is clear. The modern welfare state provides services and some cash to you when you are young, extracts a large amount of tax from you when you are middle-aged, and then provides you with a lot of services and cash when you are old. The table shows that in 2020, a middle-aged person will receive education, health, and benefits worth about £3,000 on average, whereas someone over 65 receives about £18,000 worth – which is a lot more than the £10,000 of public services and benefits received by someone under 18.

At any one moment it may look as if *we* (the workers) are paying *them* (the young and the old), but really we are all contributors and beneficiaries at different stages of our lives. In the wise words of LSE professor Nick Barr, we should think of much of the modern welfare state not so much as Robin Hood but more as a piggy bank.[12] The best estimate of the balance of these roles is that it is three-quarters piggy bank and one-quarter Robin Hood.[13] (The piggy bank does not need to have a separate fund; it just has to be a programme that we have a reasonable expectation of receiving from as well as paying for.) Most Western countries distinguish explicitly between social security, which is the contributory piggy bank, and means-tested welfare for the poor, which is Robin Hood. Britain's debate about social policy gets unusually muddled because we have lost sight of this important distinction and now all spending on benefits is called 'welfare'.[14]

One research project measured how much poverty and inequality affected the size of the welfare state in advanced Western countries. If the welfare state had a Robin Hood function you might expect it to grow when there were wider disparities of income. But the research did not find any such correlation. It is the piggy bank which matters more.[15] Of course, there are very important arguments about how the welfare state could do the job better and not undermine key values such as work or saving or family. There are also arguments about whether this redistribution across the life cycle has to be done by the state. You could imagine a society where this smoothing-out of income across the life cycle was achieved differently. You would borrow lots of money when you were young in order to finance your education, repaying the loan in your peak years of earning, and then, after you have done that, setting money aside to pay for your pension and the social care you need. That is increasingly how university education is financed. But by and large toddlers cannot walk into a bank and borrow £100,000 for their education, paid for out of future earnings. In the language of the economists, capital markets are not perfect. And there is another twist as well. Men by and large earn more than women, and partly for this very reason women tend to receive more than men. But men are not as reliable at providing this support through families as we used to be. The modern welfare state has developed because sadly it is not just capital markets that are imperfect – so are marriages.

This account does not capture everything that the government does. There are also the classic functions of the nightwatchman state – maintaining our security through the police, the legal system, and the armed forces. Nevertheless our account of transfers between the generations does describe a lot of what government does now. Even though it has not loomed so large in political theory, it certainly matters to real people. Education and health are consistently high on voters' lists of priorities for government action, suggesting that this shift of resources across the life cycle is crucial for them. You do not have to be a socialist to think that these are quite useful functions.

We have described them as shifting resources across the life cycle. But at any one moment, if you take a snapshot of what the government is doing, it is shifting resources between generations. It is sometimes compared with a chain letter or a Ponzi scheme, but that is misleading because – provided each generation keeps its side of the deal – it can usually be sustained. A classic paper by the Nobel Prize-winning economist Paul Samuelson set out the conditions for this model to work: it includes the key statement, which ties in with the argument in our previous chapter, that 'giving goods to an older person is figuratively giving goods to yourself when old'.[16] This is a powerful example of the contract between the generations.[17] You can think of it as shifting an individual's resources across the life cycle. But that is only possible because at any given moment it is also an exchange between different generations.

In a stable world it comes down to the same thing. This account of how the welfare state works is not therefore of itself evidence of any unfairness between the generations. We all take out, pay in and then take out again, and overall a typical life might expect that this broadly averages out. What could possibly go wrong with that? Quite a lot actually.

First, modern welfare states operate with a different balance of these transfers than within families in primitive societies and even today. It may be the consequence of industrialization or the democratic power of older voters, but instead of the historic pattern of flows from old to young, modern government shifts resources upwards to older people. The value of the pension and the healthcare exceeds the cost of schools and child benefits. That is very different from the flows within our own families. How much care and attention has been devoted to children as against your parents in your own family? Probably more to the children. But then think of what the welfare state does. And don't the voluntary flows show what we really want?[18] Perhaps the way government is shifting resources across the life cycle does not actually match our needs or preferences. Even if it nets out across the life cycle and it is fair across the generations, it may not maximize our well-being. We might be too parsimonious when we are young and redistribute too much to ourselves when we are old. So we freeze spending on Child Benefit while we boost state pensions with a triple lock. Perhaps spending a given amount of money differently would match better our actual priorities, as shown in the voluntary behaviour of real families.

There is one ingenious reply to this line of argument. It starts from the point that families have shifted their focus on to children and away from elderly relatives. This is because in an increasingly unequal and competitive world, parents are investing more and more in their children as it matters more. Attention to old people suffers. Indeed they are increasingly co-opted into childcare roles. The welfare state then has to adapt and devote more resources to the old to offset the increased voluntary transfers to the young. If we measure the fiscal transfers alone it looks like we are favouring the old, while the informal transfers within the family are favouring the young. Economists try to measure all this in national transfer accounts, and as they are developed for the UK we will be able for the first time to see the aggregate effects of these types of transfer. Meanwhile, in the next chapter we will investigate in more depth this significant increase in the attention and effort we voluntarily offer to our children.

This still leaves however the fundamental challenge to this model. It can be seen as maintaining fairness between the generations when circumstances are stable. Economists love nothing more than a stable equilibrium. But the world is not stable. In particular it comes under a lot of pressure when there are differences in the sizes of successive generations. Governments as custodians of the contract between the generations can exploit their power to favour one generation over another. Governments have to understand the contract between the generations and be committed to it if they are to avoid the temptation to raid the piggy bank. Even a policy which appears neutral may actually favour a particular generation.

Generations which Gain or Lose From the Welfare State

A good example of how a big generation can enjoy palpable economic gains, without even realizing it, comes from the impact of changes in the size of generations on the balance of tax and spending. Imagine a government has a simple rule that it must balance the budget across the economic cycle. That sounds quite prudent. And imagine as well that public spending policies just respond to changes in demand. So there is higher pension expenditure when there are more old people and less spending on education when there are fewer children, but spending per pensioner or per child just grows with the economy. If you have cohorts of equal size working their way through the system then there is fiscal equity across the generations. Overall it is in balance.

Now what happens if you stick to your balanced-budget rule but the big Baby Boomer cohort works its way through? When this big cohort are all children then public spending on services for children will rise. As you have got a balanced-budget rule, taxation will rise to allow for this, paid by the working population. Then that big cohort gets to working age. There is a reduction in demand for public services because there is a smaller cohort behind them, with fewer youngsters in schools for example.

At the same time tax revenues are buoyant because there is a surge in the number of taxpaying workers. So you can save on public expenditure, cut taxes, and still balance the budget over the economic cycle. This is the fiscal and economic sweet spot when a big generation are in the middle of their lives. But then they get older, claim their state pensions, and become heavy users of the NHS. This pushes up public spending and hence taxes. These effects are then magnified as there are fewer workers behind them, so tax per worker goes up even more. This example shows how the balanced-budget rule would actually work very neatly to the advantage of the Baby Boomers' generation and the disadvantage of their successors. They could enjoy low taxes when they were working taxpayers and then demand higher taxes from the next generation. The Baby Boomers enjoy the benefits of good public expenditure programmes when they are young and when they are old. But in their middle age they also enjoy the benefits of 'prudent' tax cuts. This is how the Boomers can gain at every stage from apparently responsible management of the public finances. If you have got big changes in the relative size of cohorts then a seemingly neutral balanced-budget rule is not enough to deliver fairness across the generations.

That is assuming constant policy. But if a big generation use their democratic power to vote themselves extra public spending which meets their needs at their stage of the life cycle, the generational imbalance can be even worse. Professor Sir John Hills has led the attempts to measure these effects, and the Resolution Foundation's Intergenerational Commission applied his methodology to the latest data. We have subsequently converted the figures into cash (the basis for the calculations is in the next endnote), and the result is set out in the table below. It clearly shows the Boomers doing better out of the welfare state than generations before or after them. Boomers may say they are entitled to all their benefits and public services because of how much they contributed, but they are actually taking out about a quarter of a million pounds more than they put in. The biggest gainers are people born in 1956, in the middle of the baby boom – which just so happens to include me. We enjoy a welfare state dividend of £291,000. It is rather chastening to think that, after a significant proportion of my adult career devoted to social policy, we should end up in a situation where exactly my own age group does better out of the welfare state than anyone else.[19]

Table 18: Net lifetime withdrawals from the welfare state by birth cohort[20]

Cohort	Lifetime net withdrawal	Cohort life expectancy based on 2016-based projections – England and Wales (male and female average)	Lifetime tax paid based on years of life and OBR tax curve (£)	Lifetime welfare receipt (£)	Welfare dividend (£)
1931	12%	79	903,000	1,016,000	113,000
1936	15%	81	915,000	1,050,000	136,000
1941	20%	83	926,000	1,112,000	186,000
1946	25%	84	931,000	1,162,000	231,000
1951	27%	85	936,000	1,188,000	252,000
1956	31%	86	941,000	1,231,000	291,000
1961	28%	87	945,000	1,213,000	268,000
1966	28%	88	950,000	1,216,000	266,000
1971	28%	88	950,000	1,212,000	262,000
1976	21%	89	954,000	1,154,000	200,000
1981	22%	90	958,000	1,169,000	210,000
1986	21%	90	958,000	1,161,000	203,000
1991	19%	91	962,000	1,142,000	180,000
1996	14%	91	962,000	1,095,000	132,000

These figures account for the history of the welfare state to date, changing age profiles of taxation and spending over time, rising longevity for successive cohorts, and a host of other things.

Because they span overlapping lifetimes they are best expressed as percentages in relation to GDP per capita. But to put rough cash numbers to these figures we take the Office for Budget Responsibility's profile of the average amount of tax paid per person at each age from its 2017 *Fiscal sustainability report*. This profile peaks in a person's late forties, when they pay an average of £20,000 in tax per year. We can also take each cohort's life expectancy – averaging over males and females. So, for example, a member of the 1956 cohort would live to age 86. In that case, then according to the OBR's tax profile, this person's lifetime tax contribution would be around £941,000 in today's money (and on the basis of today's tax profile by age). So based on the results of the Resolution Foundation's update of John Hills's analysis in the scenario where welfare spending doesn't ratchet up for ever due to rising health spending, we can say that an average person born in 1956 put in £941,000 but got out £1,231,000 – a welfare dividend of £291,000. The equivalent figures for all cohorts in this illustrative example are provided in the table.

One generation, the Boomers, always seem to be in the right place at the right time – enjoying low taxes when they are of working age and then claiming an increasing amount of public spending when they are old. That is to use the power of the modern welfare state not to deliver intergenerational fairness but to unbalance it.

The Tipping Point

For the past 30 years Britain has enjoyed a demographic sweet spot, with a surge in working-age Boomers and relatively few pensioners and children. This has been the backdrop to Britain's generally strong growth from the early 1980s right up to the financial crisis. We benefitted from lots of workers paying tax and lower pressures on public spending. Politicians talked as if tax cuts were the normal state of British politics. But we are now at a tipping point because the Boomers are growing old and there are fewer people of working age coming on behind. Our demographics, our economy, and our public spending will now move in a new direction. There are three tipping points, illustrated in the chart below, which add up to a very different trend line for the UK.

Figure 10: Three measures of the demographic tipping point[21]

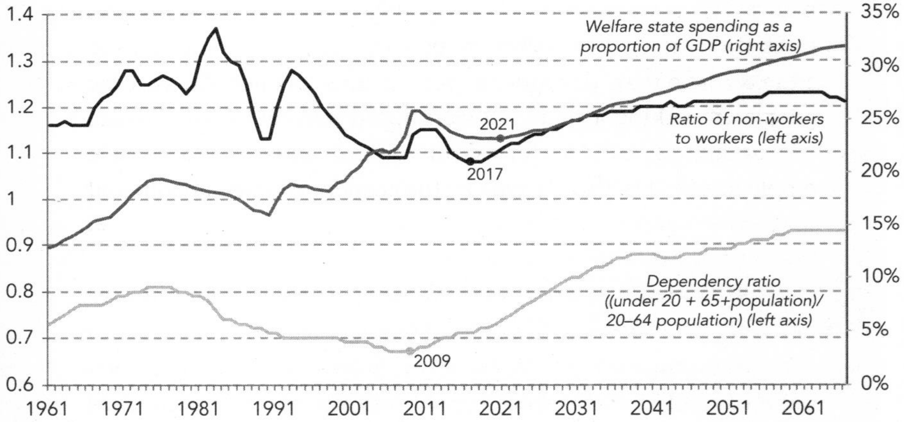

First is the simple demographic tipping point when the number of under-20s and over-65s starts to rise relative to the number of 20- to 64-year-olds. It is often described as a demographic dependency ratio, though this brings with it assumptions that the pensioner still in paid work or busy caring for a grandchild may not share. Nevertheless it does capture an underlying change in the overall demographic balance of the population. A high point of 81 young and old relative to 100 working-age adults was reached in the mid-1970s (partly because of the number of Boomer children), after which there was a long steady decline in the ratio to a low point of 67 'dependents' reached in 2009. That 30-year period from the IMF crisis to the financial crash saw genuine improvements in the performance of the British economy. Now the trend has reversed and the ratio is rising faster than it fell. The number of dependents per 100 non-dependents went back up through 70 in 2013, and in 2019 it stands at 72. It will go past its previous peak of 81 in 2028 and carry on rising toward 90 by the mid-century.

There will be a significant number of adults aged 20–64 who are not in paid work, perhaps because they are studying or unemployed or retired. And some of these 'dependents' may be in paid work. So we can move from demographics to economics and track the ratio of non-workers to people actually working. This is a higher ratio than 'dependents' versus 'non-dependents', as some people of working age are not working. It reflects the underlying demographics but also, for example, the gradual rise of female employment. It is also affected by the economic cycle of boom and bust, which does not appear to have been abolished by anyone, so the historic line moves around more.

This ratio reached a peak of 128 non-workers to workers in 1971 and another peak of 137 in 1983 when unemployment was very high. Since then it has been on a long-term decline, and reached a low point of 108 non-workers to workers in 2017 and 2018. This historic low was achieved by the favourable demographics driving the dependency ratio, combined with the success of the British labour market in absorbing more workers. But the big generation of Boomers who have boosted the labour market over the last 30 years are now retiring. While pensioners are doing more paid work, this has delayed rather than fully halted the underlying demographic trends. The year 2019 was when the ratio of non-workers to workers started rising.

These turning points also bring with them pressures for public spending to increase which is the third line in the chart. There is more detail in the table below, which shows the movement in key welfare state programmes – social security, education, and the NHS. Again it moves around because of specific decisions. Recently for example we have been offsetting demographic pressures by cutting benefits for working-age families and increasing the pension age. But inexorable demographic pressures put up public spending not just on benefits for pensioners but in other areas such as the NHS. The Resolution Foundation estimates that after a mini high point in the crash, a low point of public spending on benefits, healthcare, and education will be reached in 2021. That year it is projected to be down to 23 per cent of GDP. But then it will start rising to 25 per cent in 2030 and 27 per cent by 2040. So we are entering a period when just maintaining the existing welfare state promise is going to cost more and more. By the end of the next decade this cost will rise by £36bn a year. By 2040 it will rise to an extra £83bn.[22]

The table below gives the OBR forecasts in more detail. These are long-term forecasts and so are inevitably speculative. They assume no change in policy though do include forecasts for NHS costs continuing to rise.

Table 19: Projected future spending and tax with no change in policy (% of GDP)[23]

	2017–18	2027–8	2037–8	2047–8	2057–8	2067–8
Health and long-term care	8.3	9.7	11.5	13.1	14.5	15.7
Education	4.3	4	3.8	3.8	3.9	3.8
Pensions and pensioner benefits	7.9	8	8.8	9.3	9.5	9.7
Other welfare benefits & credits	4.8	4.5	4.3	4.2	4.2	4.2
Other spending	11.4	10.9	11	11.2	11.2	11.2
Total public spending excl. interest	36.7	37.1	39.4	41.4	43.3	44.6
Total tax receipts	36.3	36	35.9	36	36.1	35.9

This is a very different fiscal backdrop than we have been used to for the past 30 years. Politics is going to be very different as the Baby Boomers age. The age of tax cuts is over; instead, politics will be about who pays more and how much they pay. So far our attempts to address this challenge have been clumsy, and responses to them hysterical – we all remember the 'mansion tax' in 2015 and the 'dementia tax' in 2017. When I first made a speech with this evidence in 2018, a senior Tory assured me that it would still be possible to cut taxes because as we cut rates, more revenues would be collected – a particularly optimistic interpretation of the Laffer Curve is back. Meanwhile the Labour Party argues that it is possible to increase public spending on top of these trends, all financed by taxes on the rich with nobody else having to pay more. This suggests both main political parties still have some way to go in absorbing the significance of these trends.

The Burden of National Debt

We have seen how even an apparently prudent financial rule like balancing the budget over the cycle can deliver big shifts between different generations. We have also seen how the cost of these commitments is going to grow in the future. But so far we have ignored the burden of debt. This can offset these trends or magnify them. Government debt shifts the burden of paying for today's public expenditure on to the next generation. A big cohort that is at the height of its prosperity should repay debt so as to reduce the burden when it is a heavy user of the welfare state. That is the responsible thing to do. But if even in the demographic boom times it builds up debt then it really can impose a heavy burden on others.

Perhaps a forensic media inquisitor can get to the bottom of what is happening. In 1958, a lively young reporter called Robin Day was selected to conduct the first TV interview ever given by a Governor of the Bank of England. People were worried about the size of the national debt, so Robin Day asked what it was. Here is Governor Cobbold's reply:

Cobbold: The national debt represents the sums of money
which the government have over the years borrowed from
the public, mainly in this country and, to some extent,
abroad. That is really the amount of expenditure which
they have failed over the period to cover by revenue.
Day: Have we paid for World War Two?
Cobbold: No.
Day: Have we paid for World War One?
Cobbold: No.
Day: Have we paid for the Battle of Waterloo?
Cobbold: I don't think you can exactly say that.[24]

So these are deep issues. (Incidentally, we finally repaid our
remaining Second World War debt to the US in 2006.)

The burden of public debt has shot up enormously from 35 per
cent of GDP in 2007–8 before the financial crash to a peak of 85
per cent in 2016–17. This is a massive increase in the national
debt, tantamount to the burden of fighting a major war. It will
leave a debt burden to be paid by younger generations for decades.
You can argue, as we saw in the previous chapter, that they will be
richer and can afford it. But they will be bearing this extra burden
at a very bad time, when the Boomers are retiring and generating
further pressures on public spending. In fact, prudently
managed economies were trying to run budget surpluses in the
good times, so they were better prepared for these burdens. We
should, as George Osborne puts it, have fixed the roof when the
sun was shining. The consistent and principled position is to be
worried about imposing on future generations both the cost of
government debt and public spending on the Boomers as they get
older. That is before we add in other extra costs such as adjusting
to environmental change.

The counter-argument is that it is OK for governments to
borrow when interest rates are low and when it is using the money
to invest in assets for the future. We could have spent more in

the past decade, for example building more affordable housing, when borrowing costs were low and the economy had the capacity. Issuing more debt for this purpose might have been justifiable, though there are always limits to what the markets will fund – and governments do not wish to go through the nasty experience of finding they have breached that limit. And now we face a very unpalatable combination of circumstances. With debt at the still-elevated ratio of 84 per cent of GDP, government has much less room for manoeuvre when the next recession comes along and debt rises even higher. But at the same time the public sector has not got many assets to show for its surge in debt. In fact its net asset position is exceptionally poor.

Public sector net worth – government assets less government liabilities, measured as a share of net national income – fell sharply over the course of the two world wars. But then economic growth, the nationalization of several key industries, and a large-scale programme of social housing construction resulted in public-sector net worth shifting from a low of negative 190 per cent of national income in 1947 to 107 per cent by 1981. It has been on a steady downward trajectory since, however. First came the programme of privatization and council house sales during the 1980s, which helped to lower the net worth ratio to roughly 20 per cent by the mid-1990s. Then, having edged back up to 30 per cent of national income ahead of the financial crisis, the public sector's net worth fell once again, this time as a result of the rapid and large increase in public liabilities associated with government borrowing. The upshot is that public-sector net worth has turned negative once again, standing at minus 24 per cent in 2015.

The flipside of this 40-year fall in public-sector net worth is a marked upward drift in private net worth. Indeed the net assets of private households are so high that the UK's overall net worth ratio stands at around 600 per cent of national income. That's not the highest level on record, but it is better than anything we've seen in the last 100 years. But in order to be reassured by this statistic, we need to be entirely unconcerned about the distribution and composition of wealth. The *World Inequality Report 2018* argues that negative public-sector net worth potentially 'limits government ability to regulate the economy, redistribute income and mitigate rising inequality'. There are dangers in so much private inheritance as a means of passing on wealth. At the moment the state's enormous national debt, with few offsetting assets, means the state is passing on liabilities to all of us and the family is passing on assets to rather fewer of us.[25]

Is there a Contract Between the Generations at all?

Edmund Burke believed we are all bound by mutual contracts between the generations. Thomas Jefferson had a very different philosophy. He was a believer in the autonomy of each generation: 'Each generation is as independent of the one preceding, as that was of all which had gone before. It has then, like them, a right to choose for itself the form of government it believes most promotive of its own happiness'.

Ironically, the US Constitution which he himself helped to shape is one of the most powerful refutations of his belief – successive American generations have not dissolved their government and started again. But Jefferson was at least consistent and applied his principle to debt born by successive generations:

> The earth belongs in usufruct to the living... no man can by natural right oblige the lands he occupied, or the persons who succeed him in that occupation, to the payment of debts contracted by him. For if he could, he might during his life, eat up the usufruct of the lands for several generations to come, and then the lands would belong to the dead, and not to the living... The conclusion, then, is that neither the representatives of a nation, nor the whole nation itself assembled, can validly engage debts beyond

what they may pay in their own time; that is to say, within thirty-four years from the date of the engagement.[26]

Jefferson is arguing there is no intergenerational contract – so each generation is unencumbered and can make its own way, free to remake a political settlement but also free of debts left by the dead. But there is an intergenerational contract and we can leave debts for the next generation, provided we leave assets too with a fair balance between them. In the remaining four chapters we will look at practical examples of how this contract between the generations is changing as we go through the different stages of our lives.

9

TIME FOR CHILDHOOD

For many people, raising children is the most profoundly satisfying thing we do. It can give dignity to work and purpose to a marriage. It rests on deep-seated and admirable human instincts. It is what we do for the future. Rites of passage such as weddings or funerals are often a shared celebration of that achievement. It is deeply democratic as well – you can mess up despite great privileges, or you can do brilliantly despite facing great adversity. Having parents committed to this project is just about the greatest single advantage a child can have.

Nowadays we seem to be making heavy weather of it. Parents worry about how they are doing.[1] The charge is that we are failing to pass on to the next generation the values, the knowledge, and the skills which will enable them to thrive. If we cannot do this then we are indeed in deep trouble.[2] For parents it can feel as if they are battling in a hostile environment. Allison Pearson's novel *I Don't Know How She Does It* captures vividly what it is like to be a parent of young children in Britain today. Parents feel harassed, pummelled, and judged like never before. And being affluent is no protection from these pressures.

Some simple economics can help us understand what is going on.[3] As productivity improves over the long term, so returns from an hour of work increase. The cost of leisure time – the income we forego by not working – therefore increases. That means we cut our leisure time until the more intense leisure experiences which are left yield as much return as our paid work. Indeed sometimes we become so focused on trying to extract the maximum output from every hour, that we lose any ability to distinguish between work and leisure time – neatly captured in one man's description of modern family life as like running a small business with an ex-girlfriend.[4]

It used to be assumed that as we earned more per hour, so we would need to do less work – what the economists call the income effect. Keynes looked forward to his generation's grandchildren facing mankind's real problem: 'how to use his freedom from pressing economic cares, how to occupy the leisure, which science and compound interest will have won for him, to live wisely and agreeably and well'.[5] Nowadays some utopians believe that AI means we will finally have to confront Keynes's challenge. But if we earn more per hour, we also have an incentive to work even longer hours and cut out less rewarding activities – the substitution effect. What has happened for many well-paid people is that, contrary to what was expected, the substitution effect has turned out to be more important than the income effect. This is a key reason why modern life feels so pressured and the quality of life suffers. Earning more money does not solve this problem. In fact, it can make it more acute: as we become better paid we need to get higher returns – not just out of an hour of work but an hour of leisure or an hour in the home. (Think of the issue as what taxi drivers do when it rains, boosting their returns to an hour's work. If they head off home early as they have achieved their target takings for the day, then it is the income effect that matters. If they keep on the road as an extra hour's work is earning them a lot, then it is the substitution between work and leisure which matters. Reasonable people differ on this crucial issue.)[6]

Because we all feel busier it is easy to assume that time for children has lost out. One survey showed that 80 per cent of adults think parents spend less time with their children than in the past.[7] This is one reason parents get blamed for not raising their children well, even though for parents it can feel like they are working very hard indeed. We used to worry about the generation gap, but now we worry about the parenting deficit and fear that harassed parents are not able to devote enough time to their children. These anxieties are reinforced by the belief that a child's experience in their early years determines their future.

One reason we worry about the time parents devote to their children is that now we understand how malleable the brain of a young child is. If a songbird has not learned how to sing in the crucial months of its development as a fledgling then it will never be able to. Eric Knudsen of Stanford has shown wise old owls cannot learn things that young owls with their more flexible brains can learn.[8] Before about 12 months, babies brought up in the US can detect the difference between certain sounds common in the Hindi language which after 12 months they cannot distinguish; around a year old is when the first synaptic pruning takes place.[9] This is of course the natural process of neurological and language development. But there is emotional development as well – secure attachments help a child to develop the capacity for empathy or self-control, and hence a robust sense of his or her own identity. The early years do matter. However, the good news is that we are discovering that the brain is more malleable for longer than we assumed – particularly teenage brains.[10] Even adult brains can change and develop. So I have argued, for example, that the three years a person spends at university can change them as much as the first three years of their life.[11]

Some theories of child development are, however, rivalled only by cosmology in the determining power they attribute to early events. Then we fall into what has been called infant determinism.[12] In the past people used to think our fate was determined by the stars or the gods; now we believe it is determined in the playpen. As a result 'parent' is no longer just a noun but a verb. Parents feel under ever more pressure. One survey found that the key words used by parents to describe child-rearing were 'demanding, thankless, and exhausting'.[13] Whenever there is a social problem, from obesity to knife crime, there is one obvious group in the firing line – the parents. It is parents above all who are supposedly failing at their obligation of raising children who will grow into mature adults. But are parents all doing such a bad job? And is the problem too little parental supervision, or too much?

We need to look at what parents are really doing with their time. Over the past 50 years, in one of the great social research projects in the UK, 60,000 people have filled in a diary recording minute by minute how they have used their time.[14] It is an excellent way of mapping social change. We will use their UK data to compare time use in 1974–5, 2000–1, and 2014–15. We will focus on parents in couples with children under the age of five, looking at time devoted to various activities in minutes per day, averaged over a seven-day week. Both working and non-working parents are included; we are simply comparing the average time that mothers and fathers in two-parent families were able to devote to children in those three periods.

The evidence is dramatic. The average amount of time a mother devoted to caring for a child under the age of five has increased over the past 40 years from 78 minutes to 160 minutes, an extra hour and a quarter per day. For fathers, the increase in time is from 14 minutes to 86 minutes, a slightly smaller absolute increase but a bigger percentage. This confirms what experts such as Professor Jonathan Gershuny and Frank Furedi have reported, and conflicts with the conventional wisdom that somehow parents are too busy to devote time to their children. Parents are spending more time with their young children than before. Whereas nearly a quarter of mothers of young children devoted less than half an hour to childcare in the 1970s, only around a tenth devote so little time more recently.

When we look at how mothers with young children have found that extra hour and a quarter a day, it is clear that investment in domestic labour-saving equipment has been crucial. The following table identifies all the areas where time has been saved – both columns are changes from the 1974–5 base.

Table 20: Saving in time of mothers of young children between 1974–5 and 2000–1 and 2014–15 (minutes per day)[15]

	2000–1	2014–15
Housework	33	44
Cooking, eating, and washing up	49	57
Relaxation	39	45
Watching TV	11	22
Shopping	10	8
Total time saved	143	176

Those 176 minutes in 2014–15 went into an extra 82 minutes of childcare and an extra 46 minutes of paid work per day over a seven-day week. Mothers with young children do paid work on average five and a half hours longer per week than they did in the mid-seventies.

So far we have been averaging across two-parent families in different circumstances. Now let us compare the time devoted to childcare for working and non-working parents and also by educational background. (Less-educated means having left school at 16 whereas well-educated means having a qualification beyond A level, so we are excluding a significant group in the middle.)

Table 21: Amount of time devoted to care of young children by different categories of mother (minutes per day)[16]

	1974–5	2000–1	2014–15
High-educated working mother	64	159	144
Low-educated working mother	43	114	112
High-educated non-working mother	106	179	221
Low-educated non-working mother	74	148	129

This shows that the transformation in the amount of time for childcare is spread across working and non-working mothers, be they well-educated or not. In fact it is such a dramatic increase that a well-educated mother who is in paid work now spends almost 50 per cent more time on childcare than she would have done as a non-working mother 40 years ago and has more than doubled the time compared with a working mother like her then. Here we can see how she has managed it:

Table 22: Absolute amount of time spent on different activities by a working well-educated mother in 1974–5 and difference from that level in 2000–1 and in 2014–15 (minutes per day)[17]

	1974–5	2000–1 difference	2014–15 difference
Cooking and eating	185	−49	−48
Sleep	556	−59	−49
Housework	100	−21	−42
Shopping	42	−10	−13
Relaxation/hobbies	187	−37	−27
Paid work	110	+30	+55
Childcare	63	+96	+80

It is less time cooking, doing housework, less relaxation, and less sleep, so there are 179 more minutes available, which goes into extra paid work (up by almost seven hours a week) and above all 80 minutes' extra childcare per day by 2014, more than double the one hour per day devoted to childcare back in 1974–5. Babies and young children are gaining from an investment of parental time on a scale which very few young children appear to have had when the Baby Boomers were parents – or indeed children. It is a massive shift to more parental investment in children.

This overwhelming picture of an increased amount of childcare by parents, especially mothers – be they working or not – is supported by very similar evidence from other advanced Western countries. In America the argument that parents were not spending enough time with their children was advanced by Sylvia Ann Hewlett in *When the Bough Breaks*.[18] The empirical refutation came out five years later and got much less attention. Actually, average hours per day spent in childcare by white married mothers in the US went up per child from 32 minutes in 1924–31 to 49 minutes in 1975 and one hour in 1981. The conclusion of the researchers was clear: 'The public as well as many policymakers perceive that modern families have failed their children and that their mothers and grandmothers did more. Our analysis provides evidence to the contrary.'[19] In the Netherlands it is a very similar story, with the time mothers devote to childcare up from 61 minutes to 147 minutes (an increase of 86 minutes) and for men up from 22 minutes to 63 minutes (an increase of 41 minutes).[20] We are dealing here with nothing less than a transformation of the amount of time that Western parents are devoting to the care of their young children. This is a very welcome trend of increased intergenerational investment.

There is, incidentally, no equivalent increase in the time that British parents devote to teenagers. The evidence is less clear because the time-use survey asks about time devoted to childcare and that may seem odd applied to older children, so the data is not so reliable. But the data does suggest that parents devote very little time to direct engagement with their teenaged children. This is reinforced by the evidence from teenagers themselves, who report very little time in direct contact with their parents. Indeed, British teenagers spend more time with their peers and less with their parents than in other European countries.[21]

Our upbringing of children is now focused very much on early years; we leave teenagers to their peers. The irony is that it looks as if the amount of time that parents spend with their teenagers does significantly influence their behaviour, whereas some experts are not sure how big the effect is from spending more time with children in their early years.[22] And the balance between supervised and unsupervised time with peers matters for teenage behaviour as well.[23]

This may be a consequence of the focus on the early years, which can undervalue parenting as a longer-term commitment extending to the teenage years. And as parents' earnings rise as they get older, so the opportunity-cost of time for teenagers may be higher than for young children. Whatever the reason, it means we have a widening gap: intense parental investment in the early years and then a dramatic fall, with much more importance for peers whose influence peaks at the age of 15. The challenge to parents is not to do better when our children are young, small, and cuddly, but when they aren't.

So far we have focused very much on the evidence for mothers. Let us now look at what has happened for fathers. It is a good test of the widespread expectation that as we got richer we would work less. Our alternative account says that the more you earn per hour, the greater the rewards of spending your time that way so you will work more. What has happened? In 1970, less-skilled men with jobs and with children under five worked on average 7 hours 1 minute a day, while well-educated men worked for 5 hours 50 minutes a day. (These may seem rather low but these averages do include weekends.) By 2001 the more-educated man with children under five worked more (6 hours 36 minutes), but the less-skilled worker had cut his work to just less than that – 6 hours 32 minutes. In 2015 the balance shifted modestly back, with the less-educated man working a bit more than the more-educated. The hours of less-educated men have declined over the past forty years but the hours of more-educated men have increased so now they are very close.

If we categorize our men not by education but how well paid their jobs are, we get a very similar pattern. Using admittedly rather patchy data, it looks as if in the mid-eighties less well-paid fathers with young children used to work 54 minutes a day more than the highest-paid quarter of fathers. Now they work 68 minutes less. This is real evidence for the aphorism that the leisured classes have less leisure and the working classes less work.[24]

There is also some modest evidence for the 'new' man. The average father of a child under five has also moved from doing around 12 minutes of housework each day to 28 minutes a day in 2015. (This contrasts with reduced time for personal grooming, which suggests the metrosexual new man who moisturizes may be a myth – or perhaps he cannot manage it if he has young children.) They also spend more time cooking and less time eating with the family.

Table 23: Time devoted to household activities by fathers of children under five (minutes per day)[25]

	1974–5	2000–01	2014–15
Food	91	103	99
Housework	12	24	28
Childcare	17	70	84
Shopping	12	19	23
Relaxation	179	168	169
TV/radio	139	136	122
Paid work	368	254	244
Sleep	468	507	502

Before men get too pleased with themselves about this modest increase in housework, separate research shows that women do the housework that is time-inflexible such as preparing meals and doing the laundry, and which can affect their employment prospects. Men still tend to do more flexible weekend jobs such as gardening or home repairs.[26]

Still, once you add in the time saved by fathers sleeping, relaxing, and grooming less, it adds up to a big increase in time for childcare from fathers. In the early 1970s fathers spent on average around a quarter of an hour with their young children each day. By 2015 they were spending an hour and a quarter. This trend covers all fathers but it is distributed across the week very differently. During the busy weekday, the more-educated man manages an hour, and at the weekend two hours. By contrast the less well-educated fathers, whose time pressures are apparently not as uneven, spend about 50 minutes with their very young children every day.

There is one uncomfortable implication in all this. We have been focusing on couples with children. Insofar as we have got a 'new' man who contributes a modest increase in time spent cooking, doing housework, and being with his children, then the cost of being a lone parent (who are usually women) has increased. Lone parents do their best in difficult circumstances, investing enormous quantities of time into their children, but this evidence suggests that a father does not just contribute his pay packet but increasing help with childcare as well.

What we are seeing here is a near-doubling of parental investment in children within one generation. And that investment could be paying off in better cognitive and emotional development for those children. One of the most hotly debated issues in human development is the so-called Flynn effect, named after Professor James Flynn from New Zealand, who was the person to observe that IQ was rising across advanced Western countries.[27] Many different explanations have been offered for this. One possibility is that the early-years investment could be having an effect after all, as the improvements in IQ scores measured by Flynn seem to match the increase in parental time for children, which in turn is influenced by the spread of labour-saving household appliances. Thus we may have found a new explanation of the Flynn effect – it is the spread of household technology, increasing the time available for parents to devote to their children, which is crucial. The microwave oven has raised IQ.

So we have very encouraging evidence that parents are actually investing more in the younger generation, and we may be seeing the payoff in higher IQs. But it is not the whole story. All those reports warning about the quality of childhood in Britain are on to something. To understand what is going on we have to see what is happening to trust within and between the generations.

Trust and the Changing Character
of Childhood

Children can generate trust; 70 per cent of parents said they had met people or made friends through their children.[28] Walking through a park is a far more social experience if you have a child (or of course a dog). Children can also be the victims of a loss of trust. This loss of trust takes many forms. Even though it is not clear that there has been an overall loss of trust within our society, there does seem to be a specific loss of trust in other adults playing a role in raising our children.

The evidence from voluntary groups suggests that, not least because of worries about paedophiles, it is harder to get other adults to take a role in supervising children. There is a waiting list of 30,000 youngsters who would like to join the Scouts but cannot because of a shortage of adult volunteers. The commitment that men make to the Scouts has also subtly changed. It is less likely to be long-term commitment and more likely to be a commitment to helping out during the short period when one's own child is involved. The pressure to be better parents has also made us worse citizens, as parents withdraw from civic activities. Time pressures mean parents do less voluntary activity. One estimate showed a 25 per cent fall in the time devoted to voluntary activity simply in the five years 1995–2000.[29] The process may go the other way too: as we lose trust in other adults, so we take on more of the burden of raising children ourselves.

It is not just a loss of adults' confidence in other adults. There is also a growing distrust and wariness of adults other than their parents among children. This is deliberately encouraged by the authorities. Police visit schools warning of 'stranger danger' and telling children not to speak to any stranger as they are a potential threat. However, the reality is that children may feel threatened by other children and want to turn to an adult as a source of protection and support. As Margaret Atwood observes in her novel *Cat's Eye*,

'Little girls are cute and small only to adults. To one another they are not cute. They are life sized.'

As we track down this breakdown of trust within and between generations, we can also see that adults have lost confidence in other people's children. Again, there is powerful evidence showing this is more acute in Britain than in the rest of Europe. One survey asked adults in different countries if they would intervene if they saw 14-year-olds vandalizing a bus shelter: 65 per cent of German adults would; 52 per cent of Spanish adults would; the British figure was 34 per cent.[30]

It all comes together in a loss of confidence in public space. They are seen as places of risk and danger. There is some empirical evidence behind this: 43 per cent of gangs actually gather in children's play areas.[31] Parents do not want their children playing in places where graffiti, bottles, and syringes reveal territory belonging to teenage gangs. (There are, however, subtle ways of fighting back. One council has found teenagers do not like sandpits as they are bad for their trainers – so play areas that include sandpits are less likely to be taken over by gangs.) Children have withdrawn from public open spaces. A recent survey found three-quarters of UK children spend less time outside than prison inmates – 74 per cent of 5- to 12-year-olds spent less than 60 minutes playing outside each day, whereas prisoners have an entitlement to an hour a day. Most of the parents polled said their children had fewer opportunities to play outside than they did when they were young.[32]

This all adds up to very powerful evidence about how the contract between the generations is changing. It is more intensively focused on the particular relationship between parents and children, especially when they are young. There is much less confidence in other adults or other children. So each individual family feels they are on their own. Other adults are not trusted, and other children are seen as competition and perhaps even as a threat. This is a key element in the breakdown of contact and trust between the generations. In 2005, 1.5 million Britons thought about moving house to escape young people hanging around.[33] Similarly, young people are far more likely to suspect that a man whose behaviour is in any way out of the ordinary is somehow a threat to them. This loss of trust in others in turn erodes the quality of childhood.

Tim Gill, who was director of the Children's Play Council and has thought deeply about childhood and play, invites adults to look back on some of the magic moments of their childhood. One hopes there are good family times – Christmas or holidays, or moments of particular kindness and closeness with our parents. But often we have other sorts of memories as well – incident and excitement when we were out on our own or with a group of other children. These are what he calls the everyday adventures that help give childhood much of its special meaning. I think of cycling around the suburbs with my friends. My parents did not know where we went; we just had to be back for our mealtime. It was not an idyll from an Enid Blyton adventure – it was Birmingham, after all. But, looking back, I was incredibly lucky to enjoy such a mixture of freedom and security. A childhood like that, enjoyed by many Boomers, is what is disappearing. We are moving from free-range to supervised childhood. And toy consumption is not the same as play.

We have also become far more demanding and restrictive when it comes to the behaviour of children. As the president of our local Scouts when I was MP for Havant, I opened an exhibition at our local museum to mark a century of scouting. Some of the Scouts of previous decades had kept diaries of their activities. Here is an extract from an account of a Scout trip in the 1920s:

> On Easter Monday a very large party of our Scouts and Rover Scouts paid a most enjoyable visit to Kingley Vale... arriving at the Vale about 11.30. We then started the day's sport in earnest. Six of us started a battle: suddenly we discovered we were pursued by several others. We hid

amongst the bushes and pounced out on them as they came along. After this a fierce battle ensued: trousers and shirts were torn: a few cuts and bruises and the battle was won. We then sat down to a good meal and rested a bit.

Later the patrol leader describes a fight with another group: 'one was armed with an ugly scalping knife and the other with a catapult'; then he adds, 'so there was no serious damage done'. This description of a Scout trip now constitutes a list of criminal offences, for at least some of which campaigners now want a mandatory jail sentence. In 2006, three children from the West Midlands, none of whom had ever been in trouble before, were arrested and DNA tested for building a treehouse in a cherry tree on public ground. In another incident a group of boys were building go-karts from bits of junk; neighbours contacted the boys' families to complain and to move them on. In the US, Lenore Skenazy faced public opprobrium for letting her nine-year-old son ride the subway alone, and ended up writing a book about it called *Free-Range Kids: Giving Our Children the Freedom We Had Without Going Nuts with Worry*.

In the words of Tim Gill: 'Activities and experiences that previous generations of children enjoyed without a second thought have been relabelled as troubling or dangerous, while the adults who permit them are branded as irresponsible.'[34] This is matched by a failure of the authorities to distinguish between everyday children's activities and serious antisocial behaviour which is not tackled effectively either. Boys in particular need to be able to let off steam or they will be more violent later on. For girls, the expression of these pressures is different. For girls it is sadness – and there is nothing sadder than a sad child: 'Boys externalize their problems as bad behaviour, girls internalize them as sadness.'[35]

Children spend more and more of their time being supervised and managed. In fact, we have reached the stage where a good parent has to be permanently on the lookout for risk and danger.

Even if a child is not directly in our view, we need to know where he or she is. Parents worry if their child is out without their mobile and they cannot be in touch all the time. New products feed this anxiety. A company is launching children's clothes fitted with tiny transmitters linked to a geo-stationary satellite so a parent will always know where the child is. The following table shows how the age when a child is allowed out unsupervised has increased in a generation.

Table 24: Age when a child could be allowed out unsupervised[36]

	Age at which adults went out as children (%)	What adults think for children now (%)
Under-8s	16	3
8–10	23	14
11–13	27	36
14+	32	43

Children are more supervised and managed by their parents than ever before, because their parents feel the outside world is dangerous and other adults are not trusted. At the same time, all the other adults are worried about other people's children: research has found that nearly 80 per cent of Britons and 99 per cent of those over 55 think that 'young people today have too much freedom and not enough discipline'.[37] Jeremy Bentham famously designed a model prison – his panopticon – so that prisoners could be kept permanently under watch; we seem to be doing something similar for our children.

Children respond by finding new ways of escaping parental supervision. A child's bedroom has become the new territory that enables them to escape supervision; 90 per cent of children from poor families have a TV in their bedroom, and half of children in middle-class families do.[38] They have their own smartphones or laptops. And children may be more at risk online than out in the playground – one in three children has received unwanted or nasty sexual comments online, but only 7 per cent of parents are aware of this.[39]

The decline in confidence in public space also increases the importance of organized outside activity instead. Parents drive their children to sports matches and other such activities. This may mean they are sometimes over-supervised and over-organized, but at least it is an opportunity for children to get physical exercise. It is likely to depend on access to a car, parental commitment, and perhaps going to a school where there is more of such activities. In the past, poor children were skinny and active, endlessly outside, even if they were cold. It was the rich kids who were inside and plump. But now it is the poorer kids who are more likely to be inside watching TV in their bedrooms, while the more affluent kids are out playing competitive sport. We can test this hypothesis against our evidence on time use. In 1984–9, male teenagers from the poorest quarter of families watched 169 minutes of TV per day, as against 201 minutes watched by male teenagers from the most affluent quarter of families. But 20 years later this relationship has been reversed. Teenagers from the poorest families are watching about the same amount – 163 minutes – but for teenagers from the most affluent families it is down to 118 minutes. Television-viewing by teenagers from poor families has fallen over the last 20 years from 21.5 hours to 20.5 hours per week, while for rich teenagers it is down far more – from 27.5 hours to under 18 hours.[40]

This reduction in time for more affluent children watching TV may be offset by more time on laptops and smartphones. But there is another significant change as well. Thirty years ago, poor children were more likely to spend their time engaged in sport than children from more affluent backgrounds. In 1985–9, male teenagers from the poorest households spent 20 minutes every weekday playing sport, mostly at school. They still do. But the time they spend playing sport at weekends has fallen from 56 minutes per day to 47 minutes. The most affluent teenagers have increased their time playing sport at school from 12 minutes per day to 28 minutes. And at the weekend it has shot up from 12 minutes per day to 60 minutes. Boys from wealthier families used to do under 2 hours of sport a week; they now do more than 4. For poorer teenage boys, it has gone down from 3.5 to about 3 hours per week. Now teenagers from poor backgrounds do less sport than their middle-class contemporaries. And playing outside, including in team sports, is one way you learn the soft skills which are so important not just for a job but in order to study effectively.

This is a case study of how a change in relations between the generations (an intergenerational shift) can also change the distribution of advantage within generations (intra-generational). The loss of confidence that adults have in other adults and in public space is much more of a blow for a child from a poorer background than for one whose parents have the money to organize alternative activities instead. This is delicate territory. It is not that poor families are incompetent and uncaring. Nor is it a sin for an affluent family to drive their children to a sports club or a ballet class or do anything else they can to invest in them. But it does show the impact of the different constraints and environments facing different families. We are beginning to see one of the reasons why it is important to recreate a sense of adventure and enable more children to enjoy outdoor activities.

Piaget, Flynn, and Shayer

Jean Piaget realized that experiencing the world in three dimensions is what enables us to develop even some of our most abstract concepts. Kicking a football, throwing stones, standing at the sink helping with the washing-up, or jumping on hopscotch squares all help develop these cognitive skills. If children increasingly retreat from a three-dimensional to a two-dimensional world, it is much harder to develop these capacities. Thomas Friedman wrote a bestselling book in praise of globalization entitled *The World is Flat* – and often that means digitized. But in a child's world that is bad news: when the world is flat, the child is fat. It goes beyond that. Children may have digital dexterity and hand-eye co-ordination that is faster than ever; they may be adept at manipulating the symbols flashing up on their screens. These skills even show up as higher IQs. But their wider ability to interact with the world in 3D may be declining. We end up with what have been called 'screenagers'.

Professor Michael Shayer of London University recorded how children have mastered the fundamental concepts they need in order to understand the world around them. For example, you pour water from a tall, thin beaker into a short, squat beaker and ask if it is the same volume or not. After decades of responses being broadly stable, there appears to have been a downturn since the mid-1990s, when children's conceptual grasp has deteriorated dramatically: 'My findings show that 11- and 12-year-old children in year 7 are now on average between two and three years behind where they were 15 years ago in terms of cognitive and conceptual development.'[41] This evidence appears to contradict Flynn's optimism about rising IQ and suggests that children today may lack the basic conceptual equipment to master living in a three-dimensional world.

How is Shayer consistent with Flynn? This gets to the heart of the conflicting messages we receive about childhood. As well as Sue Palmer warning us about a toxic childhood, there is Steve Johnson saying our kids are smarter than ever and all those flat-screen computer games we worry about are actually good for you.[42] Our explanation of what parents are up to shows how both observations can be true. Parents have been liberated above all by domestic appliances to spend more time caring for their children when they are young. This extra investment has yielded good results. The bad news is, however, that they have lost confidence in other adults so their children are spending more time indoors and under closer supervision. This combination of extra time supervised by parents but less free-range experience of the world in 3D may explain why IQ appears to be rising but grasp of fundamental physical concepts appears to be declining.

This is reinforced by international evidence. The Flynn effect is a universal phenomenon across all developed countries. The Shayer effect is a British problem – there is no equivalent decline in the US for example. The spread of household appliances liberating parental time affects all Western countries, but the loss of trust in other adults, and hence the restrictions on children, is a much more specific British problem.

Moreover, we saw earlier there has been no increase in the amount of time parents spend with teenagers. While early years are important for neurological development, the teenage years are just as neurologically significant. One reason why, despite all the misery it shows, we love the optimism of the film *Slumdog Millionaire* is that it is about how you can escape appalling childhood adversity. Some brain areas, in particular the prefrontal cortex, continue to develop well beyond early childhood. Kevin the teenager's brain is rebooting, or at least installing new software – 12-year-olds do literally have more grey matter than 15-year-olds. The adolescent brain can function oddly as a result. One experiment presents adults and adolescents with an option such as swimming with sharks and asks them to click on 'good idea' or 'not a good idea'. It takes adolescents rather longer to work out it is not such a good idea.[43]

This opens up an unusually wide gap between teenagers and adults in Britain. It might affect cognitive development. The latest evidence from Professor Flynn does suggest a loss of progress for IQ in 12- to 15-year-olds. For 14.5- to 15.5-year-olds he shows a loss of 1.88 IQ points between 1979 and 2009.[44] The unusual dependence of British teenagers on their peers could well be behind this; indeed, Flynn hypothesizes this is linked to teenage subculture not being cognitively demanding: 'Up until the age of nine and ten the home has a really powerful influence, so we can assume parents have been providing their children with a more cognitive challenging environment in the past 30 years. After that age children have become more autonomous and they gravitate to peer groups that set the cognitive environment.' He concludes with a powerful warning: 'I look forward with some trepidation to what the next century has in store.'[45]

This warning from the researcher who gave his name to the extraordinarily optimistic finding of rising IQs is very salutary. It means we have not just been riding a favourable demographic trend but a favourable cognitive trend too. We do not know to what extent our post-War GDP growth has depended on demographic growth, let alone IQ growth. We have not yet begun to contemplate a world where these trends could go into reverse. Parents are doing their best, but as citizens we are making life tougher for the next generation.

10

EDUCATION AND SOCIAL MOBILITY

Education for our Children or for Everyone's?

Nowadays we all believe in a society which is open and mobile. You should be able to get qualifications and a job and make your way in the world because of your own abilities. Of course we want to do the best for our own children, but we also want a society where what you do is not determined by what your parents did. This argument was first put by Benjamin Franklin, 250 years ago, when he said that America would be a 'land of opportunity'. Then he was drawing a bold contrast with what he saw as the stale, hereditary systems of Europe. Now every politician promises to spread opportunity.

We aim to give the best chance to the next generation as a whole, not just one by one within our own individual families. This is not only a moral argument. In a modern market economy we are part of intricate networks of specialized labour. We depend on many other people delivering goods and services: it matters to us that they should be suited to their jobs and do them well. We cannot expect to be a successful, dynamic economy if we waste talent. Indeed, one study suggested that the Western countries with high social mobility have enjoyed an economic growth rate over the past century of 2.43 per cent a year as against 1.77 per cent for the low-mobility economies.[1] Blocking opportunity is worse than a sin – it is a mistake.

It is a good thing that families invest in their children, but we have to balance it by opportunities for everyone. Defining the right balance between these alternative principles of heredity and opportunity is not straightforward. After all, most of us are British citizens by right of inheritance. Ten per cent of British graduates follow the career of their father. If their performance were below that of their fellow professionals it would suggest nepotism, but if anything their earnings grow by more than those of their fellows, suggesting some genuine transmission of skill and human capital. Whatever one may think of the survival of the 92 hereditary peers in the House of Lords, they are not the only example of heredity determining occupation. Twenty-five per cent of farmers' sons go into farming; for medicine it is 17 per cent; and for the law 14 per cent. Self-employed entrepreneurs are also strongly hereditary, suggesting access to capital is an issue. There are businesses that are proud to call themselves '& sons' and increasingly, one hopes, '& daughters'.[2]

The previous chapter showed that we lavish more attention on our own kids – while public policy and the public realm are much less favourable to young people as a whole. So we also support planning restrictions which make it harder for them to get a house and we accept that their pay has stopped advancing and their benefits are more restricted. We have become better parents and worse citizens. Some will say that this is what happens if the private realm triumphs over the public realm: we think the best way we can help the next generation is one by one, and do not trust any collective action. Maybe we think we have to do more as parents to invest in them, to compensate for the weakening of the wider social contract. If we think our children will be operating in a tough competitive environment when they are adults then it is even more important that they have personal resources to draw on. More cynically, perhaps we think that we have a better chance of success for our efforts for our kids if the wider realm provides less support for other people's.

There is no grand moral claim which is going to trump the profound urge of parents to do the best for their kids. And we all gain if parents don't just make babies but make adults – well-socialized, imaginative, hard-working, morally rooted young people. I believe parents are producing more and more young adults like that. But is there a point at which this investment in our own children comes at the expense of everyone else?

These issues are most vivid and acute in education. It is the difference between being well-educated and being top of the class. Being well-educated is not a zero-sum game, won at someone else's expense. Top of the class is different. Not everyone can have prizes. And one way to get the prizes is for parents to get more resources for their own children's education than their young rivals have. At any one point in time there are limits to the number of schools with the most highly qualified teachers, and limits to the number of places at the most prestigious universities. So education has become an arms race of intensifying competition to get into the best schools and get the best grades, so as to get into the most selective universities. A generation ago there were still other routes into well-paid jobs and professions. When I arrived at the Treasury as a civil servant in 1978, one of the most senior officials had begun as a clerk and worked his way up. That is much harder nowadays. Higher education has become the main path to well-paid jobs, and as a result getting into university, especially a prestigious one, is more important than ever. Ninety-seven per cent of parents of children born in the Millennium year want their children to go to university.[3] There are lots of high statements about what schools are for, but in reality the purpose of schools in England is simple and overwhelming – to get pupils into university, and the more prestigious the better.

Does this have any effect on social mobility? How strong are the ties linking children's income to their parents'? Researchers have estimated the strength of the economic connection: the answer is about 0.35.[4] Imagine two children born in the same year. If one had parents who earned 100 per cent more than the other, then 30 years later that child would on average be earning approximately 35 per cent more than the child of the less affluent parents. It is what economists call the elasticity of income with regard to parental earnings. It includes every possible method by which parents can help their children, from the genetic inheritance of ability to buying an expensive house near a good school which gets lots of its students to university – or feeds one which does. We may think some of these ways of transmitting individual affluence to the next generation are better than others. And of course there is a lot of luck involved. That is what makes the debate on social mobility so fraught.

A society where there were no family ties whatsoever would be so rootless it would be almost as unbearable as the opposite – a caste society. This may be why popular attitudes are quite mixed: 69 per cent believe parents' income plays too large a part in children's life chances, but 50 per cent of people believe opportunities for social mobility are about right and a third believe they are too low.[5] This is heavily affected by where you are on the class scale: 58 per cent of people in social classes A and B believe it is about right, as against 41 per cent of people in social classes D and E. We have stronger views on inequality, with 74 per cent believing income differences are too great. Perhaps people will accept less mobility if there is more equality. They might also accept more inequality if there were more mobility too. The trouble is the world does not work like that: if anything, the Western societies with less mobility are the ones with less equality too. The reason is that social immobility means a pernicious process of passing disadvantage from one generation to the next, which increases inequality. And greater inequality means you have further to travel to catch up with the people ahead of you, so it makes mobility harder.

Even if the inequities you worry about are within generations, they are transmitted across generations. We live in a society where your weight at birth is a powerful predictor of how long you will stay in education.[6] As soon as we look seriously at poverty and deprivation, we have to face the powerful effects of inherited disadvantage. So the vertical transmission of disadvantage across generations helps to shape its horizontal distribution within one generation.

We used to think that there was an inevitable trend to increased mobility in modern capitalism. The author of Labour's 1945 manifesto, Michael Young, coined a word for it – 'meritocracy' – in his book *The Rise of the Meritocracy*, published in 1958.[7] He defined merit as IQ plus effort. He thought it was inevitable that in the future, merit would rise to the top. He mischievously argued, however, that when personal inadequacy was the only reason for lack of achievement, failure would be more cruel than before and this meritocratic society would not be a happy place. F. A. Hayek's humane response was that there was no reason why the pattern of rewards in a market economy should be seen as a judgement on merit or moral worth.[8] That reminder is even more relevant today, with our worship of worldly success.

Young predicted that meritocracy would be achieved but we would not like it. But things have turned out exactly the other way round. Now the word he coined in order to mock it has come to stand for something desirable but unexpectedly difficult to achieve. Let us look at the evidence of what happened to the children born in the year his book appeared.

What is Happening to Social Mobility?

We used to assume social mobility would steadily improve. That is why it was such a shock when in 2005 evidence came out that social mobility had declined. Steve Machin, Paul Gregg, and Jo Blanden took children born in 1958 and 1970 and looked at where they were on the income scale 30 years on, compared with their parents.[9] The tables below summarize the evidence, focusing on the children with parents in the poorest 25 per cent of the income scale (or quartile) and then children with parents in the richest 25 per cent. They measured the chances of a child born to parents in these quartiles of the income scale then ending up in each quartile of the income scale. In a completely frictionless society where outcomes were completely unaffected by where you started, you would find that 25 per cent of the children from the poorest quartile would themselves end up in the poorest quartile and so on, with 25 per cent of those children ending up in the richest quartile. But the real world is not frictionless; it is sticky. Moreover, and this was the most striking result, children in the 1970 birth cohort from the poorest quartile were more likely to stay there than the 1958 cohort, as the table below shows.

Table 25: Income mobility for children of parents in the poorest quartile (%)

Year of birth of child	1958	1970
Chances of staying in poorest quartile	31	38
Chances of moving to the richest quartile	17	16

Table 26: Income mobility for children of parents in the richest quartile (%)

Year of birth of child	1958	1970
Chances of staying in richest quartile	35	42
Chances of moving to poorest quartile	17	11

That single piece of research had a massive impact on the debate around social mobility because it showed the trend going in the wrong direction.

The evidence has been challenged and questioned. For a start, two points do not make a trend. Moreover, it looks back at people who are now middle-aged – we are like astronomers studying the light of a long-dead star. In response the researchers tried to carry forward their findings and found that social mobility appears to have stopped declining. But nobody is seriously claiming that social mobility in Britain has suddenly massively improved again.

If anything the consensus is that the higher mobility in 1958 was exceptional. The children born in the year when Michael Young wrote his book were the products of a society more meritocratic than before or since. The result for children born in 1970 is thought to be more typical of British society.

The evidence of falling and low social mobility caused such a stir because it is easy to assume that there must be more social mobility as more young people get more education and as the traditional working classes shrink and more people join the middle class. This is where the sociologists come in. They look at social class, not just income. The economists' measure with which we began this chapter ensures that social mobility must be a zero-sum game, because there is always going to have to be a quarter of the population in the bottom quartile of income. But unlike fixed slices of the income scale, the size of different social classes can change. And these social categories reveal more of the reality of how we live our lives. A graduate starting in a white-collar job with promotion and more training ahead of her and a middle-aged man doing manual work in a shrinking industry may earn the same pay but actually have very different prospects.

In the golden age of social mobility after the War there was a surge in the number of white-collar managerial and professional jobs, while the number of traditional manual working-class jobs fell. These changes in the social structure delivered improvements in social mobility as the sons and daughters of manual workers became white-collar office workers. Professor John Goldthorpe, the doyen of social mobility researchers, has measured how people have done relative to the changes in the social structure around them.[10] He shows that people have floated up the social scale as the types of occupation have changed, but there has been no further social mobility on top of that. So social mobility has just been driven by changes in the types of job people do.

Over the 60 years between 1951 and 2011, the working class fell from 55 per cent to 30 per cent of the male workforce. Meanwhile the managerial and professional occupations rose from 11 per cent to 40 per cent of all male jobs. There is a similar story for women.[11]

Most of this transformation of the social structure happened in the first 40 years. So when the Boomers were entering the jobs market, social and economic change meant they were getting on an escalator taking more of them into white-collar middle-class jobs than ever before. But more recently there has been a hollowing-out of the intermediate jobs which can be a stepping stone to those white-collar jobs, and the share of people aged 18–29 in lower-paying occupations has risen from 30 to 40 per cent.[12] That means that it is going to be harder for younger generations to achieve social mobility on the scale enjoyed by the Boomers.

There is a further effect which follows from the arithmetic of what has happened. Social mobility means moving up and moving down as well. When there were so many in working-class jobs and so few in white-collar jobs, most movement was up. But now there are many more parents in white-collar jobs who face the risk of their children going down the escalator. Between 1946 and 1980–4, the proportion of men originating in social classes 1 and 2 tripled from 13 per cent to 39 per cent, and the proportion originating in social classes 6 and 7 halved from 54 per cent to 26 per cent.[13] Younger generations are now in an environment where the risks of downward social mobility are greater. And that is what has been happening. 'While men in the 1946 birth cohort were at age 27 about twice as likely, and at age 38 almost three times more likely, to have experienced upward rather than downward mobility... for men in the 1980–4 cohort at around 27 the chances of having been upwardly or downwardly mobile are more or less equal.'[14] This is a big shift in the experience of social mobility for different generations. And it helps explain the intensifying parental arms race of investment in children's education.

Access to the leading white-collar jobs in the professions is itself becoming harder for young people from less affluent backgrounds. Research for an official Panel on Fair Access to the Professions found that 'Younger professionals (born in 1970) typically grew up in a family with an income 27 per cent above the average family, compared with 17 per cent for today's older professionals (born in 1958).' Lawyers born in 1970 grew up in families 64 per cent above the average family's income; doctors 63 per cent; journalists 42 per cent; accountants 40 per cent; and bankers 32 per cent above average. These gaps are often far wider than they were only a decade or so earlier (for a fuller breakdown, see the endnote).[15]

There is one response to these worries about falling social mobility which is not talked about in polite society. It is a widely shared but unspoken belief about heredity. Let us put the argument starkly – it goes like this: In a flexible market economy bright people tend to earn more; they also tend to have bright kids who in turn earn more; so what the critics denounce as social immobility is really genuine meritocracy plus genetic inheritance. How do we know that we are not living in a genuinely open and meritocratic society with inheritance of ability?

The biologists reply to this with evidence about regression towards the mean: bright parents or tall parents tend to have children who are closer to average intelligence or average height. But smart parents can then invest in their less smart children so as to preserve the gains the parents have won. That is why if you are from a poor background you need an IQ 15 percentage points higher to succeed.[16]

That still does not rule out a meritocratic explanation of the decline in mobility between 1958 and 1970. What if society got better at sorting us by our intelligence, and as this was partly hereditary we would get less mobility as a result? The evidence, however, is very clear – cognitive skills do not explain the fall. Our society did not spot or reward intelligence better and so inadvertently rewarded heredity as well. If anything, the relative importance of ability in predicting educational attainment actually declined.[17] Instead it was soft skills which mattered more.

Mobility declined because soft skills had a powerful double impact.[18] First, soft skills bypassed education to have a greater direct impact on your earnings – in a service economy, for example, being good at dealing with people might matter more. And second, softer skills like application became more important, compared with IQ, in predicting your educational attainment.

These softer skills are good qualities. They include empathy and emotional intelligence, but it is misleading to call them all soft. 'Grit' is a better name for the key attribute.[19] Michael Young did specifically include effort in his definition of merit. But he probably did not expect that effort would become more important relative to IQ. It means you study and stick at things even if you do not get good results straight away. It is about valuing the future and deferring gratification, as we saw in Chapter 7: 'Underachievement among American youth is often blamed on inadequate teachers, boring textbooks, and large class sizes. We suggest another reason for students falling short of their intellectual potential: their failure to exercise self-discipline.'[20] This is not hereditary – even though it is shaped by our experiences of family life as well as the world around us. And there is no evidence self-control has deteriorated – but it might be more important.

We have still, however, not quite got to the root of the popular belief in the inheritance of ability. Clearly genetic inheritance matters, but it may loom particularly large because our view of the world is shaped by our experience within our peer group; it takes a leap of imagination to think outside the group. Compare your height with that of your friends. It is very possible that the main explanation of the difference in height between you as individuals is genetic. But why are you taller than your parents were at the same age? Or people in a much poorer area? The explanation of that is not genetic; it is environmental. Imagine living in a community where the environment was so bad that it restricted growth. You would observe that, in general, taller parents had taller children and shorter parents had shorter children. Then your diet is transformed and people grow to be much taller as adults. You would still see directly the genetic influence on people's height, but everybody might be six inches taller and that would be explained by a change in the environment. This is the clue that helps us understand how a society can feel both competitive and meritocratic, yet also not be genuinely open and mobile.

If, for example, you are working in the City, it might look like a world of intense meritocratic competition with some inheritance of ability. But if you shift from the micro to the macro, the City may be part of a wider society which is far from open. Travelling the distance from being a child in East London to working in the City skyscrapers you saw from the school playground may require a journey of almost epic proportions. The competition for jobs in the professions is like English tennis: a competitive game, but largely one the middle classes play against each other.

Schools

If there is one institution which we expect to make that journey easier it is the school. Education is the single most important way in which society as a whole invests in the future. We hope we can transmit a culture, ways of thinking, and a body of knowledge to the next generation. It is not for individuals through personal experiment to discover a tiny fraction of the world's knowledge for themselves. Schools work best when both teachers and students are confronting a body of knowledge and thought which is far greater than any one individual. But this does not mean passivity and deference. It is so that each generation can then advance for itself. We are indeed dwarves standing on the shoulders of giants. Then we can draw on what Edmund Burke called the 'stock of wisdom' of the ages, regardless of your background or that of your parents.

Spreading social mobility is not the only task of schools, and they are not the only institution with this responsibility. But we do expect that social mobility should be one benefit of a strong education system. But a child from a modest background is like a salmon trying to get upstream against a raging torrent. At every stage it is tough. Indeed, we have seen how there has been no improvement in social mobility, apart from changes in social class because of changes in the structure of the economy. This suggests education has not delivered the politicians' hope of driving social mobility, apart from any role it has played in changing the shape of the economy. And the pressures on schools to do better actually increase the incentives for them to recruit the pupils who would perform best. There were objections to treating pupils as consumers of education but this missed the point – they became more like employees whose job was to boost the school's performance. The pupil premium was originally introduced by the coalition to encourage schools to recruit more students from poor backgrounds. But the pressures on schools to show good results meant that the prospect of a thousand pounds for such students was more than outweighed by the risk that they would underperform. Instead, the rationale of the pupil premium was changed to the argument that it cost more to educate children from tough backgrounds and it was important to shift resources to the schools which did this – the money was moving, not the students.

The optimists would argue however that education really did change the structure of the economy even though it did not start like this after the War. The expansion of white-collar jobs in the 1950s and 1960s if anything preceded and was on a greater scale than educational expansion. John Goldthorpe points out that men getting to the managerial level of the salariat then were not well-qualified. (Two-fifths had no formal qualifications at all.) And of men in professions, only one-fifth had a degree. (This might actually be a reason for our economic underperformance then, of course.)

The Robbins expansion of higher education began in the 1960s so that more of the first surge of Boomers could go to university, and thereafter the number of graduates rose fast. That in turn led to further changes in occupational structures. Even if, initially, demand for people to fulfil managerial roles preceded supply, later it was increases in the supply that led to changes in the type of jobs available. The world of work was being redesigned around the Boomers and their educational achievements.

There is some recent evidence for this. Richard Blundell of the Institute for Fiscal Studies suggests that an increase in the number of graduates makes a more decentralized business structure possible.[21] The big expansion of higher education was associated with the surge of Boomers into the jobs market in the 1970s and 1980s. They were not tied to the old industries by apprenticeships and instead had the flexible cognitive skills necessary for the new service industries. They made Thatcherism possible.

We might hope this effect is not over and we can continue to find ways in which our labour market can absorb highly educated people. As one example, we only spend about 1.7 per cent of our GDP on R&D compared with the government target of the internationally respectable figure of 2.4 per cent (and the 3 per cent typical of high-growth advanced economies).[22] Achieving any increase on those lines would require many more highly skilled employees and the continuing expansion of higher and further education to deliver them. That is the optimistic case. There is a bleaker view that education is an important defensive investment in a world where the risks of downward mobility are greater.

In fact, far from offsetting the advantages of children who are invested in by their parents in their early years, schooling seems to magnify these effects. There is a shocking destruction of talent as the cognitive skills of bright children from modest backgrounds steadily decline during their years at school, compared with more affluent children who start off with lower cognitive skills. Our education system is actually entrenching social advantage rather than spreading it.

The Millennium study of children born in 2000 shows children from poor backgrounds are already behind when they start school. And that is not because of some genetic inheritance; it is because they have been falling behind as soon as they come into contact with the outside world. Schools never manage to offset this. Even if you assume away that problem and take children of the same cognitive abilities at the age of 11, you then find that the children from more modest backgrounds are less likely to get to an academically good school than equally able children from a more affluent background.

One study analysed the likelihood of a child going to their nearest school depending on how good the school is and whether they are on free school meals. Children from poor families are more likely than average to end up at their local school if it is bad and less likely to end up there if it is good.[23] The Sutton Trust has assembled powerful evidence on the social background of children at the 200 English state schools which are best academically. Sadly it does look as if not many children from poorer families get to these schools. On average, 14 per cent of pupils are on free school meals across the country as a whole. In the areas where the 200 most academically successful schools are located, this falls to 12 per cent. But only 3 per cent of pupils in these schools are on free school meals, so while the standard of their education is excellent, it is not benefiting many poorer students.[24] Some say it is the abolition of grammar schools which explains what has been happening to social mobility. But the loss of grammar schools was just part of a deeper problem, as traditional pedagogy lost out to progressive teaching fads that let down a generation of children. Moreover, grammar schools are themselves very socially selective, just as other academically successful schools are, with few children from poor families going to them even if they have done well at school so far. The Sutton Trust report that 'in selective local authorities, 66% of children who achieve level 5 in both English and Maths at

Key Stage 2 who are not eligible for free school meals go to a grammar school compared with 40% of similarly high achieving children who are eligible for free school meals'.[25]

This dense interconnection of family investment and access to good schooling lies behind our low social mobility. The only way forward is for more children to have a chance of getting to good schools. That means increasing the number of good schools, as has happened most successfully in London. It is also why back in 2007 I originally proposed making it easier to create new schools. I argued that if we simply issued vouchers for an unreformed education system, that problem of social selection for school would be repeated in spades. It would be as if we were focusing on the details of exactly what free railway tickets we should hand out to people without tackling the problem that the trains which people want to take are full to bursting already, health and safety regulations make it very hard to add extra carriages, and planning rules obstruct the building of new track. We needed to make it easier to set up new schools if the school system was to provide fairer opportunities to the next generation. That, by and large, is what has happened.

The University Route – and How to Pay for It

There is a lively, high-minded debate about what schools are for, but the answer nowadays – certainly for England – is actually quite clear and straightforward. The purpose of schools is to get their students into a prestigious university. And if the school does not itself teach students of an age to get to university, the school's aim is to get them into the senior schools which in turn do get their students into university. This is how many parents assess schools. And it is how governments assess them too, as most of the indicators are indirectly about this (A-level grades) or even directly – the proportion of school students getting into a Russell Group university is now an official Department for Education performance metric. It means the educational pressures on young people now are much greater than for previous generations.

The educational arms race is the result of the rise of educational credentialism, with a degree required for many more jobs and the status of the university granting that degree counting more than ever. This arms race is particularly intense in the UK for historical reasons. Our system is susceptible to this kind of pressure because of its special features – and even educationalists do not always recognize how unusual the English system is. Centuries of an Oxbridge duopoly have given those universities a special prestige. There is no right to attend a local civic university if students get above a certain mark in a school leaving exam. This has long been the English system, but it was not so significant when many people did not go to university and many employers were downright suspicious of university graduates. But getting a university degree has become an increasingly important condition for getting a well-paid job in a profession or in a leading company.[26] It is a rite of passage taking you into the middle class.

The competition has to an extent been alleviated by the big increase in the number of university places – indeed universities are the part of the education system that has expanded most in the past 50 years. Robbins reported in 1963 that 5 per cent of young people were going to university; now 50 per cent of people have gone into higher education by the age of 30. At every stage of this growth the sceptics have tried to call a halt, but the remorseless urge for more education pushes it on further.

University is probably the stage of education that has made the most positive contribution to social mobility, because university is the only stage of education where children from poorer areas perform best.[27] A student from a state school is as likely to get a good degree as an advantaged student from a private school whose A-level grades are a bit higher.[28] It looks as if getting away from a poor neighbourhood to a residential university really does help those students. But when they go out into the labour market afterwards they cannot fully overcome their disadvantage, and for any given level of university degree they are likely to earn less than a more advantaged graduate. Moreover, only 20 per cent of young people from disadvantaged backgrounds go to university. That is better than the 10 per cent a decade ago but it is still way short of the 60 per cent of young people from advantaged backgrounds living in prosperous areas. If there is a problem of too many people going to university, it is found not in Hull or Havant but in Kensington and Winchester.

The fear was that fees of £9,000 would put off students from poor backgrounds. But, fortunately, the proportion of young people from disadvantaged backgrounds getting to university is going up. Nevertheless, that rise in fees in 2012 was very controversial and one of the most powerful objections was that we were letting down the younger generation by obliging them to pay fees when Boomers had a free education. I was regularly asked what as the author of *The Pinch* I thought of my policies as the universities minister. Weren't £9,000 fees one of the most egregious examples of the coalition government breaking the intergenerational contract? There are three reasons why I believe these fears are misplaced.

First, it is not a scheme in which students pay upfront for their university education. Young people are not paying. We, the generality of taxpayers, provide them with the money for their education. In fact it does not go through their hands at all – it is instead a model in which we provide the funds to the university and then the students pay back after they graduate. And it is not a commercial debt like a mortgage or an overdraft. Instead they pay back through PAYE at a rate of 9 per cent above a high threshold – such as the £25,000 set by Theresa May when she was prime minister. Worried parents would say to me that it was going to affect their child's ability to take out a mortgage and so would stop them getting on to the housing ladder. But the Council of Mortgage Lenders understand it is not like that at all. It is not a conventional debt but a fixed outgoing, and quite a modest one – if a graduate is earning £30,000 a year then with a threshold of £25,000 she will be paying back 9 per cent of £5,000 or £450 per annum which is £37.50 a month. This low rate spreads the repayments over a working life rather than front-loading them on young people when they are starting off in their careers.

Second, there are still several ways in which the generality of taxpayers across the generations contribute to the cost of higher education. Taxpayers write off the repayments that are not collected from graduates who for whatever reason have low-paid jobs and do not pay back in full – with the exact amount of the write-offs depending on where the repayment threshold is set. Then there are still direct grants to university for the extra costs of lab-based disciplines which require expensive kit – from medicine to engineering. We also used to provide means-tested maintenance grants to help low-income students with their living costs, until they were abolished in 2016. The system is sufficiently flexible that all these forms of taxpayer support can be adjusted according to exactly how much other generations wish to share the burden with cohorts of graduates. And putting money into these types of support is a better use of public money than a general subsidy to all students.

Nevertheless, it is still a scheme in which members of today's generation going to university are expected ultimately to pay towards their higher education. Even if it is less burdensome than many people fear, it is nevertheless a cost they face which previous generations did not. This is where the third reason comes in. When taxpayers met more of the costs of higher education, many fewer people went. Higher education has never been a priority for public spending, so as the numbers of young people wanting to go to university went up, controls were introduced on the number who could go to each university and the resource behind each student fell. But there are still very substantial gains both to individuals and to society from more people going to university. The edusceptics challenge this, and there are always some individuals for whom it is not suitable, but overall the returns are good. These returns are both individual and social, and both economic and non-economic.[29] One of the best things we can do for the younger generation is to ensure that more of them get more education. As the number of young people from disadvantaged groups lags behind, it is much better to grow the total rather than expecting them to displace students from more advantaged backgrounds. That really would be a fraught zero-sum game.

There is always a temptation for the incumbents to pull up the ladder after them – 30 per cent of graduates support a reduction in the number of university places compared with 11 per cent of those who are less-educated.[30] It is not very nice but it is understandable – a ruthless maximizing of advantage that involves trying to restrict the number of others who are able to benefit from higher education. Perhaps one of the reasons that the Boomers who bought their own houses then voted for planning restrictions to make it harder for the next generation to do the same was that this boosted house prices and made them richer. There is a similar approach to education: polls show it is graduates who are keenest to restrict the numbers going to university. Many parents keen for their own children to go to university believe it is other people's children who should not.

There is one historically disadvantaged group which is undoubtedly seizing the opportunity of higher education. Women are now significantly more likely to go to university than men. This is a fundamental shift from the world pre-Robbins, when men were more likely than women to attend. If we are to have a balanced scorecard of the experiences of successive generations, the extension of opportunities to women is one of the greatest advances enjoyed by younger generations. And it feeds through into pay.

During their twenties, the gender gap in median hourly earnings was 16 per cent for female Boomers, 9 per cent for women in Gen

X, and 5 per cent for Millennials. At age 30, however, progress has stalled: here the gap is 21 per cent for Boomers, 10 per cent for Gen X, and 9 per cent for Millennials.[31] So women still face a lifetime earnings penalty, associated with long-term costs from withdrawing from work for a time if they have children.

The classic route from A levels to university is familiar, straightforward, and well-signalled. It is now travelled by about 400,000 young people a year. It is like jumbo jets laden with passengers accelerating down a runway and taking off. It is a good mix of personal choice (what to study and where) and completely standardized processes from A levels and UCAS. And it works. It is the main form of managed transition to adulthood in the UK and indeed in most advanced Western countries. But what about those who don't take it? Are we offering a fair deal to those young people?

The Non-university Route

Higher education has superseded a recognized vocational route from apprentice to journeyman and then master of a craft. The Victorians developed a network of mechanics institutes and colleges financed by local employers which trained people for the local trades. Some of them are now thriving as universities. Our further education colleges, the Cinderellas of our education system, are also heirs to that tradition – which also depended on independent accreditation bodies such as the City and Guilds giving you a vocational qualification which employers would value and recognize. It was not perfect, but at least the routes were well understood and clearly marked. It was the world which my family came from, rooted in the different Birmingham trades of gun-barrel makers, glaziers, and silversmiths.

This all ties in with the picture of our country with which we started this book – no authority and no relative would allocate you to a job. Instead we had to look out to open institutions, and indeed we were leaders in open exams and meritocratic selection processes. This gave us what was widely admired as one of the Western world's more socially mobile societies. Those who look at things with a more sceptical eye might say we then used these institutions to protect the interests of their members and obstruct mobility and markets. But regardless of the history, the non-university route is not working as well as it ought now.

One conventional explanation of what has gone wrong is low aspirations. This views the problem as young people themselves lacking ambition or drive and ending up hanging around on street corners. But there does not appear to have been any decline in ambition among young people. And so the problem may be the disengagement of adults from offering guidance for members of the next generation, leaving a young person with much less advice and mentoring than in the past – and just when the choices they have to make have become less straightforward.

A fascinating series of interviews with young people not in education, employment, or training showed that these young people had remarkably normal aspirations: a job, a home, a car, a family. They wanted conventional jobs such as chef, solicitor, holiday rep, bar worker, plumber, soldier, etc. But 'it was also clear that they did not have a planned trajectory for achieving those aspirations' and they were pessimistic about where they would be in 10 years' time. In the words of the researchers: 'The issue is perhaps less about raising aspirations, and more about providing the means to realise existing aspirations.'[32] Many young people believe in the light at the end of the tunnel, but they cannot find the tunnel.

Instead of giving adult guidance we leave our teenagers unusually dependent on their friends and peers, as we saw in the previous chapter. The influence of peers peaks at the age of 15 – and is greater in the UK than in most other advanced Western countries, where parents have more engagement with their teenaged children. We are close to the bottom of the league for the number of 15-year-old girls who find it easy to talk to their mother, but top of the league for the number of them who have three or more close friends.[33] Forty per cent of 13-year-old boys spend four or more evenings per week with friends, which is well above the international average of 29 per cent. The Netherlands ranks top for life satisfaction of 13- and 15-year-olds, perhaps because it is close to top of the league for ease of speaking with both mother and father.

What we might think of as the English school-to-job system worked because of its mechanisms for transferring knowledge, expertise, and advice down through the generations. Apprenticeships were a widespread and effective way of passing knowledge and skill from one generation to the next – the intergenerational contract in practice. Careers advisers in schools knew what was available and how to make your way through the system. Firms themselves took on young recruits for life and invested in them accordingly, steering a promising employee through night school and developing their career. It was not nepotistic but it was, in the best sense of the word, paternalistic. These sorts of mechanisms have broken down, but no modern equivalent has been put in their place. It has left adrift teenagers who do not necessarily want the conventional academic route.

Here are three things we can do for them.

One answer is to revitalize the apprenticeship. That is now underway. For many young people it was an alternative to the university route. My former constituency of Havant was on the fringes of Portsmouth, and for the post-War period the model was clear: straight after school the young men on the big local council estate went to work as an apprentice in Portsmouth dockyard. Some still do take that route. Engineering is one of the areas where apprenticeships still thrive: there were about 60,000 engineering and manufacturing apprenticeship starts in 2017–18.[34] That is fantastic. But it is less than 10 per cent of the annual flow of young people.

When people think of apprenticeships they often imagine a man in a brown coat like the one Ronnie Barker wears in the

'Four Candles' sketch. He has a pencil behind his ear and is explaining to a rather awkward youngster how to operate a lathe. It is one of the most powerful images of training, and one reason it is so powerful is that it is a great example of the contract between the generations. The older man (and it usually is a man) is passing on a lifetime's knowledge and experience. But there are not many apprenticeships like that now. Successive governments have tried to increase them but they always face the dilemma that there are not many of them that are defined rigorously in the traditional way, and to get more of them the definition has to be much wider. Less than half of apprenticeships are equivalent to A levels: the majority are GCSE-equivalent and in business sectors such as retail.

Classic industrial apprenticeships of the sort they still have in Germany depend on a structure of the economy which we do not have anymore. Germany has an unusually big manufacturing sector (over 20 per cent of GDP, rather than 10 per cent as in the UK). Moreover it has a much more regulated labour market, with many more trades protected behind licences to practise. (Calling yourself an electrician is unrestricted in the UK but highly controlled in Germany.) Instead of apprenticeships, liberal market economies such as the UK and US tend to have high levels of participation in higher education. They provide the broader cognitive skills that make it easier to move between jobs and sectors during a longer working life.

That is why a second option is to accept the reality that most young people aim to go on into higher education, probably at a university but possibly delivered at some other institution like a college in partnership with a university (68 per cent of English 14- to 19-year-olds are planning to go to university[35]). So that can also be a place where vocational training is delivered. Already, over 40 per cent of university students are doing degrees which are vocational – practical courses often required in order to get a licence to practise a profession or trade, such as nursing – or at least are associated with a right to join a professional body such as estate management. These courses do end with an honours degree, which enhances the sense that they are academic qualifications. English education qualifications are classified between different levels rather like a multi-storey car park, with A levels at level 3 and honours degrees at level 6. England tends to offer fewer level 4 and level 5 qualifications than other OECD countries, and it could be made easier to offer these in a university (or indeed elsewhere).

The third option is to fund FE (further education) colleges better so that they can deliver a wider range of recognized qualifications. One way to finance this would be to extend the entitlement to the loans scheme to these qualifications too. But the problem is that the jobs they lead to are not necessarily well-paid, so they do not score well on repayment. An alternative would be to have a universal system of grants, but then we are also paying grants to undergraduates, many of whom could have repaid a loan. So it looks as if instead there has to be a mixed system, with increased public spending to fund grants to FE colleges to deliver these sorts of courses. That would be a good public investment in young people, whereas for university there is a viable graduate repayment system.

These options can complement each other and they would all have to be supplemented by something else – more support for more education and training during a longer working life.

Lifelong Learning and Who Gets Trained

The next chapter will show how pay has underperformed. One reason for this is that it looks as if younger people are stuck in low-paid occupations. This problem has been exacerbated by the crash. Pay is also underperforming because the rate of increase of educational qualifications has slowed down. On top of this there has been a big fall in employers' willingness to fund further education and training for their employees. All this suggests we cannot just boost educational opportunities first time round – we need to carry on investing.

Education is not just for children and young people. Even if things don't work out at school there should always be a second chance. There is a particularly bleak neurological determinism which says the only way our intellectual capacity can go is down. We used to believe that we were born with a fixed number of brain cells – of which many thousands were supposed to be killed with every glass of whisky. But now we know that our brains can grow and regrow – what they call neurogenesis.[36] A leading researcher is optimistic: 'Research on neural plasticity suggests that the brain is well set up for life-long learning and adaptation to the environment, and that educational rehabilitation in adulthood is possible and well worth investment.'[37]

We can perhaps draw some encouragement from the London taxi driver. Their hippocampus – the enlarged section of the brain which is necessary for navigation – has gone into popular mythology. London taxi drivers were not all born with brains like that. They developed that way in response to need and opportunity.

Stanley Baldwin, who was actually expelled from school, had his own rather quirky explanation of this capacity to carry on learning: 'the English schoolboy, for his eternal salvation, is impervious to the receipt of learning, and by that means preserves his mental faculties further into middle age and old age than he otherwise would (and I may add that I attribute the possession of such faculties as I have to the fact that I did not overstrain them in youth)'.[38]

One bold experiment to promote adult learning was the individual learning account, introduced by David Blunkett. It was weakly regulated and fraud killed it, so any funding would have to go towards a course at a recognized education institution or training provider. But the basic concept was a good one. Imagine a pot of money made available after education and training, to help increase your education and skills. It could help mothers in particular to overcome barriers to resuming their careers if they have taken time out of the jobs market while their children were young. Education would no longer just precede a job, a home, and a family but be intermingled with them. And that is the stage of our lives to which we now turn.

11

HOUSES AND JOBS: GENERATION CRUNCH

Modern Life is So Slow

Stanley Kubrick's film *A Clockwork Orange*, based on the novel by Anthony Burgess, remains one of the most powerful accounts of a nihilistic youth culture. We follow the exploits of a gang led by Alex (Malcolm McDowell in the film) as they attack, steal, and rape, to the music of Beethoven's Ninth Symphony. It has everything about youth culture which so shocks adults – random violence, an outlandish dress code, an exclusive language of its own, and a predatory attitude to women. The film generated great controversy when it came out in 1971. It still shocks today.

At the time all the attention was on the portrayal of the amoral behaviour by the gang. There was surprisingly little discussion of the crucial dilemma which both Anthony Burgess and Stanley Kubrick faced – how should it end? What was to happen to these 20-year-olds? We might easily assume they would turn out to be criminals and social outcasts for the rest of their lives. But there are fewer 50-year-old tearaways than 20-year-olds. Somehow young people make the transition to adulthood. Even if the clothes and hairstyle have not changed, we know when we see a 50-year-old dressed up like a Hells Angel at a motorway service station today, his wife riding with him and a packed lunch in his pannier, that they are about as likely to beat us up with a bike chain as is the elderly couple in their caravanette parked alongside.

Stanley Kubrick based the film on the American edition of the novel, which ends with the bleak assumption that the cycle of violence and exclusion from society will carry on indefinitely. But the original British edition of the novel had a further chapter, which showed how one of the droogs from Alex's gang has married and rejoined mainstream society and persuades Alex to do the same. The American publisher removed this ending because it was too optimistic. Anthony Burgess deliberately planned this final chapter about commitment and coming to adulthood as number 21. The film is so bleak because it has no 21st – no transition to adulthood.

Shaping the route to adulthood is one of the most important tasks of any society. All of us have to navigate this life course, and the freedoms we enjoy in the West today make it more complicated. We cannot automatically expect to have got there by the age of 21 – though in 1962 when Anthony Burgess published his novel that might not have been so fanciful. (Since then, the research on delinquent young men has shown that the novelist's insight was right. The most important single factor in getting male delinquents to change their behaviour is their forming a stable relationship.) The fundamental transitions of the life course – from living in one's parents' home to forming a new household with a partner – have got longer, messier, and more expensive. And children can boomerang back to parents too. Then we blame them – the kidults who have not grown up – when it is us who have made the route to growing up to independence much harder.[1]

A group of American experts on social policy, from across the political spectrum, tried to reach a consensus on how young people in the US could avoid long-term welfare dependency. Their conclusion was that you needed to follow three rules: do not drop out of school; do not have a baby until you have a long-term partner; and get a job, any job – even if very low-paid – because at least it is a start.[2] If you followed these three maxims then you would be on your way to being an independent adult and most unlikely to end up trapped on welfare. This is easy to say but it can be a lot harder to do.

Choosing a career and getting a job, deciding where to live and getting a place of your own, forming a solid relationship and having a baby. These are the big decisions of life – what, where, and who. They don't always feel like decisions, but more like events and accidents. Even getting the order right can be a challenge. And the very idea of a right order can seem unrealistic – the middle-aged trying to impose suburban domesticity on rebellious youth.[3] But almost 80 per cent of young adults want to marry and have children.[4] We saw in the previous chapter that even young people who are not in education, employment, or training (NEETs) have mainstream aspirations for a job and a career. We might be shocked by drunken young men and, nowadays, women fighting in our high streets, but deep down most of them want a decent job, a place of their own, to be in a stable relationship, and to have children. One charity working with NEETs said a young man had confessed that his great ambition was to receive a utility bill addressed to him personally. That would mean he was an adult.[5]

We try to avoid confronting the full scale of Britain's housing policy disaster by persuading ourselves that young people do not wish to own a home anymore, but the evidence is overwhelming: 77 per cent of 18- to 40-year-olds (and 72 per cent of 18- to 24-year-olds) said that, longer term, they would prefer to own their own home, either outright or with a mortgage or loan. And they cite the classic reasons: 'Four in five (80%) felt that owning a property made it feel more like home, and three-quarters (75%) felt that it meant feeling more settled in an area... Just over two-thirds (69%) of respondents reported that owning their own home was essential to feeling that they had succeeded in life, and a slightly higher proportion (73%) said that owning their home had made or would make them feel grown up.' And when asked to rank the importance of home ownership against other key milestones such as getting married, having kids, and achieving career aims, 24 per cent put home ownership ahead of all the rest.[6] The trouble is that moving through these stages in the transition to adulthood can look to a 20-year-old as daunting as scaling Mount Everest.

Countries manage these transitions differently – which goes right back to the diversity of family structure we started with in Chapter 1. In parts of Europe, the welfare state does more and for longer. In Germany parents can receive child benefit for children (if they are in education) up to the age of 25.[7] And Scandinavian states offer more generous benefits for independent young adults. In Southern Europe it is the family which is expected to do more for longer. In Italy, for example, the legal responsibility of parents for their children carries on to 26, and 60 per cent of people aged 18–29 live with their parents – the so-called *bambiccioni* ('big babies').[8]

Our historic model is for young people to leave home quite soon and go out into the market economy. For many young people, the modern equivalent of that historic English transition to adulthood via an apprenticeship is to go away to university. This is a contrast with many other Western countries, where you are more likely to stay with your parents and go to the local university.

Such transitions are becoming more difficult in Britain. It is not all bad news – teenage parenthood is down and so is youth unemployment. But the big transitions to adulthood – owning your own home and getting a secure job – are tougher and more difficult. We will focus first on the challenge of getting a place of one's own. It is a key stage in the route to adulthood. It is also, alongside the pension, the biggest asset most of us ever own. So it shapes routes to adulthood as well as the distribution of assets across the generations. Then we will turn to jobs and pay, and see that making progress in a career is no more straightforward than home ownership.

Along the way we will tackle challenges to this line of argument. One is that it is the fault of young people themselves because they are feckless and self-indulgent compared with earlier generations, who had a rough-hewn prudence and self-discipline. A different objection is that the traditional routes to adulthood are actually just petit-bourgeois behaviour promoted in a particular post-War economic and social environment which has now gone, liberating many marginalized groups in the process. We cannot oblige young people to subscribe to the values of their parents, and there would be little human progress if we could. But we have seen that young people still aspire to homes and careers and we have made it harder to achieve that. Whatever one's view of the desirability of these changes, there is a common theme – younger people are bearing far more risk than they did in the past.

Housing

Home ownership is the most vivid example of the advantages enjoyed by the Baby Boomers compared with other generations. We saw in Chapter 4 that the Boomers achieved higher levels of home ownership than the Silent Generation who came before them and Generation X after them. The Millennials are doing even worse: today's young people are half as likely to own a home aged 30 as Baby Boomers at the same age. The chart on page 73 shows that at age 30 the home ownership rate was 40 per cent for the Silent Generation, 53 per cent for Baby Boomers, 44 per cent for Gen X and 28 per cent for Millennials. The peak rate for any age group ever is 77 per cent for Baby Boomers at age 67.[9] This post-Boomer decline in home ownership applies across all parts of the country and all income levels. Some other Western countries have lower levels of home ownership, but no other advanced country has seen home ownership reach such a high level and then shrink so fast.[10]

Figure 11: Generational home ownership rates by age-group of head of family[11]

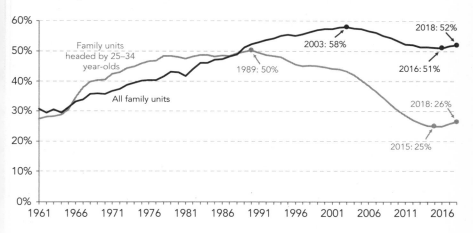

The chart above shows what has happened to families as a whole and to younger people. The proportion of families[12] owning their own home grew steadily up to 2003, when it reached a peak of 58 per cent. Within that, ownership by families with mortgages peaked in 1996, after which the growth was all in older people owning outright. Home ownership hit a low of about 50 per cent in 2016 and has been concentrating among older households, as ageing home-owning Baby Boomers replace Silent Generation tenants, while younger home ownership has declined. Since then there has been a slight recovery. Home ownership among 25- to 34-year-olds increased from a low of 25 per cent in 2016 to reach 26 per cent in 2018. This is good news, and the modest increase could go further – though the percentage will still stay below that of the Boomers.[13]

As home ownership declined, the alternative to it changed as well. Social housing (including council houses and housing associations) grew after the War, but then council house sales successfully gave the Silent Generation a late opportunity to become homeowners. However there was not much new building for social tenancy, and instead private renting has grown. Social housing peaked at 29 per cent of families in 1981 and is now down to 14 per cent. The private rented sector went to a low of 8 per cent in 1989 and is now up to 18 per cent.[14]

There had always been a period of early adulthood when successive generations stayed in flexible short-term private tenancies, which are well-suited to that stage of life. But now that stage lasts far longer, and indeed for many it may last their entire adult lives. This is a shift to a more precarious way of living, with greater risk being borne by younger families. The snapshot below shows how big the changes have been over 30 years.[15]

Figure 12: Housing tenure of 18–29 year olds, UK[16]

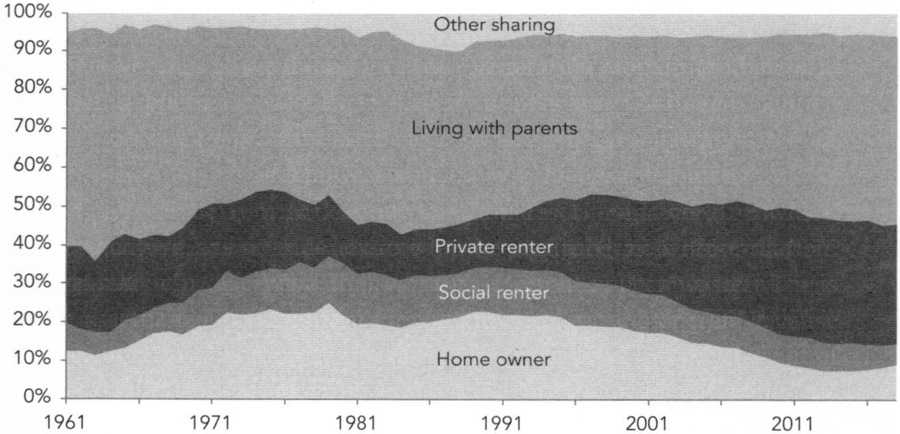

By the age of 30, only 1 in 10 Baby Boomers rented privately, compared with 2 in 10 of the Silent Generation and Generation X and 4 in 10 Millennials. This means that for the first time since the War there are now significant numbers of young families in the private rented sector. The number of households with children renting privately in England has close to tripled in the last 14 years, from 600,000 to 1.6 million; whereas the number of owner-occupied households with children has declined in the same period from 4.5 million to 3.8 million.[17] The ratio of owners to private renters with dependent children has therefore shifted from almost 8:1 to 2:1 just since the early noughties. This is a big change in the environment in which children are being raised.[18] These tenants have relatively weak rights and most can be asked to leave with two months' notice. This uncertainty is much more of an issue for a family when there is a child at a local school than for a young mobile individual. Private tenants are less tied to a local community and it is the form of tenure least likely to be on the electoral roll – down at 63 per cent registration. This says something about attitudes to voting, but also the barriers to registration for people moving around – either way, it is about transience.[19]

Whatever the form of housing, it has got more expensive. This cost presents itself in different ways. For owner-occupiers it is the high cost of a deposit. In Chapter 4 we saw the massive increase in the value of assets relative to GDP. This is not some esoteric point of economic theory. It becomes very real when one sees what it has done to the cost of a house relative to income, and this in turn shows up most vividly in the cost of a deposit of say 5 per cent of the value of the property relative to what people earn. It would have taken a typical family headed by someone aged 27–30 around three years to save for an average-sized deposit in the 1980s. Today it is 18 years.[20] That is a high barrier to entry even while interest rates are at historic lows, and the mortgage itself may be less of a burden once one has become a homeowner.

There is one way out of this trap: the bank of mum and dad. Family and friends contributed about £6bn to help two-thirds of home-buyers under 35 in 2017.[21] This is a massive voluntary transfer from the Boomers to their children. It is both a great example of solidarity across the generations and a threat to social mobility. We are slowly becoming a caste society, in which property ownership is hereditary. Back in the 1990s, a 30-year-old whose parents were property owners was twice as likely to be a homeowner than someone whose parents were not – and this is after stripping out other effects such as parental income or education. Now you are three times as likely to be a homeowner because your parents were.[22]

The value of a house also shows up in the rent that can be charged to earn a return on that asset. So rents are high relative to earnings as well. The chart below shows that more of a young person's income is going on housing costs than at any previous point – it is on average now a quarter of their income – one of the highest rates in Europe.[23] Baby Boomers did indeed have quite high housing costs if they started on the housing ladder at one of those mad times when inflation and interest rates were very high. But the rate of inflation was high as well, and so the real value of the mortgage debt rapidly eroded. There is no sign of the real size of a mortgage or the real cost of rents being eroded like that for today's young people. The Baby Boomers who are owner-occupiers with the mortgage paid off are now mostly insulated from these housing costs.

Figure 13: Proportion of income spent on housing costs by age and generation (UK)[24]

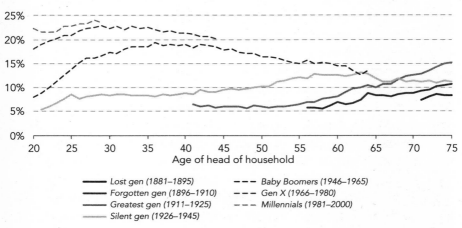

This increase in the cost of housing is not because the younger generation are getting better-located and more spacious housing. It is the opposite. Housing they can afford is further from where they work, so younger people are spending more time commuting – Millennials will spend 64 more hours (or well over a working week) commuting in the year they turn 40 than Boomers at the same age.[25] And the physical space which younger families occupy is actually falling. Each person now living in the private rented sector has on average eight square metres less space than in 1996. By contrast, owner-occupiers enjoy an extra four square metres.[26] As young households are more likely to be renters and owners are increasingly older households, this adds up to less space for young people and more for old people. And it means that as well as the bank of mum and dad there is another social phenomenon too – the warehouse of mum and dad, who keep the stuff for which the younger generation do not have enough space.

This all adds up to compelling evidence of housing failing to deliver our hope that younger generations will have better-quality lives than the generations before them. Instead they are spending more to occupy less space. They have much poorer prospects of becoming homeowners even though it is what many of them aspire to. In a pessimistic scenario, Millennials could end up with home ownership rates below 50 per cent at age 45, and in an optimistic scenario it would be just over 60 per cent compared with over 70 per cent of Baby Boomers. How have we let this happen? And is there any prospect of things improving?

Some of it is to do with changes in the way young people live their lives. More time in education delays entry to the labour market. The age at which they want to have children has increased. But these trends only explain about a third of the decline in home-ownership rates for young people since the mid-1980s. It is the failure to build enough housing which is key. Since the 1970s there have been about 160,000 new homes built each year in England, whereas we need to build about 225,000–275,000 to keep up with household growth and gradually tackle the backlog.[27] This long-term failure shows up in the UK having far fewer dwellings relative to its population than most other comparable countries. And we have gone backwards: in the peak year of 1998 there were 861 dwellings to every 1,000 families in England; today that figure stands at 825 dwellings.[28]

This decline reflects deep hostility to building more houses from people who already have one. It is a contrast to the 1950s and 1960s, when building 300,000 houses a year was a big political plus for the Conservatives. The older generation were willing to build on green fields to accommodate the Boomers, but then in turn occupants of those houses objected to house-building on a similar scale for the younger generation coming along behind. As an MP I would have a young couple coming to my constituency surgery: he might be a nurse and she would be working at Tesco. They were desperate for a house because they were still living in a spare room in his parents' house with their baby in a tiny cot at the foot of their bed. Then I would go to a meeting of a local residents' association full of decent people – governors of local schools and older people giving their time to local charities – who were nevertheless vociferously opposed to any new housing development in their area. Frustration at that gap in understanding the position of young people was one reason I wrote *The Pinch* in the first place. The good news is that attitudes are beginning to change. The pollsters ask the key question: Would you support more homes being built in your local area? Back in 2010 only 28 per cent agreed; in 2017 it was 55 per cent.[29] That shift in attitudes makes it possible to deliver a sustained effort to get more houses built. But even so, we are still behind the annual increase in demand – let alone catching up with the backlog.

It is not just a matter of supply. There are other problems which affect the cost of housing and hence demand. A combination of tax and regulation has favoured Baby Boomer possessors as against younger acquirers. The consumption of housing is under-taxed relative to other forms of consumption. There is no VAT on new house-building and no income tax on the value of the imputed rent we receive from occupying our homes (it seems far-fetched now but it was a feature of the British tax system until the 1960s). Council tax is charged at a much lower rate on high-value properties, with reduced rates for second homes. This tends to favour Baby Boomer owner-occupiers, while young renters in low-value properties pay council tax at a much higher rate relative to their property's value.

The regulatory regime has also favoured the Boomers both as young buyers and now as older borrowers. The regulation of lending was relaxed in the 1980s – just when the second peak of Baby Boomers were entering the housing market. It made it easier to get a loan of up to 100 per cent of the value of a property, and was a good way of shielding young buyers from what would otherwise have been increases in deposits as house prices rose. There was also greater use of interest-only mortgages. The Mortgage Market Review of 2014 moved in the opposite direction, however, making interest-only mortgages much harder to obtain. (Lenders have to be comfortable that the customer has a credible repayment strategy before providing an interest-only mortgage. It includes more stringent affordability checks and restrictions on lenders' average loan to value ratios.)

Back in the 1980s and 1990s, the median first-time buyer needed to find only 5 per cent of the purchase price for a deposit – now it is an average of 15 per cent.[30] Interest rates will rise and it is right to protect people from this future pressure, but regulation has gone too far. Meanwhile at the other end of the scale, for Boomers facing the prospect of repaying interest-only mortgages the regulatory barriers to lifetime mortgages have been removed.

This all adds up to a much tougher deal for today's young people getting started on the housing ladder than the two generations before them. It is not a direct conspiracy against them – though the opposition of Baby Boomers to new building is close to that. But it all adds up to a series of policies which could have been designed to make it harder for the younger generation even if that was not the deliberate intention. And it has happened because until recently we did not really focus on what this means for younger people. And when these effects became clear there was a significant shift in public attitudes towards more support for house-building.

There is one other reason why young people have done so badly in the housing market: it is because they have been doing badly in the jobs market. We saw in Chapter 4 how poorly their pay has performed. There is a widening gap between the price of the asset – the house – and the wage needed to pay for it. So now we must turn to the pay commanded by young people in their twenties, just when they are trying to get started on the housing ladder.

Pay

Younger generations have lower living standards because more of their income goes on housing costs than for previous generations. But that is only half the story. Housing is more expensive relative to their incomes not just because housing costs are high but also because their earnings are low. The chart below shows the pay of successive five-year cohorts. It is the sadly familiar pattern of increases in pay until the trend goes into reverse about 15 years ago, so now recent cohorts actually earn less in their twenties than previous cohorts did. The chart shows the effect of the 2008 crash, with earnings of all age groups drooping downwards over the past decade. But what makes it worse is that the real pay of the younger cohorts on the left of the chart is actually lower than their immediate predecessors. The two Millennial cohorts had similar earnings to the cohorts 15 years before them at the same age. This slowdown began before the crash.

Figure 14: Median real weekly employee pay by age and cohort: UK, 1975-2017[31]

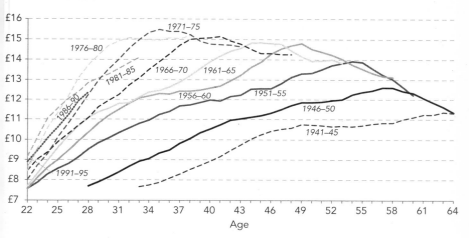

This feeds through into household incomes, though there are some favourable offsetting trends. The employment rate among young people is high. There are fewer workless households and more two-earner couples, which boosts average household incomes. Women's earnings are continuing to catch up with men's, as we saw in the previous chapter, though having kids does still knock back female lifetime earnings.[32] And one reason for this closing of the gender pay gap is how badly male earnings have done. Overall the picture is clear: the incomes of young households are falling further behind pensioner incomes, as the chart on page 90 showed.

Once again, the Boomers manage to be in the right place at the right time. When they were young, the incomes of young people were high relative to pensioners and the big social problem was pensioner poverty. Now that the Boomers are old, it is pensioners who are doing well and the big social problem is the low pay and incomes of young people.

The poor performance of young people in the jobs market is even more of a surprise than their difficulties in the housing market. If a country does not build enough homes for two decades then yes, prices rise, and it is the young people starting on the housing ladder who lose out. But it is even more unsettling that the economy can be growing and yet young people's pay can actually be falling in real terms – and this started even before the decade of economic underperformance since the crash.

There are three main explanations. First, human capital has not increased at the same rate as before, and this has fed through into lower productivity for younger workers. Second, young people today are more likely than previous generations to be working in the low-paid sectors of the economy. Third, they are unusually loyal to their employers and are failing to move on and up, which is how to boost your pay when you are in your twenties. We will look at these in turn and see there are close connections between them.

The starting point for explaining low pay is low human capital. The British labour market is very vulnerable to this, as we do poorly at training the 50 per cent who do not go on to higher education. We have for a long time scored quite badly on the OECD measure of skills of young workers. But we compensated for that by employers then investing in their own employees, so their skills grew. That process has now stopped working as it did because employers have cut back on spending on training their workers.[33] Governments have done the same – adult literacy and numeracy programmes have been cut despite their very high returns, in response to the widespread belief that it is the early years which matter despite the lack of reliable evidence of significant benefits from these interventions.[34] The one piece of good news is that the proportion of young people going to university continues to increase, though the rate of increase has fallen. But overall, as the table overleaf shows, improvements in human capital have slowed – especially for getting the crucial level 3 qualification.

Figure 15: Highest qualification held at age 25–28 by cohort: UK[35]

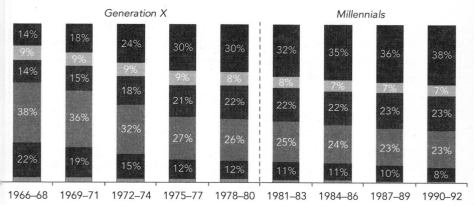

Generation X | Millennials

	1966–68	1969–71	1972–74	1975–77	1978–80	1981–83	1984–86	1987–89	1990–92
	14%	18%	24%	30%	30%	32%	35%	36%	38%
	9%	9%	9%	9%	8%	8%	7%	7%	7%
	14%	15%	18%	21%	22%	22%	22%	23%	23%
	38%	36%	32%	27%	26%	25%	24%	23%	23%
	22%	19%	15%	12%	12%	11%	11%	10%	8%

- Degree or higher
- Level 4/5 (Some higher education)
- Level 3 (A level equivalent)
- Level 2 (GCSE A*–C equivalent)
- Below GCSE/No qualifications
- Other

This trend is reinforced by changes in the business sectors in which young people work. They are heading into low-pay, low-skill, low-training jobs. Previous generations of young people, even if they had relatively low skills, moved into the growth sectors – manufacturing in the 1960s, financial services in the 1980s. Now they are concentrated in retail, hospitality, and social care – often providing services to affluent older people. There is a logic to that, given everything we have seen about the incomes of the older generation. But these are not sectors which are organized to offer great career opportunities. Meanwhile, it is older workers who are in the best sectors. Young workers pile into caring and leisure jobs (up 32 per cent and 19 per cent respectively from a decade earlier), whereas the fastest-growing occupational sectors for workers in their late fifties have been the three highest-paying.[36]

The obvious response of a young person in these circumstances should be to move out and move on. That is the way to better pay.

In 2018, the typical pay rise for someone who remained in their job was just 0.6 per cent, whereas job changers received a typical pay rise of 4.5 per cent.[37] But the rate of job moves among today's young workers is unusually low. And there has been a bigger fall in moves from one region to another, which is a particularly effective way of boosting earnings. One reason is that housing costs are now so high in the areas where pay is better that there is no boost to living standards. However if they do stay with their current employer, the rewards for loyalty have fallen and their pay increases are less than in the past.[38] Meanwhile more young people are in the gig economy with zero-hours contracts.[39] It is still very much a minority and such arrangements may suit some of them. But it does mean they are more exposed to risk – the ups and downs of customer demand which in the past were borne by the employer are now borne by the individual whose hours are highly sensitive to changes in flows of business.

Young people are having to bear more risk than previous generations. They are insecure private sector tenants. More of them are in defined contribution pension schemes in which they individually face investment and longevity risks which used to be covered by the employer. And some of them are bearing more risk in the labour market too. That adds up to a lot of risk and uncertainty to handle. So maybe they are at their limit, and when they do get a stable employment contract they hold on to it for dear life. They won't risk job and career moves which previous generations were up for. This is just a hypothesis and it has not yet been empirically tested, but it does make sense of the evidence we face.

There is another very different explanation however. It is one that appears plausible and indeed is widely believed. It links the problems which young people face in both the housing and the jobs market, and it offers the Boomers an alibi. The timing is right, because it comes into play a few years before the crash. Maybe young people have been hit by large-scale immigration.

Housing and Pay – Is Immigration the Problem?

Immigration affects different people in very different ways. It is not unambiguously and equally good for everyone. One could argue that it seems to work better for the Baby Boomers than it does for the younger generation coming on behind. If you are one of the British-born young workers facing more intense labour competition, it does not feel very beneficial for you. Would that smaller cohort of 20- to 30-year-olds who entered the British labour market in the last few years have enjoyed a tighter labour market with higher pay were it not for intense competition from a large influx of workers from abroad? Baby Boomers had tight immigration controls when they were entering the jobs market, but then relaxed them when they wanted more workers coming along behind. One of the leading experts on the economics of migration summarized the evidence in the subtitle of one of his articles: 'Affluent Americans gain; poor Americans lose'.[40] The economic logic is that more workers increases returns to capital and holds wages down so it rewards property owners. But as we saw when we considered Charles Goodhart's version of this argument in Chapter 4, it applies across the entire international open-trading system. Young British workers are competing with Chinese and Indian workers, regardless of whether they physically live in the UK or not. The important question is whether the products of their labour can be sold in the UK. The objection to free movement of labour is really an objection to free trade. That may be why economists have not been able to find a significant effect from migration on wages – the effect is from globalization itself.

Stephen Clarke of the Resolution Foundation shows that while the increase in inward migration coincided with the stagnation and then fall in real earnings, the effect of migration on pay was actually very small: a 'drag on hourly wages in skilled trades of £0.04p per annum'.[41] Putting this annual impact in context, it is clear that the effects on wages have been minimal, at least compared to other forces. For skilled trades there was a pay squeeze of 5.0 per cent in the period 2009–16, and of this 2.1 percentage points is migration. In caring and leisure there was a 9.7 per cent fall in real pay and 1.4 percentage points of this is migration.[42] Recent work by the Migration Advisory Committee, perhaps the most comprehensive analysis of migration impacts to date, finds that although there is evidence that migration may have had a negative impact on the wages of some British workers, the impacts are small. By contrast, the fall in the value of the pound after the EU referendum raised prices by around 2 per cent. They conclude that this has had a larger impact than the effect on wages of UK residents from all the EEA migration since 2004.[43] So there are effects gradually building up over time, but even so they are not the main explanation of what is going on. And we have already identified domestic reasons why wages should have underperformed without any impact specifically from migration.

Migration is however widely seen as the reason not just for low pay but also pressure on public services and on housing. Migrants can act as an alibi for the Boomers – on this basis the problems facing the younger generation are not directly caused by Boomer policies favouring older generations, but by large-scale migration. If Boomers have any responsibility it is indirect, through their role in the decisions to open Britain up to substantial migration.

And so migration is a popular all-purpose explanation for many social problems. Here is a personal example of how it works from my time as MP for Havant. A local Labour councillor brought to my constituency surgery a disabled woman who was having terrible problems getting any disability benefits. I was serving in the coalition Cabinet at the time, and the councillor expected me to have a tough time defending austerity. The meeting opened as the councillor hoped, but then my constituent really got going and said, 'I know why I can't get my benefits. It's because you're letting in all these migrants. They're claiming all the benefits and there's nothing left for people who have lived here all their life.'

I could have levelled with her and said that her problems with her benefits had little to do with migrants, who were far more likely to be taxpayers than benefit claimants. I could even have helped head off Brexit by adding that EU migrants have particularly high employment rates, whereas it is lower for migrants from the rest of the world as there tend to be more female non-workers.[44] But instead I took the easy way out and described what the coalition was doing to tighten up the immigration regime while the Labour councillor went rather quiet. I was complicit in a deceit. And I don't believe it was just me. I suspect there have been many thousands of these moments, when worries about the impact of austerity were diverted into an argument about migration. There is certainly a plausibility to the argument that more people means more pressure on public services, more need for housing, and more competition for jobs. In some ways it is the same as the assumption that a big generation is bound to have a tough deal when it has turned out to be the other way round.

This belief that migration is to blame is not just superficially plausible. It also helps divert the debate about what to do. One of the replies I get when I make the case for more house-building goes like this: 'I would agree with more house-building if I thought it was for our children. But it isn't for them. It is for the migrants who should never have been let in at all and now we're supposed to build on our green fields for them.' The belief that the problems our children face come from migration gets in the way of us discharging our obligations to them.

One of the flashpoints around immigration is its pressure on housing. In their study of social attitudes in the East End, Geoff Dench and Kate Gavron identified housing as one of the key sensitivities:

> There was yet another matter about which the white East End working class found itself baffled and resentful. We have already seen that many lost their traditional jobs, to be reduced again to the welfare dependency they believed

they had shaken off for ever, and that their children often failed to make the critical jump into the knowledge economy and the meritocratic society. On top of this, they found their traditional paths to housing blocked by new obstacles, which seemed to them systematically to favour the newcomers over themselves.[45]

One investigation concluded that net migration of 190,000 a year increased housing costs by 13 per cent over 20 years. Professor Stephen Nickell, one of our leading academic experts, forecast a decade ago that 'if the current rate of house building is sustained for the next 20 years, house prices will rise to 9.3 times average income if there is zero net migration. But if there is 190,000 net immigration each year, house prices will rise to 10.5 times average income – 13% higher than they would be with zero migration.'[46] Moreover, many immigrants are not eligible for social housing – at least not until they have been employed in the UK for a year.

It is the case that areas with lots of migrants can have very high housing costs, with London being the conspicuous example. But the direction of causation may not be migration pushing up housing costs – it might be high housing costs bringing in migrants. This reversal of the direction of causation is counter-intuitive but here is how it works.

Why does it seem easier to move to London from, say, Cracow, than from the rest of England (say, Liverpool)? How come so many immigrants go to London, yet that is where housing pressures are already so intense and housing is more expensive than in the rest of England and most of the rest of Europe? Greater London has almost half of all Britain's foreign migrants, and 38 per cent of London's population was born abroad.[47] London has the most expensive housing and the most immigrants. High house prices do not deter immigrants – they suck them in.

Imagine two people doing the same job in London. One has travelled from Poland and the other has come from Liverpool.

Imagine that they are each earning, say, £500 per week, which is slightly more than they would get working a 40-hour week on minimum wage. Each individual's basic living costs such as food, transport, and clothes add up to, say, £200 a week. The biggest item by far in their spending is housing. This is what makes the difference. Imagine there is a two-bedroom flat with a total rent of £400 a week. The Liverpudlian occupies one room, for which he pays a rent of £200 a week. This means that after his rent and his living costs he has got £100 left over. The second bedroom is occupied by the Pole, and he installs a bunk bed so that he can share the room with a friend. That means his rent is down to £100 a week. He has got £200 of disposable income left over. That is double the disposable income of the Liverpudlian.

The young man from Liverpool does not see why he should live in more cramped conditions than his family back in Liverpool. The Pole may have been in a cramped Soviet-period flat. He may be more willing to make sacrifices so that he can gain from the opportunities he has in London. His willingness to be under-housed gives him a labour market advantage, and it is greater if house prices are higher. (Of course, in different economic times it can be the other way round – *Auf Wiedersehen, Pet* was about seven British builders who went to West Germany in the 1980s to find work and had to live together in a cramped hut.)

There is something else the Pole can do with the money, and this is the biggest single reason why he is willing to be under-housed. He can send the money back home to his family. The Liverpudlian may wish to send some money back home as well – £50 in Liverpool buys a bit more than £50 in London, but not massively more. They are part of the same national pricing structure for many consumer goods. But £50 sent back home to Poland may be worth a lot more, especially when the pound was stronger relative to other currencies. It might keep elderly parents. It might help finance the purchase of a flat. We have to compare the combined earning power of money spent in London and Liverpool with the combined earning power of money spent in London and Poland. It is clearly worth more if it is divided between London and Poland, and because it is worth far more back in Poland the returns on the sacrifice of under-housing yourself in London are much greater. So it is not that our Liverpudlian is somehow a bad person compared to our Pole. It is that he cannot capture similar benefits for his family by under-housing himself in London. The paradox is that the larger the proportion of earnings consumed by housing costs, the greater the benefit of under-housing and the greater the price advantage of immigrant labour. And so it was not *despite* the high cost of housing that immigrants came to the house-price hotspots in Britain to make a living – it was *because* of them.

If you have been served at a bar by a man from Slovakia, had your house cleaned by a woman from Brazil, had your house repainted by a Polish decorator, or your children taught by an Australian, they probably have living arrangements which are far more cramped than anything a typical British barman or cleaner or builder would accept. And this is crucial to their economic advantage.

There is some evidence for this hypothesis from the figures for average household size. In 2006 the mean household size across the UK was 2.4 and the median was 2. But in households with a head from the EU accession countries it was a mean of 3.0 and median of 3. International migrants tend to live in larger households.

In 2015, the average household size in England if the HRP (household reference person) was born in the UK was 2.3 residents per household. The average household size if the HRP was born outside the EU was 3.0 residents per household, which is slightly higher than that for households where the HRP was EU-born (2.6 residents).

But people are not willing to accept under-housing for ever. It may be bearable if you are single and in your twenties or early thirties. You might be able to manage it if you are with a partner who is also working full-time. But it is much harder having a baby in such circumstances. And it is why one of the biggest uncertainties in the debate on immigration is whether or not immigrants will stay. If the aim is to send remittances back home and then to go back and raise a family there, then this surge in immigration may reverse itself. This seems unlikely on any scale, although there has been a noticeable decline in the numbers of EU migrants coming to the UK since the Brexit referendum – partly because they feel less welcome but also because the fall in the pound relative to the euro reduces the value of remittances.

Putting these effects together begins to reveal the pattern of population movement in Britain. Young immigrants are sucked into London using the competitive advantage they get from high house prices (60 per cent of all Londoners were aged 20–49, compared with only 49 per cent across the UK as a whole).[48] Couples with families move out from London to the areas fringing the M25 or beyond. And older people sell their houses to them as they downsize or move abroad.

Jack Rosenthal did a delightful comedy film in the 1980s called *The Chain*, tracing a set of property transactions on a single day across London. But nowadays the real chain stretches across Europe and beyond. It is a young Pole or Australian moving to London and willing to share cramped accommodation with a group of friends. It is a middle-aged couple moving out from London to a place where they may think the schools are better and houses are a bit cheaper. And it is an old person selling their house in order to downsize or move out to the Costa Brava or France. In 2017–18, 625,000 people immigrated to the UK and 351,000 emigrated.[49] And at the heart of this was a kind of convection effect, with people being sucked in at the bottom of the labour market and prosperous retirees emigrating at the top. This movement has reshaped the character of London.

Big cities such as London or New York are key in accepting migrants and integrating them. And it can create incredibly dynamic and creative areas with concentrations of young people. They move in because of the high house prices and their willingness to be under-housed. Because they are under-housed they do not stay in their accommodation. Instead they are out in pubs and clubs and so on. That in turn drives the dynamism of the street culture and the nightlife. At its extreme there is hot-bedding, with beds effectively allocated in 12-hour shifts. That feeds and makes the 24-hour city possible, with people willing to work at night and sleep in the daytime.

At its most successful, the sheer experience of living in one of the world's great cities can itself be integrating. Young people come together, new relationships are formed, and in London even if people are not sure that they are English they are sure that they are Londoners. We can observe similar effects but on a smaller scale in other great cities like Birmingham, Manchester, and Leeds. And if all of these immigrants are working and their partners are working too, then there is very likely to be a boost to GDP per capita. Of course it does not always work like this. It can create enormous social pressures, especially in battles over housing. But migration is still not the reason for the housing pressures. Quite simply, we have not built enough houses for the younger generation.

12

3G

Grandparents Matter

Human progress surged forward about 50,000 years ago. For the first time, we had a diversity of tools; we started fishing, cooking, drawing; we advanced out of Africa and across the globe. Although *Homo sapiens* had been around for 300,000 years or so, this – the Upper Palaeolithic Revolution – was nothing less than the start of human culture.

So what happened? The fossils left in the caves and encampments of our early ancestors are a crucial clue. They suggest that human development really took off when the ratio of old to young was transformed. The campsites of early *Homo sapiens* yield up many more jawbones of under-15s than over-30s. But about 50,000 years ago that ratio shifts dramatically so that there are twice as many jawbones for over-30s as for under-15s. A modest improvement in life expectancy meant a big increase in the chances of three generations living together – from dying at 30 with no grandchildren when your child is 15, to surviving to 35 when your child is 20 and your grandchild is 5. This was a massive change in society and is key to culture and civilization.[1]

So while the parents might be busy hunting and gathering, the children could learn from the grandparents. Useful knowledge embodied in a culture was being transmitted across three generations. The ability to pass on what you have learned, as a tradition, is what makes human progress possible. And that is what grandparents did.

Grandparents are the custodians of the intergenerational contract today as well. They can play an enormous role in the lives of their grandchildren, in terms of both time and money, and they are partners in three of the four contracts between the generations which we described in Chapter 5 (see page 113). Accounts of old age usually begin with worrying figures for dependency ratios. We can reverse that, and instead recognize the contribution that older people make to society through exchanges between the generations, captured beautifully by Michael Young and Peter Wilmott in their classic study, *Family and Kinship in East London*:

> And so it goes on – the daughter's labours are in a hundred little ways shared with the older woman whose days of child-bearing (but not of childrearing) are over. When the time comes for the mother to need assistance, the daughter reciprocates... by returning the care she has herself received.[2]

These exchanges flourished in the strong working-class neighbourhood Young and Wilmott studied, even though the three generations of a family did not necessarily live in the same house.

The classical tradition of sociology, from Durkheim to Parsons, assumed that family relations beyond the nuclear household would wither away. The small nuclear family of Britain and Northern Europe was the future, because it was most compatible with modern capitalism – Talcott Parsons argued, for example, that small nuclear families could move about more as part of a flexible labour market. And as the fertility rate has fallen and families break up, so average family size – measured as people physically living together – has indeed shrunk. Children have fewer siblings. They are even less likely to have sprawling networks of uncles and cousins, as we discussed in Chapter 1.

But something else has been happening too. Children are much more likely to have living grandparents, because life expectancy has improved faster than the age at which mothers give birth. As a result the family has changed its shape, and far from withering away it has become, if anything, more significant. A 15-year-old born in 1910 would typically have one grandparent alive, while a 15-year-old born in 1990 would on average have 2.5 grandparents alive.[3] We have already seen that the amount of time devoted by parents to their children has increased but it also looks as if the time devoted by grandparents to childcare is rising fast – up from 6.1 million hours to 9.2 million hours from 2009 to 2013 in the UK, increasing the weekly average from 5.2 to 8 hours.[4]

At the same time there has been a decline in intergenerational mixing outside the family and the formal structure of the school. Teenagers and adults under 34 have less than half the amount of intergenerational contact outside the family that would be expected given the demographic mix of the areas in which they live.[5] So families have shifted from broad horizontal networks of siblings and cousins to tall thin beanpoles linking generations.[6] This vertical intergenerational family has become more important as society overall has become more horizontally segregated by age.

One way to offset this is initiatives to promote intergenerational mixing, such as linking primary schools and nurseries with old people's homes. The media coverage of such initiatives tends to be on the benefits for old people but Channel Four's *Old People's Home for 4 Year Olds* focuses more on the kids, and as well as being really rather uplifting it shows substantial progress. The children get meaningful play and a reading buddy. They also have to adjust their behaviour for someone very different from them, and their social and emotional development is enhanced as a result. Old people get exercise, reasons to be alert, and a boost to their sense of well-being.[7]

Other initiatives promote links between young adults and old people. Nesta funds intergenerational projects which link up young professionals (with many connections but no deep roots in an area) and older residents (who have deep roots but fewer connections). The evaluation of these projects showed that 76 per cent of older neighbours felt less isolated and 98 per cent of young people said they felt closer to the community.[8] GoodGym sets young people the mission of running to an older person's house to join other runners in some physically demanding household chores or working in the garden, after which they run home. It gives exercise a purpose and once again bridges the gaps between the generations. And Homeshare UK links older people living on their own who need some help and have a spare room with younger people who need a place to live and can commit some hours a week to help with the shopping or gardening.

These are valuable initiatives to overcome the gaps between the generations, albeit very limited in Britain at present. And they are examples of the intergenerational contract at its most direct and practical. Every nursery, school, and university should aim to have a link to a care home, and every care home should link to a place for young people.[9] There is also a plausible argument that age diversity, just like other forms of diversity, is good for the performance of businesses and organizations. But it is not always like this. One study found that where there was a large age gap between younger managers and older workers, the employee 'tended to report more negative emotions, such as anger or fear'.[10] Companies can however boost productivity by creating environments that enable older workers to continue to work productively – floors easier on the joints, easy-to-use magnifying glasses – as BMW did very successfully at its Bavarian plant.[11]

Grandparents are the new housewives. One survey asked parents of young children about who had helped with childcare in the past week. A quarter had been helped by a grandparent as against 10 per cent by a friend or neighbour and 8 per cent by a day nursery.[12] Grandparents had helped 45 per cent of employed mothers with childcare as against 37 per cent who had used formal providers.[13] According to a separate, later survey, two-thirds of grandparents claim to provide at least some informal childcare for their grandchildren; 19 per cent of grandmothers and 14 per cent of grandfathers provide 10 or more hours of childcare; and 16 per cent of school-age children are cared for by grandparents during school holidays.[14] Estimates of the value of the childcare provided by grandparents range from £3.9bn to £50bn.[15] That may be one reason why now we say, 'Darling, let's have babies while our parents are young enough to look after them.' And those ethnic minorities with different family traditions do also have intergenerational living – one in four Indian families live with the paternal grandparents.[16]

The early Boomers were such young parents in the 1960s that they became unusually young grandparents. Thus the proportion of grandparents in the population is higher: more than half of the British population are now grandparents by the age of 54.[17] The average number of grandchildren they have is lower, which may be a reason for more engagement with their grandchildren – 58 per cent of grandparents describe themselves as friend/confidant to their grandchildren.[18] As women live longer than men and as wives tend to be younger than husbands, the grandparent the child is likeliest to get to know is the maternal grandmother. So maternal grandmothers make up 35 per cent of the living grandparents of 10- to 19-year-olds, and over 50 per cent of the living grandparents of grown-up grandchildren.[19] This may be significant in giving them an important role as custodians of the intergenerational contract – both contributing most to it and then benefiting from it. They can be a source of advice for teenagers when communication with their parents is weak. Maternal grandmothers are the older person who is by far the most likely to be cited by teenagers as a source of 'good advice' – 35 per cent of 11- to 16-year-olds say they can share things with their mum's mum which they cannot talk to their parents about.[20]

The rise in the value of houses relative to earnings also matters because houses represent wealth which can be acquired by inheritance – or gift – from old people. We saw earlier that the economic significance of the assets owned by parents and grandparents has increased relative to earnings. There is also evidence from surveys of substantial financial transfers between living generations: 16 per cent of grandparents in their sixties and one-third of grandparents in their seventies provide financial support to their grandchildren.[21] Twelve per cent of grandparents estimate they have spent over £1,000 on their grandchildren in the past 12 months, and a further 17 per cent say they have spent between £500 and £1,000. That suggests a total of about £8bn a year going from grandparents to grandchildren.[22]

It is not just specifically to grandchildren. More than a third of British families are now receiving financial help from grandparents, and 37 per cent of parents said they relied on financial contributions from grandparents to cover living costs.[23] Evidence from the former East Germany shows the strength of these transfers. East German pensioners enjoyed the greatest gains in income immediately after unification. Their total pensions were still lower than in West Germany but the gap was smaller than for younger people in work. What did they do with this extra income? They transferred a lot to their middle-aged children: 31 per cent made transfers in one year, compared with 23 per cent in West Germany. Children aged 40–55 were the main recipients. The researchers who uncovered this effect concluded that 'part of the public transfers from the employed population to the elderly in the form of pensions are handed back by them to their family descendants'.[24]

This account might apply in the UK as well. While public policy may be shifting power and resources to the older generation, they are then using voluntary transfers to younger generations to offset this.[25] It might even be that the process starts with us devoting more time to our kids and so less time caring for our elderly parents, which causes the state to step in and deliver more services to older people. There is certainly an important change going on in the balance of different types of exchange – as we showed in Chapter 9.

Voluntary transfers of time and money from old to young are therefore increasing. This strengthening of ties between the generations within the family is in many ways a good thing, but there are downsides. More childcare provided by grandparents is for example linked to a greater risk of child obesity, confirming every parent's suspicion that grandparents are indeed softer about giving out sweets.[26] These financial transfers may bring power and influence as well: it is pay to play. But perhaps, even while taking the money, the children and grandchildren remain impervious to the values of older people and get their advice from elsewhere. One survey showed that 90 per cent of British grandchildren would rather turn to Google and Wikipedia for advice on simple household tasks than a living grandparent.[27]

These ties are a vivid example of that dilemma at the heart of modernity – to be rooted or mobile. We saw in the previous chapter that one reason for the low pay of young adults is that they stay put rather than move on and move up. And young people may be more reluctant to move to new jobs because of financial and practical dependence on older relatives nearby. Seven in 10 grandparents live within 10 miles of their grandchildren; 87 per cent of 6-year-olds have at least one grandparent living nearby.[28] When the bank of mum and dad help their adult children fund a house purchase, they try to influence location so it is nearer to them. This ties us to families more closely than before, even when we are no longer physically sharing the same house. Social mobility is weakened if the time and money provided by grandparents comes to matter so much. Stronger intergenerational connections mean the modern family is less able to fulfil the role in modern capitalism allocated to it by Talcott Parsons.

One hard-bitten analysis suggests this type of behaviour by the older generation means they are following the advice of an American bumper sticker: 'Be nice to your kids – they will choose your nursing home.' And it is very shrewd advice. Such exchanges between the generations are a good test of the account of the social contract in Chapter 5. A study by the Centre for Population Change at Southampton has looked at how the amount of informal care elderly parents get from their children is affected by the amount of support those parents provided to their children – notably financial support when those children were adults. If these intergenerational relations are purely altruistic, the amount of help the adult child received should be irrelevant to the help subsequently given to their elderly parent – or it could be that they believe in the intergenerational contract regardless of their own experience. But if it is an exchange relationship based on reciprocity, the amount of support received as a young adult should make a difference to their subsequent willingness to care for parents. The survey found widespread intergenerational support – 75 per cent of adult children had received help from their parents and 55 per cent were giving it. A lot of it was altruism but there was also a strong element of reciprocity on top. Among adult children who had received financial support from parents, 57 per cent of sons and 60 per cent of daughters provided support to their parents in later life, compared with 49 per cent of sons and 47 per cent of daughters who had not received such support. The odds of providing support to their parents for sons who had received support in terms of accommodation were 1.25 of the odds among sons who hadn't. Among daughters who had received help with childcare the odds of providing support to parents were 1.7 times higher than among daughters who hadn't. So reciprocity did matter, and it mattered most for daughters when their children, the third generation, were also involved, suggesting that is a particularly strong form of intergenerational contract.[29]

Three Ways of Ageing

You may be wondering how grandparents managed to contribute their share of these intergenerational exchanges in the past, when everyone died so much younger. We are told that the average life expectancy was only 30 in the Middle Ages and 40 in the nineteenth century, for example.[30] This suggests that there were not many old people around then. And with our patterns of late marriage and childbearing that means there would not have been many grandparents. If this is true it would raise serious questions about our whole account of the historic English family – why hang around not marrying and delaying having kids until your mid or late twenties if you are going to die by the time you are 40? Can we explain this puzzle?

The explanation is that conventional figures for life expectancy are deeply misleading and can easily lead us to misunderstand the relations between the generations. Contrary to the impression given by these familiar measures of life expectancy, older people have always been fundamental to communities – even primitive societies – and certainly in Britain throughout our recorded history. By the seventeenth century, 9 per cent of England's population was aged over 60.[31] That was probably the pattern for at least 500 years, with the exception of the demographic surge in the turbulent years of the nineteenth century when the proportion of older people may for a time have fallen to 7 per cent. (We saw in Chapter 1 that pre-industrial England had late marriage and a low birth rate, and that, unusually, the early stages of industrialization in Britain are associated with an increase in the birth rate.)[32]

We need to disentangle the different ways in which a society can grow older. It can happen in at least three different ways, each with very different economic and social implications. Take six people. One of them dies as a child aged five. One dies of TB aged 20. The third dies in an industrial accident aged 50. The remaining three work until they are 65 and die at the age of 75. That gives those six people an average life expectancy of 50 years. It is what Britain, and many other countries, used to be like. But the average life expectancy of 50 did not mean that there were very few old people. Average life expectancy was pulled down by the dismal attrition of death during childhood or early adulthood. Indeed, our illustrative figures would have been even more dramatic if we had counted deaths in very early infancy and used them to reduce the average even further. But once you were an adult you had a reasonable chance of getting through into your sixties, thus ensuring a good mix of generations. Given our pattern of late marriage and few children, England in particular would never have felt like a particularly young country. (One might even speculate that this high proportion of old people combined with a low birth rate may be a factor in our historic political stability.)

Medicine then improves so that fewer children die and we reduce the incidence of TB. Factories become safer as well. Now imagine that all six of the people in our illustration work until they are aged 65 and all die at the age of 75. Average life expectancy therefore rises from 50 to 75, but it is not the case that everyone used to die aged 50 and now does so aged 75. Instead of different people dying at different ages there is a much greater chance of getting through into old age and a much narrower bunching of the ages when people die. This is what the demographers call the rectangularization of life expectancy, because instead of a drooping curve of survivors to old age we all die at about the same age.

This is the first way of improving life expectancy. It does not produce lots of extra years of senility and decay. Most of the extra years added to life are years of working adulthood, giving if anything a boost to the economy. That form of improvement in life expectancy has now been almost exhausted – if everyone in Britain today made it to 65, life expectancy would only rise by a further one month. Because growing life expectancy in the twentieth century took the form of eliminating many of the causes of early death, the experts kept on predicting that the increase in life expectancy would slow down. What surprised them was that improvements in life expectancy then took a further, very different form.

Now, instead of everybody dying at say 75, most make it through to 80 instead, and then on to 85. It is this type of improvement in life expectancy, pushing out the boundary, that does indeed take the form of people who were already old – judging by the standards of their time – living to be even older. This is the much more exceptional achievement of raising life expectancy at the age of 65, which is the figure that has been rising, as the table below shows. However the table also shows that the increases are getting smaller. Indeed recently there has been a pause in improvements in life expectancy for people aged 65 and aged 80. This has happened in several Western countries. The UK had unusually big improvements in the first decade of the Millennium, followed by one of the bigger slowdowns – a 21 per cent improvement in mortality for men aged 80 and over between 2001 and 2011 was followed by a 2 per cent increase in the following six years.[33] One reason may be that we did badly in predicting the mutation of the flu virus and failed to defeat the A/H3N2 virus, so the winter flu vaccination programme was unusually ineffective. This led to a serious research effort to raise our game, and it looks as if the flu vaccine did much better in the winter of 2018–19 with a big fall in excess winter deaths, which may lead to an uptick in life expectancy.[34] But the Australian winter of 2019 saw a virulent new strain of flu which could then lead to another deterioration.

Another explanation is that many people have now given up smoking and this boost has weakened, or it could be that there are now diminishing returns to classic health programmes, and the next round of big increases will come from radical medical innovations such as cell therapies as we learn how to replace diseased cells. Then there is the science of life extension, and on the horizon is the bolder dream of transhumanism combining technology and biology massively to extend lifespan. It is associated with West Coast billionaires but could well enter the mainstream. In Chapter 4 we conducted the thought experiment of a pill extending life by 10 years. The table below shows that is almost what has been achieved since the Second World War. And I expect that future research will enable us to slow down the process of cell damage, which is what ageing is. These are exciting prospects, though of course they raise many deep ethical questions if expensive procedures are only available to the few.[35]

Table 27: Average cohort life expectancy at the age of 65[36]

	1950	1960	1970	1980	1990	2000	2010	2016
Male	11.4	11.5	12.0	13.4	15.6	18.0	19.7	20.5
Female	15.1	16.1	17.4	18.4	19.0	20.7	22.0	22.7

We might have thought we were genetically programmed to die at 75, but that now looks unlikely. To understand why there is no such genetic programme we have to go to the ingenious application of the insights of Malthus and Darwin by gerontologists such as Professor Tom Kirkwood. Malthus described a world in which nature has a tendency to what he regarded as overpopulation. Darwin discerned that while this might appear wasteful, it is actually a precondition for enabling evolution to operate because it means there is an intensely competitive environment – out of which the fittest can be selected and with many more tiny genetic experiments to choose from. In this environment you don't die of old age – you die of cold or starvation or from predators. This means in turn there is no selection for a longevity gene which, like a switch, would turn you off at a certain age. So there is not a natural age of death fixing our lifespan. That is why we can indeed imagine a world where we live far longer than we do today.

One way to track this sort of ageing is to say we are old when we have reached the age at which we have a 1 per cent chance of dying in the next year, and older age sets in when there is a 10 per cent chance of dying. In 1955, men had a 1 per cent chance of dying in the next year when they reached 52, whereas in 2015 men were 63 before they reached that risk. (It is the statistical background to that genre of magazine headlines such as '60 is the new 50!'.) And the age at which men have a 10 per cent chance of dying is up from 77 to 86. For women, the 1 per cent chance threshold has gone from 58 to 68 and the 10 per cent chance up from 80 to 88 over the same period. For classic mid-Boomer men born in 1955, the age when they get to a 10 per cent risk will be 91. A boy born in 2015 can expect to reach 75 before onset of later life, and 98 before older old age sets in.[37]

We fear these extra years will be years of morbidity and ill health. On this there is conflicting evidence from different countries, perhaps because there is no authoritative measure of good health, so a lot depends on self-reporting. But I'm one of the optimists and believe that by and large we die fitter: medical science is making progress in tackling the diseases of morbidity as well as mortality. The table below shows extraordinary progress over 20 years – especially if you are a woman. And a later analysis suggests that the extra years of good health have grown since then, at least in proportion to total life expectancy.[38] So it might be even better – as dementia rates are falling, for example. One reason for this particular improvement is that the incidence of dementia is lower among those with more education and also lower among those with lower cholesterol. As more people get more education and we get better at managing cholesterol, so dementia rates fall. Dementia itself also varies according to which generation you belong to.[39]

Table 28: Changes in healthy life expectancy (LE) at the age of 65 for males (M) and females (F) in years[40]

	M total LE	M healthy LE	F total LE	F healthy LE
1983	13.3	10.1	17.3	12.1
2003	16.5	12.5	19.4	14.4
Increase	3.2	2.4	2.1	2.3

The conventional wisdom is that people aged over 75 need a lot of healthcare. So if people live five years longer, the pessimists say, they are going to need five more years of expensive healthcare. But this is to misunderstand what is going on. (In fact, Professor Kirkwood has been systematically studying the quality of life of a socially representative group of over-85s. He found that 80 per cent of them needed little care and rated their quality of life as either good or excellent.)[41] Intensive healthcare is not delivered to people because they are aged 75; it is delivered to people because they are in the last year of their lives. One estimate is that – for people over the age of 65 – 60 per cent of medical costs are incurred in the last 12 months of life. As people live to be 80 instead of 75, they still need expensive healthcare but the healthcare will be needed in the last year, which is five years later than before. So on this model, rising life expectancy, even in the form of extra years of old age, delivers a short-term saving in healthcare costs as it delays the moment when people start needing expensive medical assistance.[42]

This second form of ageing can, other things being equal, change the ratio of over-60s to under-60s, but that is simply a numerical relationship. It is wrong to get into the mindset of regarding this as a 'dependency ratio'. There is no rule of God or man that says that people aged over 60 have to be dependent. In fact, the research with which we began this chapter took such a ratio and interpreted it the opposite way round – with an increase in the number of older people seen as crucial to human development. Older people do not just make a massive contribution to society; they can also continue making a direct measured economic contribution: 1.3 million people aged 65 and over are now in employment, up from just 0.5 million 15 years before.[43] Income from earnings is 7 per cent of the total income of single pensioners and 20 per cent for couples. (Though that includes couples where one adult is below pension age.)[44]

So far we have looked at two very different long-term trends, both of which can be regarded as a society ageing. What really adds the drama is the third form of population ageing – and it is what is going on now. It can happen alongside the other two trends, and it can offset them or enormously magnify them.

This third form of ageing is when the population ages because a big cohort works its way through society over time, like a pig swallowed by a python, and gets to the later stages of life. If it is followed by a younger cohort which is smaller, then society will age even without the other two effects we have just looked at. In fact, the average age of a country can rise without any change in an individual's life expectancy.

It is this form of population ageing which is now hitting us as the Baby Boomers reach pension age and beyond. Imagine a society with a steady birth rate where life expectancy is slowly rising because of the first two trends we identified – that sets the trend line. Then, on top of that, there is a boom in the birth rate followed by a bust. While the big cohort is young, the average age of that society is younger than it would otherwise have been. As the cohort grows old, society ages more rapidly than it otherwise would have. Then, when the large and small cohorts die out, it eventually gets back to its underlying trend in life expectancy. It enjoys a temporary tailwind of lots of younger workers lowering the median age and then a headwind as median age rises rapidly to reach the level which puts it back on trend. The table below shows how young Britain was in the 1970s and 1980s, and how rapidly it is growing older now.

Table 29: Median age of population[45]

1950	1955	1960	1965	1970	1975	1980	1985	1990	1995	2000	2005	2010	2015
34.9	35.1	35.6	35.1	34.2	34.0	34.4	35.4	35.8	36.5	37.6	38.7	39.6	40.2

As the cohort ahead of the Boomers is quite small, we had a couple of decades up to the early noughties with very little increase in the number of pensioners. In 2007 the women from the first peak of the baby boom reached the then pension age of 60, and in 2012 men reached their pension age of 65. That, incidentally, was the very year when the retirement age of 65 was finally removed. It is a case study in the political power of a big cohort. Meanwhile 2017 was the year of the 70th birthday of this large group of Boomers.

One way to respond to these ageing trends is to raise the pension age or the retirement age. These are often confused – and that is Beveridge's fault. He designed a social security system which stepped in when someone was not earning a wage. The pension was therefore a retirement pension, which you only received after you retired. This created an incentive for older people to stop work, as otherwise they lost some or all of their pension. That earnings rule was abolished in 1989 – the state pension ceased to be a retirement pension. But the concept of retirement survived in labour market legislation. Successive governments made it harder for employers to sack people but a crucial exemption from these protections was reaching the age of 65, after which you could be told to retire.

During the early days of the coalition, the government commissioned policy advice on how to cut back on employee rights. If that is your aim, the limited protections for over-65s were the model to aim for. But at the same time as the media were full of stories about the coalition deregulating the labour market, the first peak of the baby boom – the million babies born in 1947 – reached the retirement age of 65. They did not want to be compulsorily retired off, and with very little fuss or debate the retirement age was abolished. This meant that all the existing labour market protections were extended to over-65s. Some of the same newspapers which wanted to see the labour market deregulated also welcomed the extension of all these protections to over-65s. The interests of the 65-year-olds facing retirement trumped any ideological belief in deregulated labour markets. Now there is no remaining role for retirement age in public policy – a good thing, as there is no fixed amount of work to be done and getting rid of it boosts total employment.

Neville Chamberlain introduced in 1928 a single state pension available to men and women from the age of 65. (Beveridge added the retirement condition.) During the War a special married couple's allowance was introduced to incentivize second earners for the war effort, and in return the female pension age was reduced to 60. For the past 20 years, successive British governments have raised the female pension age – and at rather a fast pace for some women born in the early 1950s – so Boomers don't always get things their own way. Female pension once more matched that for men in 2018.

This was followed by a moment whose significance was that it went unnoticed. On 6 December 2018, men and women reaching the age of 65 should have started receiving their pension. But it did not happen. Instead, men and women born after 6 December 1953 received their pension on 6 March 2019. The male pension age is now rising for the first time since it was set in 1928, and female pension age is rising alongside it. They are going up by a month every two months and will get to 66 in 2020. The broad aim is that roughly about a third of adult life should potentially be in retirement, with changes limited to once per decade.[46] Another way of setting the pension age would be to set a certain number of years with a pension based on life expectancy. We are familiar with the RPI – X formula: this would be RIP – X.

Pensions

A pension is the intergenerational contract in its most explicit form. We might just think it is simply a matter of our own pension and our own savings, but that does not really capture what is going on. The bread which you might eat as a pensioner in 20 years' time does not yet exist. You cannot bake it now and store it for the future. Instead we need a way of registering our claim to bread and other resources in the future, when they will be produced by the younger generation.

A traditional way to do this is via the family, with working members of the family sharing their wages with elderly parents. In China there is still an expectation that a son will maintain his parents; a daughter's obligations are to her in-laws. This pension arrangement is why the one-child policy has led, via abortion and infanticide, to a massive surplus of 34 million more men than women. (China's high savings ratio is also partly families saving to pay the rapidly rising bride price for a wife.) If China had property rights and funded pensions, families' future incomes would not be so dependent on their children. An English parent amazed by the sheer hard work and commitment to education of the Chinese family at their local school, should remember that the origins of this behaviour lie in a system where your child – especially your son – is your pension. China's tiger mothers who focus on their child's education are investing in their pension scheme.

The English family has not traditionally functioned like the Chinese. Our unusually small families, with more limited obligations between the generations, may be one reason why financial products such as insurance and annuities flourished here. The historical evidence is that: 'By about 1600 it was possible to purchase a lifetime annuity in the marketplace for oneself and one's wife.'[47] We needed such financial instruments because we do not spread claims on future resources through extended families. Instead we make a claim on these resources through a pension fund, which might, for example, own shares in businesses and so take the value of some of the output as profit and dividends. This is of course generated by the younger generation.

Some of the output goes to shareholders such as pension funds, so they can pay out to their elderly members. One advantage of such a fund is that it is better able than national governments to take a stake in the production of workers in other countries with very different demographics from ours. Another way future pensioners can make a claim on resources is via the state. The government does not need to run an equity fund and collect the dividends, because it can tax the output of the next generation of workers and pass some of it on to the older generation. Either way, whether the money is being claimed via pension funds or taxes, the bread which is being baked by the working generation is ending up in the mouths of older people. And successive generations of workers accept it because they know their turn to be a recipient will come.

These promises can last a long time – in fact, pension promises are some of the most long-lasting we can make. The American Civil War veterans' pension fund made its last payment to a veteran's widow in 2001, almost 140 years after it was first set up in 1862. (She had married a veteran in the 1920s when he was very old and she was very young. Such marriages were quite widespread, and we might speculate on what was in it for both parties. In 2019 payments were still being made to Irene Triplett, the elderly daughter of a Civil War veteran who fathered her at the age of 83.)

We still tend to assume that old people are likely to be poor. But that has all changed. In 2010 the income of the typical pensioner actually overtook the typical family of working age after allowing for housing costs. Typical pensioner income is now £20 per week higher than non-pensioners, whereas in 2001 it was £70 per week lower. And the poorest working-age households now have lower incomes than the poorest pensioners. By 2016–17 poor working-age households (at the 20th percentile of the income distribution) were managing on £12,300, whereas similar poor pensioner households were on £14,500.[48] By 2021, post-crash per-person benefits will be 13 per cent higher for pensioners, but for families they will be down 9 per cent and for children down 15 per cent.[49] Now it is younger people who are more likely to be poor.[50] A big generation like the Boomers can gain: when they are of working age they pay low taxes for low pensions, and when they grow old they benefit from higher pensions paid for by higher taxes on the generations after them.

From free travel cards for the over-60s to free TV licences for the over-75s, public policy has been designed around the assumption that pensioners are more likely to be poor than the rest of us, but that is no longer the case and we must break free from this way of designing public policy. The most egregious example is the triple lock, which boosts state pensions by prices or earnings or 2.5 per cent – whichever is highest – while at the same time many benefits for working-age families are frozen in cash terms. Between 2010 and 2018, the value of state benefits per pensioner stayed constant in real terms, compared to a fall of 13 per cent in working-age and children's benefits per person.[51]

Now that earnings are growing and inflation is low, the triple lock is (for a time) less significant. One could just about argue that it was necessary, to reverse the long-term decline in the real value of the basic pension (even though pensioners had other sources of income as well). The state pension was 26 per cent of earnings in 1979, down to 16 per cent by 2010, and is now back up to 24 per cent.[52] But in that case, having reached this kind of level, the triple lock should be replaced by a link to earnings – perhaps with a temporary boost when earnings growth is low, which is unwound when they grow more rapidly.

The other case for the triple lock is that if the younger generation are patient they too will gain from it. This is like the intergenerational defence of fagging at Eton – you might not like being on the receiving end, but be patient and you will eventually be a beneficiary. We still have to decide if this scale of income shifting between different ages makes sense. Many young people think the state pension will not be around for them to enjoy, whereas on the evidence of the past few years it has a lot of life left in it – indeed, at over £100bn a year it is one-seventh of total public spending and substantially exceeds the value of the entire education budget. It is going to carry on for some time – but the question is at what scale.

Young generations were clearly the losers from the coalition government's big pension reform: the single-tier pension which replaced earnings-related supplements to the basic pension with a new higher-rate basic pension. The rights to higher earnings-linked pensions were protected for Boomers, but younger workers lost the increased claims they had already built up and will instead have to settle for the new single pension. The new system is cost-neutral over time, but only because the boost to today's pensioners who got a new single pension higher than their previous entitlement was paid for by younger workers getting less in future. By 2060 55 per cent of pensioners will be worse off as a result of the new system. It is a case study in using public policy to deliver an intergenerational transfer to the Boomers.[53]

There are different pension crises, depending on where you are looking from. The one which dominated the headlines was companies who made promises of pensions linked to earnings and payable to their retired employees above a fixed age, which have turned out to be far more expensive than they expected. As we saw in Chapter 4, these defined benefit (DB) pensions are very valuable and they have made a big contribution to the wealth of the Boomers, partly because of improvements to life expectancy. The classic response of a company to these costs and uncertainties has been to close its final salary pension scheme, protecting the rights of the Boomers who were in the scheme but depriving younger generations of access to such a generous promise in the future.

Younger generations are moved instead to a defined contribution (DC) scheme. Often these new schemes have much lower contributions. Total contributions average 21 per cent of earnings for DB with 16 per cent coming from the employer, but just 5 per cent contributions for DC with 2.9 per cent from the employer.[54] So it is much less likely that the younger employees will end up with the size of pension enjoyed by the generations ahead of them. But there are other crucial differences between these two types of pension which have profound effects on the distribution of resources between men and women and young and old.

In a DB scheme the employee and the employer pay in during the employee's working life, and when they retire they get a pension usually related to their final salary. This is financed out of the big shared pot which is the company pension scheme. They carry on getting this pension, possibly uprated by inflation, for the rest of their life. Their widow or widower has a continuing entitlement to half your pension as long as she or he survives. This is in effect the company acting as a mini welfare state. Its pension scheme is taking a risk on how long the employee and their partner will live. It is also promising to protect them from the uncertainties of inflation and the death of a partner.

The company could only afford to do this because the employer thought it would carry on as a big business. It is a good rule of thumb that companies with 'British' or 'Imperial' in their title tend to have a big pension problem. They assumed successive generations of younger workers would be paying contributions that kept the whole thing going – these company schemes were closer to a pay-as-you-go pension than they were willing to admit. They were usually set up with much less generous promises but successive governments legislated to increase inflation protection or the rights of widows – and above all to make these pension claims cast-iron property rights which companies had to meet. This turned what was an intergenerational risk-sharing scheme into a one-off special offer for the Boomers, who voted themselves all these extra protections which will never be repeated as they cost so much they brought the schemes down.

It now looks an extraordinary set of responsibilities for a company to bear, and only the public sector and a few very big corporations are willing to do so any longer. Even this type of generous arrangement has its losers as well as its gainers, at least in relative terms. Early leavers, for example, may not do very well. Another group who do relatively badly are those who may not expect to live for very long, having paid in a lot – such as smokers. But the biggest losers are the young workers in companies which used to offer such pensions but now are closed to them. They are working to generate revenues to plug deficits in schemes they won't even belong to.

We looked into this at the Resolution Foundation. Non-wage elements accounted for 13 per cent of total labour compensation in the year 2000 but rose to 17 per cent in 2007, peaking at 18 per cent in 2012 and then 17 per cent in 2016. Of the £37bn increase of non-wage compensation in 2016, £26bn was employer pension contributions – even while occupational scheme coverage was falling. (These were both increased 'normal' contributions and also 'special' contributions to plug historic deficits.) This reduced pay for employees in private-sector companies with DB schemes by £145–225 per year or about 0.2 per cent. The biggest effect is on young employees who have never been members of the scheme. Of the 10.9 million members of DB schemes, 40 per cent are already in retirement and just 1.6 per cent are under 30 and actively contributing.[55]

The Pensions Commission chaired by Adair Turner contributed enormously to pension reform in 2002–6, but did not propose ways in which these costs on DB pensions could be reduced to make them viable in the future, or how new hybrid schemes could be created. As a minimum these pensions should now be uprated by CPI not RPI, which would bring them in line with the authoritative measure of inflation and reduce their costs. Instead the focus was all on promoting DC saving instead. A defined contribution scheme is very different. You have a personal pot of pension saving. You build it up during your working life, usually with some contribution from your employer as well.

There are pros and cons to both forms of pension, but a shift from one to the other involves gainers and losers. We saw for example that a final salary pension is required by law to protect your spouse after you die with an entitlement to half your pension.

But there is no such requirement if you have a personal pension. Instead you have a choice. You do not now need to take out an annuity: if you do you can either buy an income just for yourself during the rest of your life or you can buy one for your possible future widow too. The choices men make – and it usually is men – are some of the best real-world evidence about the ability of the family to act as a mini welfare state. It makes uncomfortable reading: two-thirds of people in these circumstances opt for an annuity which just covers them and not their widow or widower too.[56]

The personal pension is likely to be small compared with what you could have built up in a traditional company scheme. That means losses for the younger generation, who are not going to build up a pension with anything like the value they would have had in the old company scheme. The gap between the pension of older employees and younger employees gets even wider.

Above all, the individual pension pot is bearing much more risk. Instead of a big ocean liner we are each in our own craft – and in such a small craft there might not even be room for one's own spouse. For some this is invigorating, free of messy and hidden redistribution. For others it means potential losses. The good news is that a lot of us at least have some DC pension provision because 10 million people have auto-enrolled. Auto-enrolment has almost doubled the participation of 22- to 29-year-olds in pension schemes from 36 per cent in 2011–12 to 72 per cent in 2015–16.[57] So the good news is coverage is wide, but the bad news is that it is shallow. Unless the amounts saved are boosted, one can see the shape of a future pensions crisis. It will come over the next decades, when people expect to retire and find that their new-style defined contribution is worth a pittance. They will refuse to leave or will demand something better. And this is when the real battle over resources begins.

But there is a mechanism here which governments can use in future to boost the value of pension savings – by for example boosting the Exchequer Contribution for the under-40s if they make matching increases in the amount they are saving.

There is one other way forward: a hybrid approach somewhere between the full-blown DB and the atomized risk-bearing DC. These are collective defined contribution (CDC) schemes, which have been developed for the Post Office. CDCs have fixed contribution rates from the employer and members of the scheme. Unlike pure DC, they pool investment and longevity risk between members. There is a target for what the employee will receive but it is not guaranteed. There is no compulsory annuity. It is trust-based like classic DB. There is a pension adjustment mechanism for all members – actives, deferred, and pensioners. A broad legislative framework is provided in the Pensions Schemes Act but as yet no regulations. Expert modelling by the Pensions Policy Institute shows that they can deliver a better return than DC (replacement rate of 27–30 per cent not 12–21 per cent). The big risk with them is intergenerational unfairness, if any adjustment is all borne by young workers and older pensioners are always protected – so clear rules need to be established to share the burden of making reductions if times are tough.[58]

Inheritance and Social Care

As the Boomers enter old age they hold more housing and pension wealth than any generation before them. One might hope this is what progress looks like and successive generations will be even richer. But the wealth enjoyed by the Boomers is unique, and generations after them are very unlikely to enjoy such gains. The underlying performance of the economy has not increased to match this increase in wealth, nor is it a reward for unusual amounts of saving: these are passive gains from restrictions on house-building, legislation to increase the value of the pensions promised to them, and quantitative easing after the crash. The overall value of the national wealth might even fall back from its peak of seven times the national income and be spread more evenly so it is never again concentrated so egregiously in the hands of one generation.

The question now is what the Boomers are going to do with this wealth as they age. And what about the younger generation waiting to inherit while facing higher taxes to fund the Boomers' pensions and health and social care? If the ageing Boomers do give some of their wealth to their children during their lives, will their children behave like Cordelia or like Goneril and Regan to their King Lear?

The Boomers might pass their wealth on to their children and grandchildren when they die. The total amount that is inherited each year is indeed growing. The real value of estates passing on death has more than doubled over the past 20 years from £38bn to £87bn, and will double again by 2035 when it is set to peak. The average inheritance per person per year has gone up from £470 to £910. A broadly stable 2.5 per cent of adults are inheriting each year. The average they inherit is up from £20,000 to £43,000. Two-thirds of money inherited goes direct from parents to their children.

Because home ownership was democratized so successfully for the Boomers and because housing is heritable, there is an optimistic view that this wave of inherited wealth is going to be spread more widely than ever before. Fifty-five per cent of the lowest income quintile of 20- to 35-year-olds have at least one parent with property wealth so can expect some inheritance to come. Although absolute per-sibling parental property wealth levels are 3.8 times as high for the highest income quintile of 20- to 35-year-olds, they are less unequal than incomes which are 6.6 times as high. Relative to income, inheritances are on average greatest for those with lowest incomes, though this is driven by a small minority of low-income households receiving substantial amounts. And it is still a lot less than richer families are going to inherit. The most affluent 40-to 59-year-olds inherited three times as much as the poorest did (£5,900 versus £2,400), and it is rich families who can afford to give away some of their money earlier. These patterns of inheritance also provide a vivid example of assortative mating. Those coupled adults under the age of 50 who expect not to get any inheritance are with partners who expect an average inheritance of £25,000. Those who expect to get an inheritance of £500,000 or more have partners with an inheritance expectation of £190,000.[59]

Inheritances are not growing as fast as they would be if they represented the full value of the surge in wealth belonging to old people. Chris Hammett of King's College London analysed the estates people leave.[60] He found they contain fewer houses than was expected. In the early 1970s, 140,000 properties a year were being left. We had high expectations of wealth cascading down the generations. Yet 40 years later 187,000 houses were being left in estates.[61] That is an increase but it is not as great as might have been expected given what has happened to wealth over the same period.

One possibility is therefore that we Boomers are instead spending our wealth on ourselves – what the financial services industry calls decumulation. It rests on the life-cycle model of personal spending (economists focus on the life cycle and sociologists focus on cohorts). It says we smooth our income across the life cycle, so first we build up our savings when we are most prosperous and then we run them down. (We are supposed to spend our last day sipping our last martini paid for with the last pound in our bank account as the mortgage on the house hits 100 per cent and we hit our credit card limit.) It is the economic theory behind the behaviour of the 60-somethings going bungee jumping in New Zealand paid for by the money the kids thought was going to be their inheritance. For some Boomers the whole of retirement becomes the holiday of a lifetime. This model of behaviour has a very simple explanation of inheritance – it is a mistake. The mistake is made because sadly we do not know quite when we will die, so we end up with surplus assets in case we live longer than we do. Inheritance is like the tiresome foreign banknotes left over at the end of an overseas holiday which we give to BA for charity.

One use of all this money might be to tax it to pay for the services such as the NHS which Boomers need. Taxing their wealth might be better all round than taxing the earnings of workers. But inheritance tax receipts are growing over the period 2006–7 to 2022–3 at less than a quarter as fast as inheritances themselves. They are now up to about 5 per cent of the value of estates but could fall again, so there is a case for reforming inheritance tax. At the moment it is a classic bad tax; at a high rate (40 per cent) above a very high threshold. It could be cut to a lower rate but over a wider range of inheritances. Australia provides interesting evidence of how much inheritance tax matters to old people and their children. When inheritance tax was cut after a fixed future date in Australia there was a fall in death rates, as sick old people held on until the new tax regime came into force. Tax affects behaviour so much it can even delay death.

Another explanation for where the wealth is going that is not inherited is that we are giving more away to our children and other good causes while we are alive. There is no tax on inter vivos transfers of up to £3,000 per beneficiary per annum, or gifts which are financed out of current income. Transfers are hard to tax and hard to measure but they are the economic reality behind, for example, the estimated £8bn of transfers from grandparents discussed earlier in the chapter. It is easier for more affluent couples to makes these kinds of transfers. At least they reach young people sooner. The most common single age at which people will inherit is 61; that is rather long to wait.

There is one other possibility, and it is the shadow hanging over this debate – funding social care. Old people may be holding on to their wealth in order to meet the costs of social care. For some this will end up as a heavy expense. Chris Hammett's research suggested that 30,000–50,000 properties every year are now being sold to pay for care. These are cases where the value of the inheritance is reduced because old people need the money themselves to pay for their own care. One estimate is that by 2025 about 12 per cent of the over-65s will be medium- or high-dependency.[62] More old people will need care at some point in their lives but, even so, many will not. So it is very wasteful to be saving for what is basically a risk against which we should insure. The trouble is that some old people cannot afford to insure, especially as the unlikely but high-cost scenario pushes up everyone's insurance costs. That is why thoughtful experts such as Kate Barker or Andrew Dilnot suggest a model with dual protection. First there is a cap on the maximum costs and individual pays – after say £150,000 of cost, public spending takes the burden (though housing assests would no longer be excluded from the means test for domiciliary care). Second they suggest that a basic amount of everyone's savings, such as £50,000, should be protected. With this cap and floor, individuals can either take the risk themselves or insure against it.

This would involve both more private spending and public spending on social care. The public spending cost could be £2bn or perhaps more – exactly the kind of thing which could be financed out of a reformed inheritance tax. If this were a trusted, stable, long-term solution it would lift a lot of anxiety from old people and might also reduce the need for their holding on to assets to cover this risk – assets which could instead be distributed to younger generations.

Ageing Better

The Boomers have accumulated extraordinary wealth. When challenged, Boomers justify it – as they justify all their actions – by arguing it is not luck or favourable public policy but a reward for virtue and prudence. The increase in the value of the house is because they spent hard-earned money on a conservatory, and their pension is worth so much because they worked so hard and saved so much. But the truth is that the assets they have accumulated are way ahead of any earnings or savings. This increases the strength of the claim that other generations have to be provided with opportunities to acquire wealth of their own. There is however another side of the case. Boomers are not bad people. They may have tilted the playing field in their own favour, but even so they are entitled to a decent life and a decent old age. And as increasing numbers face the prospect of a 100-year life, enhancing the quality of the last 40 years really matters.[63]

There is an opportunity for Boomers to age better than any generation before them, and it has three key elements. First, enjoying good health and good care when they need it. That means we must all accept taxes are going to have to increase to fund them as they get older. And we must keep on researching and tackling the threats they face – from Alzheimer's to the evolutionary adaptations of the flu virus. Second, they can look to financial security. The combination of funded pensions and generous state pensions offers that. Third, there is social engagement which makes life worthwhile, and often its most deeply satisfying form is when it is across the generations.

None of these three elements can be achieved without the support of younger generations coming after the Boomers. The Baby Boomers can expect everyone to support their health, security, and engagement. And the evidence is that young people do feel an obligation to the old. But in return the Boomers themselves have an obligation to use some of their own exceptional wealth to help meet their costs, rather than loading them on to less affluent generations behind them. And Boomers also have a reciprocal obligation to help younger generations enjoy the same kind of opportunities enjoyed by the Boomers themselves.

CONCLUSION

For me, *Blade Runner* used to be the film with the most powerful vision of the future. But now I think instead of two rather unlikely films set deep in rural France: *Jean de Florette* and its sequel, *Manon des Sources*. Since their release in the 1980s, these two films – based on the novels of Marcel Pagnol – have touched deep French fears about the prospects of the next generation.

Yves Montand plays the role of César Soubeyran, a prosperous farmer. He and his unappealing nephew Ugolin want to take over the neighbouring farm and its fields fed by a spring. They try to buy it but the old farmer refuses. When he dies it is taken over by a newcomer, Jean, acted by Gérard Depardieu. He struggles heroically to make the farm a success, but Soubeyran and Ugolin have secretly blocked up the spring on the farm. His increasingly desperate search for water ultimately results in his death.

Jean's daughter, Manon, discovers what Soubeyran and Ugolin have done and seeks revenge for her father's death. By the end of the film Ugolin has hanged himself and Soubeyran has the shock of discovering that Jean, the man he worked so assiduously to destroy, was actually his own son. Soubeyran had been determined to continue the male bloodline through his nephew. But eventually, as a result of his own actions, the family name is extinguished with the deaths of both his nephew and his son. He dies tortured by this knowledge.

The films raise deep questions about fairness across the generations. Even though Soubeyran wanted to help his nephew and pass on his wealth to the next generation, he conspired in blocking up the spring of future prosperity and thus destroyed the lives of both his heirs. It is a melodramatic version of the strangely mixed emotions of so many middle-aged parents today, who have achieved reasonable prosperity themselves but are increasingly anxious about how their own children can ever hope to achieve anything similar. No one can, of course, know how things will turn out. And the sheer dynamism of science and technology are the best single hope we have. But we cannot simply leave to modern science the responsibility for discharging our obligations to the future. The fabric tying the generations together is woven from many more strands than that.

There are two places above all where these obligations across the generations are discharged: the family and the nation state. We saw in Chapter 1 how there are strong connections between them, with family structure influencing both the shape of civil society and the structure of our economy. Both family and nation state are by and large hereditary. They are the remaining vertical links in a world where many more of our connections are horizontal – to people in our own age group.

Our fears about our society and the strains in our economy reflect a breakdown in the balance between the generations. The equilibrium is under threat from the Baby Boomers, not because of deliberate selfishness but because of their sheer demographic and economic power. Younger generations are losing out.

The relative size of different generations has a big impact. Our short account of post-War Britain in Chapter 3 showed how the surge of young people from the immediate post-War baby boom, pouring out into adulthood, helps us understand the permissive society of the 1960s. In the 1980s the arrival of a further wave of young workers from the second peak of the baby boom made the Thatcherite transformation of Britain possible, as there were new workers who were not tied to traditional jobs in traditional industries. So these twin peaks of the baby boom drove the twin social and economic revolutions of the 1960s and the 1980s. There are some who fear that society is on an irreversible process of atomization. We can be more optimistic when we understand that some of these changes are caused by transient and unusual demographic changes when countries are youthful – and we were exceptionally youthful in the period from the sixties to the eighties.

It used to be thought bad news to be a big generation, as you have tougher competition for limited resources. But the economic and cultural evidence in Chapter 4 showed that since the Second World War the reality has been the opposite: both in Britain and throughout the West, the big Boomer generation has done disproportionately well. They own more than half of Britain's £13tn of personal wealth. They have benefitted from previous house price booms and they are also the beneficiaries of generous company pension schemes. It is now much, much harder for the younger generation to get started on the housing ladder or to build up such a pension – the two main forms of personal wealth.

One objection to this argument is that younger generations are going to be a lot better off than us. If this is the case then why shouldn't we borrow money from their future? But our obligation to provide for future generations is not extinguished if we believe they are going to be richer than us. The Victorians left us fine public buildings and infrastructure such as railways which we still use today, despite their believing, rightly, that we would be better off than they were. Moreover, while our children and grandchildren will probably be better off than us, if we, in effect, borrow from them, then their prosperity will be blighted. And that is just what we have been doing. The Boomers have been pinching too big a share of the wealth and income being generated.

The massive rise in asset prices in the past 20 years made us all feel richer but it favoured the possessors. Thus there was a shift in wealth to the Baby Boomers, as the generation that owned the housing and pre-crisis pensions. But the Boomers converted a one-off surge in asset prices into higher incomes by borrowing against them. This delivered a temporary boost in living standards financed by a massive reduction in saving and imposed higher costs on the next generation, who have less to inherit. It will be the younger generation who pay the price.

The amounts we save and invest are the clearest single measure of how much we value the future. Britain's savings rate has for much of the past 30 years been one of the lowest in the Western world.[1] The personal sector is an important part of this total. One reason our banks were so vulnerable to the credit crunch which started the 2008 crash is that they had fewer savings deposits than in the past; instead they were raising funds by borrowing in the wholesale interbank market. These funds were therefore only supplied to our banks for short periods and had to be continuously re-borrowed. When they were no longer available, our banking system came close to collapse. We still need to boost personal saving.

Total physical investment in Britain is also low compared with other countries. We are not endowing future generations with the transport or energy infrastructure they need to be prosperous. Even when we do have physical assets they do not necessarily belong to us, as we have had to raise funds by selling our airports or electricity-generating capacity to foreign companies. Cross-border transactions are part of the modern global economy and they neither could nor should be stopped by government controls. But this sale of our assets is a result of fundamental imbalances – particularly a dependence on funds from abroad to finance our balance-of-payments deficit – which are now going to have to be addressed. Meanwhile successive generations are not going to be able to enjoy the benefits of an income from these assets. The output we produce in Britain will not necessarily yield revenues for British people.

The social contract is an important part of Western political thought and I believe it is really a contract between the generations. These intergenerational contracts are at the heart of the family and the welfare state. They depend on reciprocity, and we saw in Chapter 5 how advances in game theory and in understanding the evolution of human behaviour have helped us see how reciprocity sustains co-operative behaviour and gives people a sense of well-being. Mutual exchanges between the generations are particularly fruitful in strengthening civil society. Much of what we experience as social breakdown arises from the loss of trust between the generations.

This focus on generations is a strand of thought which begins with the first sociologist, Auguste Comte, and runs through to the great twentieth-century thinker Karl Mannheim, whose essay 'The Problem of Generations'[2] is about how the succession of different generations shapes modern life. His insight is that in pre-modern societies the vertical links of family and tribe are what matter. When a culture is stable, successive generations are indistinguishable. In the modern world the crucial ties are horizontal: you are linked to other members of your generation by the particular cultural, social, and economic experiences you share. This can weaken co-operation between the age groups, who regard each other as alien creatures.

Increasingly neighbourhoods and workplaces comprise people of the same age. When there are concentrations of very young people with very few adults, antisocial behaviour flourishes. We saw in Chapter 6 how this helps explain not just the instability of countries going through their demographic transition but also the troubles on our own housing estates. Indeed, we have managed on our tough estates to create environments with such large numbers of children relative to adults that demographically they are closer to developing countries at the start of their demographic transition – *Lord of the Flies* is all about what happens in the extreme case of when there are no adults at all.

One way to break out of these misunderstandings between the generations is to think of other generations as like one's own but at different stages of their lives. The fundamental process of moving through the life cycle gives life its rhythm – ask people about the events which have meant the most to them over the past year, the highs and the lows, and they won't talk about politics but rather a wedding, the death of a relative, or children's birthdays – events which mark the stages of the life cycle.

We may attach a lot of importance to future generations but conventional discount rates – the classic way economists measure value in the future – do not. They do not really attach much value to anything more than about a generation ahead. The environmental movement has led to new thinking about how we should value future generations. Chapter 7 investigated this issue and suggested a curving discount rate in the shape of a hyperbola, as a way of reconciling conventional economic analysis which values the short term with the need to attribute some value to the interests of our grandchildren. We may well be optimistic about our long-term prospects, especially given the extraordinary dynamism of modern science and technology. But there is a predictable and clear pinch point which appears to be most acute in the period 2030–50. Even if we do not care about future generations, most of us will be around then, when these pressures – notably, of course, climate change – are most intense. It is in our self-interest to tackle them. We just have to have the imagination to think of ourselves at different stages of the life cycle.

The world is no longer simply an America, with unlimited resources just waiting for our enterprise. We have, for example, been mining water without, as the accountants would say, properly allowing for the cost of depreciation; water stress could be a growing issue. It will be 2030 when demographic pressures are intense, as the Boomers age in the West and Asia and the youthful population surges in Africa. Demographic pressures, climate change, energy security, pressures on water and food supplies – all this adds up to a time of peril for humanity. It has rightly been called the 'long emergency'. Beyond these material issues, the challenge of conveying our culture from one generation to the next seems much harder with the decline of confidence in a cultural canon and the rise of militant Islam.

Our story in Chapter 8 of successive generations going through the life course provided an account of a lot of what government does. By and large the system takes money from middle-aged people and redistributes it to children and older people, not just through benefits but also in education and healthcare. This is rather like the redistribution that has traditionally been undertaken by the family and which to an extent still is. But as the family has shrunk, so the welfare state has found itself doing more. And the welfare state tends to focus principally on the older generation, to which we do of course have inescapable obligations, whereas historically the flow of resources in families from both parents and grandparents has been to the younger generation.

For many young people, negotiating the route from childhood to independence – getting started on the housing ladder, settling down, and having children – is very hard indeed. Twenty-somethings become trapped in a kind of semi-adulthood. For them modern life is not fast but actually very slow. The transitions into stable employment and a stable relationship take longer now than at any time since the War. This is easily misinterpreted by older generations as a rejection of these aspirations. Generally, it is not. The aspirations remain, but they are harder to achieve. It is this movement through the stages of the life course which we followed in the final four chapters. Instead of post-modern invented narratives, this is deeply rooted in the patterns of human experience.

The old generation gap – the mutual incomprehension of parents and children – is disappearing. The personal ties between parents and children are if anything stronger, but the economic gaps are getting wider and financial dependence lasts for longer. Parents may do their best for their own children but there is still the task of ensuring a fair deal for the younger generation as a whole. A good example is the extra time parents devote to their young children even while the quality of childhood is declining. The explanation of this paradox of extra parental time and poorer-quality childhood is that although parents are devoting more time to their own children, they have lost trust in other adults. They are anxious about the safety of public space and so are reluctant to let their children play freely. As a result our children are either inside in an unsupervised screen-based culture or they are outside and active but supervised. Free-range childhood has disappeared in a generation.

The growing significance of parents compared with other adults helps us to explain low social mobility in our country. The opportunities to break free from family influence are shockingly weak. The route from school to work is especially tricky for young people who do not have strong family backing. Getting a house of one's own is also far harder for the younger generation, unless of course they have access to the bank of mum and dad. The higher cost of housing for young people is in fact as heavy a burden as if the government had more than doubled the national debt in a decade and left the younger generation to pay it off with higher taxes. But a fall in house prices is not making it much easier for younger people to get on to the housing ladder, because of tight rules on access to credit.

We have focused on the obligations we have to younger generations. But intergenerational justice is a richer idea than that: it covers all stages of the life cycle and includes obligations to older people as well as the young and the middle-aged. In 2012, men from the first peak of the baby boom become pensioners, and the number of pensioners will surge over the next 20 years, partly dampened by increases in the pension age. The pensions crisis means that people who retire in 10 or 20 years with a personal pension will receive much less per year than someone with a traditional final salary pension. They may have to 'eat their house', which means there will be less for the next generation to inherit. Alternatively, they will vote for parties promising them higher state benefits and more spending on the NHS, financed by the younger generation.

The central argument in this book is that we are not attaching sufficient value to the claims of future generations. This is partly because a big disruptive generation of Baby Boomers has weakened many of the ties between the generations. But it is also an intellectual failure: we have not got a clear way of thinking about the rights of future generations. We are allowing one very big generation to break the intergenerational contract because we do not fully understand it. This is where politics comes in.

Politics can sometimes seem like a cacophony of conflicting opinions. Although politicians may appeal to ideology, most people are not particularly ideological, so it leaves them cold. Montaigne expressed the scepticism which many voters feel about such deductive politics: 'It seems to me that there is a great deal of self-love and arrogance in judging so highly of your opinions that you are obliged to disturb the public peace to establish them.'[3]

That is why I have been trying to go back to fundamental experiences – the pattern of our lives as we move through the different ages of the life cycle; the changing balance of the generations and the ties between them. This is an attempt to root politics in things which are natural and human. The family is key as it is the human universal but it also helps us to understand the distinctive traditions and practices of our own society.

At its best, government helps maintain the balance between the generations and helps shift resources between the different stages of the life cycle in a way that complements what families do. However, it can also allow itself to be captured by particular generational interests that exploit this power. The big age gap in the Brexit vote is the latest and most significant example of this. But this is not inevitable. Public policy can make a difference.

And that means politics – good politics. What are the underlying principles that should shape what a politician does? You might say that there aren't any shared principles because political argument is about the principles we disagree on, but that isn't the whole story. We should share a belief in the basic principles of a modern liberal democracy. Can we go beyond that? What is it that enables us to distinguish between a good politician – a statesman if you like – and a bad one who is just playing the game? Look at some of the obvious historical comparisons. Why is Pitt the Younger a greater figure than Walpole? Why is Attlee a greater figure than Wilson? Why is Thatcher a greater figure than Macmillan? Why is Churchill above all the rest? The explanation is surely that the great leaders did far more to shape the future of our country, even if it meant short-term sacrifices. Good politics is about a contract between the generations in which the interests of the present generation should not automatically come first.

One opinion survey showed that more than half of voters wanted political parties to follow policies which would do good in the long term, rather than for the next year or two. This was the highest level of approval for any party political characteristic, and much higher than the 13 per cent of people who would support a party for its ideological principles.[4] This means helping to sustain the family, where these obligations are discharged one by one. It also means ensuring that no one generation uses the state for its own interests. If being a good politician is to mean anything other than being technically accomplished, it has to mean valuing the future and maintaining the contract between the generations. This lies behind our instinctive judgement about the difference between a statesman and a mere politician. As Disraeli is supposed to have said, 'A politician thinks of the next election. A statesman thinks of the next generation.'[5]

Visionaries may hope that government will wither away. Edmund Burke replied to them in his *Reflections on the Revolution in France*, one of the classic conservative texts. He did not, as one might expect, justify government as a guarantor of order and security. Instead he positioned government as the custodian of the contract between the generations. It is a beautiful statement of the central theme of this book:

> Society is indeed a contract. Subordinate contracts for objects of mere occasional interest may be dissolved at pleasure – but the state ought not to be considered as nothing better than a partnership agreement in a trade of pepper and coffee, calico or tobacco, or some other such low concern, to be taken up for a little temporary interest, and to be dissolved by the fancy of the parties. It is to be looked on with other reverence; because it is not a partnership in things subservient only to the gross animal existence of a temporary and perishable nature. It is a partnership in all science; a partnership in all art; a partnership in every virtue, and in all perfection. As the ends of such a partnership cannot be obtained in many generations, it becomes a partnership not only between those who are living, but between those who are living, those who are dead, and those who are to be born.[6]

So here we are. We have appealed to a contract between the generations. We have explained how it rests on reciprocity and how this is the origin of our moral sense. We have shown how the Boomers have ended up with a large share of the national wealth and we have set out some of the economics behind this. We have tried to address the argument that future generations will be richer, arguing that this does not extinguish the obligation. And as there is a pinch point coming we cannot be so confident about their prosperity over the next few decades. We have offered a concession and proposed that even if we just think about the rest of our own lives there is still a problem we have to face. We have then expanded that argument by suggesting we think of other generations as being like us but at different stages of the life cycle. We have been flattered as good parents and then challenged to be better citizens. We have appealed to our sense of self-preservation by asking what future generations will do for us when we are old and must depend on them if we do not provide for them now. We have hoped for good politics – the statesmanship that comes from valuing the future. Is any further appeal left?

There remains the appeal of narrative, of tradition in its best and most sophisticated sense. We have already seen that the best way to learn responsibility and master oneself is to have a project for the future which gives purpose to one's behaviour in the present and makes sense of what was done in the past. That is what drives us to reduce public debt or preserve the environment or improve educational standards. And this ties together the arguments in this book. If we value the future then we can co-operate for the simple reason that we can value reciprocal benefits we hope to receive in the future. That makes reciprocity and co-operation possible. Vice versa, it is through our first experiences of such reciprocity that we can learn the value of future benefits. If someone, probably a parent, reciprocates, we begin to learn how our behaviour can bring future consequences, be they good or bad. It is hard to envisage the accumulation of social capital unless we value the future. The more we value the future, the wider the circle of co-operative reciprocal arrangements that become possible for us.

The problems of obesity or antisocial behaviour or credit card debt are not separate; they are all part of the same challenge of making self-control worthwhile. It can be done if we see what we do today as part of a story linking past, present, and future. That is what we can do in a family and in a nation and perhaps even globally. It is what T. S. Eliot described in his great essay, 'Tradition and the Individual Talent'. He was writing about the process of artistic creation but it also applies to our sense of who we are and what it means to inherit a tradition and pass it on:

the historical sense compels a man to write not merely with his own generation in his bones... No poet, no artist of any art, has his complete meaning alone. His significance, his appreciation is the appreciation of his relation to the dead poets and artists... He must be aware that the mind of Europe – the mind of his own country... is a mind which changes, and that this change is a development which abandons nothing en route... he is not likely to know what is to be done unless he lives in what is not merely the present, but the present moment of the past, unless he is conscious, not of what is dead, but of what is already living.[7]

Those statements are not just true for artists; they are true for all of us. The modern condition is supposed to be the search for meaning in a world where unreflective obligations to institutions or ways of doing things are eroded. The link between generations past, present, and future is a source of meaning which is as natural as could be. It is both cultural and economic, personal and ethical. We must understand and honour those ties which bind the generations.

EPILOGUE

POLICY AND POLITICS

Ten years on from the original publication of *The Pinch* we are still not delivering the promise that successive generations will be better off. There are qualifications, of course. This is about averages. Some older people endure with great forbearance lives in which they struggle in very tough circumstances. Some younger people enjoy surging prosperity. Meanwhile the wheels of modern capitalism continue to turn, with innovation, entrepreneurship, and new technology generating new products and services. But nevertheless there is overwhelming evidence that on key indicators of material well-being, younger generations are not enjoying the improvements which the Boomers enjoyed – and on some key measures they are actually going backwards:

- The incomes after housing costs of the Millennials are no better than Generation X before them, who in turn enjoyed nothing like the progress on incomes enjoyed by the Boomers over their predecessors.

- The assets of the Millennials are lower for longer: in particular, Millennials are only half as likely as Boomers to own a home by the age of 30.

- The Millennials live in less space, have longer commutes, and consume less relative to older generations.

This is not because of bad behaviour by young people. They are studying more, drinking less, consuming less, and sticking with their employers for longer. Nor are they just victims of brute luck. The surge in the value of pensions and houses and the changes in the distribution of benefits between different generations are the result of political decisions – making company pensions more generous, restricting planning permission for new houses, increasing benefits for pensioners and cutting them for families. These have had the effect of disadvantaging young people. As a result, we are failing to honour the promise of modern liberal market economies to successive generations. That is a worry which older generations share. Indeed I'm surprised that young people don't have more of a sense of grievance, given the way they are being treated.

That leaves two crucial questions. What can we actually do about it? And even if we come up with policies which would have an effect, are they politically possible?

We will look at these questions in turn. First, here is a policy agenda organized around four key themes: the future shape of the state and how we fund it; spreading property ownership; a better deal on education, pay, and productivity; and finally, boosting contact between the generations.

The Future Shape of the State

If we carry on as we are, we end up with a health and pensions state. The British state is already a very peculiar shape – like a body distorted by only exercising one set of muscles. When it comes to pensions and health it is a brash big ambitious state taking on public responsibilities which are, if anything, above the OECD average. It pays out pensions so high that even before private occupational pensions are included, very few pensioners are so poor they need means-tested social assistance. It also runs one of the Western world's biggest health systems, with a non-contributory promise of free healthcare for every citizen which is exceptional in its generosity. These are big muscular programmes uninhibited by any doubts about the role or capacity of the state. And these are primarily funds and services for the over-60s. They take up 40 per cent of all public spending, higher than in many other OECD countries.

The rest of the British state is by contrast a puny weakling, so our total public spending ends up at about the OECD average. The question for the Boomers who are on track to be the main beneficiaries of these massive state programmes is how they are to be funded. Can they realistically expect younger generations of workers to pay higher taxes for services for older people when they are clearly having a hard time themselves and are receiving very little of their taxes back from the state at their stage of the life cycle?

The voting power of the Boomers means that there has to be something for the older generation. And indeed it is right to provide for them. Polling shows that one of the many admirable qualities of younger people is that they want granny to have a decent state pension and a well-funded NHS. So we start with a three-point offer to old people:

1. **The state pension increases with earnings.** This replaces the triple lock of increases by prices, earnings, or 2.5 per cent (whichever is higher). Instead it settles for the obvious basic principle that the incomes of non-earners should roughly grow alongside earners. It is wrong to have a long-term ratchet whereby they grow by more. But it can be difficult for pensioners if there is a period when prices are growing more than earnings, so there could be an additional protection with the state pension increased by inflation when it is higher than earnings. This increase would be recouped when earnings are more than inflation, until the long-term stable ratio to earnings is re-established. (And if this ratio were to be increased, the presumption is that the state pension age would be increased to pay for it.)

2. There is a new settlement for social care with more public funding. One of the biggest worries of older people is how they will pay for their social care, and we should lift that anxiety from them. There should be a minimum level of personal assets below which no contribution to social care is collected – of say £50,000. Above the £50,000 there would be a tapering level of contribution but with an upper limit to the total cost which the individual pays (of say £100,000); and above that, public funding steps in. This broadly follows the structure of the proposals of the Dilnot Review. These parameters could be even more generous if there were agreement on the tax increases or other savings to fund it.[1] It involves significantly greater protection for old people than they enjoy currently, as there is a higher minimum level of protected assets and for the first time a maximum too. But this package covers both domiciliary and residential care, so there is no automatic protection of the house – though there could be a postponement of the payment by making it a charge on the property at death. If either cost rises above the maximum, or savings fall to the minimum, then the taxpayer steps in. Over half of pensioners would be exempt from all care costs in this proposed system.[2]

3. We accept that the cost of the NHS is going to rise as this big Boomer cohort grows old, and this means increased taxation to fund increases in public funding for the NHS ahead of inflation. The NHS is one of our most popular and respected institutions, and the bulk of its resources are devoted to older people. All the forecasts show public spending rising because of a combination of more old people and upward cost pressures. It is right to pledge to fund the NHS properly.

This adds up to a powerful combination of three policies that give older people an unprecedented level of protection from the financial anxieties which often plague them. They get guarantees for their income, social care, and healthcare.

Then we turn to the difficult question of how to pay for this. If old people can afford to, they should contribute in some way to this triple guarantee of public services from which they, above all, benefit. Some may argue the case for a bolder reform, shifting more responsibility to private provision and payment. The trouble is that even the boldest advocates tend to say these policies are for young generations, because it is too late to tell a 60-year-old to shift to private payment for their care. But the spending pressures come from older people, so private payment by the young is not a credible alternative to higher taxes. And it would mean they would be paying taxes towards a service for older people that they themselves would not be able to enjoy.

Means-testing the basic pension or access to the NHS is another option which is very hard to justify, so well-designed taxes to fund increased spending on the NHS look a lot better. These taxes should ensure that affluent older people make a proper contribution. After all, this is to raise resources going directly into services that are mainly for old people. We are not proposing increased taxes to pay for some eccentric social experiment – this is for their pensions and their healthcare.

The obvious answer appears to be to increase income tax. Affluent older people do pay income tax. Indeed, one in five income tax payers is aged over 65, as pensioner incomes have increased. But even so, the bulk of income tax comes from the working-age population. It might appear to be the ideal candidate to fund the extra spending but it would not be as fair as it seems, because of two crucial changes in the patterns of income and wealth.

The first change is the rise of the occupational pension as a significant source of income. Occupational pensions are now about 30 per cent of total pensioner incomes.[3] Pensioners do not pay National Insurance contributions on these pensions when they are received. Employee contributions were included in the income-paying National Insurance when they were levied but not employer contributions, and this made it tax-efficient for most of occupational pensions to be financed out of employer contributions.

We should shift to a regime in which pensioners pay employee National Insurance contributions on their occupational pensions when they receive them and the original contributions are exempt from National Insurance. There will be some who could object that this means they will have paid National Insurance contributions twice. To offset this, these National Insurance contributions could be at a lower rate – say 6 per cent – and the threshold for payments could be set at the income tax threshold, not the lower National Insurance threshold.

Employee National Insurance contributions should also be charged on the earnings of pensioners. This ends the unfairness that if two people are working side by side for the same pay, the pensioner will be taking home more as they won't be paying National Insurance. This exemption goes back to the founding doctrine of the Beveridgean welfare state that National Insurance was to pay for your pensions, which were compensation for loss of income when you retired. But he also set the condition that you had to have retired to collect the pension. Now that the retirement condition has gone, so should the exemption from National Insurance.

Taken together, these changes could raise over £2bn in 2020. They could even be badged as an NHS levy, as that is what they would be funding.[4] Eighty per cent of this revenue would come from the most affluent 20 per cent of pensioners, who tend also to be the younger ones. So it is very progressive – it does not hit the 80-year-old struggling to heat her home in the winter. Successive governments have increased National Insurance even when they have been cutting income tax. This has had the unintended effect of shifting the relative tax burden away from pensioners, who are largely exempt from National Insurance. These proposed changes restore a fairer balance between the generations.

There is another fundamental change in the balance of our economy which our tax system needs to respond to. We have already seen how assets have shot up in value relative to income. Our national wealth is now more than six times our national income (roughly £13tn of assets relative to £2tn of GDP). But even though our wealth has shot up, the proportion of our tax which comes from taxing wealth has not increased. So capital is under-taxed relative to earnings. I do not begrudge people their wealth and do not wish to tax it out of a sense of grievance. But if we have to raise taxes to pay for services for an older generation who are the prime holders of this wealth, it is reasonable to expect some contribution from their assets before we tax the earnings of the working-age population. A good place to start is council tax. This is after all a local tax, and social care is a local obligation. It has ended up much more regressive than was intended because of the failure to revalue properties, and also because it needs to fund local services so areas with low-value properties have to charge higher rates than rich areas with high-value properties. As a result, someone living in a property worth £100,000 ends up paying about five times the effective rate of council tax relative to the value of their house compared with someone in a property worth £1m. Younger people tend to be in the low-value property and older people in the high-value property, so once again there is an unintended generational effect as well. There should be a local property tax which is more proportionate to the value of a property.

There should in addition be an allowance exempting the first part of the value of the property, like the income tax allowance. The property tax might be set at about 1 per cent of value of the property per year. Older people may be asset-rich and cash-poor, so taxes like this can be a genuine source of anxiety. To address this there should be a clear national policy that these taxes can be deferred as a charge on the estate. In turn, councils should be free to borrow additionally against this future revenue. The aim should be to increase local property tax revenues by up to £5bn.

These tax increases are not to fund ambitious projects to extend the welfare state. The only increase in public responsibility is in social care, and that is specifically to help older people – the NHS is likely to need more resources just to stand still, given the increase in the number of old people. Nor are these taxes proposed with any relish. It would be much more convenient if the forecasts showed long-term public spending trends going downward. But they don't. Conservatives are the main tax-cutting party but the beneficiaries of our biggest public spending programmes are older people, who tend to be Tory voters, so it is hard to see even the party of fiscal rectitude cutting these programmes. The only realistic approach therefore is to try to find a way to pay for them that is fair across the generations.

This is a handsome offer to the Boomers. It is a promise that they will have a decent old age with higher incomes and better-funded public services than any previous generation of pensioners. They really will be a lucky generation. But these services have to be paid for. I do not like raising taxes, but borrowing money just to meet the benefits bill and pay for the day-to-day running of the NHS is wrong. Taxes are going to have to rise and they should be fair across the generations – rather than just falling on the younger working population. That means taxing more fairly the incomes of older people: extending National Insurance to the earnings of older workers; applying National Insurance to their occupational income; and reforming council tax to make it a better-designed, more fair property tax.

So far we have proposed a fair fiscal settlement to guarantee services to old people. It would also mean that the young would dodge the bullet of big increases in their taxes to pay for pensions and healthcare for an older generation who in many ways have better chances than them. But we have to do more for the younger generation, and that leads to our next proposal.

Spreading Property Ownership

Imagine a society where incomes are distributed less unequally than wealth. There is no change in the distribution of either, but wealth rises in value relative to income. That changes the character of the society profoundly. For a start, it feels more unequal, even if this does not show up in either the distribution of income or of wealth. But also it means that acquiring an asset out of income gets harder. And this is bad for social mobility. It means inheritance becomes a more important way of getting property compared to working for it.

This is a simplified account of what has happened in the UK over the past 30 years. The point at which it all gets very real is when a young person is trying to save out of their earnings to put down a deposit to buy a house. The underlying trend is that property has become more important and harder to obtain. The great vision of the property-owning democracy is in retreat.[5]

Looking back over the evidence in the last four chapters, a second trend is discernible as well – a shift in risk to the younger generation. As home ownership declines, so more young people and families find themselves in private rented accommodation with little security of tenure. Their jobs come with fewer protections too. They are saving into a pension but it is not the old sort of occupational income enjoyed by the Boomers, with a promise of a pension related to earnings for the rest of your life. Instead it is a pot of money, and how much of a pension it will buy depends on a range of factors from how long you are expected to live to the state of the financial markets on the day you use it to buy an annuity. The big employers have not just closed their defined benefit pension schemes; their apprenticeship programme has been cut back as well, and your chances of long-term employment with them as they train you up are much lower. So instead of signing on for a steady job with them, you are navigating a much more complex environment of multiple qualifications and fewer long-term jobs. This adds up to a massive transfer of risk to the individual.

Some risk is good. And it is necessary in a modern, flexible labour market. But perhaps there is only so much risk we can take. Volvo drivers are supposed to feel so safe that they drive faster to achieve their target level of risk. Maybe young people have so much risk exposure that they then reduce it in areas where they ought to take risks – sticking with their employers in low-pay sectors for far too long, for example.

One of the ways people can cushion themselves from risk is to have some savings or other assets to fall back on. That is why these two trends of less property and more risk combine to put the younger generation under real pressure. We need to do something about these trends in order to help young people – giving them the opportunity of property ownership and reducing their vulnerability to some of the risks they face.

Young people emerge from education and depend on private rented accommodation, but may well struggle to find the deposit the landlord requires. As for the deposit to buy a house – saving for that is going to take years. And it is made harder by the increased proportion of their pay going on paying the rent – probably on a buy-to-let property owned by a Boomer. Some sceptics say that the world has changed and ownership matters less to younger generations – experiences are supposed to matter nowadays, not stuff. There has indeed been a clear shift in attitude away from owning a motor car but there is still an aspiration to own your own home: we need to do better at enabling young people to fulfil that aim.

It is a high priority for public policy to enable more homes to get built. Macmillan made his reputation in the 1950s with 'applied Beaverbrookism' to achieve the target of 300,000 homes both for private ownership and for council and social ownership. Achieving that again means that we must ease planning rules and planning processes. We should also liberalize borrowing rules so councils and housing associations can build more too. High rates of stamp duty are also blocking the operation of the housing market and should be reformed. Meanwhile, we should improve the protections for those who are private-sector tenants. We should also do more to link the savings of the Boomers in their pension funds to house-building for their kids, by promoting build-to-rent. There are obscure but significant barriers to build-to-rent programmes, such as stamp duty being borne by the entire development as an aggregate rather than unit by unit. These sorts of barriers need to be removed.

It is not all bad news for young people. Their chances of employment are better than ever. But they may be trapped in a low-pay sector. Moving on to a new job is difficult without getting the right vocational qualification, and FE colleges are strapped for cash and require you to pay upfront for qualifications specifically linked to a job (such as long-distance lorry driver). Young people might want to set up their own business instead, but it is hard to get the basic resources together to do this unless their parents can help them out. Just a few thousand pounds to fund that new qualification or to get their business started could make all the difference. We saw earlier in the book that entrepreneurship is hereditary because of constraints on access to capital. There is American evidence that people taking out patents are more likely to have affluent parents.[6] We need to broaden access to start-up capital.

The successful roll-out of auto-enrolment means that more young people than ever have some form of pension savings. Again, that is good news. But behind this there is once again the shift in risk – the impact of an increase in life expectancy is to increase the value of a defined benefit promise, as it pays out for longer, whereas with a defined contribution pot the impact is to lower the annual payments when any given pot is converted. Moreover, the bad news is that there is not much in these savings accounts. But this framework could be used to promote savings, so the government should gradually increase the NEST contributions expected by all three parties – Exchequer, employer, and individual.

So young people struggle to find the deposit for a house, to fund retraining, to start a business, or to build up a pension pot. Put all this together and it is absolutely clear that they need a cushion of financial assets to set them on their way. Assets increase options. Owning some kind of asset makes it easier to absorb the risks and enables young people to take the kind of risks that boost their prospects. The assets held by the younger generation are pitifully small. Indeed for many their net assets are negative. That is why, as well as specific initiatives for more home ownership and more pension savings, the Intergenerational Commission which I chaired proposed a distribution of £10,000 each for young people financed out of inheritance tax reform. (The Intergenerational Commission proposed a gradual roll-out, starting in 2020 with £1,000 for 34- and 35-year-olds and then increasing the amount by £1,000 and going down two years each year until £10,000 for 25-year-olds is reached in 2030. My version here is a simpler version of this scheme.) That £10,000 would be put into an account from which a young person could draw on it for four uses:

- education or training;
- a deposit for renting or buying a house;
- the start-up costs for a new business, supported through a recognized entrepreneurship scheme;
- investment in a pension.

It puts young people on the road to property ownership and gives them some financial resilience with the risks they face. Some of them are fortunate to have parents or grandparents or rich uncles who help in precisely that way. This spreads that kind of support more widely. Critics of this type of proposal say it is a silly gimmick which would not change young people's lives. 'What could you get for £10,000?' the affluent pundits ask. The question reveals how poorly we understand the plight of today's young people. It is shocking how much of an impact it makes. That £10,000 would double or more the assets of almost two-thirds of 25- to 29-year-olds in the UK. It would provide two-fifths of the average home deposit of a first-time buyer. In half the regions and nations of the UK it would cover more than half the average first-time buyer's deposit.[7] Alternatively, if put into a DC pension scheme at the age of 25 it could add an extra £45,000 to pension pots at the age of 68.

One of the classic roles of the state is to pool risk, and we do that for the old. For them the state takes on ever more responsibility, but for the young we are doing less – socialism for the old and libertarianism for the young. I believe that there continues to be a real challenge of lifting some of the risk young people now face and giving them the opportunity to go out into what is a tough, competitive world. There are about 700,000 young people reaching the age of 30 each year, so this scheme would cost about £7bn a year – which is less than 1 per cent of public expenditure and is dwarfed by the £100bn we spend on the state pension. It would be paid for in part by the tax measures listed earlier, which would yield more than is probably necessary to fund social care. In addition, inheritance tax should be reformed to yield more revenue. At the moment it is a classic bad tax, with a very high rate (40 per cent) above a very high threshold. The value of inheritances is rising much faster than the revenues from them. There are also substantial exemptions, such as for agricultural land. Capital gains tax liability is extinguished on death and inheritance tax is currently a weak substitute for it. A new, lower rate of 20 per cent tax on inheritances worth more than £250,000 is one option. The Intergenerational Commission proposed reforming inheritance tax so it was a tax on amounts of money received not amounts left – a bequests tax, in effect. This would encourage affluent parents to spread their wealth around. (A rate of 20 per cent on bequests between £125,000 and £500,000 and 30 per cent above that would initially raise an additional £5bn and would increase over time.)[8]

We need bold measures to halt the retreat of property ownership. Margaret Thatcher did it by council house sales and selling shares in privatized industries – with discounts in both cases. Now that the public sector's assets are much reduced we cannot repeat what she did but this proposal is in the same spirit. The amount of wealth inherited from parents will continue to increase. That is fine. But we need to be good citizens as well as good parents, and this proposal ensures all young citizens inherit something as well.

Education, Productivity, and Pay

So far we have focused on a fair deal for older generations and reversing the decline of property ownership among younger generations. Now we need to turn to the key investment we make in the younger generation: in their education and their capacity to work productively. Again there is good news – education has been prominent in public debate and public policy, and the quality of education is probably improving. There has been a welcome shift to greater school autonomy, and London in particular has seen a transformation in the quality of its schools. Universities have been put on a sound financial footing and given stronger incentives to focus on the quality of teaching. But there have been failures too. Funding for 16- to 18-year-olds has fallen between a pledge on school spending for the under-16s and the boost to post-18 education from fees and loans for university students. Compared with spending on healthcare, education has done badly. Non-university vocational training remains stubbornly hard to fix. And, after all this, the productivity of British workers per hour worked has barely increased since the crash, so it takes us five days to earn what a French or German worker can earn in four days. Meanwhile the mini baby boom at the beginning of the Millennium is inexorably working its way through the system. The pressures of growing numbers of students are now being felt at secondary schools, and will reach universities and colleges in the next five years.

There are three things we can do to boost education and training for young people. First, embrace the reality of growth of education as one of the best features of modern life. More young people are going to get more education in a wider range of settings. And that is a good thing. Too often a pledge to protect education spending in real terms applies to the total spend and therefore means a reduction in spend per person. We should end the preoccupation with early years and instead focus on the teenagers who are left to their own devices with their peer group. We should do more for FE colleges, which are the poor relations. We also need to promote the level 4 and 5 qualifications such as HNCs and HNDs, which are above A levels but less than honours degrees. And we should give up on the reactionary fantasy that somehow the growth of universities is a bad thing and can be stopped. At every stage of the growth in higher education participation – from 5 per cent to 50 per cent – there have been objections, but it just carries on. In fact the challenge now is to prepare for the next surge of growth, which will come from a combination of demographic trends and the growing expectations of disadvantaged groups. At the moment, 400,000 people go to university as undergraduates; we will reach 500,000 in a decade and it will be terrible if we look back and say we failed to prepare for it by, for example, promoting the creation of new universities. The edusceptics talk about 'over-education'. I hate the concept. It is under-education we should worry about. It should be a clear priority for any government to help more young people get more education and more training.

Secondly, there is a right way and a wrong way to promote vocational education. The wrong way is to sort the sheep from the goats as early as possible. The right way is to promote a broad education for longer. Early specialization is the bane of English education. It is now obligatory for young people to be in education or training up to the age of 18, but there is no broad measure of their education to aim for. A levels are an emanation of universities, designed by them for the purpose of selecting who can best benefit from higher education. And because of the power of individual faculties in deciding who to admit, specialized prior knowledge is rewarded. We need a much broader education to the age of 18, which includes maths and the arts but also incorporates more vocational courses for those who want that type of training. We need a new school-leaving exam at age 18. Given the value and prestige of A levels we should keep the name. Indeed we love A levels so much we want young people to have the opportunity to do more of them – say six across a range of disciplines. Each would obviously have to be reduced somewhat to make this viable. Vocational equivalents such as BTECs and T levels should also be explicitly included in the structure of qualifications aimed at 18-year-olds.

The third educational proposal is aimed at tackling the failure to provide adult education opportunities. We have seen how one of the biggest problems facing young people is that they are trapped in poorly paid jobs in low-pay sectors. They are finding it hard to get promotions or move across to a different sector; employers are cutting back on training; and FE colleges have been under such financial pressure that they find it harder to help. We need a much wider range of opportunities for young people to retrain. That is why one use of the £10,000 citizen's inheritance is to fund more adult education and training.

More Mixing Between the Generations

So far we have been looking at financial transactions and decisions about the use of public resources. They are the unavoidable economic realities of the contract between the generations. And they can be measured. It is hard for a government to say it is serious about obligations to younger generations if it is systematically shifting scarce resources to older people. But there is something else which is harder to measure but just as important. It does look as if we spend more time with our peers and less time with people of other generations. Most of our dealings with people from different generations are structured interactions in institutions such as schools, hospitals, shops, and offices. The informal intergenerational relationships are increasingly found within the family. It is where we have less to do with our siblings as family size shrinks, and more to do with other generations as life expectancy improves. Grannies replace cousins. But apart from that there is less interaction between different generations. The decline of the high street and of public space is part of this.

After more than a decade of being involved in intergenerational politics, I am shocked by the crude caricatures generations have of each other. In particular older generations, when confronted with the cold evidence of how hard younger generations are finding things, fall back on explaining it by caricatures of how young people behave – they are extravagant or hypersensitive or unwilling to save. These caricatures thrive in environments where these older generations just don't come across many young people. So we need to promote more intergenerational contact.

There are some interesting initiatives linking up the very young and the very old – nurseries and nursing homes. The regulatory regime is very age-specific, and it is not straightforward designing a single facility aimed at providing services to people of very different ages. This is what the charity Uniting the Generations is trying to do. It is also what innovative social enterprises such as the Bromley by Bow Centre are trying to do. It should be easier to place young lodgers with older landlords. We saw in Chapter 12 that the way social housing is allocated leads to segregation of ages, so age mixing needs explicitly to be taken into account in social housing, particularly to ensure that children do not outnumber adults.

Politically Possible?

This adds up to an agenda for making our country fair between the generations and breaking down the barriers between them. I think it is the kind of country most people, whatever their age, want to live in. But is it really politically possible? In particular, it requires real shifts of resources to the younger generation. Given the power of the Boomers, can't they use their power to block anything like that? I hope that Boomers will be swayed by an appeal to the contract between the generations from which we all gain. But the uncomfortable evidence is that our politics is increasingly divided by age. It has replaced class as a crucial determinant of voting behaviour.

The chart on page 320 shows that voting support for Labour and Conservative is now evenly distributed across different social classes. It is age that is the new political divide. In 1974, a 30-year-old was as likely to vote Labour as a 70-year-old. In 2017, they were twice as likely to. In 1974, a 70-year-old was 1.4 times as likely to vote Tory as a 30-year-old. In 2017, they were 2.2 times as likely. This shows up clearly in the Brexit referendum as well, as the chart below shows. Behind the Leave/Remain divide are a host of social and cultural beliefs which divide the generations. Conservatives are becoming the party of old, even though paradoxically older people are the main beneficiaries of the big state.

Figure 16: EU referendum 2016 voting by age[9]

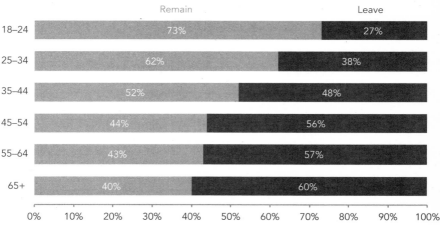

Figure 17: Proportion of voters voting Conservative or Labour by age,
October 1974 and 2017 general elections[10]

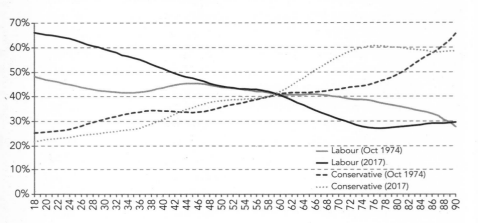

It is older voters who pack the most powerful political punch,
because they have the double advantage of being a big cohort
with a higher propensity to vote (not least because they are owner-
occupiers and it is easier for them to register). Every Boomer votes
alongside 530,000 voters of the same age. Every Millennial votes
alongside 400,000 voters of the same age.[11] So we cannot make
progress by attacking Boomers – we have to win them over. We
should not pursue intergenerational fairness as if we hate old
people or their money. By and large, the older generations do care
about the prospects of their children and grandchildren. Indeed
this is one of our most fundamental values, widely shared across
different cultures and social groups. It is something that unites us
– which makes it particularly important in these divided times.
This is not about promoting generational warfare; instead it is
an appeal to our highest principles. It is the contract between the
generations which holds a society together.

One thing we can do now is to provide much more information
about the position of the different generations. Many people, for
example, believe that benefits for unemployed people cost as much

as benefits for pensioners. They think young people are spending all their money eating out. The Resolution Foundation (generously supported by the Nuffield Foundation) is trying to illuminate this debate by publishing a yearly audit of the balance between the generations – a responsibility of our new Intergenerational Centre. The government should go further by publishing generational accounts every year, showing the balance of public spending and taxes between the generations. It should show that the people in the middle are paying the taxes out to recipients who tend to be at each end of the life cycle. That is no bad thing. It is what should happen. But it will also reveal the balance between the support for young and old, and we can also start to track trends over time. And this is just part of a wider set of generational accounts showing the full scale of transfers between the generations. James Sefton of Imperial College London is our national expert on these, and the Resolution Foundation is working with him to ensure they are properly accessible and publicized.

The options set out above may not be politically possible today. But they might be tomorrow. The boundaries of political acceptability are not eternally fixed; they can be moved by persuasive and determined advocacy. That includes showing what is in it for all of us if we stick to the intergenerational contract. Boomers have the votes and the power. There has to be something in it for them. So as well as an appeal to their better natures, it must also be an appeal to the enlightened self-interest of the Boomers themselves.

It is not just young people who lose out from the current dispensation. Boomers, however big and powerful they appear now, are vulnerable as their cohort ages and shrinks. Their incomes increasingly come from resources generated by younger generations which are redistributed via dividends or rents or taxes to them. Thus they need younger people who will be happy to fund them. In particular, Boomers are becoming more and more dependent on public services paid for by the younger generation. Already the failure to come up with a coherent policy for social care is an increasing source of anxiety to older people and their families. They must also hope their pensions are protected.

As they grow older, the Baby Boomers will become increasingly eloquent advocates of the intergenerational contract, particularly the obligations of young to old. But we all have a lot to gain from a stronger, better-balanced contract between the generations.

We are all in this together.

BIBLIOGRAPHY

Arber, Sara, and Claudine Attias-Donfut (eds), *The Myth of Generational Conflict: The Family and State in Ageing Societies*, Routledge, 2000.

Ashworth, Tony, *Trench Warfare 1914–1918: The Live and Let Live System*, Pan Books, 2000.

Axelrod, Robert, *The Evolution of Co-operation*, Basic Books, 1984.

Baldwin, Stanley, *On England* (1926), Penguin, 1937.

Barbour, Jerome, Leda Cosmides, and John Tooby (eds), *The Adapted Mind: Evolutionary Biology and the Generation of Culture*, Oxford University Press, 1992.

Barr, Nick, *The Welfare State as Piggy Bank*, Oxford University Press, 2001.

Binmore, Ken, *Natural Justice*, Oxford University Press, 2005.

Bricker, Darrell, and John Ibbitson, *Empty Planet: The Shock of Global Population Decline*, Crown Publishing, 2019.

Bristow, Jennie, *Stop Mugging Grandma: The 'Generation Wars' and Why Boomer Blaming Won't Solve Anything*, Yale University Press, 2019.

Brooks, Arthur, *Gross National Happiness and How America Can Get More of It*, Basic Books, 2008.

Bukodi, Erzsébet, and John H. Goldthorpe, *Social Mobility and Education in Britain: Research, Politics and Policy*, Cambridge University Press, 2019.

Burke, Edmund, *Reflections on the Revolution in France* (1790), Everyman, 1976.

Bynner, John, Peter Elias, Abigail McKnight, Huiqi Pan, and Gaelle Pierre, *Young People's Changing Routes to Independence*, Rowntree, 2002.

Chandler, A., *Scale and Scope: The Dynamics of Industrial Capitalism*, Belknap Press, 1994.

Charles, Enid, *The Twilight of Parenthood* (1933), Watts & Co., 1936.

Cott, Nancy, *Public Vows: A History of Marriage and the Nation*, Harvard University Press, 2000.

Coupland, Douglas, *Generation X: Tales for an Accelerated Culture*, St Martin's Press, 1991.

Darwin, Charles, *The Descent of Man*, John Murray, 1879.

de Waal, Frans, *Primates and Philosophers: How Morality Evolved*, Princeton University Press, 2006.

BIBLIOGRAPHY

Dench, Geoff, Kate Gavron, and Michael Young, *The New East End: Kinship, Race and Conflict*, Profile Books, 2006.

Drescher, Seymour, *Tocqueville and England*, Harvard University Press, 1964.

Dupré, John, *Darwin's Legacy: What Evolution Means Today*, Oxford University Press, 2003.

Easterlin, Richard, *Birth and Fortune: The Impact of Numbers on Personal Welfare*, Basic Books, 1980.

Frey, William, *Diversity Explosion: How New Racial Demographics are Remaking America*, Brookings, 2014.

Frum, David, *How We Got Here: The 70's: The Decade That Brought You Modern Life – For Better or Worse*, Basic Books, 2000.

Fukuyama, Francis, *Trust: The Social Virtues and the Creation of Prosperity*, Hamish Hamilton, 1995.

Gallie, Duncan, Catherine Marsh, and Carolyn Vogler (eds), *Social Change and the Experience of Unemployment*, Oxford University Press, 1994.

Giddens, Anthony, *Modernity and Self-Identity: Self and Society in the Late Modern Age*, Polity Press, 1991.

Goldstone, Jack, Eric Kaufmann, and Monica Duffy Toft (eds), *Political Demography: How Population Changes Are Reshaping International Security and National Politics*, Oxford University Press, 2012.

Goodhart, David, *The Road to Somewhere: The Populist Revolt and the Future of Politics*, Penguin, 2017.

Gordon, Robert, *The Rise and Fall of American Growth*, Princeton University Press, 2016.

Gosseries, Axel, and Lukas Meyer (eds), *Intergenerational Justice*, Oxford University Press, 2009.

Green, Andy, *The Crisis for Young People: Generational Inequalities in Education, Work, Housing and Welfare*, Palgrave Macmillan, 2017.

Haidt, Jonathan, *The Righteous Mind: Why Good People Are Divided by Politics and Religion*, Random House, 2012.

Hansen, Randall, *Citizenship and Immigration in Postwar Britain*, Oxford University Press, 2000.

Harari, Yuval Noah, *Sapiens: A Brief History of Humankind*, HarperCollins, 2014.

Haskel, J., and S. Westlake, *Capitalism Without Capital: The Rise of the Intangible Economy*, Princeton University Press, 2017.

Haste, Helen, *Mapping Britain's Moral Values*, Nestlé, 2000.

Hayek, Friedrich, *The Fatal Conceit: The Errors of Socialism*, Routledge, 1988.

Hills, John, *Good Times Bad Times: The Welfare Myth of Them and Us*, Policy Press, 2017.

——, *Inequality and the State*, Oxford University Press, 2004.

Himmelfarb, Gertrude, *Poverty and Compassion: The Moral Imagination of the Late Victorians*, Vintage, 1992.

——, *The Roads to Modernity: The British, French and American Enlightenments*, Vintage, 2005.

Howker, Ed, and Shiv Malik, *Jilted Generation: How Britain has Bankrupted its Youth*, Icon Books, 2010.

Hume, David, *A Treatise of Human Nature* (ed. L. A. Selby-Bigge), Oxford University Press, 1975.

Ipsos MORI, *Millennial Myths and Realities*, 2017.

Ipsos MORI, *Beyond Binary: The Lives and Choices of Generation Z*, 2018.

Jackson, Richard, and Neil Howe, *The Graying of the Great Powers: Demography and Geopolitics in the 21st Century*, Centre for Strategic and International Studies, 2008.

Johnson, Paul, Christopher Conrad, and David Thomson (eds), *Workers versus Pensioners: Intergenerational Justice in an Ageing World*, Manchester University Press, 1989.

King, Gregory, *Two Tracts* (ed. G. E. Barnett), Johns Hopkins Press, 1936.

Klinenberg, Eric, *Going Solo: The Extraordinary Rise and Surprising Appeal of Living Alone*, Duckworth Overlook, 2013.

Koch, Adrienne, and William Peden (eds), *The Life and Selected Writings of Thomas Jefferson*, Random House, 1944.

Kotlikoff, Laurence J., and Scott Burns, *The Coming Generational Storm: What You Need to Know about America's Economic Future*, MIT Press, 2004.

Kurt Wolff (ed.), *From Karl Mannheim*, Transaction, 1993.

Landes, D., *The Unbound Prometheus: Technological Change and Industrial Development in Western Europe from 1750 to the Present*, Cambridge University Press, 1969.

Langford, Paul, *Englishness Identified*, Oxford University Press, 2001.

Laslett, Peter, and James S. Fishkin (eds), *Justice Between Age Groups and Generations*, Yale University Press, 1992.

Lawson, Nigel, *An Appeal to Reason: A Cool Look at Global Warming*, Duckworth Overlook, 2008.

Leadbeater, Charles, *Up the Down Escalator*, Viking, 2002.

Lee, Ronald, and Andrew Mason, *Population Aging and the Generational Economy: A Global Perspective*, Edward Elgar Publishing, 2011.

Lewin, C. G., *Pensions and Insurance before 1800: A Social History*, Tuckwell Press, 2003.

Macfarlane, Alan, *The Riddle of the Modern World*, Palgrave, 2000.

——, *The Culture of Capitalism*, Blackwell, 1987.

——, *The Origins of English Individualism*, Blackwell, 1978.

Macnicol, John, *Age Discrimination: A Historical and Contemporary Analysis*, Cambridge University Press, 2006.

——, *The Politics of Retirement in Britain, 1878–1948*, Cambridge University Press, 1998.

Macunovich, Diane J., *Birth Quake: The Baby Boom and its Aftershocks*, University of Chicago Press, 2002.

Mason, Andrew, and Georges Tapinos (eds), *Sharing the Wealth: Demographic Change and Economic Transfers between Generations*, Oxford University Press, 2000.

McRae, Susan (ed.), *Changing Britain: Families and Households in the 1990s*, Oxford University Press, 1999.

Mischel, Walter, *The Marshmallow Test: Understanding Self-control and How to Master It*, Bantam Press, 2014.

Morland, Paul, *The Human Tide: How Population Shaped the Modern World*, Hodder and Stoughton, 2018.

Norberg, Johan, *Progress: Ten Reasons to Look Forward to the Future*, Oneworld, 2016.

O'Hara, Kieran, *After Blair: Conservatism Beyond Thatcher*, Icon Books, 2005.

O'Rourke, P. J., *The Baby Boom: How it Got That Way... And It Wasn't my Fault... And I'll Never do it Again*, Atlantic Monthly Press, 2014.

Oakeshott, Michael, *Rationalism in Politics*, Methuen, 1962.

Offer, Avner, *The Challenge of Affluence*, Oxford University Press, 2006.

Oxford Martin Commission, *Now for the Long Term: The Report of the Oxford Martin Commission for Future Generations*, Oxford Martin School, 2013.

Parfit, Derek, *Reasons and Persons*, Oxford University Press, 1992.

Paul, Kathleen, *Whitewashing Britain: Race and Citizenship in the Postwar Era*, Cornell University Press, 1997.

Phillips, Melanie, *The Sex Change State*, Social Market Foundation, 1997.

Pinker, Steven, *The Better Angels of Our Nature: Why Violence Has Declined*, Viking Books, 2011.

——, *The Blank Slate: The Modern Denial of Human Nature*, Penguin Putnam, 2002.

Putnam, Robert, *Bowling Alone: The Collapse and Revival of American Community*, Simon and Schuster, 2000.

Rawls, John, *A Theory of Justice*, Oxford University Press, 1972.

Resolution Foundation, *A New Generational Contract: The final report of the Intergenerational Commission*, May 2018.

Ridley, Matt, *The Rational Optimist: How Prosperity Evolves*, HarperCollins, 2010.

——, *The Origins of Virtue*, Viking, 1996.

Roberts, Andrew, *History of the English-Speaking Peoples Since 1900*, HarperCollins, 2008.

Rosling, Hans, *Factfulness: Ten Reasons We Are Wrong About the World – and Why Things Are Better Than You Think*, Flatiron Books, 2018.

Rowlingson, Karen, Ricky Joseph, and Louise Overton, *Inter-generational Financial Giving and Inequality: Give and Take in 21st Century Families*, Palgrave Macmillan, 2017.

Schuller, Tom, and David Watson, *Learning Through Life: Inquiry into the Future for Lifelong Learning*, NIACE, 2009.

Scott, Andrew, and Lynda Gratton, *The 100-Year Life: Living and Working in an Age of Longevity*, Bloomsbury, 2016.

Seabright, Paul, *The Company of Strangers: A Natural History of Economic Life*, Princeton University Press, 2004.

Skyrms, Brian, *The Stag Hunt and the Evolution of Social Structure*, Cambridge University Press, 2004.

Smith, Adam, *A Theory of Moral Sentiments*, Oxford University Press, 1976.

——, *The Wealth of Nations*, Oxford University Press, 1976.

Strauss, William, and Neil Howe, *Generations: The History of America's Future 1584 to 2069*, William Morrow, 1991.

Taine, Hippolyte, *Notes on England*, Henry Holt and Co., 1885

Thane, Pat, *Old Age in English History*, Oxford University Press, 2000.

Thomson, David, *Selfish Generations: How Welfare States Grow Old*, White Horse Press, 1996.

Tocqueville, Alexis de, *Democracy in America*, Vintage Classics, 1990.

Todd, Emmanuel, *After the Empire. The Breakdown of American Order*, Columbia University Press, 2003.

——, *The Explanation of Ideology: Family Structures and Social Systems*, Blackwell, 1983.

Twenge, Jean, *iGen: Why Today's Super-Connected Kids Are Growing Up Less Rebellious, More Tolerant, Less Happy – and Completely Unprepared for Adulthood*, Atria Books, 2017.

Waite, Linda, and Maggie Gallagher, *The Case for Marriage: Why Married People are Happier, Healthier, and Better-Off Financially*, Broadway Books, 2000.

Walker, Alan (ed.), *The New Generational Contract: Intergenerational Relations, Old Age and Welfare*, UCL Press, 1996.

Wellings, Kaye, Julia Field, Anne Johnson, and Jane Wadsworth, *Sexual Behaviour in Britain*, Penguin Books, 1994.

Whitelock, D., *English Historical Documents 500–1042*, Routledge, 1979.

Will, George, *Statecraft as Soulcraft: What Government Does*, Simon and Schuster, 1983.

Willetts, David, *A University Education*, Oxford University Press, 2017.

——, *Civic Conservatism*, Social Market Foundation, 1995.

——, *Modern Conservatism*, Penguin, 1992.

Wilmot, Michael, and William Nelson, *Complicated Lives*, Wiley, 2003.

Wilson, James Q., *The Moral Sense*, Free Press, 1993.

Wuthnow, Robert, *Loose Connections*, Harvard University Press, 1998.

Young, Michael, *The Rise of the Meritocracy*, Thames and Hudson, 1958.

Zak, Paul (ed.), *Moral Markets*, Princeton University Press, 2008.

Zweiniger-Bargielowska, Ina, *Austerity in Britain: Rationing, Controls, and Consumption, 1939–1955*, Oxford University Press, 2000.

NOTES

Preface to the New Edition
1. Speech in 2005.
2. See Robert Gordon, *The Rise and Fall of American Growth*, Princeton University Press, 2016.
3. Jean Twenge, *iGen: Why Today's Super-Connected Kids Are Growing Up Less Rebellious, More Tolerant, Less Happy – and Completely Unprepared for Adulthood*, Atria Books, 2017.
4. Ipsos MORI analysis of Social Attitudes 2011, 'Millennials are around half as likely to take pride in the welfare state as Boomers'.
5. Stephen Clarke, *A Brave New World: How reduced migration could affect earnings, employment and the labour market*, Resolution Foundation, August 2016.
6. Resolution Foundation Report of Intergenerational Commission, p. 26, fig. 1.1.
7. Office for National Statistics, Birth Characteristics (England and Wales); NRS, Births Time Series Data (Scotland); NISRA, Live births, 1887 to 2015 (Northern Ireland).

Introduction to the First Edition
1. Alexis de Tocqueville, 'Of Individualism in Democratic Countries', *Democracy in America*, vol. II, book II (chap. 2), Vintage Classics, 1990, p. 99.
2. Herodotus, *The Histories*, vol. I: 29–34, Oxford University Press, 1998. Another, more rigorous translation is 'Until he is dead he is not happy, only lucky.'
3. 'The Long Now' is a powerful expression coined by Brian Eno and is the name of a foundation set up by him and others. They use the idea far more ambitiously than in this volume, to shift the way we think about the future so we value time spans of thousands of years. For them the year of publication of this book is 02019.

NOTES

1. Who We Are

1. Alan Macfarlane, *The Culture of Capitalism*, Blackwell, 1987, p. 151.
2. The key table is 'A scheme of the Income and Expense of the several families of England calculated for the year 1688', in Gregory King, *Two Tracts* (ed. G. E. Barnett), Johns Hopkins Press, 1936, p. 31.
3. Alan Macfarlane, *The Origins of English Individualism*, Blackwell, 1978. The quotation is from p. 163 and the figures from pp. 95 and 96.
4. F. W. Maitland, *Constitutional History of England*, quoted in Macfarlane, *Culture of Capitalism*, p. 188.
5. L. Lancaster, 'Kinship in Anglo-Saxon Society', Part II, *British Journal of Sociology*, 9(4), 1958, p. 375.
6. 'Family ties and the insurance they provide can only work if extended families live close to each other and therefore geographical mobility is lower.' A. Alesina and P. Giuliano, *The Power of the Family*, Centre for Economic Performance Discussion Paper, April 2007.
7. 'Sermon of the Wolf to the English', in D. Whitelock, *English Historical Documents 500–1042*, Routledge, 1979, p. 931.
8. 'The Thegns' Guild of Cambridge', in ibid., p. 604.
9. 'The Ordinance of the Bishops and Reeves of the London District', in ibid., p. 426.
10. Macaulay, quoted in Gertrude Himmelfarb, *Poverty and Compassion: The Moral Imagination of the Late Victorians*, Vintage, 1992, p. 186.
11. The dissolution of the monasteries in 1536–40 removed long-established provision for the poor and needy. A legal framework for parish-based relief in its stead was developed over the next 60 years. The first Poor Law Act was passed in 1552. The first legislation for a compulsory local tax to pay for it was passed in 1576. This Elizabethan legislation was then consolidated in the 1601 Poor Law, which remained largely unchanged for two centuries.
12. David Seawright, 'One Nation', in K. Hickson (ed.), *The Political Thought of the Conservative Party since 1945*, Palgrave Macmillan, 2005, p. 71.
13. Montesquieu quoted in Paul Langford, *Englishness Identified*, Oxford University Press, 2001, p. 5.
14. Benjamin Franklin, letter from London, 1773, quoted in Bolingbroke's *Political Writings* (ed. Bernard Cottiot), Macmillan, 1997.
15. Montesquieu, *Spirit of the Laws*, quoted in Alan Macfarlane, *The Origins of English Individualism*, p. 170.
16. *New Scientist*, 17 November 2008.
17. Emmanuel Todd, *The Explanation of Ideology: Family Structures and Social Systems*, Blackwell, 1983.
18. W. D. Rubinstein, *Capitalism, Culture, and Decline in Britain 1750–1990*, Routledge, 1993.
19. Paul Morland, *The Human Tide*, John Murray, 2019, p. 45.
20. A. Chandler, *Scale and Scope: The Dynamics of Industrial Capitalism*, Belknap Press, 1994; and D. Landes, *The Unbound Prometheus: Technological Change*

and Industrial Development in Western Europe from 1750 to the Present, Cambridge University Press, 1969.

21. Friedrich Engels, *The Origins of the Family, Private Property and the State*, quoted in Macfarlane, *Origins of English Individualism*, pp. 121–2.

22. French inheritance law was updated in 2015 to comply with EU regulations. It enables citizens of other EU countries living in France to opt out from their inheritance law, but forced heirship remains a fundamental feature of French inheritance law.

23. N. Bloom and J. van Reenen, *Measuring and Explaining Management Practices across Firms and Countries*, CEP Discussion Paper No. 716, March 2006, p. 35.

24. *Economist*, 7 December 2017. See Office for National Statistics, *Experimental data on the management practices of manufacturing businesses in Great Britain: 2016* and *Management practices and productivity in British production and services industries – initial results from the Management and Expectations Survey: 2016*, April 2018.

25. N. Bloom and J. van Reenen, 'Why Do Management Practices Differ across Firms and Countries?', *Journal of Economic Perspectives*, 24(1), 2010, pp. 203–24. See pp. 217–18.

26. T. Nicholas, 'Clogs to Clogs in Three Generations? Explaining Entrepreneurial Performance in Britain since 1850', *Journal of Economic History*, 59(3), 1999, p. 709.

27. 'Poor management is another feature of family firms. Britain emerges badly from the World Management Survey in this respect: only 37% of managers in its family-owned, family-run companies have degrees, whereas 48% do in companies with a diverse shareownership. In Germany, 49% of managers in family-run and family-owned firms have degrees, rising to 70% in companies with a wider ownership.' *Economist*, 7 December 2017.

28. Emmanuel Todd, *After the Empire. The Breakdown of American Order*, Columbia University Press, 2003, p. 50.

29. Dr Johnson quoted in Lawrence Stone, *The Family, Sex and Marriage in England 1500–1800*, Pelican, 1979, p. 173. When Laurence Shirley, the 4th Earl Ferrers, was tried and hanged for the murder of a servant in 1760, his brother Washington succeeded him as the 5th Earl and inherited all of his estates. Holland was probably the only other European country of the period where an aristocrat could be tried for murdering a commoner and where the lines of family inheritance would be completely unaffected. I apologize to my dear brother Peter for this point.

30. Gertrude Himmelfarb, *The Roads to Modernity: The British, French and American Enlightenments*, Vintage, 2005.

31. Institute for Social and Economic Research, *Understanding Society 2015–17*.

32. Andrew Roberts, *History of the English-Speaking Peoples Since 1900*, HarperCollins, 2008.

33. Tocqueville, *The Old Regime*, quoted in Francis Fukuyama, *Trust: The Social Virtues and the Creation of Prosperity*, Hamish Hamilton, 1995, p. 55.

NOTES

34. Tocqueville, quoted in Seymour Drescher, *Tocqueville and England*, Harvard University Press, 1964, p. 63.
35. Tocqueville, *The Old Regime*, quoted in Alan Macfarlane, *The Riddle of the Modern World*, Palgrave, 2000, p. 212.
36. Nancy Cott, *Public Vows: A History of Marriage and the Nation*, Harvard University Press, 2000. Chapter 1, 'An Archaeology of American Monogamy', explains the links between the American Revolutionaries' political model and their account of the family – a consensual union resting on a social contract.
37. Tocqueville, quoted in Drescher, *Tocqueville and England*, p. 6.
38. Gilles Duranton, Andrés Rodríguez-Pose, and Richard Sandall, *Family Types and the Persistence of Regional Disparities in Europe*, Working Papers No. 2008–07, Instituto Madrileño de Estudios Avanzados (IMDEA) Ciencias Sociales, 2008.
39. Fahmida Rahman and Daniel Tomlinson, *Cross Countries: International comparisons of intergenerational trends*, Resolution Foundation, February 2018.
40. The expressions come from Benedict Anderson, *Imagined Communities*, Verso, 1983; Linda Colley, *Britons: Forging the Nation: 1707–1837*, Yale University Press, 1992; Eric Hobsbawm and Terence Ranger (eds), *The Invention of Tradition*, Cambridge University Press, 1983.
41. Adults aged 16–75. Source: Ipsos MORI.
42. Hippolyte Taine, *Notes on England*, Henry Holt and Co., 1885, p. 4.

2. Breaking Up

1. Fifty per cent of elderly individuals live with adult children in Japan, 42 per cent in Italy, and 40 per cent in Spain. By contrast, less than 15 per cent of elderly individuals live with their children in France, Germany, the UK, and the US. See *The 2003 Aging Vulnerability Index* published by the Center for Strategic and International Studies, Washington DC. This does broadly match the divide between very low birth rates and rather higher ones.
2. Source for these figures and for the chart: Office for National Statistics, Families and households in the UK.
3. Kathleen Kiernan, 'Lone Motherhood, Employment and Outcomes for Children', *International Journal of Law, Policy and the Family*, 1996, 10(3), pp. 233–49; shows that the educational attainments and economic outcomes for the children of lone parents are worse if the parent is not working than if he or she does. This effect is particularly marked for daughters.
4. There is a new data set beginning in 1996 when 20.5 per cent of households were workless, after which date there is a slow decline in numbers of workless households. Because of methodological inconsistencies we cannot be sure when the peak was, but the early 1990s is a reasonable suggestion. See Paul Gregg and David Finch, *Employing new tactics: The changing distribution of work across British households*, Resolution Foundation, 2016.
5. Richard Dickens and David T. Ellwood, 'Child Poverty in Britain and the United States', *The Economic Journal*, 113(488), 2003, pp. 219–39.

6. Arthur Brooks, *Gross National Happiness and How America Can Get More of It*, Basic Books, 2008, shows that by and large the people who try to keep these traditions going are happier than the more liberal-minded. But there is nothing to gloat about. In such a confused and fragmented world, extremists tend to be happier too.

7. Eurobarometer, *Satisfaction and Dissatisfaction with Quality of Life*, SP003, 2018. In terms of 'satisfied with the life you lead', the EU as a whole is Very 23 per cent and Fairly 59 per cent.

8. Eunice Yu and Jianguo Liu, 'Environmental Impacts of Divorce', *Proceedings of the National Academy of Science*, 104(51), 2007, pp. 20629–34.

9. Linda Waite and Maggie Gallagher, 'The Wages of Wedlock', *The Case for Marriage: Why Married People are Happier, Healthier, and Better-Off Financially* (chap. 7), Broadway Books, 2000, pp. 97–109.

10. A recent examination of this trend is Eric Klinenberg, *Going Solo: The Extraordinary Rise and Surprising Appeal of Living Alone*, Penguin, 2012.

11. J. Hudson, 'Inequality and the Knowledge Economy: Running to Stand Still', *Social Policy and Society*, vol. 5(2), pp. 207–22.

12. Ray Hall, Philip E. Ogden, and Catherine Hill, 'Living Alone: Evidence from England and Wales and France for the Last Two Decades', in Susan McRae (ed.), *Changing Britain: Families and Households in the 1990s* (chap. 11), Oxford University Press, 1999, p. 274.

13. Maria Evandrou and Jane Falkingham, 'Demography', *Annual Report of the Chief Medical Officer 2015: On the State of the Public's Health, Baby Boomers: Fit for the future* (chap. 2), p. 29

14. Inequality by household composition, Resolution Foundation analysis of Households Below Average Income data, 2016.

15. Anthony Giddens, *Modernity and Self-Identity: Self and Society in the Late Modern Age*, Polity Press, 1991, p. 6. See also chap. 3, 'The Trajectory of Self and the Brief Discussion of Family Obligations', p. 98.

16. Robert Putnam, *Bowling Alone: The Collapse and Revival of American Community*, Simon and Schuster, 2000, p. 224.

17. A good example of the optimist argument is Charles Leadbeater, *Up the Down Escalator*, Viking, 2002. For the pessimist case see Melanie Phillips, *The Sex Change State*, Social Market Foundation, 1997.

3. The Baby Boom

1. Office for National Statistics, Live births in Great Britain. A historic low point of 667,000 was reached in 1933.

2. Enid Charles, *The Twilight of Parenthood*, 1934, Watts & Co., (subsequent editions retitled *The Menace of Under-Population*).

3. Advice from the Government Actuary in 1936. See John Macnicol, *The Politics of Retirement in Britain, 1878–1948*, Cambridge University Press, 1998, p. 264.

4. T. S. Eliot, 'The Idea of a Christian Society', in *Selected Prose of T. S. Eliot*, Faber and Faber, 1975, p. 285.

5. J. M. Keynes, 'Some Economic Consequences of a Declining Population', The Galton Lecture, *Eugenics Review*, 29(1), 1937.

6. Royal Commission on Population: His Majesty's Stationery Office, Cmd.7695, June 1949; National Advisory Committee on the Employment of Older Men and Women, First Report, The Watkinson Report, Cmd.8693, October 1953; Report of the Committee on the Economic and Financial Problems of the Provision for Old Age, The Phillips Committee, Cmd.9333, December 1954.

7. From December 2018, the state pension age for both men and women is increasing to reach 66 by October 2020. Then it rises to 67 between 2026 and 2028, having been brought forward by a decade. Under the current law, the state pension age is due to increase to 68 between 2044 and 2046. Following the Cridland Review the increase to 68 is currently set to be accelerated to 2039, but a further review to be completed by 2023 will be undertaken before any legislation to this effect is enacted. See Cridland Review, *Independent Review of the State Pension Age: Smoothing the Transition: Final Report*, March 2017.

8. Ina Zweiniger-Bargielowska, *Austerity in Britain: Rationing, Controls, and Consumption, 1939–1955*, Oxford University Press, 2000, shows just how low calorie intake was. The calorie intake of the middle classes fell from approximately 3,725 kcals per day in 1932–5 to a low point of 2,307 in 1947. For the working classes the figure also fell, but from 2,859 in 1932–5 to 2,308 in 1947. It is also striking that calorie intake became so equal across social classes.

9. John Hobcraft, 'Fertility in England and Wales: A Fifty-Year Perspective', *Population Studies*, 50(3), 1996, p. 490.

10. The average age of first intercourse fell from 21 years old for women born 1931–5 to 20 for women born 1936–40 and 19 for women born 1941–5. See Kaye Wellings, Julia Field, Anne Johnson, and Jane Wadsworth, *Sexual Behaviour in Britain*, Penguin Books, 1994, p. 37.

11. Philip Larkin, 'Annus Mirabilis', in *High Windows*, Faber and Faber, 1979.

12. Office for National Statistics: Marriages in England and Wales, 2015; and Live births within eight months of marriage, 2012 to 2015.

13. Joanna Burke, 'Housewifery in Working Class England 1860–1914', *Past & Present*, 143, May 1991, p. 168. The comparison between all women and then wives is imperfect, but there are limits on the data and the underlying point still holds.

14. Pennsylvania State University researcher Dr Stacy Rogers interviewed 2,033 married people in 1980, 1983, 1988, 1992, and 1997 to better understand the role of income in relationships. When partners don't earn the same amount of money, the one earning less feels dependent, and the one earning more feels obligated to the other. People in either situation are less likely to divorce. This was one of the findings of the Marital Instability Over the Life Course Study: A Six-Wave Panel Study, 1980, 1983, 1988, 1992–1994, 1997, 2000. Recent British evidence found that the 1999 changes in the structure of tax credits which meant women could receive more Working Families Tax

Credit if they did not have a very low-earning or non-earning partner had a 'substantial impact' on the divorce rate among the poorest households in Britain, prompting a 160 per cent rise in separations. M. Francesconi, H. Rainer, and W. van der Klaauw, 'The Effects of In-Work Benefit Reform in Britain on Couples: Theory and Evidence', *The Economic Journal*, 119(535), 2009, pp. 66–100.

15. R. Lampard, 'An Examination of the Relationship between Marital Dissolution and Unemployment', in Duncan Gallie, Catherine Marsh, and Carolyn Vogler (eds), *Social Change and the Experience of Unemployment*, Oxford University Press, 1994, pp. 264–98. For a later discussion see Morten Blekesaune, *Unemployment and Partnership Dissolution*, ISER Working Paper 2008–21.

16. Robert Rowthorn and David Webster, *Male Worklessness and the Rise of Lone Parenthood in Britain*, Oxford Centre for Population Research, Working Paper No. 30, 2007.

17. 'Men in their early fifties with an occupational pension and in the top quartile of the income distribution are 50 per cent more likely to be displaced than a man with the same age and hourly wages but no occupational pension', Nigel Campbell, *The Decline of Employment among Older People in Britain*, LSE, CASE Paper, January 1999.

18. Taylor and Walker, *Intergenerational relations in the labour market: The attitudes of employers and older workers*, in Alan Walker (ed.), *The New Generational Contract: Intergenerational Relations, Old Age and Welfare*, UCL Press, 1996, p. 62. See also discussion in John Macnicol, *Age Discrimination: A Historical and Contemporary Analysis*, Cambridge University Press, 2006, p. 82.

19. Attributed to Gloria Steinem: 'A woman without a man is like a fish without a bicycle.'

20. Office for National Statistics, Marriage Statistics.

21. There were 990,000 births in 1963, just short of the 1,015,000 peak in 1964.

22. Kathleen Paul, *Whitewashing Britain: Race and Citizenship in the Postwar Era*, Cornell University Press, 1997, p. 86.

23. Royal Commission on Population, 1949, paragraph 329, p. 124.

24. The Colonial Secretary informed the Cabinet in June 1948 that 'the men concerned are all British subjects. The Government of Jamaica has no legal power to prevent their departure from Jamaica and the Government of the United Kingdom has no legal power to prevent their landing.' Memorandum by Colonial Secretary to the Cabinet quoted in Randall Hansen, *Citizenship and Immigration in Postwar Britain*, Oxford University Press, 2000, p. 57. Companies, notably the publicly owned London Transport, also set up direct recruitment schemes from the West Indies in the 1950s.

25. I am grateful to Chris Cook for these calculations (see table below).

Table 30: Total of UK-born 20- to 30-year-olds, based on births 20 to 30 years previously

Date	1945	1950	1955	1960	1965	1970	1975	1980	1985	1990	1995	2000	2005	2010
Number in Millions	8.7	8.2	7.3	6.9	7.3	8.2	8.2	8	8.9	9.3	8.4	7.2	6.9	7.3

26. Jumana Salaheen and Chris Shadforth, 'The Economic Characteristics of Immigrants and Their Impact on Supply', *The Bank of England Quarterly Bulletin*, 2006, Q4, Table 8, p. 379.

27. Stephen Clarke, *A Brave New World: How reduced migration could affect earnings, employment and the labour market*, Resolution Foundation, August 2016.

28. The total fertility rate is defined as the average number of children a group of women would have if they experienced the fertility rate of women of each age in that specific year through their childbearing lifespan. So you add up the rate of childbirth for a woman of 20, 21, 22, etc. in a given year and get the total fertility rate for women in that year. It is a widely used measure but it can magnify swings. Imagine that a lot of women aged 30 in 2010 decide to delay having children until they are 35 in 2015. That lowers the total fertility rate in 2010 and raises it in 2015, even if the total number of children they have ultimately remains constant.

29. Office for National Statistics, Birth Statistics.

30. Nicola Tromans, Julie Jefferies, and Eva Natamba, 'Have Women Born Outside the UK Driven the Rise in UK Births Since 2001?', *Population Trends*, 136, Summer 2009, pp. 28–42.

31. See my own article in *The Times* on 22 May 2004 for an early – perhaps the first – account of the new trend.

32. M. Brewer, A. Ratcliffe, and S. Smith, 'Does Welfare Reform Affect Fertility?', CMPO 07/177, August 2007. Useful analyses are Mike Brewer, 'Does welfare reform affect fertility? Evidence from the UK', *Journal of Population Economics*, 25(1), 2012, pp. 245–66; and Juliet Stone and Ann Berrington, *Income, welfare, housing and the transition to higher order births in the UK*, Centre for Population Change, September 2017. The UK Government's cap on the total value of welfare benefits and its subsequent limit on benefits to only two children may have changed this, though lines of causation are disputed.

33. ONS. Births in England and Wales, 2018.

34. I set out the basis for this estimate in the *Sunday Times*, 22 May 2005.

35. The classic way of measuring these effects is dependency ratios, which measure the balance between the size of different generations. The very term 'dependency ratio' for what are just figures for different age groups contains important assumptions about who is a dependant and who is not. Many a working family who can only run their lives because of support from the grandparents may feel that the dependency runs the other way. Nevertheless it is an important piece of evidence of the demographic challenges ahead.

36. Karl Mannheim, 'The Problem of Generations' (1928), in *From Karl Mannheim*, Transaction, 1993. The same volume also contains his essay 'Conservatism: A Contribution to the Sociology of Knowledge', which is one of the classic twentieth-century essays on conservatism.

37. William Strauss and Neil Howe, *Generations: The History of America's Future 1584 to 2069*, William Morrow, 1991.

38. Office for National Statistics, Birth characteristics (England and Wales); NRS, Births Time Series Data (Scotland); NISRA, Live births, 1887 to 2015 (Northern Ireland); Numbers surviving to 2015 are Office for National Statistics mid-year population estimates, 2015.

39. David Frum, *How We Got Here: The 70's: The Decade That Brought You Modern Life – For Better or Worse*, Basic Books, 2000, is an excellent statement of the argument that many of the changes we associate with the sixties really happened in the seventies.

40. Douglas Coupland, *Generation X: Tales for an Accelerated Culture*, St Martin's Press, 1991.

41. One survey showed approximately 25 per cent of American Millennials did not believe that the Apollo mission had got man to the moon. See Jeff Foust, *The Space Review*, 2 January 2007.

42. Jean Twenge, *iGen: Why Today's Super-Connected Kids are Growing up Less Rebellious, More Tolerant, Less Happy – and Completely Unprepared for Adulthood*, Atria Books, 2017.

4. Spending the Kids' Inheritance

1. Richard Easterlin, *Birth and Fortune: The Impact of Numbers on Personal Welfare*, Basic Books, 1980.

2. The *Daily Mirror* of 29 August 2006 gave the results of a poll of members of the public; Q magazine, January 2006, gave the top 100 albums as selected by music enthusiasts.

3. By this method you can also work out which album is the most overrated album and the most underrated album in the *Mirror*'s top 100. Madonna's *Ray of Light* is the best performer, doing the best in spite of small cohort support, followed by Oasis, *What's the Story, Morning Glory?*, and Radiohead's *OK Computer*. Meanwhile the albums which have been carried highest by the demographic tide behind them are *Love Over Gold* by Dire Straits and *Welcome to the Pleasuredome* by Frankie Goes to Hollywood.

4. I am grateful to Chris Cook for these calculations. He explains that, using Spearman's rank correlation, there is almost no relationship between the two lists' rankings of the 38 albums. But if you rank the albums in the *Mirror* list by number of 15- to 24-year-olds, it is then possible to work out a rank for the albums reflecting the degree to which albums over- or underperformed against this demographic handicapping. Albums which do well despite being released when there are few teenagers get high rankings. Albums which do poorly despite being released when there were many teenagers plunge. Once

you make this adjustment, the Spearman's rank correlation coefficient shoots up. This is consistent with the idea that the discrepancy between the rankings of 38 albums is demographic.

5. Pew Research Centre, *Forty Years after Woodstock a Gentler Generation Gap*, August 2009. The extraordinary generational reach of the Beatles is striking. They were the second most popular musical performers for 16- to 29-year-olds, third for 30- to 49-year-olds, top for 50- to 64-year-olds and fourth for over-65s. The Rolling Stones were third, fourth, fourth, and thirteenth respectively.

6. Median real net household annual income after housing costs; CPI After Housing Costs adjusted to 2017 prices for 1931–5 cohort (Great Britain). Precise figures are £8,860 in 1962–6, median age 31; £10,805 in 1972–6, median age 41; £15,085 in 1982–6, median age 51; and £17,954 in 1988–92, median age 57. Source: Resolution Foundation analysis of Institute for Fiscal Studies: Households Below Average income; Department for Work and Pensions: Family Resources Survey. The measure is household income not pay, as the time series on pay does not go back far enough.

7. Resolution Foundation analysis of Office for National Statistics, Family Expenditure Survey; Office for National Statistics, Labour Force Survey.

8. Resolution Foundation analysis of Office for National Statistics, Wealth and Assets Survey.

9. Median real weekly employee earnings CPIH-adjusted to 2017 prices. Source: Resolution Foundation analysis of Office for National Statistics, Labour Force Survey; Annual Survey of Hours and Earnings; New Earnings Survey Panel Dataset.

10. The 1931–5 cohort reached 71 per cent home ownership in 1990–94 at a median age of 59, whereas the 1956–60 cohort reached 71 per cent in 1998–2002 at a median age of 42. Source: Resolution Foundation analysis of Office for National Statistics, Family Expenditure Survey, Labour Force Survey.

11. Median real weekly employee earnings in 2011–15 CPIH-adjusted to 2017 prices. Source: Resolution Foundation analysis of Office for National Statistics, Labour Force Survey, Annual Survey of Hours and Earnings; New Earnings Survey Panel Dataset.

12. Resolution Foundation analysis of Institute for Fiscal Studies: Households Below Average Income, Department for Work and Pensions, Family Resource Survey. CPI-AHC adjusted to 2017 prices. The figures are equivalized household income, i.e. for a given household structure. For a given household structure (e.g. two adults), a non-working adult going out to work boosts household income. If there are already female earners the trend for female earnings to rise helps too. These are tailwinds pushing up household income. But then housing costs are a headwind lowering them. Both positive and negative effects are included in this table and others on the same basis throughout the book.

13. Resolution Foundation analysis of Office for National Statistics, Family Expenditure Survey and Labour Force Survey.

14. Resolution Foundation, *Stagnation Generation*, July 2016, p. 10.
15. Office for National Statistics, *Wealth in Great Britain Wave 5: 2014 to 2016*, February 2018.
16. Office for National Statistics, *The Blue Book*, 2005, Table 6.1.9.
17. George Bangham, *Game of Homes: The rise of multiple property ownership in Great Britain*, Resolution Foundation, June 2019.
18. Office for National Statistics, *Wealth in Great Britain Wave 5*.
19. Resolution Foundation analysis of Office for National Statistics, Wealth and Assets Survey.
20. Ibid.; *Wealth in Great Britain Wave 5: 2014 to 2016*, Table 1, Breakdown of aggregate total wealth by components, July 2014–June 2016. Figures in Table 5 may not sum due to rounding.
21. Up to 1980, personal wealth averaged around 2.6 times the GDP but then it rose to 6.4 times by 2012–14. Laura Gardiner, *The million dollar be-question*, Intergenerational Committee Report 13, December 2017, p. 11. See also fig 11.1 of IGC report, p. 197.
22. Resolution Foundation analysis of Office for National Statistics, Wealth in Great Britain; Institute for Social and Economic Research, British Household Panel Survey; Office for National Statistics, UK National Accounts; D. Blake and J. Orszag, 'Annual estimates of personal wealth holdings in the United Kingdom since 1948', *Applied Financial Economics*, 9, 1999; OECD stats.
23. Laura Gardiner, *The million dollar be-question*, p. 16.
24. Resolution Foundation analysis of Office for National Statistics, House Price Index. Real (CPI-adjusted to 2018 prices) house prices by region.
25. Resolution Foundation, *Generation of Wealth*, pp. 58–9.
26. Ibid., pp. 65–7.
27. Ibid., p. 6.
28. Source for tables: Resolution Foundation analysis of Office for National Statistics, Wealth and Assets Survey. Note figures may not sum due to rounding.
29. Resolution Foundation, *Generation of Wealth*, p. 25.
30. Resolution Foundation, 'Home ownership struggle reaches Coronation Street', 2 August 2016.
31. Resolution Foundation analysis of Office for National Statistics, Wealth and Assets Survey.
32. RF analysis of ONS, Wealth and Assets Survey.
33. Andrew Benito, Jamie Thompson, Matt Waldron, and Rob Wood, 'House Prices and Consumer Spending', *Bank of England Quarterly Bulletin*, Summer 2006, p. 144.
34. This compares with the estimate of £1.8tn in the first edition. As well as underlying real changes, there has also been a key change in methodology as the previous estimate was based on the assets in both defined contribution and defined benefit pension funds. The new figure is an Office for National Statistics estimate which uses the assets in defined contribution pensions

but values the pension promise in defined benefit schemes, not the financial assets they actually hold.

35. Resolution Foundation analysis of Office for National Statistics, Annual Survey of Hours and Earnings.

36. Resolution Foundation, *The pay deficit: Measuring the effect of pension deficit payments on workers' wages*, May 2017.

37. Office for National Statistics, *Wealth in Great Britain Wave 5: 2014 to 2016*, Table 12, Percentage of employees with wealth in current occupational (defined benefit and defined contribution) pension schemes and amounts of wealth (£) held in such pensions, by age, July 2014–June 2016.

38. Resolution Foundation analysis of Office for National Statistics, Labour Force Survey.

39. Office of the Deputy Prime Minister, *Affordability and the Supply of Housing*, 2005–6, Q71.

40. HM Treasury, Pre-Budget Report, December 2004, Cm 6408, p. 96.

41. Adam Smith, 'Of the Division of Stock', *The Wealth of Nations*, book II (chap. 1), Oxford University Press, 1976, p. 281.

42. OECD, Household savings as percentage of household disposable income, 2000–2017, Household savings (indicator), 2019, doi: 10.1787/cfc6f499-en.

43. Martin Weale, 'House Price Worries', *National Institute Economic Review*, 200(1), 2007. I am grateful to Martin for the original point and his assistance with updating it. Resolution Foundation calculations based on Bank of England, *A millennium of economic data*; Office for National Statistics, *Wealth in Great Britain Wave 5: 2014 to 2016*.

44. Martin Weale, 'House Price Worries'.

45. Kate Barker, *Review of Housing Supply*, March 2004, p. 124.

46. A consistent CPIH series is available from 1989 onwards, which we project back to 1975 using changes in an estimated historic series of CPI inflation. Source: Resolution Foundation analysis of Office for National Statistics, New Earnings Survey (1975–97); Office for National Statistics, Annual Survey of Hours and Earnings (1997–2018).

47. Resolution Foundation, *Stagnation Generation*, pp. 23–4.

48. Resolution Foundation, *The kids aren't alright: A new approach to tackle the challenges faced by young people in the UK labour market*, fig. 5.

49. Department for Children Schools and Families, *NEET statistics quarterly brief*, 2009.

50. Office for National Statistics, Young people not in education, employment, or training.

51. S. Burgess, C. Propper, H. Rees, and A. Shearer, 'The class of 1981: the effects of early career unemployment on subsequent unemployment experiences', in *Labour Economics*, 10(3), 2003; P. Gregg and E. Tominey, 'The Wage Scar from Youth Unemployment', in *Labour Economics* 12(4), 2004; P. Oreopoulos, T. von Wachter, and A. Heisz, 'The Short- and Long-Term Career Effects of

Graduating in a Recession', in *American Economic Journal: Applied Economics* 4(1), 2012.

52. Resolution Foundation, *Gaining from Growth*, the final report of the Commission on Living Standards 2012.
53. L. Keister and N. Deeb Sossa, 'Are Baby Boomers Richer than their Parents?', *Journal of Marriage and the Family*, 63(2), 2001.
54. 'Can Demographics Reverse Three Multi-Decade Trends?' by Charles Goodhart, a professor at the London School of Economics and senior consultant to Morgan Stanley, and Manoj Pradhan, global economist at Morgan Stanley. See also Toby Nangle (Global Co-Head of Asset Allocation, Columbia Threadneedle Investments), 'Labour power sets the neutral real rate', an extended version of a piece originally posted on VoxEU on 09 May 2015.
55. John Bynner, Peter Elias, Abigail McKnight, Huiqi Pan, and Gaelle Pierre, *Young People's Changing Routes to Independence*, Rowntree, 2002; Peter Elias, *Pathways, Earnings and Well-being*.
56. Resolution Foundation analysis of Office for National Statistics, Annual Survey of Hours and Earnings, New Earnings Sruvey.
57. Resolution Foundation, Resolution Foundation Report of Intergenerational Commission, fig. 4.3, p.75.
58. Real household net annual income after housing costs (CPI-AHC-adjusted to 2017 prices), by life stage: UK. 'p20' refers to incomes at the 20th percentile within each age group; 'p80' refers to incomes at the 80th percentile within each age group. Dotted lines show 2016–17 nowcast. Incomes are equivalized to account for differences in household size. Source: Resolution Foundation analysis of Department for Work and Pensions, Family Resources Survey; Resolution Foundation nowcast.
59. All expenditures deflated using all-items CPIH (which has been indexed back to 1963 using historic trends in RPI), to give an indication of 'real' consumption expenditure changes over time. Source: Loughborough University / Resolution Foundation analysis using Office for National Statistics, Family Expenditure Survey and Living Costs and Food Survey.
60. Resolution Foundation, *Consuming Forces*.

5. The Social Contract

1. Jonathan Sacks, *The Politics of Hope*, Vintage, 2000; David Selbourne, *The Principle of Duty*, Sinclair-Stephenson, 1994; Alasdair Macintyre, *After Virtue*, 3rd edn, University of Notre Dame Press, 2007 (1st edn, 1981); Michael Sandel, *Liberalism and the Limits of Justice*, Cambridge University Press, 1982; Elinor Ostrom, *Governing the Commons: The Evolution of Institutions for Collective Action*, Cambridge University Press, 1990. My own earlier attempts at wrestling with this were David Willetts, *Modern Conservatism*, Penguin, 1992, and *Civic Conservatism*, Social Market Foundation, 1995.

2. Rousseau was given refuge in Britain in 1766, helped by Hume. But he then bitterly accused Hume of plotting against him. There was no such plot. But Hume was perhaps too intensely concerned to protect his reputation as Le Bon David. The dispute has gained iconic significance, with entire books devoted to it, as it reveals the difference between Rousseau's Romantic rebellion and Hume's Classical reason, a comparison made all the more vivid by their shared atheism.

3. Its significance has been brought out brilliantly by Brian Skyrms in *The Stag Hunt and the Evolution of Social Structure*, Cambridge University Press, 2004.

4. Jean-Jacques Rousseau, *A Discourse on Equality*, quoted in Skyrms, *The Stag Hunt*, p. 1.

5. David Hume, *A Treatise of Human Nature* (ed. L. A. Selby-Bigge), bk iii, section v, 'Of the Obligation of Promises', Oxford University Press, 1975, pp. 520–21.

6. I have particularly drawn on Ken Binmore's excellent *Natural Justice*, Oxford University Press, 2005; and also Paul Seabright, *The Company of Strangers: A Natural History of Economic Life*, Princeton University Press, 2004; Steven Pinker, *The Blank Slate: The Modern Denial of Human Nature*, Penguin Putnam, 2002; Matt Ridley, *The Origins of Virtue*, Viking, 1996. Friedrich Hayek has an interesting example of this type of argument in *The Fatal Conceit: The Errors of Socialism*, Routledge, 1988. The structure of this chapter draws especially on Martin Nowak, 'Five Rules for the Evolution of Co-operation', *Science*, 314(5805), 2006, p. 1560.

7. In fact much of the latest theory is really a fleshing-out of Book Three of his *Treatise of Human Nature* – it is extraordinary what he accomplished without knowledge of evolution or genes or game theory to help.

8. Elainie Madsen, Richard Tunney, George Fieldman, Henry Plotkin, Robin Dunbar, Jean-Marie Richardson, and David McFarland, 'Kinship and Altruism: A Cross-Cultural Experimental Study', *British Journal of Psychology*, 98(2), 2007, pp. 339–59. It is also described in Binmore, *Natural Justice*, pp. 103–4.

9. John Dupré has warned powerfully about this fallacy, in *Darwin's Legacy: What Evolution Means Today*, Oxford University Press, 2003. Many serious philosophers are most uncomfortable with what they dismiss as the naturalistic 'Just So stories' of the evolutionary biologists, maintaining that we cannot move from descriptions of how evolution may have worked to moral judgements about how we should behave. In response, the evolutionary biologists dismiss what Daniel Dennett has called the 'sky-hooks' on which moral philosophers suspend our religious or moral principles with no explanation of what the sky-hooks themselves are attached to. A sky-hook is the modern equivalent of the *deus ex machina*, which neatly resolved all the tricky loose ends in a plot by flying in a classical god in a theatrical machine. The alternative preferred by Dennett is a crane which lifts us up but remains firmly based on the ground itself. That is what these naturalistic accounts of our obligations to others are trying to offer. I myself favour those who believe nowadays we have to offer a naturalistic

account: it is the best type of argument to use in the public realm, whatever our
personal religious beliefs may be.

10. Quoted in Tony Ashworth, *Trench Warfare 1914–1918: The Live and Let Live System*, Pan Books, 2000, p. 146.

11. Robert Axelrod, *The Evolution of Co-operation*, Basic Books, 1984.

12. Seabright, *Company of Strangers*, p. 56.

13. Hume, *Treatise of Human Nature*, p. 521.

14. The Milgram Experiment involved an authority figure getting people to apply severe electric shocks to subjects, not knowing that they were actors who were simulating pain. And Professor Philip Zimbardo studied in the Stanford Prison Experiment the psychological effects of becoming a prisoner or prison guard. Volunteers randomly assigned to play a prisoner or guard soon absorbed the role and lived it out all too energetically.

15. Michael Oakeshott, *Rationalism in Politics*, Methuen, 1962, p. 105.

16. The barter economy analogy is from Nowak, 'Five Rules'.

17. Adam Smith, 'The Theory of Moral Sentiments', quoted in Avner Offer, 'Between the Gift and the Market: The Economy of Regard', *Economic History Review*, 50(3), 1997, p. 452.

18. Jean Twenge, *iGen: Why Today's Super-Connected Kids are Growing up Less Rebellious, More Tolerant, Less Happy – and Completely Unprepared for Adulthood*, Atria Books, 2017.

19. L. Bickman, A. Teger, T. Gabriele, et al., 'Dormitory Density and Helping Behavior', *Environment and Behavior*, 5(4), 1973, pp. 465–90. This greater co-operation in smaller halls of residence does not, however, show up as a difference in satisfaction – students living in the big crowded dorms did not report that they were less happy with their community even though there was clearly less co-operative behaviour.

20. A Parliamentary answer to the author on 19 February 2007 (Ref. 119112) showed 3.33 per cent of the school population excluded in schools with under 1,000 pupils and 6.85 per cent in the few schools with more than 1,500 pupils.

21. Leda Cosmides and John Tooby, 'Cognitive Adaptation for Social Exchange', in Jerome Barbour, Leda Cosmides, and John Tooby (eds), *The Adapted Mind: Evolutionary Biology and the Generation of Culture*, Oxford University Press, 1992.

22. E. Hermann et al., 'Humans Have Evolved Specialized Skills in Social Cognition: The Cultural Intelligence Hypothesis', *Science*, 317(5843), 2007, pp. 1360–65.

23. I am grateful to Gervas Huxley and Marloes Nicholls for this example.

24. Jane Austen, *Pride and Prejudice*, chap. 48 in particular.

25. Seabright, 'Murder, Reciprocity and Trust', *Company of Strangers* (chap. 3), pp. 48–53.

26. Steven Pinker, *The Better Angels of Our Nature: Why Violence Has Declined*, Viking Books, 2011, assembles this evidence very powerfully.

27. Charles Darwin, *The Descent of Man*, John Murray, 1879, p. 161.

28. Richard Dawkins would argue that group selection is simply the selection of what is rational self-interested behaviour by individual vampire bats.

29. Binmore, *Natural Justice*, p. 9.

30. If vampire bats are rather unappealing, you may prefer an experiment conducted by a Victorian naturalist, Sir John Lubbock. He managed to get ants intoxicated on water laced with alcohol and then observed whether these insensible ants were assisted by sober ants. 'The sober ants were somewhat puzzled at finding their intoxicated fellow creatures in such a disgraceful condition' but they carried members of the same colony back to their nest – but not drunken ants from other colonies who were dropped into water. Sir John Lubbock, *Ants, Bees, and Wasps: A Record of Observation of the Social Hymenoptera*, 1882, p. 111.

31. There is a rich literature on vampire bats and collaboration. See for example G. G. Carter and G. S. Wilkinson, 'Social benefits of non-kin food sharing by female vampire bats', *Proceedings of the Royal Society B*, 282(1819), October 2015; and also Carter and Wilkinson, 'Food sharing in vampire bats: reciprocal help predicts donations more than relatedness or harassment', *Proceedings of the Royal Society B*, 280(1753), 2013.

32. Vasyl Palchykov, Kimmo Kaski, Janos Kertész, Albert-László Barabási, and Robin I. M. Dunbar, 'Sex differences in intimate relationships', *Scientific Reports*, 2(370), 2012.

33. Helen Haste, *Mapping Britain's Moral Values*, Nestlé, 2000.

34. Avner Greif, 'Reputation and Coalitions in Medieval Trade: Evidence on the Maghribi Traders', *Journal of Economic History*, 49(4), 1989, pp. 857–82. In the words of Greif's classic paper: 'The Maghribi traders overcame the contractual problems associated with agency relationships by organizing such relationships through a non anonymous organizational framework, the coalition. Within the coalition an internal information transmission system served to balance asymmetric information and a reputation mechanism was used to ensure proper conduct. This reputation mechanism explains the observed "trust" relations among the traders. The "trust" did not reflect a social control mechanism or the internalization of norms of behaviour... rather the Maghribi traders established a relationship between past conduct and future economic reward... Since this fact was known beforehand to all traders, agents could acquire a reputation as honest agents.'

35. Binmore, *Natural Justice*, p. 11.

36. Frans de Waal, *Primates and Philosophers: How Morality Evolved*, Princeton University Press, 2006, p. 29.

37. Paul Zak, 'Values and Value', in Paul Zak (ed.), *Moral Markets*, Princeton University Press, 2008, p. 267.

38. Jefferson, quoted in George Will, *Statecraft as Soulcraft: What Government Does*, Simon and Schuster, 1983, p. 53.

39. Nicholas Humphrey, *Seeing Red: A Study in Consciousness*, Harvard University Press, 2006.

40. Robert Frank, *Passions Within Reason: The Strategic Role of the Emotions*, W. W. Norton, 1988.

41. Binmore, *Natural Justice*, p. 83.

42. Jonathan Haidt, *The Righteous Mind: Why Good People Are Divided by Politics and Religion*, Random House 2012.

43. Daria Koch et al., 'Diminishing Reciprocal Fairness by Disrupting the Right Prefrontal Cortex', *Science*, 314, 2006, p. 829.

44. De Waal, *Primates and Philosophers*, pp. 45–9.

45. Yuval Noah Harari, *Sapiens: A Brief History of Humankind*, HarperCollins, 2014.

46. Benjamin Nelson, *The Idea of Usury: From Tribal Brotherhood to Universal Otherhood*, Princeton University Press, 1949, appears to be the origin of the phrase.

47. Nicholas Humphrey, *Prospect*, September 2006, p. 68.

48. Haste, *Mapping Britain's Moral Values*.

49. James Q. Wilson, *The Moral Sense*, Free Press, 1993. Wilson finds a 'general pattern of warm familial relationships' in several separate pieces of research, p. 39. He cites Samuel P. Oliner and Pearl M. Oliner, *The Altruistic Personality: The Rescuers of Jews in Nazi Europe*, New York Free Press, 1988.

50. Nancy Folbre, *Family Time: The Social Organization of Care*, Routledge, 2004, and C. B. Mulligan, *Parental Priorities*, University of Chicago Press, 1997, cited by Sarah McLanahan, 'Diverging Destinies: How Children are Faring under the Second Demographic Transition', *Demography*, 41(4), 2004, pp. 607–27.

51. Exodus, 20:12.

52. E. Agerbo, P. B. Mortensen, and T. Munk-Olsen, 'Childlessness, parental mortality and psychiatric illness: A natural experiment based on in vitro fertility treatment and adoption', *Journal of Epidemiology and Community Health*, 67(4), 2012, pp. 374–6; cited in *The Economist*, 15 December 2012.

53. K. Modig, M. Talbäck, J. Torssander, et al, 'Payback time? Influence of having children on mortality in old age', *Journal of Epidemiology and Community Health*, 71(5), 2017, pp. 424–30.

54. Axel Gosseries makes a useful distinction between descendant and ascendant contracts in 'Three Models of Intergenerational Reciprocity', in Axel Gosseries and Lukas Meyer (eds), *Intergenerational Justice* (chap. 4), Oxford University Press, 2009.

55. A good recent summary of the philosophical debate is Gosseries and Meyer (eds), *Intergenerational Justice*. J. C. Tremmel (ed.), *Handbook of Intergenerational Justice*, Elgar, 2006, is another useful collection of essays.

56. I am grateful to Matthew Willetts for this point – itself a good example of intergenerational exchange. It does of course assume that we do not discount the interests of future generations.

57. Emily Grundy and John Henretta, 'Between Elderly Parents and Adult Children: A New Look at the Intergenerational Care Provided by the Sandwich Generation', *Ageing and Society*, 26, 2006, pp. 707–22, quotation from

p. 717. She focuses on women aged 55–69 who had at least one adult child and one living parent or parent-in-law. And also E. Grundy, 'Reciprocity in Relationships: Socio-economic and Health Influences on Intergenerational Exchanges between Third Age Parents and Their Adult Children in Great Britain', *British Journal of Sociology*, 56, 2005, pp. 233–55. She concludes: 'If you help a child, with time or money, you are more likely to help a parent and this is after allowing for class, income etc and marriage.' The data does also show stronger help among the married.

58. See for example Daphna Gans and Merril Silverstein, 'Norms of Filial Responsibility for Aging Parents Across Time and Generations', Journal of Marriage and Family, 68(4), 2006, pp. 961–76.

59. Kimberly A. Wade-Benzoni, 'A Golden Rule Over Time: Reciprocity in Intergenerational Allocation Decisions', *Academy of Management Journal*, 45(5), 2002, pp. 1011–28.

60. John Rawls, *A Theory of Justice*, Oxford University Press, 1972.

61. Ibid., sections 22, 44, and 45. David Gauthier, *Morals by Agreement*, is a conspicuous exception. I am grateful to Georgina Testa for drawing out its significance for me. The quote is from section 44, p. 284.

62. Ibid., section 44, p. 285.

63. Ibid., p. 128.

6. Ages and Stages

1. Ipsos MORI, cited in IGC Report, pp. 26 and 27.

2. Geoff Dench, 'Exploring Parents' Views', in A. Park, J. Curtice, K. Thomson, M. Phillips, and E. Clery (eds), *British Social Attitudes, the 25th Report* (chap. 5), Sage, 2009, p. 114.

3. Ipsos MORI, *Millennial Myths and Realities*, 2017, pp, 125–8).

4. In 2014, 48 per cent of the pre-War generation and 43 per cent of Baby Boomers thought immigration was an important issue, as against 33 per cent of Generation X and 26 per cent of Millennials. Ipsos MORI, *Millennial Myths and Realities*, pp. 130–1).

5. Alison Park, 'The Generation Game', in Roger Jowell, John Curtice, Alison Park, Katerina Thomson, Lindsey Jarvis, Catherine Bromley, and Nina Stratford (eds), *British Social Attitudes, the 17th Report 2000/01* (chap. 1), National Centre of Social Research, 2001, p. 103.

6. Helen Haste, *Mapping Britain's Moral Values*, Nestlé, 2000.

7. Ministry of Justice, Youth Justice statistics, England and Wales, 2016–17.

8. The exact figures for drinking are 66 per cent and 53 per cent. See Office for National Statistics, 'Being 18 in 2018: Work, family marriage – how life has changed for the children of 2000 reaching adulthood', 2018.

9. Jean Twenge, *iGen: Why Today's Super-Connected Kids are Growing up Less Rebellious, More Tolerant, Less Happy – and Completely Unprepared for Adulthood*, Atria Books, 2017, pp. 143, 145 and 152.

10. Michael Wilmot and William Nelson, *Complicated Lives*, Wiley, 2003, pp. 86–7.

11. Howard Schuman and Jacqueline Scott, 'Generations and Collective Memories', *American Sociological Review*, 54, June 1989, pp. 359–81.

12. Professor Stephen Zeldes of Columbia University, cited in *Professional Pensions*, 4 December 2008, p. 6.

13. David Bell and David Blanchflower, *What Should be Done About Rising Unemployment in the UK?*, University of Stirling, 2009, p. 16.

14. S Clarke, *Growing Pains: The impact of leaving education during a recession on earnings and employment*, Resolution Foundation, May 2019.

15. The life-cycle model of consumption was developed by Franco Modigliani, for which he won the Nobel Prize in Economics in 1985. It suggests we aim for a broadly stable level of consumption across our lives, so we borrow when we are young, save when we are middle-aged, and run down our savings when we are old. It lies behind the behaviour described in Chapter 4, and we will return to it when we discuss the role of government in Chapter 8.

16. I am grateful to Una McCormack for this point on the life course.

17. Dench, 'Exploring Parents' Views', p. 116.

18. Jacqueline Scott, 'Changing Households in England – Do Families Still Matter?', *Sociological Review*, 45(4), 1993, p. 601.

19. T. S. Eliot, *Collected Poems*, Faber and Faber, 1974.

20. Paul Seabright, *The Company of Strangers*, Princeton University Press, 2004, p. 138.

21. Alison Park, *The Generation Game*, in British Social Attitudes Survey, 2000.

22. Onward, *Generation Why*, 2019, p. 47.

23. The figures in this paragraph all come from George Bangham, *Happy Now? Lessons for economic policy makers from a focus on subjective well-being*, Resolution Foundation, February 2019.

24. Jacqueline Scott, Duane F. Alwin, and Michael Braun, 'Generational Changes in Gender-Role Attitudes: Britain in a Cross-National Perspective', *Sociology*, 30(3), 1996, p. 485.

25. Robert Putnam, 'Tuning in, Tuning out: The Strange Disappearance of Social Capital in America', *Political Science and Politics*, 28(4), 1995, pp. 664–83.

26. Michael Johnston and Roger Jowell, 'Social Capital and the Social Fabric', in Roger Jowell, John Curtice, Alison Park, and Katarina Thomson (eds), *British Social Attitudes, the 16th Report: Who Shares New Labour Values* (chap. 9), Ashgate, 1999. I am grateful to Rein Jensons for his assistance with this research.

27. Ibid., p. 188.

28. Robert Putnam, 'Social Capital: Measurement and Consequences', in *The Contribution of Human and Social Capital to Sustained Economic Growth and Well-Being*, International Symposium report, OECD and HRDC, 2000.

29. E. L. Glaeser, D. Laibson, J. A. Scheinkman, and C. L. Soutter, *What Is Social Capital? The Determinants of Trust and Trustworthiness*, NBER Paper 7216, July 1999, Table 1.

30. Robert Wuthnow, *Loose Connections*, Harvard University Press, 1998; and Les Lenkowsky, 'Review of Bowling Alone', *Commentary*, October 2000.
31. Glaeser, Laibson, Scheinkman, and Soutter, *What is Social Capital?*, pp. 21 and 22. Also you return much less if you were an only child than if you have siblings, showing again the importance of the family as the place where reciprocity is first learned.
32. Bruce Lesley, *The Racial Generation Gap and the Future for our Children*, Future Focus, January 2016.
33. William Frey, *Diversity Explosion: How New Racial Demographics are Remaking America*, Brookings, 2014.
34. Ipsos MORI, *Millennial Myths and Realities*, 2017, p. 162.
35. Ibid., p. 164. They call the Millennials 'Generation Y'.
36. Rory Fitzgerald, Eric Harrison, and Frank Steinmaier, *Age Identity and Conflict: Myths and Realities*, NatCen British Social Attitudes 27th report, 2010, chap. 8.
37. Peter Hall, 'Social Capital in Britain', *British Journal of Political Science*, 29(3), 1999, pp. 417–61, p. 433. Page 429 has a generational chart which appears to show we also have a long civic generation followed by a decline. But Hall says this is a life-cycle effect and has a chart showing more engagement with age, certainly up to 50.
38. Ben Page of Ipsos MORI.
39. Miller McPherson, Matthew E. Brashears, and Lynn Smith-Lovin, 'Social Isolation in America: Changes in Core Discussion Networks Over Two Decades', *American Sociological Review*, 71(3), 2006, pp. 353–75.
40. A survey for *Bliss* magazine, 2004. In a survey of over 2,000 students aged 13–15, only 4 per cent agreed with the statement that 'marriage is old-fashioned and no longer relevant'. C. Hill, *Sex under Sixteen?*, Family Education Trust, 2000.
41. Laura Gardiner, *Votey McVoteface*, Resolution Foundation, Intergenerational Commission Working Paper 2, September 2016.
42. Office for National Statistics, 'Being 18 in 2018: Work, family marriage – how life has changed for the children of 2000 reaching adulthood', average age at first marriage England and Wales, 2018.
43. Shelter and YouGov, 'Great Home Debate' press release, 6 June 2016.
44. *Sunday Times*, 16 October 2016, citing work by Shelter and YouGov which together show housing costs delay marriage and children by an average of 7.2 years.
45. Rosie Boycott, *Daily Mail*, 19 March 2004.
46. UN Population Division, World Population Prospects 2017, Table for Median Ages.
47. The controversial German demographer Gunnar Heinsohn has set out this theory in *Sons and World Power: Terror in the Rise and Fall of Nations*, published as *Söhne und Weltmacht: Terror im Aufsteig und Fall der Nationen*, Bern, Orell Füssli, 2003. For evidence of the interest of the US military see Patrick Hughes (Director, Defense Intelligence Agency), Evidence to the Senate

Select Committee on Intelligence, 5.2.97: 'A global threat and challenge to the United States is the youth bulge phenomenon which historically has been a key factor in instability.' An earlier, more cautious, historical account is Jack Goldstone, *Revolution and Rebellion in the Early Modern World*, University of California Press, 1991. For a sceptical warning not to forget the role of institutions and policies, see Garran Therborn, 'NATO's Favourite Demographer', *New Left Review*, 56, March–April 2009. For a more recent discussion of this phenomenon see Paul Morland, *The Human Tide: How Population Shaped the Modern World*, Hodder and Stoughton, 2018.

48. UN Population Facts, 2015/11.

49. UN Population Division World Population Prospects 2017, Table for Median Ages.

50. David Page, *Developing Communities*, Joseph Rowntree Foundation, 1994, p. 19, and David Page, *Building for Communities*, Joseph Rowntree Foundation, 1993. See also Graham Martin and Judi Watkinson, *Rebalancing Communities: Introducing Mixed Incomes into Existing Rented Housing Estates*, Joseph Rowntree Foundation, 2003.

51. See Stuart Bonar's blog post, 'The UK Riots: The Mystery of the David Willetts rule of post-war baby boom peaks'.

52. Albert Sabater, Elspeth Graham, and Nissa Finney, 'The spatialities of ageing: Evidencing increasing spatial polarisation between older and younger adults in England and Wales', *Demographic Research*, vol. 36, article 25, pp. 731–44, 8 March 2017.

53. Research by Phil Rees and Danny Dorling, cited in the *Economist*, 22 May 2004.

54. CIPD Employee Relations Report 2004, pp. 6–7.

55. McPherson, Brashears, and Smith-Lovin, *Social Isolation in America*, pp. 353–75.

56. Francis McGlone, Alison Parker, and Ceridwen Roberts, 'Kinship and Friendship: Attitudes and Behaviour in Britain 1986–1995', in Susan McRae (ed.), *Changing Britain: Families & Households in the 1990s* (chap. 5), Oxford University Press, 1999, p. 149.

57. L. J. Kotlikoff and A. Spivak, 'The Family as an Incomplete Annuities Market', *Journal of Political Economy*, 89(21), 1981.

58. Nicholas Eberstadt, 'World Population Implosion?', *The Public Interest*, Fall 1997, p. 21.

59. M. Rokeach and S. J. Ball-Rokeach, 'Stability and Change in American Value Priorities, 1961–1981', *American Psychologist*, 44(5), 1989, pp. 775–84; Daniel Kahneman and Alan B. Kruger, 'Developments in the Measurement of Subjective Well-Being', *Journal of Economic Perspectives*, 20(1), 2006, pp. 3–24.

60. Kay Hymowitz, *Marriage and Caste in America: Separate and Unequal Families in a Post-Marital Age*, Ivan Dee, 2006.

61. I am grateful to Harry Benson of the Bristol Community Family Trust for this analysis.

62. K. Kiernan, 'Childbearing Outside Marriage in Western Europe', *Population Trends*, 90(98), 1999, pp. 11–20.

7. Why Bother About the Future?

1. Then as now it is the full title that matters, and his was *An Essay on population as it affects the future Improvement of society, with remarks on the speculation of Mr Godwin, Mr Condorcet and other writers*. First published in 1798; published in Penguin Books, 1982.

2. A geometrical progression is one where the starting number is multiplied by a fixed number – if it is by 2 then your sequence would go 2, 4, 8, 16, etc. An arithmetical sequence adds a fixed number time after time. So sticking with our example using 2, it would go 2, 4, 6, 8, etc. Malthus thought 'Population, when unchecked, increases in a geometrical ratio. Subsistence increases only in an arithmetical ratio' (p. 71).

3. Matt Ridley, *The Rational Optimist: How Prosperity Evolves*, HarperCollins 2010; Johan Norberg, *Progress: Ten Reasons to Look Forward to the Future*, Oneworld, 2016; Hans Rosling, *Factfulness: Ten Reasons We Are Wrong About the World – and Why Things Are Better Than You Think*, Flatiron Books, 2018.

4. 'We won't have the rate of progress that we've had over the last few decades. I think that's inevitable with any technology; it eventually saturates out. I guess I see Moore's law dying here in the next decade or so, but that's not surprising.' *IEEE Spectrum*, 'Special Report: 50 Years of Moore's Law' (Gordon Moore, interviewed by Rachel Courtland).

5. *The Economics of Climate Change: The Stern Review*, HMSO, 2006, and Cambridge University Press, 2007.

6. *The Collected Speeches of Margaret Thatcher* (ed. Robin Harris), HarperCollins, 1997, p. 341.

7. Charles Dickens, 'Telescopic Philanthropy', *Bleak House* (chap. 4).

8. A good discussion of hyperbolic discounting is George-Marios Angleton, David Laibson, Andrea Repetto, Jeremy Tobacman, and Stephen Weinberg, 'The Hyperbolic Consumption Model: Calibration, Simulation, and Empirical Evaluation', in George Loewenstein, Daniel Read, and Roy Baumeister (eds), *Time and Decision: Economic and Psychological Perspectives on Intertemporal Choice*, Russell Sage Foundation, 2003.

9. As our economy grows, so future generations will be much richer. But how much extra happiness does Nick Stern think this will bring us? When our descendants are all millionaires in today's terms, how much will 1 per cent more income be worth to our richer descendants as against another 1 per cent of our income today? Nick Stern's model suggests that the value of both should be the same. By selecting what economists call a value for the elasticity of the marginal utility of consumption (usually called the 'eta' in the literature) of 1, Stern has assumed that an extra 1 per cent of GDP now is equal in psychological value to an extra 1 per cent of GDP in the future. Stern has a social discount rate close to zero so £1,000 now will be worth £1,000 in the future. We can also assume that we will get the same amount of utility from an extra 1 per cent of GDP today as we will from an extra 1 per cent of GDP in the future. It is when we combine these two assumptions that the real difficulties begin. The low discount rate means we are willing to incur costs today for benefits in the future – sacrificing

£1,000 of output now for £1,100 in 10 years' time looks a very good deal. But to get the same amount of happiness in that richer world we are going to need even more money than that because it may be a lower proportion of GDP. The assumption about marginal utility says that, wherever you are on the income scale, now or in the future, the psychological damage of losing 1 per cent of your income is the same. A society which lives by these two assumptions would have very high savings for the future to avoid feeling worse off. Professor Partha Dasgupta suggests, for example, that we would be saving 97.5 per cent of our national income (*National Institute Economic Review*, 199, 2007, pp. 4–7) because we would be willing to sacrifice a lot of money today to provide for the future. We would never say that we do not need to worry about people in the future because they will be richer – that is the eta assumption – but we would say that benefits in the future are worth as much as benefits today – that is the discount rate assumption. Lord Stern has replied with a concession. He accepts that actually as we get richer an extra given sum of money is worth less and less to us. So instead of an eta of 1 we could increase it to, say, 2, meaning that the marginal utility of income halves. But he then adds, rather mischievously, that his critics have made a case not just for redistributing income from rich future to poor now, but also have to accept it means redistributing from people who are rich now to people who are poor now. It is one of the oddities of the political line-up in this debate that some of the experts who are keenest on the argument that we should not be redistributing away from us to the rich future are not so keen on applying this to incomes today. That we save so little reveals that we are not valuing the future in the way which Nick Stern's model suggests. This is the key critique from leading economists such as Professors Nordhaus, Weitzman, and Dasgupta. They argue that behind Stern's technical analysis there is a moral appeal which does not accurately reflect our current behaviour.

10. A lively contribution is Nigel Lawson, *An Appeal to Reason: A Cool Look at Global Warming*, Duckworth Overlook, 2008. He makes some telling remarks about the economics of all this, though he is wrong to dismiss the scientific evidence on global warming.

11. The *South Park* episode is from April 2004.

12. This analysis draws heavily on a paper by John Beddington (Chief Scientific Adviser to HM Government), 'Food, Energy, Water and the Climate: A Perfect Storm of Global Events?', conference on sustainable development, London, March 2009.

13. World population projected to reach 7.8 billion in 2020, 9.8 billion in 2050, 10.6 billion in 2070, and 11.2 billion in 2100. Figures from United Nations, Department of Economic and Social Affairs, Population Division, *World Population Prospects: The 2017 Revision*, data acquired via website.

14. Donald Mitchell, *A note on rising food prices*, World Bank Policy Research Paper, No. 4682, July 2008.

15. UN fact sheet on water scarcity.

16. Zeke Hausfather, 'Analysis: Why children must emit eight times less CO_2 than their grandparents', *Carbon Brief*, 10 April 2019, drawing on work by

Dr Ben Caldecott of Oxford University. I am grateful to Adam Corlett for bringing this to my attention.

17. Lifetime carbon budgets in tonnes of CO_2 by birth year based on historical emissions and future 1.5C scenario. Using generation periods from the Pew Research Center and averaging the lifetime budget of all the birth years of each generation.

18. This paragraph draws heavily on an as-yet-unpublished paper by Matthew Whittaker of the Resolution Foundation.

19. Edward Woolcott, 'An international comparison of gross fixed capital formation', Office for National Statistics, 2 November 2017.

20. J. Haskel and S. Westlake, *Capitalism Without Capital: The Rise of the Intangible Economy*, Princeton University Press, 2017.

21. Office for National Statistics, UK National Accounts; and R. Thomas & N. Dimsdale, 'A Millennium of UK Data', Bank of England OBRA dataset, 2017.

22. David Laibson, 'Golden Eggs and Hyperbolic Discounting', *Quarterly Journal of Economics*, May 1997, pp. 443–77.

23. The remark is sometimes attributed to an American congressman but the earliest record of it is Sir Boyle Roche, during Grattan's Parliament in Dublin in the 1790s.

24. Estimate by Laura Gardiner of Resolution Foundation, based on Office for National Statistics, life expectancy tables, 2016.

25. The case of Phineas Gage has fascinated people ever since, and has been widely written about. It influenced the early development of neurology as it revealed different parts of the brain had different functions.

26. Adam Smith, *A Theory of Moral Sentiments*, book IV, chap. 2, para. 6, Oxford University Press, 1976, p. 189. David Hume also thought this capacity was important: 'There is no quality in human nature, which causes more fatal errors in our conduct, than that which leads us to prefer whatever is present to the distant and remote...', *Treatise of Human Nature*, book III, part ii, section vii, 'Of the Origin of Government' (ed. L. A. Selby-Bigge), Oxford University Press, 1975, p. 538. Note the title of the chapter where this point is made – Hume is considering how we get ourselves into circumstances where this sort of prudence is rewarded and gives a role for government not unlike Sunstein and Thaler have recently proposed in *Nudge*.

27. Avner Offer, 'Body Weight and Self-Control', *The Challenge of Affluence* (chap. 7), Oxford University Press, 2006.

28. George Loewenstein, Daniel Read, and Roy F. Baumeister (eds), *Time and Decision: Economic and Psychological Perspectives of Intemporal Choice*, Russell Sage Foundation, 2003, p. 204.

29. Walter Mischel, *The Marshmallow Test: Understanding Self-control and How to Master It*, Bantam Press, 2014.

30. The paper is a University of Oregon Working Paper by K. Krause and W. Harbaugh published in 1999. Alternatively, I guess children could do the experiments on adults.

31. A vivid account is Claire Fox, '*I find that offensive!*', Provocations, 2017.

32. C. Peter Herman and Janet Polivy, 'Dieting as an Exercise in Behavioural Economics', in Loewenstein, Read, and Baumeister, *Time and Decision*. The quote is from p. 478.

33. Derek Parfit, *Reasons and Persons*, Oxford University Press, 1992.

34. Shane Frederick, 'Time Preference and Personal Identity', in Loewenstein, Read, and Baumeister, *Time and Decision* (chap. 2), pp. 89–113.

35. Fifty-three was the age of your author when he wrote that, so apparently it does not get better than that cognitively. 'In cross-sectional data of prime borrowers in ten credit markets, middle-aged adults borrow at lower interest rates and pay fewer fees relative to younger and older adults. Fee and interest payments are minimized around age 53… Age-related changes in experience and cognitive function provide the leading explanation for the patterns that we observe.' Sumit Agarwal, John Driscoll, Xavier Gabaix, and David Laibson, 'The Age of Reason: Financial Decisions over the Lifecycle', 21 October 2008, Social Science Research Network, http://ssrn.com/abstract=973790.

36. Christian Jarrett, 'Children of today are better at delaying gratification than previous generations', British Psychological Society Research Digest, reporting the findings of John Protzko at the University of California, Santa Barbara.

37. Maybe the involvement of these two different parts of the brain helps to explain hyperbolic discounting – we value $10 tonight over $11 tomorrow, yet $111 in a year and a day over $110 in a year. See Samuel McClure et al., 'Separate Neural Systems Value Immediate and Delayed Monetary Rewards', *Science*, 306(5695), 2004, p. 503.

38. James Tobin, 'What Is Permanent Endowment Income?', *The American Economic Review*, 64(2), May 1974, pp. 427–432.

39. Oliver Hauser, David Rand, Alexander Peysakhovich, and Martin Novak, 'Co-operating with the future', *Nature*, 511, July 2014, pp. 220–3.

40. The examples in this and the following paragraph come from Kimberly A. Wade-Benzoni, 'Legacies, Immortality, and the Future: The Psychology of Intergenerational Altruism', *Ethics in Groups: Research on Managing Groups and Teams*, 8, pp. 247–70.

8. What Governments Do

1. Hillard Kaplan and Michael Gurven, 'The Natural History of Human Food Sharing and Co-operation: A Review and a New Multi-Individual Approach to the Negotiation of Norms', in Herbert Gintis, Samuel Bowles, Robert Boyd, and Ernest Fehr (eds), *Moral Sentiments and Material Interests: The Foundations of Cooperation in Economic Life*, Massachusetts Institute of Technology, 2005.

2. There is an excellent review of these arguments in Ronald Lee, 'Intergenerational Transfers and the Economic Life-Cycle: A Cross-Cultural Perspective', in Andrew Mason and Georges Tapinos (eds), *Sharing the Wealth: Demographic Change and Economic Transfers between Generations*, Oxford University Press, 2000.

3. John Hills, *Good Times Bad Times: The Welfare Myth of Them and Us*, Policy Press, 2017.
4. £127bn on benefits for pensioners compared with £101bn of spending – including tax credits and disability benefits – on children and working-age adults in 2019–20. See *An OBR guide to welfare spending* on the Office for Budget Responsibility website.
5. Author's estimate.
6. Figures from HM Treasury, *Public Expenditure Statistical Analysis*, Cm 9648 2018, Table 5.2: Public sector expenditure on services by sub-function 2013–14 to 2017–18.
7. Office for National Statistics, Distribution of median and mean income and tax by age range and gender 2015–16. As the breakdown is for 2015–16 and the total is for 2017–18, there is a slight discrepancy in the figures.
8. Personal tax credits, Child Benefit, maternity pay and Income Support.
9. Figures from HM Treasury, *Public Expenditure Statistical Analysis*, table 5.2.
10. Office for Budget Responsibility, *Fiscal Sustainability and Public Spending on Health*, September 2016, Chart 2.3.
11. Office for Budget Responsibility, *Financial Sustainability Review*, January 2017. Tax is all tax, not just income tax.
12. Nick Barr, *The Welfare State as Piggy Bank*, Oxford University Press, 2001. Strictly speaking, the piggy bank function involves both mutual insurance against misfortune and personal accounts, which directly link what you pay in when you are working and what you get out when you are, for example, a pensioner.
13. John Hills, 'Distribution and Redistribution', *Inequality and the State* (chap. 8), Oxford University Press, 2004, p. 197.
14. Lloyd George, assisted by Winston Churchill, introduced the contributory principle for healthcare in 1911 having introduced non-contributory means-tested pensions in 1909. We then spent the next half-century reversing this arrangement and moving to a contributory pension system and a non-contributory NHS. The pre-War arrangement still leads some people to believe that their National Insurance contributions pay for the NHS, which in turn may be one reason for the relative popularity of National Insurance over income tax. Some other advanced Western countries such as Germany and the USA have kept the contributory principle for healthcare.
15. The researchers did not find 'a positive impact of income heterogeneity on the size of these programmes'. F. Breyer and B. Craig, 'Voting on Social Security: Evidence from OECD Countries', *European Journal of Political Economy*, 13(4), 1997, pp. 705–24.
16. Paul Samuelson, 'An Exact Consumption-Loan Model of Interest with or without the Social Contrivance of Money', *Journal of Political Economy*, LXVI, December 1958, pp. 467–82. The quotation is from p. 471.
17. Avner Offer in his paper 'The Economy of Obligation: Contract Ambiguity and the Welfare State' (July 2009, unpublished) argues that maintaining these pay-as-you-go contracts is a key function of government.

18. Rational expectations theory says that families adjust their behaviour to government issues of debt, recognizing that it means higher taxes in the future and that deficit-financed spending has not made them any better off really. This theory is therefore arguing that ultimately it is families who decide the balance of costs between the generations and they will adapt their behaviour to offset what governments do. It is an interesting idea but given the scale of the government flows we are considering here, it looks implausible.

19. The programmes covered in the calculation are health, education, and social security. The table does not include future increases in healthcare costs; instead it takes health spending per head at each age held constant. See discussion in George Bangham, David Finch, and Toby Phillips, *A welfare generation: Lifetime welfare transfers between generations*, Resolution Foundation, 14 Feb 2018.

20. Resolution Foundation analysis of Office for Budget Responsibility, Fiscal Sustainability Report, January 2017; HM Treasury, Public Expenditure Statistical Analyses; Office for National Statistics, 2016-based midyear population estimates and 2016-based population projections; John Hills, *Inequality and the State*.

21. Resolution Foundation analysis of Office for National Statistics, Mid-year population estimates and population projections; Office for Budget Responsibility, Fiscal Sustainability Report, July 2018.

22. Resolution Foundation estimates based on Office for Budget Responsibility, Financial Stability Report, July 2018.

23. Office for Budget Responsibility, Financial Stability Report, July 2018.

24. Reported in a speech by Mervyn King, Governor of the Bank of England, 21 October 2008.

25. I am grateful to Matt Whittaker of the Resolution Foundation for the research underpinning this and the previous paragraph.

26. Thomas Jefferson, letter to James Madison, 6 September 1789, in Adrienne Koch and William Peden (eds), *The Life and Selected Writings of Thomas Jefferson*, Random House, 1944, pp. 488–93. The issues in the letter have been widely discussed. See W. Andrew Achenbaum, 'Public Pensions as Intergenerational Transfers in the United States', in Paul Johnson, Christopher Conrad, and David Thomson (eds), *Workers versus Pensioners: Intergenerational Justice in an Ageing World* (chap. 7), Centre For Economic Policy Research and Manchester University Press, 1989. It is also discussed in Victor Muniz-Fraticelli, 'The Problem of a Perpetual Constitution', in Axel Gosseries and Lukas Meyer (eds), *Intergenerational Justice* (chap. 14), Oxford University Press, 2009. The Jefferson quote further up is from a letter to Samuel Kercheval, 12 June 1816.

9. Time for Childhood

1. A UNICEF report in 2007 showed Britain at the bottom of the league table of advanced countries for quality of childhood. Their subsequent report in

2013 showed us 16th out of 29. We were doing better for children's sense of well-being and for no further deterioration of child obesity but badly for numbers staying on for post-sixteen education and training and infant mortality.

2. Report Card 7, 'Child Poverty in Perspective: An Overview of Child Well-Being in Rich Countries', UNICEF, 2007. Sue Palmer, *Toxic Childhood: How the Modern World is Damaging Our Children and What We Can Do About It*, Orion Books, 2006, sets out the arguments very well.

3. Staffan Linder, *The Harried Leisure Class*, Columbia University Press, 1970, was a path-breaking account of these ideas.

4. A further example of this is the extraordinarily packed CVs young people now present. Assuming they are not works of fiction, they are spending their time far more intensely and purposefully than the Boomers did. Robert Putnam suggests one reason for the apparent increase in voluntary activity by young people is that they are improving their CVs, having learned that employers value it.

5. John Maynard Keynes, 'Economic Possibilities for our Grand-children', in Keynes, *Essays in Persuasion*, W. W. Norton and Company 1931, p. 367.

6. Admittedly, one piece of empirical research, on New York taxi drivers, did suggest they had a target income and all went home when it rained. See George Loewenstein, Daniel Read, and Roy Baumeister (eds), *Time and Decision: Economic and Psychological Perspectives on Intertemporal Choice*, Russell Sage Foundation, 2003, p. 468.

7. Future Foundation, *The Changing Face of Parenting: Professional Parenting, Information and Healthcare*, Experian report for Calpol, August 2006.

8. Eric Knudsen, 'Sensitive Periods in the Development of the Brain and Behaviour', *Journal of Cognitive Neuroscience*, 16(8), 2004.

9. Sarah-Jayne Blakemore and Suparna Choudhury, 'Development of the Adolescent Brain: Implications for Executive Function and Social Cognition', *Journal of Child Psychology and Psychiatry*, 47(3/4), 2006, pp. 296–312.

10. An excellent account is Sarah-Jayne Blakemore, *Understanding Ourselves: The Secret Life of the Teenage Brain*, Hachette, 2018.

11. David Willetts, 'Which Three Years?', *A University Education* (chap. 6), Oxford University Press, 2017.

12. Two powerful critiques of early-years determinism are Jerome Kagan, *Three Seductive Ideas*, Harvard University Press, 1998, and John Bruer, *The Myth of the First Three Years*, Free Press, 2002.

13. ICM, 1999, cited in Frank Furedi, *Paranoid Parenting*, Allen Lane, 2001, chap. 5.

14. I am grateful to Professor Jonathan Gershuny at Oxford University, our leading expert on time use, for providing raw data from the most recent Multinational Time Use Studies (MTUS) surveys on which this chapter draws. The data was analysed by Chris Cook, and subsequently by George Bangham for the second edition. I am most grateful to both of them. The organization responsible is the ESRC Centre for Time Use Research, now based at UCL and directed by Professor Jonathan Gershuny and Professor Oriel Sullivan.

15. Resolution Foundation analysis of data from Jonathan Gershuny and Kimberly Fisher. (2013) Multinational Time Use Study. Centre for Time Use Research, University of Oxford.
16. Resolution Foundation analysis of data from Jonathan Gershuny and Kimberly Fisher. (2013) Multinational Time Use Study. Centre for Time Use Research, University of Oxford.
17. Resolution Foundation analysis of data from Jonathan Gershuny and Kimberly Fisher. (2013) Multinational Time Use Study. Centre for Time Use Research, University of Oxford.
18. Sylvia Ann Hewlett, *When the Bough Breaks: The Cost of Neglecting Our Children*, Basic Books, 1991.
19. W. Keith Bryant and Cathleen D. Zick, 'Are We Investing Less in the Next Generation? Historical Trends in Time Spent Caring for Children', *Journal of Family and Economic Issues*, 17(3/4), 1996, pp. 365–92.
20. Using the same international MTUS dataset as the UK figures.
21. Kirsten Asmussen, Judy Corlyon, Hanan Hauari, and Vincent La Placa, *Supporting Parents of Teenagers, Research Report No. 830*, Policy Research Bureau, March 2007.
22. 'The amount of "parent time" – the time mothers and fathers spent together engaged in activities with their teens – was linked to fewer behavioral problems, higher math scores, less substance abuse, and less delinquent behavior among adolescents.' Melissa A. Milkie, Kei Nomaguchi, and Kathleen E. Denny, 'Does the Amount of Time Mothers Spend with Children or Adolescents Matter?', *Journal of Marriage and Family*, 77(2), 2015, pp. 355–72, cited in Policy Research Bureau note, 'Time with Parents Key for Adolescents', 24 April 2015.
23. 'On occasions when youths spent more unsupervised time with their peers *than usual*, they also engaged in more problem behaviors and experienced more depressive symptoms *than usual* in the following year and... on occasions when youths spent more supervised time with their peers *than usual*, they also showed better school performance *than usual* in the following year.' Chun Bun Lam, Susan M. McHale, and Ann C. Crouter, 'Time with Peers from Middle Childhood to Late Adolescence: Developmental Course and Adjustment Correlates', Child Development, 85(4), 2014, pp. 1677–93.
24. Calculations by Chris Cook from the MTUS dataset.
25. Resolution Foundation analysis of data from Jonathan Gershuny and Kimberly Fisher. (2013) Multinational Time Use Study. Centre for Time Use Research, University of Oxford.
26. Mark Bryan and Almudena Sanz, Does Housework Lower Wages and Why? Evidence for Britain, ISER Working Paper 2008–3.
27. James Flynn, *What is Intelligence?*, Cambridge University Press, 2007.
28. Claire James and Sally Gimson, *Families and Neighbourhoods*, Family and Parenting Institute, 2007.
29. Perry Francis and Harwinda Tiwana, 'Unpaid Household Production in the United Kingdom 1995–2000', *Economic Trends*, January 2004, p. 58, shows a 25 per cent fall in gross unpaid household production of voluntary activity.

30. Survey conducted by UCL Jill Dando Institute of Crime for ADT, May 2006.
31. Clare Sharp, Judith Aldridge, and Juanjo Medina, 'Delinquent Youth Groups and Offending Behaviour: Findings from the 2004 Offending, Crime and Justice Survey', Home Office Online Report 14/06.
32. Damian Carrington, 'Three-quarters of UK children spend less time outdoors than prison inmates', *Guardian*, 26 March 2016.
33. Julia Margo and Mike Dixon, with Nick Pearce and Howard Reed, *Freedom's Children: Raising Youth in a Changing World*, Institute for Public Policy Research, 2006, p. 13.
34. Tim Gill, *No Fear: Growing Up in a Risk Averse Society*, Calouste Gulbenkian Foundation, 2007, pp. 157 and 158, cited in Sue Palmer, *21st Century Boys: How Modern Life is Driving Them off the Rails and How We Can Get Them Back on Track*, Orion Books, 2009.
35. Palmer, *21st Century Boys*.
36. Richard Layard and Judy Dunn, *A Good Childhood: Searching for Values in a Competitive Age*, Penguin, 2009, p. 38.
37. Margo and Dixon, *Freedom's Children*, p. 14.
38. 97 per cent of children from deprived backgrounds and 48 per cent of children from affluent backgrounds have a TV in their bedroom; 93 per cent of children from deprived backgrounds have a DVD or video player in their room compared to 41 per cent of affluent children. Deprived children are classified as children living in part of the 15 per cent most-deprived areas in the UK; affluent as in the 15 per cent most-affluent areas in the UK. Source: Agnes Nairn and Jo Ormond with Paul Bottomley, *Watching, Wanting and Wellbeing: Exploring the Links*, Family Parenting Institute, 2007, p. 14.
39. Sonia Livingstone and Magdalena Bober, *UK Children Go Online: Final Report of Key Project Findings*, LSE, 2007, p. 3.
40. Calculations by Chris Cook from the MTUS dataset.
41. Economic and Social Science Research Council, 'Children are Falling Behind in Maths and Science', *The Edge*, March 2009, which draws on M. Shayer, *Have the Norms for Volume and Heaviness for Year 7 changed since the Mid-70s?*, Report to the ESRC RES-000-22-1379.
42. Steve Johnson, *Everything Bad is Good for You: How Today's Popular Culture is Actually Making Us Smarter*, Riverhead, 2005.
43. Sarah-Jayne Blakemore's research shows how malleable teenagers' brains are. Sarah-Jayne Blakemore and Suparna Choudhury, 'Development of the Adolescent Brain: Implications for Executive Function and Social Cognition', *Journal of Child Psychology and Psychiatry*, 47(3/4), 2006, pp. 296–312, and Sarah-Jayne Blakemore, *Brain Development during Adolescence and Beyond*, The Institute for Cultural Research, Monograph Series No. 51, 2006.
44. James Flynn, 'Requiem for Nutrition as the Cause of IQ gains: Raven's Gains in Britain 1938–2008', Economics and Human Biology, 2009.
45. James Flynn, quoted in the *Sunday Telegraph*, 8 February 2009.

10. Education and Social Mobility

1. John Hassler and Jos. Vincente Rodríguez-Mora, *IQ, Social Mobility and Growth*, CEPR Discussion Paper Series No. 1827, March 1998.
2. Arnaud Chevalier, *Just Like Daddy: The Occupational Choice of UK Graduates*, University College, Dublin, and Centre for Economic Performance, LSE, 2002.
3. Institute for Education, Centre for Longitudinal Studies, Millennium Cohort Study, *Fourth Survey: A user's guide to initial findings*, 'Millennium mothers want a university education for their children', press release, 15 October 2014.
4. Jo Blanden, Alyssa Goodman, Paul Gregg, and Stephen Machin, *Changes in Intergenerational Mobility in Britain*, Centre for Economic Performance Discussion Paper, December 2001, p. 4.
5. Ipsos MORI and the Sutton Trust, Social Mobility, 2008.
6. Marcus Richards, Rebecca Hardy, Diana Kuh, and Michael Wadsworth, 'Birth Weight and Cognitive Function in the British 1946 Birth Cohort', *British Medical Journal*, 322, 2001, pp. 199–203.
7. Michael Young, *The Rise of the Meritocracy*, Thames and Hudson, 1958. New edition with a new introduction by the author, Transaction Publishers, 1994.
8. F. A. Hayek, 'Equality, Value and Merit', *Constitution of Liberty* (chap. 6), Routledge and Kegan Paul, 1960.
9. Steve Machin, Paul Gregg, and Jo Blanden, *Intergenerational Mobility in Europe and North America*, Sutton Trust, 2005.
10. The following paragraphs draw heavily on John Goldthorpe's latest book summarizing years of research. Erzsébet Bukodi and John Goldthorpe, *Social Mobility and Education in Britain: Research, Politics and Policy*, Cambridge University Press, 2019.
11. Ibid., fig. 2.1, p. 36.
12. Resolution Foundation, *An Intergenerational Audit for the UK: 2019*, p. 19.
13. Bukodi and Goldthorpe, *Social Mobility*, p. 43.
14. Ibid., p. 41.
15. Panel on Fair Access to the Professions, *Unleashing Aspiration: The Final Report of the Panel on Fair Access to the Professions*, July 2009, p. 20; *Phase 1 Report: An Analysis of the Trends and Issues Relating to Fair Access to the Professions*, April 2009, p. 21; and *Fair Access: Good Practice, Phase 2 Report*, May 2009, p. 20. The original figures come from a paper by Lindsay Macmillan, *Social Mobility and the Professions*, Centre for Market and Public Organisation, University of Bristol. Here is a summary of her key table based on the average monthly net family income at the age of 16 of people who are subsequently in various professions aged 33/34. It shows how much higher these family incomes were than the national average for 16-year-olds in 1958 and then in 1970. Some of the changes are very striking indeed – such as for accountants and journalists.

Table 31: Difference in family income above national average for people who join professions (%)

	1958	1970
Doctors	43	63
Lawyers	40	64
Lecturers and professors	21	11
Teachers	18	17
Bankers	13	32
Artists, musicians, writers	13	8
Stockbrokers and traders	11	14
Engineers	9	17
Scientists	8	16
Journalists and broadcasters	6	42
Nurses	4	10
Accountants and actuaries	0	40

16. John Goldthorpe, 'Class Inequality and Meritocracy: A Critique of Saunders and an Alternative Analysis', *The British Journal of Sociology*, 50(1), pp. 1–27.
17. Fernando Galindo-Rueda and Anna Vignoles, 'The Declining Relative Importance of Ability in Predicting Educational Attainment', *Journal of Human Resources*, 40(2), 2005, pp. 335–53.
18. Jo Blanden, Paul Gregg, and Lindsey Macmillan, 'Accounting for Intergenerational Income Persistence: Non Cognitive Skills, Ability and Education', *Economic Journal*, 117 (519), 2007, pp. 43–60.
19. Yvonne Roberts, *Grit: The Skills for Success and How They are Grown*, Young Foundation, 2009.
20. Angela Duckworth and Martin Seligman, 'Self-Discipline Outdoes IQ in Predicting Academic Performance of Adolescents', *Psychological Science*, 16(12), 2005, pp. 939–44.
21. See David Willetts, *A University Education*, Oxford University Press, 2017, p. 131.
22. See official website of UK Research and Innovation, 'Increasing the UK's investment in R&D to 2.4% of GDP'.
23. The research shows 'A pupil from a poor family is 17 percentage points less likely to go to a good school.' S. Burgess and A. Briggs, *School Assignment, School Choice and Social Mobility*, CMPO 06/157.
24. Sutton Trust, *Rates of Eligibility for Free School Meals at the Top State Schools*, October 2005, p. 4.
25. Sutton Trust factsheet on grammar schools. It also states that in grammar schools 'only 3% of their entrants receiving free school meals compared with an average of 18% of pupils entitled to free school meals in their surrounding area'.

26. 'Opportunities to become a professional via a no-graduate route are becoming rarer... Only 27 of *The Times* Top 100 Employers accept alternative entry routes.' The Panel on Fair Access to the Professions, *Phase 1 Report: An Analysis of the Trends and Issues Relating to Fair Access to the Professions*, April 2009, p. 45.
27. Willetts, *A University Education*, p. 401, footnote 53.
28. Ibid., pp. 176 and 200.
29. Ibid., chap. 5.
30. Ibid., p. 183 and p. 398, footnote 19, citing British Social Attitudes Survey 2011.
31. Laura Gardiner, 'Is the gender pay gap on the brink of closure for young women today?', Resolution Foundation, January 2017.
32. 'At the workshops with young people, all of the participants expressed some form of aspiration, many of which were highly specific.' Based on 36 workshops across the UK with young NEETs. Geoff Hayward, Stephanie Wilde, and Richard Williams, *Engaging Youth Enquiry: Consultation Report, Rathbone/Nuffield Review*, 15 October 2008.
33. World Health Organization, *Inequalities in Young People's Health: Health Behaviour in School-Aged Children: International Report from the 2005/06 Survey*, ed. Candace Currie, Saoirse Nic Gabhainn, Emmanuelle Godeau, Chris Roberts, Rebecca Smith, Dorothy Currie, Will Picket, Matthias Richter, Antony Morgan, and Vivian Barnekow, University of Edinburgh: Child and Adolescent Health Research Unit, 2008. England has the highest number of 11-year-olds with three or more close friends and the highest number of 15-year-old girls with three or more close friends at 91 per cent. But we are in the bottom half of the league table for all ages for the number of children who find it easy to talk to their mother – 72 per cent of 15-year-old girls compared with an average of 77 per cent. Only 50 per cent of 15-year-old girls find it easy to talk to their father, again below the average. I am grateful to Ryan Shorthouse for this point.
34. House of Commons briefing paper 06113 on apprenticeship statistics England, 11 February 2019.
35. Willetts, *A University Education*, p. 178 and p. 397, footnote 8.
36. Jonah Lehrer, *Proust was a Neuroscientist*, Houghton Mifflin Harcourt, 2007.
37. Sarah-Jayne Blakemore, *Brain Development during Adolescence and Beyond*, Institute for Cultural Research Monograph Series No. 51, 2006.
38. Stanley Baldwin, *On England* (1926), Penguin, 1937, p. 13.

11. Houses and Jobs: Generation Crunch

1. There is now a rich literature on the subject of transitions to adulthood stimulated in the USA by Jeffrey Arnett's work on 'Emerging Adulthood'. A good guide to the British debate is John Bynner's article 'Rethinking the Youth Phase of the Life Course: The Case for Emerging Adulthood?', *Journal of Youth Studies*, 8(4), 2005, pp. 367–84, which includes references

to evidence on the stabilizing effects of long-term relationships, especially with non-delinquents. Professor Gill Jones, *Young Adults and the Extension of Economic Dependence*, the National Family and Parenting Institute policy discussion paper, is another useful guide. One radical argument is that the source of the problem is the modern idea of adolescence, which should be abolished – as argued by the leading American psychologist, Robert Epstein, in *The Case against Adolescence: Rediscovering the Adult in Every Teen*.

2. Michael Novak, John Cogan, et al., *The New Consensus on Family and Welfare*, American Enterprise Institute Press, 1987.

3. Some critics might object to the idea of a 'right' order. A good example is Professor Gill Jones writing for the National Family and Parenting Institute: 'It is not feasible to talk in terms of successful or unsuccessful transitions to adulthood, since "success" and "failure" are likely to be constructed differently by young people, their parents and policy makers' (*Young Adults and the Extension of Economic Dependence*, policy discussion paper). The risk with this relativism is that it can enable older generations to shed their responsibility for unhappy and delayed transitions to adulthood.

4. Civitas in 2006 found 76 per cent of all 20–24s want to marry. Marriage Foundation/Seddons 2012 survey of 2,000 adults conducted by One Poll (private analysis by H. Benson, not published) found 77 per cent of unmarried 18–24s want to marry. I am grateful to Harry Benson for this information.

5. Author's conversation with Sandy Campbell of Working Rite.

6. Lydia Marshall and Neil Smith, *First-time buyers: An early life crisis: Britain's homeownership aspirations*, NatCen report for Yorkshire Building Society, March 2016.

7. CESifo Database for Institutional Comparisons in Europe, Family Benefit and Child Benefit, 2014.

8. 'In 2007, the then economy minister, Tommaso Padoa-Schioppa, caused anger in Italy by referring to adults living at home as *bambiccioni* (big babies). The term stuck, and today suggests that some remain at home for the convenience of free room, board and housekeeping by a doting mother.' Andrea Vogt, 'Third of Italian adults live with their parents, report finds', *Guardian*, 19 September 2012.

9. Resolution Foundation Analysis of Office for National Statistics, Labour Force Survey.

10. Resolution Foundation, *Cross countries: International comparisons of intergenerational trends*, February 2018, p. 7.

11. A 'family unit' is a single adult or couple, and any dependent children. Source: Resolution Foundation analysis of IFS, Households Below Average Income (1961–83); Office for National Statistics, Annual Labour Force Survey (1984–91) and Quarterly Labour Force Survey (1992–2018).

12. 'Families' here means benefit units. That means it excludes young adults living with their parents.

13. Office for National Statistics, Labour Force Survey 1998–2018, analysed by Lindsay Judge of the Resolution Foundation. For a full account of data sources

for this and subsequent housing statistics summarized as the Labour Force Survey, see Lindsay Judge, *Home Affront: Housing across the generations*, Intergenerational Commission Report, 9 September 2017, annexes 1 and 3.

14. Ibid.
15. Office for National Statistics, Labour Force Survey 1998–2018.
16. Eighteen-year-olds that live with parents and are not full-time students are not counted as separate family units and do not appear in these statistics. These people are likely to be in education at sixth form or college, and so are still 'dependent children'. Source: Resolution Foundation analysis of IFS, Households Below Average Income (1961–83); Office for National Statistics, Annual Labour Force Survey (1984–91) and Quarterly Labour Force Survey (1992–2018).
17. English Housing Survey 2017 to 2018.
18. IGC Report, p. 147.
19. See discussion in Laura Gardiner, *Votey McVoteface*, Resolution Foundation Intergenerational Commission Working Paper 2, September 2016, p. 14.
20. IGC Report, pp 57–8, and John Wood and Stephen Clark, *House of the rising son (or daughter): The impact of parental wealth on their children's homeownership*, December 2018. Number of years of saving 5 per cent of income required to get a first-time deposit for households headed by person of that age. The low point was 2.6 years in 1985 and 1986 and only 2.8 years by 1996, but it had increased to 11.6 years by 2006 and 19.2 years in 2016. By 2018 it had improved modestly to 18 years.
21. John Wood and Stephen Clark, *House of the rising son (or daughter)*, p. 3, citing figures from Legal and General.
22. Stephen Clarke, *Lender of last resort? The Bank of Mum and Dad and Britain's millennial housing crisis*, Resolution Foundation, 4 December 2018. The figures for 1991–2003 were a 38 per cent chance of a 30-year-old being a homeowner if their parent had property wealth, and 18 per cent if they did not. For 2004–17 it is 24 per cent relative to 8 per cent – a threefold gap even against an overall decline. See also Jo Blanden and Stephen Machin, *Home Ownership and Social Mobility*, CEP Discussion Paper No. 1466, January 2017.
23. Resolution Foundation, Report of Intergenerational Commission, p. 59.
24. This analysis refers to households, not families as in our analysis of tenure. Source: RF analysis of Institute of Fiscal Studies, Households Below Average Income; Department for Work and Pensions, Family Resources Survey.
25. Resolution Foundation, IGC report, p. 65.
26. Adam Corlett and Lindsay Judge, *Home Affront*, Resolution Foundation, September 2017, p. 47.
27. DCLG, 'Fixing our Broken Housing Market', Cm 9352, February 2017, p. 9. See also Centre for Policy Studies.
28. Lindsay Judge, *The one million missing homes?*, Resolution Foundation, June 2019.

29. Ministry of Housing, Communities and Local Government, *Public attitudes to house building: Findings from the 2017 British Social Attitudes Survey 2017*, June 2018, p. 4.

30. UK Finance Industry Tables, Table ML2.

31. Source: RF analysis of ONS, New Earnings Survey (1975–97); ONS, Annual Survey of Hours and Earnings (1997–2018) CPIH-adjusted to 2017 prices.

32. IGC Report, p. 50.

33. Resolution Foundation, *Skills Audit*, March 2019.

34. See David Willetts, *A University Education*, Oxford University Press, 2017, chap. 6.

35. Resolution Foundation analysis of Office for National Statistics, Labour Force Survey.

36. Resolution Foundation, *Study, Work, Progress, Repeat? How and why pay and progression outcomes have differed across cohorts*, Intergenerational Commission Report Paper 5, February 2017.

37. N. Cominetti, The Resolution Foundation earnings outlook, Q3 2018, February 2019.

38. IGC Report, p. 52. The cohort born 1975–7 received an annual pay rise of 6.9 per cent when they remained with their employer, compared with 3.9 per cent for the cohort born 1987–9.

39. Ibid., p. 47; 1 per cent of the 1986–90 cohort reported being on a zero-hours contract aged 21, as against 6 per cent of the 1991–5 cohort.

40. George J. Borjas, 'The New Economics of Immigration', *The Atlantic Monthly*, 278(5), November 1996. See also David Goodhart, *The Road to Somewhere: The Populist Revolt and the Future of Politics*, Penguin, 2017.

41. Stephen Clarke, *A Brave New World: How reduced migration could affect earnings, employment and the labour market*, Resolution Foundation, August 2016, fig. 9.

42. Ibid., fig. 12.

43. Migration Advisory Committee, https://assets.publishing.service.gov.uk/government/uploads/system/uploads/attachment_data/file/741926/Final_EEA_report.PDF

44. Clarke, *Brave New World*.

45. Geoff Dench, Kate Gavron, and Michael Young, *The New East End: Kinship, Race and Conflict*, Profile Books, 2006, p. 155.

46. House of Lords, Select Committee on Economic Affairs, *First Special Report*, 2008, para. 171.

47. Between 2002 and 2017 40 per cent of all migrants to the UK settled in London. Stephen Clarke, *London Stalling: Half a century of living standards in London*, Resolution Foundation, June 2018, p. 26.

48. Ibid.

49. Office for National Statistics, *Migration Statistics Quarterly Report*, November 2018, Table 1. Figures are for year to June 2018.

12. 3G

1. The conclusion of the research is: 'We therefore think significant longevity came late in human evolution and was a fundamental component tied to the population expansions and related behavioural innovations associated with modern humans.' Rachael Caspari and Sang-Hee Lee, 'Old Age Becomes Common Late in Human Evolution', *Proceedings of the National Academy of Sciences of the United States of America*, 101(30), 27 July 2004, pp. 10895–900.
2. Quoted in Geoff Dench and Jim Ogg, *Grandparenting in Britain: A Baseline Study*, Institute of Community Studies, 2002, p. 8. One of Michael Young's many insights was the importance of grandparents for intergenerational exchange – the pressure group Grandparents Plus has been called his last brainchild – and one of his intellectual companions, Geoff Dench, is responsible for much research on grandparents.
3. Nigel Keohane, *Longer Lives, Stronger Families? The changing nature of intergenerational support*, Social Market Foundation, February 2016, p. 20.
4. Grandparents Plus, *Grandparents Today 2017*, p. 25.
5. United for All Ages, *The Next Generation: How intergenerational interaction improves life chances of children and young people*, January 2019, p. 11; The Challenge, *British Integration Survey 2016*, published using Ipsos MORI data.
6. J. Griggs, *The Poor Relation? Grandparental Care: Where Older People's Poverty and Child Poverty Meet*, Grandparents Plus, 2009.
7. United for All Ages, *The Next Generation*. See also A-La Park, 'The impacts of intergenerational programmes on the physical health of older adults', *Journal of Aging Science*, 2(3), 2014, pp. 1–5, a literature review suggesting 'intergenerational interactions can at least be helpful in slowing down some aspects of the ageing process'.
8. Katy Rutherford and Carrie Deacon, The Cares Family evaluation.
9. United for All Ages wants 500 sites where older and younger people come together. The UK Centre for Intergenerational Practice, supported by the Beth Johnson Foundation, is a useful source of practical examples here.
10. F. Kunze and J. Menges, 'Younger supervisors, older subordinates: An organizational-level study of age differences, emotions, and performance', *Journal of Organizational Behavior*, 38(4), pp. 461–86.
11. Christopher Loch, Fabian Sting, Nikolaus Bauer, and Helmut Mauermann, 'The Globe: How BMW is Defusing the Demographic Time Bomb', *Harvard Business Review*, March 2010.
12. Caroline Bryson, Anne Kazimirski, and Helen Southwood, *Childcare and Early Years Provision: A Study of Parents' Use, Views and Experience*, DCSF Research Report No. 723, 2004. They state: 'Almost nine in ten (86 per cent) families had used some form of childcare or early years provision – be it regular or ad hoc – within the last year. Over that period, a greater proportion of families (67 per cent) had used informal care than formal care (57 per cent). Of all providers, families were most likely to have used grandparents. Half of families (49 per cent) had done so at some point in the last year... Two-thirds of families had used childcare in the last week: 41 per cent had used formal

care, and 42 per cent had used informal care. As with use over the last year, out of all the childcare providers, families were most likely to have used a grandparent for childcare during the past week (26 per cent). Used by 12 per cent of families, out of school clubs (on or off school sites) were the most commonly used type of formal provision in the last week.'

13. Grandparents Plus, *Rethinking Family Life: Exploring the Role of Grandparents and the Wider Family*, 2009, p. 11.
14. *Grandparents Today 2017*, p. 23.
15. *Rethinking Family Life*, p. 5.
16. Ibid., p. 35.
17. Dench and Ogg, *Grandparenting in Britain*, p. 32.
18. Ben Page, *Families and Children Key Issues*, Ipsos MORI, Age Concern Research Services, 2006.
19. Dench and Ogg, *Grandparenting in Britain*, p. 37.
20. *Rethinking Family Life*, p. 14; A Buchanan and J. Griggs, *My second mum and dad: The involvement of grandparents in the lives of teenage grandchildren*, Grandparents Plus, September 2009.
21. *Rethinking Family Life*, p 15.
22. *Time to care: Generation generosity under pressure*, July 2014, poll by IPSOS MORI for Grandparents Plus.
23. *Grandparents Today 2017*, p. 31, citing ILC 2017.
24. Martin Kohli, Harald Künemund, Andreas Motel, and Marc Szydlik, 'Families Apart? Intergenerational Transfers in East and West Germany', in Sara Arber and Claudine Attias-Donfut (eds), *The Myth of Generational Conflict: The Family and State in Ageing Societies* (chap. 5), Routledge, 2000, pp. 88–99.
25. Martin Kohli, 'Private and public transfers between generations: Linking the family and the state', *European Societies*, 1(1), 1999, pp. 81–104.
26. *Grandparents Today 2017*, p 15.
27. Survey by Dr Beckmann, March 2013.
28. *Grandparents Today 2017*, p. 9.
29. Maria Evendrou, Jane Falkingham, Madelin Gomez-Leon, and Athina Vlachantoni, 'Intergenerational flows of support between parents and adult children in Britain', *Ageing and Society*, 38(2), 2018, pp. 321–51. They use NCDS 1958 so they can follow exchanges through time, starting with child leaving full time education.
30. In 1901, according to the Office for National Statistics, baby boys were expected to live for 45 years and girls 49 years. US life expectancy of a white male at birth was 38 in 1850 and 42 in 1890, according to the US Department of Health and Human Services Vital Statistics Reports.
31. Pat Thane, *Old Age in English History*, Oxford University Press, 2000. See especially her excellent opening chapter 'Did People in the Past Grow Old?' She points out that 'the average age at death of the nine seventeenth-century Archbishops of Canterbury was 73 and the average age of appointment was 60' (p. 4).

32. Paul Morland, *The Human Tide: How Population Shaped the Modern World*, John Murray, 2019, p. 45.

33. Office for National Statistics, *Changing trends in mortality: An international comparison, 2000 to 2016*. See also Continuous Mortality Investigation, *Recent mortality in England and Wales*, Mortality Projections Committee Working Paper No. 83, October 2015, and Lucinda Hiam et al, 'Why has mortality in England and Wales been increasing? An iterative demographic analysis', *Journal of the Royal Society of Medicine*, 110(4), pp. 153–62.

34. L. S. Vestergaard et al, 'Excess all-cause and influenza-attributable mortality in Europe, December 2016 to February 2017', *Euro Surveillance*, 22(14), 2017; and Public Health England, *Surveillance of influenza and other respiratory viruses in the UK: Winter 2017 to 2018*, May 2018. I am grateful to Douglas Anderson, founder of Club Vita, for bringing my attention to the provisional evidence of lower winter mortality in 2018–19.

35. I am grateful to Dr Jason Hilton, research fellow at the Centre for Population Change at the University of Southampton, for drawing much of this material to my attention. I am also grateful to Dame Sally Davies, the Chief Medical Officer, and Jonathan Pearson-Stuttard, Editor-in-Chief of the CMO's Annual Report, Department of Health, for illuminating discussions around this issue and for highlighting the considerations of life expectancy contained in the CMO's Annual Report.

36. Office for National Statistics, Life expectancy projections (2016-based and predecessors), covering England and Wales only pre-1990.

37. Jane Falkingham Centre for Population Change, *The changing meaning of old age*, Briefing Paper No. 31, February 2016.

38. Cridland Review, *Independent Review of the State Pension Age: Smoothing the Transition: Final Report*, March 2017, p. 36.

39. '664,000 individuals [were] estimated to have dementia in 1991. Taking into account only the effects of population ageing this number would now be expected to be 884,000. However... the number of people with dementia in 2011 was 670,000... a reduction of 24%.' Fiona Matthews et al, 'A two-decade comparison of prevalence of dementia in individuals aged 65 years and older from three geographical areas of England: results of the Cognitive Function and Ageing Study I and II', *The Lancet*, 382(9902), 2013.

40. The table comes from the DWP Performance Indicator 31: Increase in healthy life expectancy at age 65. By contrast, the Institute for Health Metrics and Evaluation in the US extended its seminal work on the Global Burden of Disease to focus specifically on the UK. The findings are that while our mortality rates and years of life lost have decreased substantially over the last 20 years in the UK, our increased years of life are more likely to be spent in poor health. This research is cited in Department for Health, *Living Well for Longer*, 2013. In 2018, as part of the Ageing Challenge, the government set a mission to ensure that people can enjoy at least five extra healthy, independent years of life by 2035,while narrowing the gap between the experience of the richest and poorest.

41. Quotes from Peter Hetherington's interview of Tom Kirkwood, 'Research dispels old myths about ageing', *Guardian*, 30 May 2012.

42. The Treasury applied this argument in its 2006 report on long-term fiscal trends. It did not increase its forecast for life expectancy but it managed to cut its forecast of long-term NHS spending by 1 per cent of GDP. It did this by taking account of the 'finding that a high proportion of lifetime utilisation of healthcare costs is concentrated in the final year of life'. HM Treasury, *Long-Term Public Finance Report: An Analysis of Fiscal Sustainability*, December 2006, p. 34. It was taking a transitional saving on public spending from improving life expectancy. Nowhere in the document is the effect of this assumption explained.

43. Figure for the final quarter of 2018, Office for National Statistics, Labour Market Statistics.

44. Department for Work and Pensions, *Pensioners' Incomes Series*.

45. UN, World Population Prospects.

46. Pension age was equalized in 2018 and is to increase to 66 by 2020 and then to 67 by 2028. It is supposed to reach 68 in 2046 but could come sooner. Cridland Review, *Smoothing the Transition*.

47. C. G. Lewin, *Pensions and Insurance before 1800: A Social History*, Tuckwell Press, 2003, p. 134.

48. Resolution Foundation analysis of Department for Work and Pensions, Family Resources Survey.

49. Resolution Foundation, February 2017.

50. There was a 31 per cent increase in pensioner incomes between 2001–2 and 2014–15. One-quarter was because of employment; half was increases in private pension and investment income; and the rest was a rise in benefits, which was mainly pre-triple lock. Adam Corlett, *Intra and Inter-generational equality*, Intergenerational Committee Report 4.

51. Resolution Foundation analysis of Department for Work and Pensions, Benefit expenditure and caseload tables 2016; Office for National Statistics, Mid-year population estimates and 2014-based population projections; Office for Budget Responsibility, Economic and Fiscal Outlooks.

52. Cridland Review, *Smoothing the Transition*, p. 85.

53. A lifelong low earner retiring in the 2050s will receive less state pension under the new scheme because the flat-rate additional pension in the old system would have allowed them to build up a greater entitlement. See IGC Report, pp. 174–5 and fig 10.1, and also David Finch and Laura Gardiner, *As good as it gets*, Intergenerational Committee Report 12, November 2017, p. 23.

54. Resolution Foundation, *Stagnation Generation*, July 2016, p. 38.

55. Brian Bell and Matt Whittaker, *Pay lower because of plugging pension deficits*, Intergenerational Committee Report 6, May 2017.

56. Jackie Wells, *Pension Annuities: A review of consumer behaviour*, report prepared for the Financial Conduct Authority, January 2014, Fig. 5: Proportion of annuity sales single v. joint life.

57. Pensions Policy Institute, Briefing Note No. 105, February 2018.

58. Pensions Policy Institute, *What is CDC and how might it work in the UK?*, November 2018.

59. All the figures in this and the previous paragraph come from Laura Gardiner, *The million dollar be-question*, Intergenerational Committee Report 13, December 2017, and Adam Corlett, *Passing on: Options for reforming inheritance taxation*, Intergenerational Committee Report 21, May 2018.

60. Research by Chris Hammett of King's College London.

61. Figure for 2015–16 HMRC, Inheritance Tax Statistics.

62. A. Kingston, A. Comas-Herrera, and C. Jagger, 'Forecasting the care needs of the older population in England over the next twenty years: Estimates from the Population Ageing and Care Simulation (PACSim) modelling study', *Lancet Public Health*, 3(9), 2018, pp. 447–55.

63. See Andrew Scott and Lynda Gratton, *The 100-Year Life: Living and Working in an Age of Longevity*, Bloomsbury, 2016. The UK has an excellent organization, the Centre for Ageing Better, which is devoted to this cause. In the US the Sightlines Project at Stanford has identified the three elements for a better old age listed here in the main text.

Conclusion

1. Office for National Statistics reply to Parliamentary Question by the author, 16 January 2008, and Ray Barrell and Martin Weale, *Fiscal Policy: Fairness between Generations and National Saving*, National Institute of Economic and Social Research, September 2009. Imagine an economy which is generating an output of £1tn a year from a fixed capital of £6tn. For its output to grow by 3 per cent a year, its capital also has to grow by about 3 per cent, which is £180bn a year in this example. That means 18 per cent of its output has to be set aside for investment. Those are the kind of figures other advanced Western countries achieve for their levels of net investment and saving. We fall far short of them.

2. Karl Mannheim, 'The Problem of Generations', in Kurt Wolff (ed.), *From Karl Mannheim*, Transaction Publishers, 1993, pp. 351–98.

3. Montaigne quoted in Kieran O'Hara, *After Blair: Conservatism beyond Thatcher*, Icon Books, 2005, p. 49.

4. A survey for the Fabian Society by YouGov in 2004.

5. Another attribution is to James Clarke.

6. Edmund Burke, *Reflections on the Revolution in France* (1790), Everyman, 1976, pp. 92–3.

7. T. S. Eliot, 'Tradition and the Individual Talent', from *The Sacred Wood: Essays on Poetry and Criticism*, Methuen, 1920.

Epilogue: Policy and Politics

1. Dilnot Commission, *Fairer Funding for All*, Report of the Commission of Funding of Care and Support, 2103. It proposed a higher protected level of assets of £100,000 and a smaller maximum contribution of £35,000. How to calibrate these two key parameters depends on the overall fiscal position.
2. Resolution Foundation, *A New Generational Contract: The final report of the Intergenerational Commission*, pp. 196–200.
3. Adam Corlett, *As Time Goes By: Shifting incomes and inequality between and within generations*, Resolution Foundation, February 2017.
4. Ibid., pp. 200–4.
5. This section draws heavily on Resolution Foundation, IGC Report, pp 207–12.
6. A. M. Bell at al., *Who Becomes an Inventor in America? The Importance of Exposure to Innovation*, NBER Working Paper No. 24062, November 2017 (revised January 2019).
7. IGC Report, p. 212.
8. See ibid., p. 208.
9. Source: Lord Ashcroft Polls, EU Referendum 'How Did You Vote' poll, 21–23 June 2016.
10. Source: Resolution Foundation Analysis of British Election Study.
11. Laura Gardiner, *Votey McVoteface*, Resolution Foundation IGC paper, September 2016.

INDEX